Praise for the Previous Editions

"Theologically informed, lucid, supremely accessible: no wonder McGrath's introduction to the Reformation has staying power!" *Denis R. Janz, Loyola University*

"Alister McGrath . . . is one of the best scholars and teachers of the Reformation. . . . [this book] is more than one dared ask for. . . . How teachers will rejoice in this wonderfully useful book." *Teaching History*

"Vigorous, brisk, and highly stimulating. The reader will be thoroughly engaged from the outset, and considerably enlightened at the end." *John Platt, Pembroke College, University of Oxford*

"Highly recommended." *Choice*

"A remarkably fine introduction to the study of the Reformation and its theological ideas; it is exceptionally well thought out, fully up to date in its scholarship, fair in its presentation, and simply pellucid in its explanations. Highly recommended." *ADRIS*

D0869800

Also by Alister E. McGrath from Wiley-Blackwell

Historical Theology: An Introduction to the History of Christian Thought, Second Edition (2012)

Reformation Thought: An Introduction, Fourth Edition (2012)

Theology: The Basic Readings, Second Edition (edited, 2012)

Theology: The Basics, Third Edition (2012)

Luther's Theology of the Cross: Martin Luther's Theological Breakthrough, Second Edition (2011)

Darwinism and the Divine: Evolutionary Thought and Natural Theology (2011)

The Christian Theology Reader, Fourth Edition (edited, 2011)

Christian Theology: An Introduction, Fifth Edition (2011)

Science and Religion: A New Introduction, Second Edition (2009)

The Open Secret: A New Vision for Natural Theology (2008)

The Order of Things: Explorations in Scientific Theology (2006)

Christianity: An Introduction, Second Edition (2006)

Dawkins' God: Genes, Memes, and the Meaning of Life (2004)

The Intellectual Origins of the European Reformation, Second Edition (2003)

Christian Literature: An Anthology (edited, 2003)

A Brief History of Heaven (2003)

The Blackwell Companion to Protestantism (edited with Darren C. Marks, 2003)

The Future of Christianity (2002)

Christian Spirituality: An Introduction (1999)

The Foundations of Dialogue in Science and Religion (1998)

The Blackwell Encyclopedia of Modern Christian Thought (edited, 1995)

A Life of John Calvin (1990)

Reformation Thought

An Introduction

Fourth Edition
Alister E. McGrath

A John Wiley & Sons, Ltd., Publication

This fourth edition first published 2012
© 2012 John Wiley & Sons Ltd

Edition history: Blackwell Publishers Ltd (1e, 1988; 2e, 1993 and 3e, 1999)

Wiley-Blackwell is an imprint of John Wiley & Sons, formed by the merger of Wiley's global Scientific, Technical and Medical business with Blackwell Publishing.

Registered Office
John Wiley & Sons Ltd, The Atrium, Southern Gate, Chichester, West Sussex, PO19 8SQ, UK

Editorial Offices
350 Main Street, Malden, MA 02148-5020, USA
9600 Garsington Road, Oxford, OX4 2DQ, UK
The Atrium, Southern Gate, Chichester, West Sussex, PO19 8SQ, UK

For details of our global editorial offices, for customer services, and for information about how to apply for permission to reuse the copyright material in this book please see our website at www.wiley.com/wiley-blackwell.

The right of Alister E. McGrath to be identified as the author of this work has been asserted in accordance with the UK Copyright, Designs and Patents Act 1988.

Library of Congress Cataloging-in-Publication Data

McGrath, Alister E., 1953-
    Reformation thought : an introduction / Alister E. McGrath. – 4th ed.
        p. cm.
    Includes bibliographical references and index.
    ISBN 978-0-470-67283-9 (hardback) – ISBN 978-0-470-67281-5 (paperback)
    1. Theology, Doctrinal–History–16th century. 2. Reformation. I. Title.
    BT26.M37 2012
    270.6–dc23

                            2011046042

A catalogue record for this book is available from the British Library.

This book is published in the following electronic formats: ePDFs ISBN: 9781444354850; Wiley Online Library ISBN: 9781444354881; ePub ISBN: 9781444354867; Mobi ISBN: 9781444354874

Set in 10.5 on 13 pt Galliard by Toppan Best-set Premedia Limited

6 2017

Contents

Detailed Contents

List of Figures

Preface to the Fourth Edition

The European Reformation of the sixteenth century is one of the most fascinating areas of study available to the historian. It also continues to be of central importance to anyone interested in the history of the Christian church or its religious ideas. The Reformation embraced a number of quite distinct, yet overlapping, areas of human activity: the reform of both the morals and structures of church and society, new approaches to political issues, shifts in economic thinking, the renewal of Christian spirituality, and the reform of Christian doctrine. It was a movement based upon a more or less coherent set of ideas, which were believed to be capable of functioning as the foundation of a program of reform.

But what were those ideas? How may their origins be accounted for? And how were they modified by the social conditions of the period? One serious difficulty – indeed, perhaps the most serious difficulty – facing today's historian of the sixteenth-century Reformation is the strangeness of the ideas underlying it. The term "theology" has been used by Christians since the third century to mean "talking about God." The word can be used to refer to both the core ideas of the Christian faith, and the academic discipline which reflects on these ideas.

Many modern students of the Reformation know little about Christian theology. For example, the great theological slogan "justification by faith alone" seems incomprehensible to many students of this era, as do the intricacies of the sixteenth-century debates over the Eucharist. Why should these apparently obscure issues have caused such a storm at the time? There is an obvious temptation for the student of the Reformation to avoid engaging with the ideas of the movement and to treat it as a purely social phenomenon.

This book is written in the conviction that there are many who will not be prepared to rest content with this superficial engagement with the ideas of the Reformation, and wish to deal with them seriously – but who are discouraged from doing so by the formidable difficulties encountered in trying to understand its ideas. Christian theology will always hold a place of importance in the study of the Reformation. To fail to have at least some degree of familiarity with theology is to lack an understanding of the culture and self-consciousness of the Reformation era. Religious ideas played a large part in the development and expansion of the Reformation. To study the Reformation without considering the religious ideas that fueled its development is comparable to studying the Russian Revolution without reference to Marxism. Historians cannot cut themselves off from the language and ideas of their era of study.

A further difficulty placed in the path of such a student is the remarkable advance made within the last generation in our understanding both of the Reformation itself, and of its background in the late Renaissance, particularly in relation to late medieval scholasticism. Some of this work has yet to filter through to the student, and there is a pressing need for a work which will explain the findings of recent scholarship, and indicate its importance for our understanding of the Reformation during the sixteenth century.

The present work aims to do just that. It assumes that the reader knows nothing of Christian theology, and aims to provide an entry-level guide to the ideas that proved to be so central to this movement in European history, while at the same time distilling the findings of much recent scholarship in its field. The book arose from many years' experience of teaching the field of Reformation studies to students at Oxford University, and I wish to acknowledge my complete indebtedness to those students. It is they who have taught me just how much about the Reformation, so often taken for granted, actually needs to be explained. It is they who have identified the points of particular difficulty which need special discussion. It is they who have recognized the need for precisely this work – and if the reader finds it helpful, it is those students who must be thanked. I am also grateful to my colleagues from the Oxford University faculties of theology and history for many helpful discussions concerning the difficulties encountered in teaching Reformation thought in the twenty-first century.

This book first appeared in 1988. It was immediately clear that it had met a real educational need. An expanded and revised second edition appeared in 1993. The third edition of 1999 offered substantially increased biographical coverage of major Reformation thinkers, and extended its coverage to include the thought of the English Reformation.

This new edition retains all the features which made those earlier editions so attractive to students, while incorporating additional material of direct relevance. In addition to general updating as necessary, reflecting scholarly developments since the last edition, the new edition has been reorganized to make it easier to use. The entire work has been revised to ensure that it is as accessible and useful as possible.

While some reviewers have suggested that the work would be improved if its scope were to be expanded to include seventeenth-century developments, most have asked that it retain its present focus on the sixteenth century. This wish – which makes good pedagogical sense – has been respected.

Alister McGrath
London, December 2011

How to Use This Book

Three words sum up the aim of this book: *introduce*; *explain*; *contextualize*. The book aims to introduce the leading ideas of the European Reformation during the first half of the sixteenth century. It is like a sketch map, which indicates the main features of the intellectual landscape: notes and suggestions for further reading will allow the reader to add finer detail later. Second, the book aims to explain these ideas. It assumes that the reader knows nothing about the Christian theology which underlies the Reformation, and explains what terms such as "justification by faith" and "predestination" mean, and why they are of religious and social relevance. Third, it aims to contextualize these ideas by setting them in their proper intellectual, social, and political context. That context includes such great intellectual movements as humanism and scholasticism, the alternative religious ideologies of the radical Reformation and Catholicism, and the political and social realities of the imperial cities of the early sixteenth century. All these factors affected the thought of the reformers and its impact upon their public – and this work aims to identify that influence and assess its effects.

A series of appendices deal with difficulties which experience suggests most students encounter as they read works relating to the Reformation. What do these abbreviations mean? How can I make sense of those references to primary and secondary sources? What does "Pelagian" mean? Where should I go to find out more about the Reformation? These questions and others are dealt with at length, making this book unique. It will be assumed that the reader speaks no language other than English, and all Latin quotations or slogans will be translated and explained. Although the text of the work draws extensively upon foreign language scholarship, unavailable in English, a select bibliography of works available in English is provided for the benefit of such readers.

On Notes and Further Reading

Notes are kept to a minimum, and are limited to identifying the source of extended quotations or scholarly studies explicitly identified in the text. For abbreviations and forms of reference to primary sources, see Appendices 3 and 4.

The best reference resource currently available relating to the thought of the Reformation is H. J. Hillerbrand, ed., *The Oxford Encyclopaedia of the Reformation* (4 vols; Oxford, 1996). This is an essential resource for anybody concerned with any aspect of the Reformation, and includes substantial bibliographies.

The bibliographies to be found at the end of each chapter do not aim to be exhaustive; their task is to identify potentially valuable studies in the English language, in order to allow readers of this work to take the topics of each chapter further.

Centers of theological and ecclesiastical activity at the time of the European Reformation

1

The Reformation: An Introduction

Many students approach the Reformation in much the same way as medieval travelers approached the vast dark forests of southern Germany – with a sense of hesitation and anxiety, in case what lay ahead should prove impenetrable, or in case they should find themselves hopelessly lost. They are often like explorers venturing into new terrain, unsure what there is to find, at times bewildered by the unmapped wilderness, at others exhilarated by unexpected vistas and valleys. Many find themselves longing for a guide who will lead them through what sometimes seems like a dense jungle.

It is tempting for such students to ignore the *ideas* of the Reformation altogether in order to concentrate upon its social or political aspects. The price of making the Reformation easier to come to grips with in this way, however, is to fail both to capture its essence as a historical phenomenon and to understand why it remains such an essential reference point for much contemporary debate in the religious world and far beyond.

It is understandably difficult for a student sympathetic to the secularism of modern western culture to come to terms with a movement that was so clearly motivated by religious ideas. It is tempting to marginalize these ideas and approach the sixteenth century with the worldview of the modern period. Like any historical phenomenon, however, the Reformation demands that its interpreters attempt to enter into *its* worldview. We must learn to empathize with its concerns and outlook, in order to understand how these affected the great flux of history. The Reformation in Switzerland and Germany was directly based upon religious ideas which demand and deserve careful consideration. Even in England,

Reformation Thought: An Introduction, Fourth Edition. Alister E. McGrath.
© 2012 John Wiley & Sons, Ltd. Published 2012 by John Wiley & Sons, Ltd.

where local conditions led to political factors having a greater influence than religious ideas, there was still a significant core of such ideas underlying developments. This book aims to explain as clearly as possible what the religious ideas underlying the Reformation actually were and how they affected those who entertained them.

The present introductory chapter aims to deal with some preliminary matters, preparing the ground for more detailed discussion of the thought of the Reformation in later chapters.

The Cry for Reform

The term "Reformation" immediately suggests that something – namely, western European Christianity – was being reformed. Like many other terms used by historians to designate eras in human history – such as "Renaissance" or "Enlightenment" – it is open to criticism. For example, the twelfth century witnessed a comparable attempt to reform the church in western Europe – but the term "Reformation" is not used by historians to designate this earlier movement. Other terms might be thought by some to be more appropriate to refer to the sixteenth-century movement we shall be studying in this work. Nevertheless, the fact remains that the term "Reformation" *is* generally accepted as the proper designation for this movement, partly because the movement was linked with the recognition of the need for drastic overhaul of the institutions, practices, and ideas of the western church. The term helpfully indicates that there were both social and intellectual dimensions to the movement which it designates.

By the beginning of the sixteenth century it was obvious that the church in western Europe was in urgent need of reform. The popular cry for "reform in head and members" both summed up the problem and pointed to a possible solution. It seemed to many that the lifeblood of the church had ceased to flow through its veins. The church legal system was badly in need of overhaul, and ecclesiastical bureaucracy had become notoriously inefficient and corrupt. The morals of the clergy were often lax and a source of scandal to their congregations.

Clergy, even at the highest level, were frequently absent from their parishes. In Germany, it is reported that only one parish in 14 had its pastor in residence. The Frenchman Antoine du Prat, archbishop of Sens, turned up for only one service at his cathedral: moreover, his presence and role at this service was somewhat passive, since it was his funeral. Most higher ecclesiastical posts were secured through dubious means, generally relying upon the family connections or the political or financial status of the candidates rather than their spiritual qualities. Thus Duke Amadeus VIII of Savoy secured the appointment of his son to the senior position of bishop of Geneva in 1451; if anyone had misgivings about the fact that the new bishop had never been ordained and was only eight years of age, they were wise enough to keep quiet about them. Pope Alexander VI, a member of the Borgia family (famous for its lethal dinner parties), secured his election to the papacy in 1492 despite having several mistresses and seven children, largely because he bought the papacy outright over the heads of his nearest rivals.

Niccolò Machiavelli put the loose morals of late Renaissance Italy down to the poor example set by the church and its clergy. For many, the cry for reform was a plea for the administrative, moral, and legal reformation of the church: abuses and immorality must be eliminated; the pope must become less preoccupied with worldly affairs; the clergy must be properly educated; and the administration of the church must be simplified and purged of corruption. For others, the most pressing need concerned the spirituality of the church. There was an urgent need to recapture the vitality and freshness of the Christian faith.

Many looked back with nostalgia to the simplicity and excitement of the apostolic Christianity of the first century. Could not this Golden Age of the Christian faith be regained, perhaps by pondering anew the New Testament documents? This program of reform was the wistful pipe dream of intellectuals throughout half of Europe. Yet the Renaissance popes seemed more interested in secular than in spiritual matters, and managed between them to achieve a hitherto unprecedented level of avarice, venality, immorality, and spectacularly unsuccessful power politics. The words of Gianfresco Pico della Mirandola (not to be confused with his uncle, Giovanni), spoken in March 1517, sum up succinctly the thoughts which preyed on many educated minds at the time: "If we are to win back the enemy and the apostate to our faith, it is more important to restore fallen morality to its ancient rule of virtue than that we should sweep the Black Sea with our fleet."

There were others, however, who added another demand to this list of long-overdue reforms – a reformation of Christian doctrine, of theology, of religious ideas. To critical observers such as Martin Luther at Wittenberg and John Calvin at Geneva, the church had lost sight of its intellectual and spiritual heritage. It was time to reclaim the ideas of the Golden Age of the Christian church. The sad state of the church in the early sixteenth century was simply a symptom of a more radical disease – a deviation from the distinctive *ideas* of the Christian faith, a loss of intellectual identity, a failure to grasp what Christianity really was. Christianity could not be reformed without an understanding of what Christianity was actually meant to be. For these men, the obvious decline of the late Renaissance church was the latest stage in a gradual process which had been going on since the early Middle Ages – the corruption of Christian doctrine and ethics.

The distinctive ideas which thinkers such as Luther and Calvin held to underlie Christian faith and practice had been obscured, if not totally perverted, through a series of developments in the Middle Ages. According to these and other reformers of that age, it was time to reverse these changes, to undo the work of the Middle Ages, in order to return to a purer, fresher version of Christianity which beckoned to them across the centuries. The reformers echoed the cry of the humanists: "back to the sources" (*ad fontes*) – back to the Golden Age of the church, in order to reclaim its freshness, purity and vitality in the midst of a period of stagnation and corruption.

Contemporary writings unquestionably paint a picture of growing ecclesiastical corruption and inefficiency, indicating how much the late medieval church was in need of reform. It is necessary, however, to enter a note of caution on the manner in which these sources are to be interpreted. It is quite possible that they document growing levels of expectation within the late medieval church as much as declining levels of performance.

The growth of an educated laity – one of the more significant elements in the intellectual history of late medieval Europe – led to increasing criticism of the church on account of the obvious disparity between what the church *was* and what it *might be*. The growing level of criticism may well reflect the fact that more people were, through increasing educational opportunities, in a position to criticize the church – rather than any further decline in the ecclesiastical standards of the day.

But who could reform the church? By the first decade of the sixteenth century, a fundamental shift in power within Europe was essentially complete. The power of the pope had diminished as the power of secular European governments had increased. In 1478 the Spanish Inquisition was established, with power over clergy and religious orders (and eventually also over bishops). Yet this was an instrument of the Spanish state, not the Spanish church. Control of this system of courts rested not with the pope, but with the Spanish king. The Concordat of Bologna (1516) gave the king of France the right to appoint all the senior clergy of the French church, effectively giving him direct control of that church and its finances.

Across Europe, the ability of the pope to impose a reformation upon his church was steadily diminishing. Even if the will to reform had been there in the later Renaissance popes (and there are few indications that it was), their ability to reform the church was gradually slipping away. This diminishment in papal authority did not, however, lead to a decrease in the power of local or national churches, which continued to exercise major influence over nations. It was the ability of the pope to control such local or national power that declined during our period. The German, Swiss, and English reformations illustrate this point well.

It is therefore important to notice the manner in which Protestant reformers allied themselves with regional or civic powers in order to effect their program of reform. Luther appealed to the German nobility and Zwingli to the Zurich city council for reform, pointing out the benefits which would accrue to both as a consequence. For reasons we shall explore presently (pp. 223–5), the English Reformation (in which political factors tended to overshadow theological issues, which were generally treated as being of secondary importance) is not typical of the European movement as a whole.

The continental Reformation proceeded by a symbiotic alliance of reformer and state or civic authority, each believing that the resulting Reformation was to their mutual benefit. The reformers were not unduly concerned that they gave added authority to their secular rulers by their theories of the role of the state or the "godly prince": the important thing was that the secular rulers supported the cause of the Reformation, even if their reasons for doing so might not be entirely straightforward or praiseworthy.

The mainstream reformers were pragmatists, people who were prepared to allow secular rulers their pound of flesh provided the cause of the Reformation was advanced. In much the same way, of course, the opponents of the Reformation had little hesitation in calling upon the support of secular authorities which felt that their interests were best served by a maintenance of the religious status quo. No study of the Reformation can overlook its political and social dimensions, as secular authorities in northern Europe saw their chance to seize power from the church, even at the cost of thereby committing themselves to a new religious order.

Nevertheless, the fact remains that certain distinctive religious ideas achieved widespread circulation and influence within western European society in the sixteenth century. The Reformation was about theology, not just social and political change. These theological ideas cannot be ignored or marginalized by anyone concerned with the study of the Reformation. It is hoped that the present work will introduce, explain, and contextualize them.

The Concept of "Reformation"

The term "Reformation" is used in a number of senses, and it is helpful to distinguish them. As used in the historical literature, the term "Reformation" generally refers to four elements: Lutheranism, the Reformed church (often referred to as "Calvinism"), the "radical Reformation" (often still referred to as "**Anabaptism**"), and the "Counter-Reformation" or "Catholic Reformation." In its broadest sense, the term "Reformation" is used to refer to all four movements. Some recent studies of this age have used the plural form "Reformations" to suggest that the Reformation was a multifaceted movement – perhaps even that it was a loosely connected set of distinct reforming movements, rather than a single coherent movement with local adaptations.

Anabaptism Literally, "re-baptism." Used to refer to the radical wing of the Reformation.

The term "Reformation" is traditionally used in a somewhat more restricted sense to mean "the Protestant Reformation," thereby excluding the Catholic Reformation. In this sense, it refers to the three Protestant movements noted above. In some scholarly works, the term "Reformation" is used to refer to what is sometimes known as the "magisterial Reformation," or the "mainstream Reformation" – in other words, the type of reformation that was linked with the Lutheran and Reformed churches, rather than the Anabaptists.

The unusual phrase "magisterial Reformation" needs a little explaining. It highlights the way in which the mainstream reformers developed a generally positive relationship with secular authorities, such as princes, magistrates, or city councils. Whereas the radical reformers regarded such authorities as having no rights or authority within the church, the mainstream reformers argued that the church was, at least to some extent, subject to the secular agencies of government. The magistrate had a right to authority within the church, just as the church could rely on the authority of the magistrate to enforce discipline, suppress heresy, or maintain order. The phrase "magisterial Reformation" is often used to draw attention to this close relationship between the magistracy and the church, which lay at the heart of the reforming program of writers such as Martin Luther or Martin Bucer.

All four senses of the word "Reformation" will be encountered in the course of reading works dealing with the sixteenth century. The term "magisterial Reformation" is increasingly used to refer to the first two senses of the term (i.e., covering Lutheranism and the Reformed church) taken together, and the term "radical Reformation" to refer to the third (i.e., covering Anabaptism). The present work is primarily concerned with the ideas of the magisterial Reformation.

The term "Protestant" also requires comment. It derives from the aftermath of the Second Diet of Speyer (February 1529), which voted to end the toleration of Lutheranism in Germany. In April of the same year, six German princes and 14 cities protested against this oppressive measure, defending freedom of conscience and the rights of religious minorities. The term "Protestant" derives from this protest. It is therefore not strictly correct to apply the term "Protestant" to individuals prior to April 1529 or to speak of events prior to that date as constituting "the Protestant Reformation." The term "evangelical" is often used in the literature to refer to the reforming factions at Wittenberg and elsewhere (e.g., in France and Switzerland) prior to this date. Although the word "Protestant" is often used to refer to this earlier period, this use is, strictly speaking, an anachronism.

The Lutheran Reformation

The Lutheran Reformation is particularly associated with the German territories and with the pervasive personal influence of one charismatic individual – Martin Luther (1483–1546). Luther was particularly concerned with the doctrine of **justification**, which formed the central point of his religious thought. The Lutheran Reformation was initially an academic movement, concerned primarily with reforming the teaching of theology at the University of Wittenberg. Wittenberg was an unimportant university, and the reforms introduced by Luther and his colleagues within the theology faculty attracted little attention. It was Luther's personal activities – such as his posting of the famous Ninety-Five Theses (31 October 1517) and the Leipzig Disputation (June–July 1519: see p. 54) – which brought the reforming ideas in circulation

justification by faith Section of Christian theology concerning how the individual sinner is able to enter into fellowship with God.

at Wittenberg to the attention of a wider (though not always appreciative) audience.

Strictly speaking, the Lutheran Reformation really began in 1522, when Luther returned to Wittenberg from his enforced isolation in the Wartburg. Luther had been condemned by the Diet of Worms in 1521. Fearing for his life, certain well-placed supporters removed him in secrecy to the castle known as the "Wartburg," until the threat to his safety ceased. (Luther used his enforced isolation to begin translating the New Testament into German.) In his absence, Andreas Bodenstein von Karlstadt (1486–1541), one of Luther's academic colleagues at Wittenberg, began a program of reform at Wittenberg which seemed to degenerate into chaos. Convinced that his own presence was needed if the Reformation was to survive Karlstadt's ineptitude, Luther emerged from his place of safety and returned to Wittenberg.

At this point, Luther's program for academic reform changed into a program for reform of church and society. No longer was Luther's forum of activity the university world of ideas – he now found himself regarded as the leader of a religious, social, and political reforming movement which seemed to some contemporary observers to open the way to a new social and religious order in Europe.

In fact, it should be noted that Luther's program of reform was actually more conservative than that associated with his Reformed colleagues, such as Huldrych Zwingli. It also met with rather less success than some anticipated. The movement remained obstinately landlocked within the German territories, and – the kingdoms of Scandinavia apart – never gained the foreign power bases which had seemed to be like so many ripe apples, ready to fall into its lap. Luther's understanding of the role of the "godly prince" (which effectively ensured that the monarch had control of the church) does not seem to have held the attraction which might have been expected, particularly in the light of the generally republican sentiments of Reformed thinkers such as Calvin. The case of England is particularly illuminating: here, as in the Lowlands, the Protestant theology which eventually gained the ascendancy was Reformed rather than Lutheran.

The Reformed Church

The origins of the Reformed church lie with developments within the Swiss Confederation. Whereas the Lutheran Reformation had its origins primarily in an academic context, the Reformed church owed its origins more to a series of attempts to reform the morals and worship of the church (but not necessarily its *doctrine*) according to a more biblical pattern. Although most of the early Reformed theologians – such as Huldrych Zwingli (1484–1531) – had an academic background, their reforming programs were not academic in nature. They were mainly concerned with reforming the practices (such as the worship) of the churches in the Swiss cities, such as Zurich, Berne, and Basle.

Whereas Luther was convinced that the doctrine of justification by faith was of central significance to his program of social and religious reform, the early Reformed thinkers had relatively little interest in doctrine, let alone this one specific doctrine. Their reforming program was institutional, social, and ethical, in many ways similar to the demands for reform emanating from the humanist movement. We shall consider the ideas of **humanism** in some detail presently (pp. 36–45); for the moment it is important simply to note that all the major early Reformed theologians had links with the humanist movement which were not shared by Luther, who regarded it with some suspicion.

> **humanism** Complex movement involving a new interest in the cultural achievements of antiquity.

The consolidation of the Reformed church is generally thought to have begun with the stabilization of the Zurich reformation after Zwingli's death (in battle, 1531) under his successor, Heinrich Bullinger (1504–75), and to have ended with the emergence of Geneva as its power base and John Calvin (1509–64) as its leading spokesman, in the 1550s. The gradual shift in power within the Reformed church (initially from Zurich to Berne, and subsequently from Berne to Geneva) took place over the period 1520–60, eventually establishing the city of Geneva, its political system (republicanism), and its religious thinkers (initially Calvin, and after his death Theodore Beza) as predominant within the Reformed church. This development was consolidated through the establishment of the Genevan Academy (founded in 1559), at which Reformed pastors were trained.

The term "Calvinism" is often used to refer to the religious ideas of the Reformed church. Although still widespread in the literature relating to the Reformation, this practice is now generally discouraged. It is becoming increasingly clear that later sixteenth-century Reformed theology draws on sources other than the ideas of Calvin himself. To refer to later sixteenth- and seventeenth-century Reformed thought as "Calvinist" implies that it is essentially the thought of Calvin – and it is now generally agreed that Calvin's ideas were modified subtly by his successors. (We shall explore this development in relation to the doctrine of predestination on pp. 202–4.) The term "Reformed" is now preferred, whether to refer to those churches (mainly in Switzerland, the Lowlands, and Germany) or religious thinkers (such as Theodore Beza, William Perkins, or John Owen) which were grounded on Calvin's celebrated religious textbook *The Institutes of the Christian Religion* or to church documents (such as the famous *Heidelberg Catechism*) based upon it.

The term "Calvinist" presents some difficulties for the intellectual historian. The term dates from the 1560s, when a significant alteration in the political situation in the German territories took place. Germany had been seriously destabilized in the 1540s and early 1550s by conflicts between Lutherans and Catholics, and it was widely recognized that such conflicts were damaging to the Empire. The Peace of Augsburg (September 1555) settled the religious question in

Germany by allocating certain areas of Germany to Lutheranism and the remainder to Catholicism – the famous principle often referred to as *cuius regio, eius religio* ("your region determines your religion"). No provision was made for the Reformed faith, which was effectively declared to be "nonexistent" in Germany.

In February 1563, however, the *Heidelberg Catechism* was published (see p. 246), indicating that the Reformed theology had gained a firm foothold in this hitherto Lutheran region of Germany. This catechism was immediately attacked by Lutherans as being "Calvinist" – in other words, foreign. The term "Calvinist" was used by German Lutherans to attempt to discredit this new and increasingly influential document by implying that it was unpatriotic. Given the original polemical associations of the term "Calvinist," it would seem appropriate for the historian to use a more neutral term to refer to this movement. The term "Reformed" is widely used for this reason, and is to be preferred.

Of the three constituent elements – Lutheran, Reformed (or Calvinist), and Anabaptist – of the Protestant Reformation, it is the Reformed wing that is of particular importance to the English-speaking world. Puritanism, which figures so prominently in seventeenth-century English history and is of such fundamental importance to the religious and political views of New England in the seventeenth century and beyond, is a specific form of Reformed Christianity. To understand the religious and political history of New England or the ideas of writers such as Jonathan Edwards (1703–58), for example, it is necessary to come to grips with at least some of the theological insights and part of the religious outlook of Puritanism that underlie their social and political attitudes. It is hoped that this work will help with this process of familiarization.

The Radical Reformation (Anabaptism)

The term "Anabaptist" owes its origins to Zwingli (the word literally means "rebaptizers"), and refers to what was perhaps the most distinctive aspect of Anabaptist practice – the insistence that only those who had made a personal public profession of faith should be baptized. Anabaptism seems to have first arisen around Zurich, in the aftermath of Zwingli's reforms within the city in the early 1520s. It centered on a group of individuals (among whom we may note Conrad Grebel, c.1498–1526) who argued that Zwingli was not being faithful to his own reforming principles. He preached one thing and practiced another.

Although Zwingli professed faithfulness to the *sola scriptura* ("by Scripture alone": see pp. 98–100) principle, Grebel argued that he retained a number of practices – including infant baptism, the close link between church and magistracy, and the participation of Christians in warfare – which were not sanctioned or

sola scriptura Phrase summarizing the theory that the practices and beliefs of the church should be grounded in Scripture.

ordained by Scripture. In the hands of such radical thinkers, the *sola scriptura* principle became radicalized (see pp. 100–1): reformed Christians came to believe and practice only those things explicitly taught in Scripture. Zwingli was alarmed by this, seeing it as a destabilizing development which threatened to cut off the Reformed church at Zurich from its historical roots and its continuity with the Christian tradition of the past.

The Anabaptists had good reason to accuse Zwingli of compromise. In 1522, Zwingli wrote a work known as *Apologeticus Archeteles*, in which he recognized the idea of a "community of goods" as an authentic Christian ideal. "No-one calls any possessions his own," he wrote, "all things are held in common." But by 1525, Zwingli had changed his mind and come round to the idea that private property was not such a bad thing, after all.

Although Anabaptism arose in Germany and Switzerland, it subsequently became influential in other regions, such as the Lowlands. The movement produced relatively few theologians – the three most significant are generally agreed to be Balthasar Hubmaier (c.1480–1528), Pilgram Marbeck (died 1556), and Menno Simons (1496–1561). This failure partly reflects the forcible suppression of Anabaptism by the secular authorities. Yet it may also reflect the fact that the movement did not have any substantial common theological basis.

A number of common elements can be discerned within the various strands of the movement: a general distrust of external authority, the rejection of infant baptism in favor of the baptism of adult believers, the common ownership of property, and an emphasis upon pacifism and non-resistance. To take up one of these points: in 1527, the governments of the cities of Zurich, Berne, and St Gallen accused the Anabaptists of believing "that no true Christian can either give or receive interest or income on a sum of capital; that all temporal goods are free and common, and that all can have full property rights to them."

It is for this reason that "Anabaptism" is often referred to as the "left wing of the Reformation" (Roland H. Bainton) or the "radical Reformation" (George Hunston Williams). For Williams, the "radical Reformation" was to be contrasted with the "magisterial Reformation," which he broadly identified with the Lutheran and Reformed movements. These terms are increasingly being accepted within Reformation scholarship, and the reader is likely to encounter them in his or her reading of more recent studies of the movement.

Probably the most significant document to emerge from the movement is the Schleitheim Confession, drawn up by Michael Sattler (1490–1527) on 24 February 1527. The Confession takes its name from the small town of that name in the canton of Schaffhausen. Its function was to distinguish Anabaptists from those around them – supremely from what the document refers to as "papists and antipapists" (that is, unreformed Catholics and magisterial evangelicals). In effect, the Schleitheim Confession amounts to "articles of separation" – that is to say, a set of beliefs and attitudes which distinguish Anabaptists from their opponents inside and outside the Reformation, and function as a core of unity, whatever their other differences might be.

The Catholic Reformation

This term is often used to refer to the revitalization of Catholicism in the period following the opening of the Council of Trent (1545). In older scholarly works, the movement is often designated the "Counter-Reformation": as the term suggests, this refers to the strategies that the Catholic church developed as a means of combating the Protestant Reformation. The Catholic church countered the Reformation partly by reforming itself from within, in order to remove the grounds of Protestant criticism. In this sense, the movement is to be seen both as a reformation of the Catholic church, as well as a critique of the Protestant Reformation.

The same concerns underlying the Protestant Reformation in northern Europe were channeled into the renewal of the Catholic church, particularly in Spain and Italy. The Council of Trent (see Figure 1.1), the foremost feature of the Catholic Reformation, clarified Catholic teaching on a number of confusing matters, and introduced much-needed reforms in relation to the conduct of the clergy, ecclesiastical discipline, religious education, and missionary activity. The movement for reform within the Catholic church was greatly stimulated by the reformation

Figure 1.1 The Council of Trent, 4 December 1563 (oil on canvas), Italian School, (sixteenth century), Louvre, Paris, France. Formerly attributed to Titian (1488–1576); 23rd session of the Council. Louvre, Paris, France/Giraudon/The Bridgeman Art Library

of many of the older religious orders and the establishment of new orders (such as the "Society of Jesus," often referred to as "the Jesuits"). The more specifically theological aspects of the Catholic Reformation will be considered in relation to its teachings on Scripture and tradition, justification by faith, the church, and the **sacraments**.

sacrament Church service or rite held to have been instituted by Jesus Christ himself.

As a result of the Catholic Reformation, many of the abuses that originally lay behind the demands for reform – whether these came from humanists or Protestants – were removed. By this stage, however, the Protestant Reformation had reached a point at which the mere removal of malpractices and abuses was no longer sufficient to reverse the situation: the demand for the reformation of doctrine, religious ideology, and the church was now regarded as an essential aspect of the Protestant–Catholic controversies. This point highlights the need to consider the religious ideas lying behind the "magisterial Reformation," which became of increasing importance to the Protestant–Catholic debate as the sixteenth century progressed.

The Importance of Printing

Recent technological developments in the field of data processing and transfer – such as the Internet – have revolutionized many aspects of modern life. It is important to realize that a single technological innovation destined to have an enormous influence over western Europe was developed on the eve of the Reformation. This innovation was, of course, printing. It would have a very substantial impact on the development and propagation of the ideas of the Reformation.

Although originally developed centuries earlier by the Chinese, the first European printed documents which can be dated reliably originate from the press of Johann Gutenberg (c.1398–1468) at Mainz around 1454. In 1456, the same press produced a printed Latin Bible. This was followed in 1457 by the so-called Mainz Psalter, which established the custom of identifying the printer, the location of the press, and the date of publication on the title page of the work. From Germany, the technology was taken to Italy, presses being established at Subiaco (1464) and Venice (1469). Caxton set up his printing shop at Westminster, London, in 1476. The famous Aldine Press was established at Venice in 1495 by Aldus Manutius Romanus. This press was responsible for two important developments: "lower case" letters (so called because they were kept in the lower of two cases containing type) and the sloping "italic" type (so called in English-language works on account of Venice being located in Italy; Aldus himself called the type "Chancery").

Why would printing have such a major impact upon the Reformation? The following points should be noted. First, printing meant that works advocating the agenda of the Reformation could be produced quickly and cheaply. The tedious process of copying manuscripts by hand was no longer necessary. Further, the errors introduced by the copying process were eliminated; once a work was set up in type, any number of error-free copies could be run off. Anyone who could read and who could afford to pay for books was in a position to learn of the sensational new ideas coming out of Wittenberg and Geneva. For example, in England it was the literate and financially advantaged classes who knew most about Lutheranism in the third decade of the sixteenth century. Lutheran books, banned by the authorities as seditious, were smuggled in through the Hanseatic trade route to Cambridge via the ports of Antwerp and Ipswich. There was no need for Luther to visit England to gain a hearing for his ideas – they were spread by the printed word (see pp. 242–3).

This point is of interest in relation to the sociology of early **Protestantism**. In both England and France, for example, the first Protestants were often drawn from the upper strata of society, precisely because these strata possessed the ability to read and the money to pay for books (which, as they often

> **Protestantism** Term used to designate those who "protested" against the practices and beliefs of the Roman Catholic church.

had to be smuggled in from abroad, were generally rather expensive). Similarly, the greater influence of Protestantism at the University of Cambridge than at Oxford partly reflects the former's proximity to the continental ports from which Protestant books were being (illicitly) imported.

Second, the Reformation was based upon certain specific sources: the Bible and the Christian theologians of the first five centuries (often referred to as "the Fathers," or "the patristic writers"). The invention of printing had two immediate effects upon these sources, of considerable importance to the origins of the Reformation. It was now possible to produce more accurate editions of these works – for example, through the elimination of copying errors. By comparing the printed text of a work with manuscript sources, the best possible text could be established and used as the basis of theological reflection. In the late fifteenth and early sixteenth centuries, humanist scholars rummaged through the libraries of Europe in search of patristic manuscripts which they could edit and publish.

As a result, these sources were made much more widely available than had ever been possible before. By the 1520s, just about anyone could gain access to a reliable edition of the Greek text of the New Testament or the writings of Augustine of Hippo (354–430), a patristic writer particularly favored by the Reformers. The 11 volumes of the collected works of Augustine were published at Basle by the Amerbach brothers, after an editorial process lasting from 1490 to 1506. Although only 200 copies of each volume seem to have been published, they were widely used to gain access to the most reliable text of this important writer.

Erasmus of Rotterdam produced the first published text of the Greek New Testament in 1516 (see Figure 1.2). Entitled *Novum Instrumentum omne*, the work had three main sections: the original Greek text of the New Testament; a new Latin translation of this Greek text, which corrected inadequate existing translations, especially the **Vulgate** (see pp. 94–5); and, finally, an extended

> **Vulgate** Latin translation of the Bible upon which medieval theology was largely based.

Figure 1.2 Erasmus of Rotterdam in the print shop of his friend Johannes Froben of Basle. © Bettmann/ CORBIS

commentary on the text in the form of annotations. The work was widely used by those sympathetic to the cause of the Reformation. For the reformers – especially Luther and his colleagues at Wittenberg – the religious ideas of the Reformation drew largely on the Bible and Augustine. The advent of printing, linked with increasingly effective bookselling methods, meant that accurate and reliable texts of both these sources were widely available, thus facilitating both the initial development and the subsequent spread of these ideas.

The importance of printing in spreading the ideas of the Reformation cannot be overstated. Surveys of the personal book collections of French bourgeois families point to the religious implications of this trend. Jacques Lefèvre's French New Testament of 1523, pointedly addressed "to all Christian men and women," along with his French Psalter of 1524, were read widely throughout France, and were even distributed free of charge within the reforming diocese of Meaux. Copies of these works, along with the New Testament commentaries of Erasmus, Melanchthon, and Lefèvre himself, are frequently to be found jostling for space on the shelves of bourgeois libraries in the late 1520s. If these books were ever read by their owners – and the evidence strongly suggests that they were – a considerable head of pressure for reform would have developed.

The Use of the Vernacular in Theological Debates

Luther had learned from Erasmus the importance of the printing press in project-ing intellectual influence within society. In 1520, he began to advance the cause of his reformation by appealing directly to the German people, over the heads of clerics and academics, through the medium of print. It was a tactic that would be imitated throughout Europe, as the power of the pamphlet became obvious to all. Luther now began to have the popular impact that he knew was essential if he was to change the shape of the church, rather than tinker with academic niceties. He would do this by using the vernacular as a means of theological communication.

Why was this development so important? The language of the academy, the church, and the state in western Europe throughout the Middle Ages was Latin. There was an obvious need for a common language to allow communication across this vast and diverse region of the world. Latin was the language of the great Roman poets, rhetoricians, politicians, and philosophers, and of highly influential Christian theologians such as Augustine of Hippo, Ambrose of Milan, and Tertullian. Luther knew that anything he wrote in Latin would be under-stood by the educated elite across Europe.

Yet Luther wanted to reach beyond an academic readership and touch the hearts and minds of ordinary people. The decision to publish in German was iconic, making a statement about the inclusive nature of the reformation that Luther proposed to pursue. To publish in Latin was to exclude the ordinary people. To publish in his native German was to democratize the debate about the future of the church by including those who were traditionally marginalized by the use of the ancient scholarly language. From that moment onward, one of the hallmarks of Protestantism would be its use of the vernacular at every level. Most importantly of all, the Bible would also be translated into the language of the people.

An example will illustrate the importance of both printing and the use of the vernacular to the propagation of the ideas of the Reformation. A crucial turning point in the French Reformation was marked by the publication of the French-language edition of Calvin's *Institutes of the Christian Religion* in 1541. Suddenly, coherently expressed and carefully justified radical reforming doctrines were avail-able within France in a language which most could understand (see pp. 247–50).

There was something approaching panic in official circles in Paris. On 1 July 1542, the Parisian *parlement* directed that all works containing heterodox doc-trines, especially Calvin's *Institutes*, were to be surrendered to the authorities within three days. Calvin's *Institutes* were thus seen as the spearhead of a Genevan assault upon the French Catholic church, mediated through the printed word in French. The reaction from the booksellers of Paris was immediate: they protested that they would face financial ruin if they were prohibited from selling such books. It seems that there was a major market for works which were considered to be dangerously unsound by the authorities – further evidence of the importance of a literate and affluent laity in promoting the ideas of the Reformation. Indeed, Laurent de Normandie, Calvin's friend and bookseller, found the contraband book trade so profitable that he emigrated to Geneva, in order that he might publish such books rather than just sell them.

This is not to say, however, that the Reformation was wholly dependent upon a technological innovation, or the use of the vernacular. The social context of the Reformation helps us understand something of its appeal at the time.

The Social Context of the Reformation

The northern European Reformation was based largely in the cities. In Germany, more than 50 of the 65 "imperial cities" responded positively to the Reformation, with only five choosing to ignore it altogether. In Switzerland, the Reformation originated in an urban context (Zurich), and spread through a process of public debate within Confederate cities such as Berne and Basle and other centers – such as Geneva and St Gallen – linked to these cities by treaty obligations. French Protestantism began as a predominantly urban movement, with its roots in major cities such as Lyons, Orléans, Paris, Poitiers, and Rouen.

It is becoming increasingly clear that the success or failure of the Reformation in these cities was dependent in part upon political and social factors. By the late fifteenth and early sixteenth centuries, the city councils of the imperial cities had managed to gain a substantial degree of independence. In effect, each city seems to have regarded itself as a miniature state, with the city council functioning as a government and the remainder of the inhabitants as subjects.

The growth in the size and importance of the cities of Germany is one of the more significant elements in late fourteenth- and fifteenth-century history. An extended food crisis, linked with the ravages of the Black Death, led to an agrarian crisis. Wheat prices dropped alarmingly in the period 1450–1520, leading to rural depopulation as agricultural workers migrated to the cities in the hope of finding food and employment. Denied access both to the trade guilds and to the city councils, discontent grew within this new urban proletariat.

The early sixteenth century thus witnessed growing social unrest in many cities, as demands for broader-based and more representative government gained momentum. In many cases, the Reformation came to be linked with these demands for social change, so that religious and social change went together, hand in hand. We must not think that religious concerns swamped all other mental activities – they simply provided a focal point for them. Economic, social, and political factors help explain why the Reformation succeeded, for example, in Nuremberg and Strasbourg, yet failed in Erfurt.

A number of theories have been advanced since about 1970 to explain the appeal of the Reformation to the cities. The German church historian Berndt

Moeller has argued that the urban sense of community had been disrupted in the fifteenth century through growing social tension within the cities and an increasing tendency to rely upon external political bodies, such as the imperial government or the papal curia.[1] By adopting the Lutheran Reformation, Moeller suggested, such cities were able to restore a sense of communal identity, including the notion of a common religious community binding inhabitants together in a shared religious life. Significantly, Moeller drew attention to the social implications of Luther's doctrine of the priesthood of all believers (see pp. 210–12), which broke down certain traditional distinctions within urban society and encouraged a sense of communal unity.

A second explanation was advanced by the American cultural historian Thomas A. Brady, based largely upon his analysis of the city of Strasbourg.[2] Brady argued that the decision to adopt Protestantism at Strasbourg was the outcome of a class struggle, in which a ruling coalition of patricians and merchants believed that their social position could be maintained only through alignment with the Reformation. The urban oligarchs introduced the Reformation as a subtle means of preserving their vested interests, which were threatened by a popular protest movement. A similar situation, Brady suggested, existed in many other cities.

A third explanation of the appeal of the Reformation to sixteenth-century urban communities centers on the doctrine of justification by faith (an idea explored in detail in Chapter 7). In a study published in 1975, the American church historian Steven Ozment argued that the popular appeal of Protestantism derived from its doctrine of justification by faith, which offered relief from the psychological pressure of the late medieval penitential system and an associated "semi-Pelagian" doctrine of justification.[3] As the weight of this psychological burden was greatest and most evident in urban communities, he argued, it was within such communities that Protestantism found its greatest popular support.

Ozment argued that Moeller had vastly exaggerated the differences between Luther and the theologians of the southwest. The early reformers shared a common message, which could be summarized as the liberation of individual believers from the psychological burdens imposed by late medieval religion. Whatever their differences, the magisterial reformers – such as Bucer, Zwingli, and Luther – shared a common concern to proclaim the doctrine of justification by faith through grace, thereby eliminating the theological necessity of and diminishing the popular concern for indulgences, purgatory, invocation of the saints, and so forth. This theory is of importance to this work because it illustrates the role of ideas in generating pressure for reform and change: the pressure for social change is, according to Ozment, the *outcome*, not the *cause*, of the new religious ideas of the age.

Each of these theories is significant, and together they have provided an important stimulus to the more detailed study of the development of urban Protestantism in the first phase of the Reformation. Equally, each has been shown to have obvious weaknesses, as one might expect from ambitious global theories. For example, in the case of Geneva, as we shall see, the social tensions which eventually resulted in alignment with the Protestant city of Berne and adoption of the Zwinglian Reformation did not arise from class differences, but from division within a common social class over whether to support Savoy or the Swiss Confederacy. The pro-Savoyard Mammelukes and the pro-Bernese Eiguenots were both drawn from a single social group, characterized by a range of identifiable shared economic, familial, and social interests. Similarly, Ozment's suggestion of a universal concern for the doctrine of justification finds little support in the case of cities within or linked with the Swiss Confederacy – such as Zurich, St Gallen, and Geneva – and overlooks the obvious hesitations concerning the doctrine on the part of many Swiss reformers.

Nevertheless, some common features emerge from a study of the origins and development of the Reformation in major northern European cities such as Augsburg, Basle, Berne, Colmar, Constance, Erfurt, Frankfurt, Geneva, Hamburg, Lübeck, Memmingen, Ulm, and Zurich. It is helpful to explore them.

In the first place, the Reformation in the cities appears to have been a response to some form of popular pressure for change. Nuremberg is a rare instance of a city council imposing a reformation without significant preceding popular protest or demand. Dissatisfaction among urban populations of the early sixteenth century was not necessarily purely religious in character; social, economic, and political grievances were unquestionably present, to varying extents, within the agglomerate of unrest evident at the time. City councils generally reacted in response to this popular pressure, often channeling it in directions appropriate to their own needs and purposes. This subtle manipulation of such pressure was an obvious way of co-opting and controlling a potentially dangerous popular protest movement. Existing urban regimes were often relatively unchanged by the introduction of new religious ideas and practices, which suggests that city councils were able to respond to such popular pressure without radical changes in the existing social orders.

Second, the success of the Reformation within a city was dependent upon a number of historical contingencies. To adopt the Reformation was to risk a disastrous change in political alignment, in that existing treaties or relationships – military, political, and commercial – with territories or cities which chose to remain Catholic were usually deemed to be broken as a result. A city's trading relationships – upon which her economic existence might depend – might thus be compromised fatally. Thus the success of the Reformation in the city of St Gallen was partly due to the fact that the city's linen industry was not adversely affected to any significant degree by the decision to adopt the Reformation. Equally, a city (such as Erfurt) in close proximity to a Catholic city (Mainz) and a Lutheran territory (Saxony) could risk becoming embroiled in military conflict with one or other of these interested parties, with potentially lethal results for the independence of that city.

Third, the romantic, idealized vision of a reformer arriving in a city to preach the gospel, with an immediate ensuing decision on the part of the city to adopt the principles of the Reformation, must be abandoned as quite unrealistic. Throughout the entire process of reformation, from the initial decision to implement a process of reform to subsequent decisions concerning the nature and the pace of reforming proposals, it was the city council who remained in control. Zwingli's Reformation in Zurich proceeded considerably more slowly than he would have liked on account of the cautious approach adopted by the council at crucial moments. Bucer's freedom of action in Strasbourg was similarly limited. As Calvin would discover, city councils were perfectly able to evict reformers from their precincts if they stepped out of line with publicly stated council policy or decisions.

In practice, the relationship between city council and reformer was generally symbiotic. The reformer, by presenting a coherent vision of the Christian gospel and its implications for the religious, social, and political structures and practices of a city, was able to prevent a potentially revolutionary situation from degenerating into chaos. The constant threat of reversion to Catholicism, or subversion by radical Anabaptist movements, rendered the need for a reformer inevitable. Someone had to give religious direction to a movement which, unchecked and lacking direction, might degenerate into chaos, with momentous and unacceptable consequences for the existing power structures of the city and the individuals who controlled them.

Equally, the reformer was someone who was under authority, one whose freedom of action was limited by political masters jealous for their authority and with a reforming agenda that generally extended beyond that of the reformer to include consolidation of their economic and social influence. The relation between reformer and city council was thus delicate, easily prone to disruption, with real power permanently in the hands of the latter.

In the case of Geneva, a delicate relationship developed between the city's reformers (initially Guillaume Farel and Calvin, subsequently Calvin alone) and the city council. Conscious and jealous of its hard-won authority and liberty, the city council was determined not to substitute the tyranny of a reformer for that of a Catholic bishop. In 1536, the city had just gained its independence from Savoy, and had largely retained that independence, despite the attempts of Berne to colonize the city. Geneva was in no mood to be dictated to by anyone, unless they were in a position to bring massive economic and military pressure to bear. As a result, severe restrictions were placed upon Calvin's activities. He was someone whose options were very limited.

The expulsion of Calvin from Geneva in 1538 demonstrates that political power remained firmly in the hands of the city council. The notion that Calvin was the "dictator of Geneva" is totally devoid of historical foundation. Nevertheless, the city council found itself unable to cope with a deteriorating religious situation in Calvin's absence. In a remarkable act of social pragmatism and religious realism, the council recalled their reformer, and allowed him to continue his work of reform. Geneva needed Calvin, just as Calvin needed Geneva.

An important difference may be noted at this point between Lutheran and Reformed thought. Luther was the product of a small Saxon town under the thumb of the local prince, but the great Reformed thinkers Zwingli and Bucer were the product of the great free cities of Zurich and Strasbourg. For these latter, the Reformation involved the identification of "citizen" with "Christian," with a great emphasis upon the political dimension of life quite absent from Luther's thought. Thus Zwingli laid great emphasis upon the need to reform and redeem a *community*, whereas Luther tended to concentrate upon the need to reform and redeem the *individual*. Luther, through his doctrine of the "Two Kingdoms," effectively separated religious ideas from secular life, whereas Zwingli insisted upon their mutual integration. It is therefore significant that the Reformed church gained its most secure power bases in the cities of southern Germany and Switzerland, which were more advanced socially, culturally, and economically than the northern cities destined to become Lutheran strongholds.

The social context of the Reformation is a fascinating subject in itself, but is noted here primarily on account of its obvious influence upon at least some of the religious ideas of the reformers. For example, there are excellent reasons for suggesting that many of Zwingli's ideas (especially his ideas concerning the societal function of the sacraments) were directly conditioned by the political, economic, and social circumstances of Zurich. Equally, some of Calvin's ideas about the proper structures of a Christian church seem to reflect institutions already in existence at Geneva prior to his arrival in that city. We shall consider this issue at a number of points in the course of this work.

The Religious Concerns of the Reformers: A Brief Overview

It is appropriate to introduce the religious ideas of the reformers at this point. These ideas will be amplified and developed throughout this study, and the present section is intended to give the reader a preliminary overview. Just as a sketch map provides a broad survey of an area in order that fine detail may be mapped in later, so the present section is intended to introduce the reader to the ideas to be encountered as this work progresses.

The fundamental conviction motivating the magisterial reformers was that Christianity could best be reformed and renewed by returning to the beliefs and practices of the early church. The first five centuries – often designated "the patristic period" – tended to be regarded as the Golden Age of Christianity. The great vision of many sixteenth-century reformers was summed up in the Latin slogan *Christianismus renascens* – "Christianity being born again." How could this rebirth take place?

The reformers pointed to the vitality of Christianity in the apostolic period, as witnessed by the New Testament, and argued that it was both possible and necessary to recapture the spirit and the form of this pivotal period in the history of the Christian church. It was necessary to go back to the New Testament and its earliest interpreters, in order to learn from them. These were the title deeds of Christendom, the fountainhead of Christian belief and practice.

Standing in the great tradition of the Old Testament prophets, the reformers laid down a challenge to the religious leaders of their day. They saw the latter as guilty of condoning additions to and distortions of the Christian faith – alterations which reflected the interests of ecclesiastical fund-raisers and which fed popular superstition. The doctrine of purgatory and the related practice of selling indulgences were singled out as representing sub-Christian cults, exploiting the hopes and fears of the ordinary people. It was time to eliminate such corruptions through the consistent appeal to the beliefs and practices of the early church, which was held up as a model for the kind of shake-up and clean-out that the church so badly needed.

This emphasis upon early Christianity as resource, a norm, and point of reference for the sixteenth-century vision of *Christianismus renascens* allows us to understand why the reformers placed such great emphasis upon the New Testament and the early Christian writers usually known as "the Fathers" or "the patristic writers." It was in these writings that a blueprint for the reformation and renewal of the church was to be found. Here could be found the original ideals of Christianity.

Thus the production of the first Greek New Testament and the first edition of the works of Augustine (regarded by most reformers as *the* patristic writer) were milestones in the sixteenth-century program of reform, and became widely available throughout Europe. For Martin Luther, the program of reform at the University of Wittenberg around 1519 could be summed up in a simple phrase: "the Bible and St Augustine."

The rise of Renaissance humanism was widely regarded as providential, in that the great advances made in Hebrew and Greek studies in relation to classical texts in western Europe paved the way for the direct engagement with the scriptural text, in place of the unreliable Latin translation of the Vulgate. The new textual and philological techniques pioneered by the humanists were regarded as holding the key to the world of the New Testament, and hence authentic Christianity. As the sixteenth century entered its second decade, there were many who felt that a new era was dawning, in which the voice of authentic Christianity, silent for so long, would be heard once more.

Simple though this program of reform might seem, it was nevertheless accompanied by formidable difficulties, which we shall be exploring in the course of this work. The agenda for the Reformation had been set, and the tools by which it might be achieved were being prepared. But we must plunge into the heady waters of fifteenth- and early sixteenth-century thought if we are to understand the backdrop to this drama in human history.

Having explored some preliminary issues, we are now in a position to engage with the Reformation. The most appropriate place to begin this encounter is by exploring the world of late medieval Christianity, to which we now turn.

Notes

1   B. Moeller, *Imperial Cities and the Reformation* (Philadelphia, 1972).
2   T. A. Brady, *Ruling Class, Regime and Reformation at Strasbourg, 1520–1555* (Leiden, 1977).
3   S. E. Ozment, *The Reformation in the Cities: The Appeal of Protestantism to Sixteenth-Century Germany and Switzerland* (New Haven, 1975).

Further Reading

Bagchi, D., and D. Steinmetz, eds, *The Cambridge Companion to Reformation Theology* (Cambridge, 2004).

Bainton, R. H., *The Reformation of the Sixteenth Century* (Boston, MA, 1985).

Bossy, J., *Christianity in the West 1400–1700* (Oxford, 1987).

Cameron, E., *The European Reformation* (Oxford, 1991).

Chadwick, O., *Pelican History of the Church*, vol. 3: *The Reformation* (London, 1972).

Eisenstein, E. L., *The Printing Press as an Agent of Change*, 2 vols (Cambridge, 1979).

Elton, G. R., ed., *New Cambridge Modern History*, 2nd edn, vol. 2: *The Reformation 1520–1559* (Cambridge, 1990).

George, T., *The Theology of the Reformers* (Nashville, TN, 1988).

Gordon, B., *The Swiss Reformation* (Manchester, 2002).

Hillerbrand, H. J., *The Protestant Reformation* (New York, 1968).

Holt, M. P., "The Social History of the Reformation: Recent Trends and Future Agendas," *Journal of Social History* 37 (2003), 133–44.

Lindberg, C., *The European Reformations* (Oxford, 1996).

Lindberg, C., *The Reformation Theologians: An Introduction to the Theology of the Early Modern Period* (Oxford, 2002).

MacCulloch, D., *Reformation: Europe's House Divided, 1490–1700* (London, 2003).

Noll, M. A., *Confessions and Catechisms of the Reformation* (Grand Rapids, MI, 1991).

Ozment, S. E., *The Age of Reform 1250–1550* (New Haven and London, 1973).

Pelikan, J., *The Christian Tradition*, vol. 4: *Reformation of Church and Dogma, 1300–1700* (Chicago and London, 1984).

Pettegree, A., *Reformation and the Culture of Persuasion* (Cambridge, 2005).

Reardon, B. M. G., *Religious Thought in the Reformation* (London, 1981).

Rupp, G., *Patterns of Reformation* (London, 1969).

Snyder, A., *Anabaptist History and Theology: An Introduction* (Kitchener, ON, 1996).

Spitz, L. W., *The Protestant Reformation 1517–1559* (New York, 1986).

Williams, G. H., *The Radical Reformation*, 3rd edn (Kirksville, MO, 1992).

2

Christianity in the Late Middle Ages

The backdrop to the Reformation is the late medieval period. In recent scholarship there has been a growing emphasis upon the need to place the Reformation movement in its late medieval context and to bring together the insights of late medieval, Renaissance, and Reformation studies. The separation of these fields – for example, through each having their own university chairs, journals, and learned societies – has greatly hindered this process of synthesis and consolidation, essential to the correct understanding of the ideas of the Reformation. In the two chapters that follow, we shall examine in some detail the two most important intellectual forces in late medieval Europe: humanism and scholastic theology. The present chapter deals with some preliminary points about late medieval religion.

The Growth of Popular Religion

Older studies of the background to the Reformation tended to portray the later Middle Ages as a period in which religion was in decline. In part, this reflected the uncritical attitude adopted by these studies toward the literature of the fifteenth century, which was critical of the church. Modern studies, using more reliable criteria, have indicated that precisely the reverse is true. Between 1450 and 1520, Germany saw a considerable increase in popular religious piety.

Toward the end of this period, on the eve of the Reformation, religion was perhaps more firmly rooted in the experience and lives of ordinary people than

Reformation Thought: An Introduction, Fourth Edition. Alister E. McGrath.
© 2012 John Wiley & Sons, Ltd. Published 2012 by John Wiley & Sons, Ltd.

at any time in the past. Earlier medieval Christianity had been primarily monastic, focused on the life, worship, and writings of Europe's monasteries and convents. Church building programs flourished in the later fifteenth century, as did pilgrimages and the vogue for collecting relics. The fifteenth century has been referred to as "the inflation period of mystic literature," reflecting the growing popular interest in religion. The fifteenth century witnessed a widespread popular appropriation of religious beliefs and practices, not always in orthodox forms.

The phenomenon of "folk religion" often bore a tangential relationship to the more precise yet abstract statements of Christian doctrine that the church preferred, but that many found unintelligible or unattractive. In parts of Europe, something close to "fertility cults" emerged, connected and enmeshed with the patterns and concerns of everyday life.

The agrarian needs of rural communities – such as haymaking and harvesting – were firmly associated with popular religion. Thus in the French diocese of Meaux in the early sixteenth century, the saints were regularly invoked in order to ward off animal and infant diseases, the plague and eye trouble, or to ensure that young women found appropriate husbands. The direct connection of religion and everyday life was taken for granted. The spiritual and the material were interconnected at every level.

The Rise in Anti-Clericalism

An important aspect of fifteenth-century German religion was the phenomenon of anti-papalism and anti-clericalism. Lower clergy were often the butt of crude criticism. Monasteries were regularly depicted as lice-infested dens of homosexual activity. The poor quality of the parish clergy basically reflected their low social status: in early sixteenth-century Milan, chaplains had incomes lower than those of unskilled laborers. Many resorted to horse and cattle trading to make ends meet.

Furthermore, illiteracy was rife among the clergy. Many had learned the Latin words of the Mass off by heart from older colleagues, and were known to make mistakes as time passed and memories failed. As levels of lay literacy soared in the late fifteenth century, the laity became increasingly critical of their clergy. One English squire of the early sixteenth century grumbled that he had distinctly heard his local priest use the accusative case, when the ablative was clearly called for. Many educated laity resented the distinction between the "sacred" and "secular" orders, which implied the clergy enjoyed a closer relationship with God than they did.

Unsurprisingly, there was hostility in some quarters toward the clergy, partly reflecting their incompetence, partly the privileges they enjoyed. The tax breaks enjoyed by clergy were the source of particular irritation, especially in times of economic difficulty. In the French diocese of Meaux, which would become a center for reforming activists in the period 1521–46, the clergy were exempted from all forms of taxation, provoking considerable local resentment. In the diocese of Rouen, there was popular outcry over the windfall profits made by the church by selling grain at a period of severe shortage.

The subsistence crisis of this period focused popular attention on the enormous social distance between the working class and the ecclesiastical establishment. For example, the vast majority of late Renaissance bishops in France were drawn from the nobility, a trend illustrated in diocese after diocese. In Meaux, the higher echelons of the ecclesiastical establishment were drawn from the urban patriciate, as were the senior clergy throughout Brie. A similar pattern can be established at Rouen, as it can at John Calvin's birthplace, Noyon, where the de Hangest family monopolized ecclesiastical affairs, exercising substantial powers of patronage as well as providing most of the bishops of the diocese over a period of more than a quarter of a century.

In the French province of Languedoc, the senior clergy were generally outsiders, often nobility imposed upon the dioceses by royal patronage. Rarely resident within their dioceses, these clergy regarded their spiritual and temporal charges as little more than sources of unearned income, useful for furthering political ambitions elsewhere. The noble background and status of the episcopacy and senior clergy served to distance them from the artisans and peasants and to insulate them from the economic subsistence crisis of the 1520s. It is this growing tension during the 1520s in the relationship between the senior clergy – largely based in the towns and cities – and the rural population which constitutes the backdrop to the origins of the Reformation in France.

Yet it is important not to exaggerate the extent of such anti-clericalism. While there were undoubtedly areas in which such hostility was particularly pronounced – mainly in cities – the clergy were often valued and respected. In rural areas, where levels of lay literacy were low, the clergy remained the most highly educated members of the local community. More importantly, many of the great monasteries of Europe were respected on account of their social outreach and their significant contributions to the local economy. Yet when all this is taken into account, a rumbling discontent remained, often expressed in what is known as the "grievance literature."

The new emphasis upon education within humanist circles throughout much of western Europe in the 1510s and 1520s led to the ecclesiastical establishment being viewed as reactionary, hostile to the new learning and threatened by both its progress and its emphasis upon the personal appropriation of faith. Literature began to appear in the 1520s suggesting that clergy had a vested interest in retaining the old, lax ways, which made few demands of them as teachers, as spiritual guides, or as moral examples or agents.

Anti-papal feelings also increased in the late Renaissance, especially in Germany. The development of this hostility toward the papacy was often linked with the perception that it was dominated by Italians. Hostility to the pope was perhaps greatest among the educated and ruling classes, who resented his interference in local ecclesiastical and political matters; hostility to the clergy was greatest among the ordinary people, especially in the towns, who resented their privileges (such as exemption from taxation) and the oppressive role often played by the clergy as landlords to the German peasants.

Studies of this tradition of anti-clerical and anti-papal feeling have pointed to the existence of what might be called an "ecclesiastical grievance literature." The list of papal and clerical abuses given by Luther in his famous reforming treatise of the 1520s, *Appeal to the German Nobility*, parallels similar lists in circulation in the previous century. Luther appears to have been tapping a tradition of long-standing complaints against the church in order to gain support for his program of reform.

In the popular German mind, Luther and others such as Ulrich von Hutten were identified as common liberators from an oppressive church. Furthermore, there is evidence which strongly suggests that German nationalism, fanned by anti-papal and anti-Italian sentiment, reached a peak in the years 1517 to 1521. A popular mythology had developed which saw in Germany a nation chosen by God to fulfill his purposes. Although this mythology was systematically discredited by humanists in the period 1530–60, it seems that many regarded the German Reformation under Luther as divinely guided and inspired. This phenomenon was not restricted to Germany, of course; the Lollard movement in England seems to have displayed much the same characteristics, for example.

One final point must be made concerning the growth of popular religion in the later Middle Ages. In part, popular religion represented an attempt to convert the abstract ideas of theologians into something more tangible. Baptism, marriage, and death became events surrounded by popular beliefs and practices – usually referred to as "folk religion" – which, although originally derived from the textbooks of Christian theologians, often came to bear little relation to them (see p. 24).

Perhaps the most important element of late medieval popular religion was a cluster of beliefs and practices concerning death, in which participation by a priest was indispensable. The expenses attending such cults of the dead were considerable, a fact reflected in the rise of religious fraternities dedicated to the provision of the appropriate rites of passage for their members. In times of economic hardship, anti-clerical sentiment was an inevitability, as noted earlier (pp. 183–5), for the clergy came to be seen as profiting from the anxiety of the impoverished living concerning their dead kinsfolk.

Central to these practices was the concept of purgatory, vividly portrayed by Dante in Book II of his *Divine Comedy*, which expressed the idea that the dead were required to undergo both punishment and purification for their remaining sins, before being allowed to enter into heaven. In effect, it was thought of as a sort of intermediate clearing-house for the dead as they awaited the final judgment. The idea held a particular popular fascination, as can be seen from the growth in the indulgence trade, which seemed to offer at worst an accelerated passage through purgatory and at best its avoidance altogether.

In Germany, trafficking in indulgences was viewed by Luther as a morally outrageous and theologically questionable exploitation of the natural affections of the common people for their dead. His Ninety-Five Theses (31 October 1517) were a direct criticism of those who asserted that a dead soul might be freed instantly from purgatory on payment of an appropriate amount to an authorized ecclesiastical tradesman. For Germans, insult was added to injury in that the fees paid by them eventually found their way to Italy, to finance the extravagances of the Renaissance papacy. Luther took particular exception to the advertising copy of Johann Tetzel, promoting indulgences:

> As soon as the coin in the coffer rings
> The soul from purgatory springs!

Luther's doctrine of justification by faith alone obviated the need for purgatory and indulgences; the dead could rest in peace on account of their faith, which made them right with God, and not on account of the payment of a sweetener to the church. In France, an indulgence campaign had also been arranged by Leo X and Francis I in 1515, with a view to financing a crusade; in 1518, however, the Parisian faculty of theology protested against some of the superstitious ideas to which this campaign gave rise. It condemned as "false and scandalous" the teaching that "whoever puts into the collection for the crusade one teston or the value of one soul in purgatory sets that soul free immediately, and it goes unfailingly to paradise." Yet, although regarded as questionable by academic theologians, such beliefs held a deep fascination for ordinary people. An "unofficial" theology came to develop, largely unrelated to the approved theology textbooks, but deeply rooted in the hopes and fears of society in general.

As the rift between popular belief and theology grew wider, so reform became an increasingly faint possibility. To reform popular belief by bringing it back into line with an "official" theology presupposed agreement upon what that theology was – and, as we shall see in the following sections, the growth of doctrinal pluralism and confusion effectively ruled out this option. In the end, the reformers cut this Gordian knot by attacking both the popular beliefs and practices *and* the theology upon which they were originally, if increasingly tenuously, based, and by undertaking a massive educational program. However, the problems facing those who wished to reform popular religion in the later Middle Ages are brought into sharp focus through the relative failure of these massive programs of the Reformation period: folk religion and popular superstition proved virtually impossible to eradicate.

The Rise of Doctrinal Pluralism

One of the most significant features of medieval religious thought is the growth of "schools" of theology. Two such schools may be noted briefly: the Thomist school, based upon the writings of Thomas Aquinas (1225–74), and the Scotist school, based upon the rather different ideas found in the writings of John Duns Scotus (c.1265–1308). The Middle Ages was a period of expansion in the universities and schools of Europe. An inevitable result of this expansion was intellectual diversification. In other words, the more academics you have, the more opinions you find in circulation as a result. By the beginning of the sixteenth century, as many as nine such schools had been established within the western European church.

Each of these schools of thought took significantly different positions on a number of major theological questions. For example, was Mary, the mother of Jesus of Nazareth, sinful (the maculist position, defended by Thomas Aquinas), or was she somehow preserved from sin (the immaculist position, defended by Duns Scotus). The schools were also divided over a number of issues relating to the doctrine of justification (to which we shall return in Chapter 7), such as what the individual had to do in order to be justified. Similar divisions existed over a whole range of questions of direct importance to both personal religion and ecclesiastical politics.

But which of these schools of thought was *right*? Which corresponded most closely to the official teaching of the church? To use the appropriate technical terms, what was merely "theological opinion," and what was "Catholic dogma"? It was clearly essential that some way of *evaluating* the reliability of the new doctrines should be brought into play. But, for reasons which we shall explore shortly, no such evaluation was undertaken. The papacy was reluctant to define, and apparently incapable of enforcing, "true doctrine." The result was inevitable: confusion. Private opinion and public policy became confused. Nobody could be quite sure exactly what the official teaching of the church was on certain matters. As one of those matters was the doctrine of justification, it is perhaps not surprising that this doctrine should have been at the center of one major movement for reform – that associated with Martin Luther.

The practical consequences of this doctrinal vagueness are easily documented. An episode from the late Italian Renaissance will serve our purposes well. During the first decade of the sixteenth century, a small group of young Italian noblemen met regularly, in order to discuss matters of religion. The members of this group shared a common concern: how to ensure the salvation of their souls. But how could this be done? What did they have to do in order to be saved? This direct question appeared to have received no clear-cut answer from the ecclesiastical authorities.

A crisis developed within the group, reaching its culmination in 1510. The group split into two sections. One group, convinced that salvation could come about only by a rejection of the world and personal denial, withdrew to a local monastery, there to work out their salvation safe from the influences of a fallen world. The second group chose to remain in the world. Somehow, they reasoned, it must be possible to remain in the world and attain salvation. But nobody was entirely sure of the official position of the church on this major question – a question which Luther later addressed in his doctrine of justification by faith.

Confusion over the official teaching of the church on justification contributed in no small manner to the origins of Luther's program of reform in Germany.

The most recent known authoritative pronouncement on the part of a recognized ecclesiastical body relating to this doctrine dated from 418, and its confused and outdated statements did little to clarify the position of the church on the matter in 1518, 1100 years later. It seemed to Luther that the church of his day had lapsed into Pelagianism (see p. 65), an unacceptable understanding of how an individual entered into fellowship with God. The church, Luther believed, taught that individuals could gain favor and acceptance in the sight of God on account of their personal achievements and status, thus negating the whole idea of grace.

Luther may well have been mistaken in this apprehension – but there was so much confusion within the church of his day that no one was able to enlighten him on the authoritative position of the church on the matter. Even within the papal sovereign enclave at Avignon, an anarchy of ideas prevailed. "Everyone has his own opinion," wrote Boniface Amerbach (1495–1562), who added further to the chaos during the 1520s by promoting the ideas of the "excellent doctor Martin" within this papal stronghold (Figure 2.1).

We can speak of a *spectrum* of thought within the late Middle Ages. A remarkably wide range of doctrines was in circulation. It is all too easy for twentieth-century writers, with the benefit of hindsight, to recognize the potential dangers of the ideas being developed by the first reformers – but *at the time* these ideas attracted little attention from the official defenders of orthodoxy. The boundary

Figure 2.1   Palace and Bridge at Avignon. The Rhone river flows by the Pont Saint-Bénézet (commonly known as Pont d'Avignon) and the medieval Palais des Papes (Popes' Palace). © Gail Mooney/CORBIS

lines between what was orthodox and what was not became so hopelessly confused that it was virtually impossible to treat individuals such as Luther as heretical – and by the time this move became necessary, the Reformation had gained such momentum that it proved difficult to obstruct it. The scene for a future religious confrontation was set by the doctrinal pluralism of the late medieval church.

A Crisis of Authority within the Church

A development in the later medieval period which is of central importance to a study of the Reformation is the growing crisis in authority, evident from the fourteenth century onward. To whom or to what should someone look for an authoritative pronouncement concerning doctrine? Who was in a position to state unequivocally that "the position of the Catholic church on *this* matter is *that*"? In a period which witnessed a remarkable growth in theological debate, it was essential that someone lay down what was mere theological speculation and what was accepted Catholic doctrine. There was a widespread recognition within the church that theological speculation was legitimate – after all, academics had to do something with their spare time, and the church was sufficiently confident in the truth of its teachings to allow them to be subjected to close scrutiny. But there needed to be some means of enforcing orthodoxy (assuming, of course, that "orthodoxy" could be defined, which became increasingly doubtful as time went on). The papacy required the means of coercing those with unorthodox views to abandon them, or at least to stop teaching them.

Two major developments within the late medieval church combined to make the definition and enforcement of orthodoxy virtually impossible in the late fifteenth and early sixteenth centuries. First, the authority of the pope was called into question through the Great Schism and its aftermath. The Great Schism (1378–1417) led to the division of western Christendom on the death of Gregory XI. An Italian faction was led by Urban VI, a French faction by Clement VII. This situation continued until 1417, when the Council of Constance elected Martin V as pope. For a brief period around 1409, there were three claimants to the papacy.

The crucial question was this: how could the dispute concerning who was *really* pope be resolved? It was widely accepted that the final arbiter in all doctrinal disputes within the church was the pope – but *which* pope could settle this dispute? Eventually it was agreed that a Council should meet, with authority to settle the dispute. The Council of Constance (1414–17) was convoked to choose between the three rival candidates for the papacy (Gregory XII, Benedict XIII, and John XXII). The Council conveniently resolved the matter by passing over all three, and choosing its own candidate (Martin V). It seemed that an important general principle had been established: councils have authority over the pope. But Martin V thought otherwise.

The scene was thus set for the development of two rival theories of authority within the church: those who held that supreme doctrinal authority resided in a general council (the "conciliarist" position) and those who argued that it resided in the person of the pope (the "curialist" position). As the recognition of the need for reform of the church grew in the fifteenth century, the conciliarist party argued that the only hope for such reform lay in calling a reforming General Council. Martin Luther reflected such a position in his 1520 *Appeal to the German Nobility*, in which he argued that the German princes had the right to convoke such a council.

The ultimate failure of the conciliarist movement is generally regarded as a central cause of the Reformation, for two reasons. First, it led to hopes being raised that the church might be reformed from within – and when such hopes were dashed, many began to look for ways of *imposing* reform upon the church, perhaps through an appeal to the secular authorities. Second, it posed a challenge to the doctrinal authority of the pope, thereby contributing to the theological confusion of the later medieval period. As it was not clear who held ultimate doctrinal authority, many theologians developed their theological opinions without asking too many questions concerning their authenticity.

The second major factor of importance here is the rise in the power of the secular rulers of Europe, who increasingly came to regard the pope's problems as of somewhat limited relevance. Moreover, the popes seem to have been reluctant to make use of the channels already available for enforcing doctrinal orthodoxy. For example, the German diocesan and provincial synods had the power to suppress heresy – but these synods were not convened when required in the early sixteenth century. The attention of many European rulers was focused initially upon the Franco-Italian war and subsequently on the Hapsburg–Valois conflict, at the time when the Reformation *could* have been forcibly suppressed, had the political will been present.

Yet the ability of the popes to call on secular rulers to enforce their religious will was ebbing away. Nationalism became an increasingly important factor in reducing papal authority north of the Alps, as the situation in France demonstrates. The dramatic victory of Francis I over the combined papal and Swiss forces at Marignano in September 1515 established him as a force to be reckoned with in Italian affairs, and enhanced his authority over the French church. The ensuing Concordat of Bologna (1516) gave Francis I the right to appoint all the senior clergy of the French church, effectively weakening direct papal control over that church. Francis, aware of the need to enforce religious orthodoxy within his realm, delegated responsibility for this matter to the Faculty of Theology of the University of Paris – a body which soon became known simply as "the Sorbonne." Francis's gradual move toward absolutism, although temporarily interrupted by his defeat at the battle of Pavia (1525) and subsequent imprisonment at Madrid, led to a corresponding decrease in papal influence over French affairs, whether state or ecclesiastical.

As a result, reforming movements within France were treated as a matter concerning Francis I, rather than the pope. Had the pope wished to intervene in the affairs of the French church, a formidable series of diplomatic and legal obstacles awaited him. Having just defeated the pope in battle, Francis showed relatively little interest in defending papal interests in France, save when they happened to coincide with those of the French monarchy.

A further illustration of the severe restrictions placed upon papal authority by secular rulers can be seen in the case of Henry VIII's attempts to divorce Catherine of Aragon, which took place from 1527 to 1530. At the time when Henry petitioned the pope for a divorce (which would normally have been forthcoming without undue difficulty), the pope found himself under enormous pressure from the emperor Charles V – who happened to be related to Catherine of Aragon. As Charles had recently sacked Rome and retained a large military presence in the region, the pope was faced with the choice of offending either the king (who had not, and was never likely to have, armies anywhere near Rome) or the emperor (who had such armies, and was perfectly prepared to use them). The outcome was a foregone conclusion. Henry VIII did not get his divorce.

There was thus a twofold crisis of authority in the later medieval church. There was obvious confusion concerning the nature, location, and manner of exercise of *theological* authority, just as there was either a reluctance or an inability to exercise the *political* authority required to suppress the new ideas of the Reformation. In the midst of this ecclesiastical confusion and powerlessness, the Reformation proceeded with increasing pace, until its local suppression was no longer a realistic possibility.

An English Case Study: Lollardy

The Reformation did not bring a church into being from nowhere; throughout Europe, it built upon existing foundations. It is increasingly being recognized that the English Reformation rests on Lollard foundations. Lollardy is therefore included in this analysis of late medieval religion as a single case study, illustrating the way in which elements of popular religion contributed toward the origins and shaping of a local reformation.

Recent studies have demonstrated the complexity of Lollardy, making generalizations concerning its basic beliefs considerably more hazardous than was once the case. For example, although some Lollards were opposed to the idea of purgatory, most appear to have been content to allow it to remain; serious opposition to the concept in England appears to have gained momentum only with the execution of John Frith over the question in 1533. However, a cluster of basic attitudes which appear to have been widespread within the movement can be summarized as follows. Lollards, in general, believed that:

1   The Bible ought to be available in the vernacular.
2   The veneration of images is unacceptable.

3   The practice of pilgrimage is open to serious criticism.
4   Every layperson is a priest.
5   The pope exercises excessive authority.
6   Christ's presence in the communion bread is purely spiritual (as opposed to the medieval doctrine of **transubstantiation**; see p. 164).

> **transubstantiation**   Doctrine according to which the bread and the wine are transformed into the body and blood of Christ in the Eucharist.

In one sense, this list of beliefs could be argued to be little more than a form of grievance literature. Yet it points to certain attitudes, prevalent within Lollard circles, which gave rise to an enhanced stage of receptivity toward Lutheran ideas when these began to make their appearance in England in the 1520s. Lutheran doctrines resonated with these attitudes. For example, Luther's doctrine of the "priesthood of all believers" was consonant with the Lollard dislike of priests and the Lollard belief that all the laity had a right to call themselves priests. Similarly, the Lutheran doctrine of justification by faith seemed (at least to the Lollards) to imply that there was no longer any need for popes, priests, or the institutional church – all of which they cordially detested – in the process of salvation. Each individual could make peace with God, without dragging the detested ecclesiastical hierarchy into the matter.

Movements similar to Lollardy appear to have existed in many parts of Europe, providing fertile seedbeds in which the ideas of the Reformation could germinate and take root. The Lollards developed nothing like the sophisticated doctrines of the priesthood of all believers or justification by faith alone. At best, they were possessed of attitudes, or a general outlook, which was severely critical of the church of their day. But Lutheran ideas, when they came, made a lot of sense to Lollardy. They resonated with these attitudes, reinforced their arguments, adding intellectual sophistication to Lollard enthusiasm and giving a new theological foundation to their criticisms of the English church.

This, then, is a brief overview of the pressures building up within the late medieval church. Instability was on the increase. It is clear that some kind of shake-up was inevitable. In the end, it took the form of the Reformation, as we now know it. A significant additional element within this process of destabilization of existing medieval religious beliefs and practices was the rise of Renaissance humanism. It was not long before the new methods of humanism were raising serious questions about aspects of medieval doctrine. We shall explore this development in the following chapter.

Further Reading

Bartlett, R., *The Making of Europe: Conquest, Colonization, and Cultural Change, 950–1350* (Princeton, NJ, 1993).

Bolton, B., *The Medieval Reformation* (London and Baltimore, 1983).

Brown, P., *The Rise of Western Christendom: Triumph and Diversity AD 200–1000*, 2nd edn (Cambridge, MA, 2003).

Cameron, E., *Enchanted Europe: Superstition, Reason, and Religion, 1250–1750* (Oxford, 2010).

Dipple, G., *Antifraternalism and Anticlericalism in the German Reformation: Johann Eberlin von Günzburg and the Campaign against the Friars* (Aldershot, 1996).

Duffy, E., *Saints and Sinners: A History of the Popes*, 3rd edn (New Haven, CT, 2006).

Dykema, P. A., and H. A. Oberman, eds., *Anticlericalism in Late Medieval and Early Modern Europe*, 2nd edn (Leiden, 1994).

Lambert, M. D., *Medieval Heresy: Popular Movements from Bogomil to Hus* (London, 1977).

Lewis, C. S., *The Discarded image: An Introduction to Medieval and Renaissance Literature* (Cambridge, 1964).

Logan, F. D., *A History of the Church in the Middle Ages* (New York, 2002).

McGrath, A. E., *The Intellectual Origins of the European Reformation*, 2nd edn (Oxford, 2003).

Oakley, F., "Religious and Ecclesiastical Life on the Eve of the Reformation," in *Reformation Europe: A Guide to Research*, ed. S. Ozment (St Louis, MO, 1982), pp. 5–32.

Oberman, H. A., "The Shape of Late Medieval Thought," in *The Dawn of the Reformation* (Grand Rapids, MI, 1992), pp. 18–38.

Ozment, S. E., *The Age of Reform 1250–1550: An Intellectual and Religious History of Late Medieval and Reformation Europe* (New Haven, CT, 1973).

Strauss, G., *Manifestations of Discontent in Germany on the Eve of the Reformation* (Bloomington, IN, 1971).

Swanson, R. N., *Church and Society in Late Medieval England* (Oxford, 1993).

Volz, C. A., *The Medieval Church: From the Dawn of the Middle Ages to the Eve of the Reformation* (Nashville, TN, 1997).

3

Humanism and the Reformation

Of the many intellectual and cultural tributaries which contributed to the flow of the Reformation, probably the most important was Renaissance humanism. Although the Reformation began in the cities of Germany and Switzerland, there are excellent reasons for suggesting that it may well have been the inevitable outcome of developments in fourteenth-century Italy, as the movement that we now know as the "Italian Renaissance" gained momentum. The present chapter will survey the ideas and methods of Renaissance humanism, in order that their relevance to the Reformation may be understood.

When the word "humanism" is used by a twentieth-century writer, it generally refers to an anti-religious philosophy which affirms the dignity of humanity without any reference to God. "Humanism" has acquired very strongly secularist – perhaps even atheist – overtones. But in the sixteenth century the word "humanist" had a quite different meaning, as we shall see shortly. Humanists of the fourteenth, fifteenth, or sixteenth centuries were remarkably religious, if anything concerned with the *renewal* rather than the *abolition* of the Christian church.

Readers should set aside the modern sense of the word "humanism" in preparing to meet this phenomenon in its late Renaissance setting. Renaissance humanism was not an ideological program, still less an anti-religious movement. It was rather a body of literary knowledge and linguistic skill based on the "revival of good letters." This is how the term "humanist" was understood from the fourteenth through to the sixteenth century. It is pointless to impose modern

Reformation Thought: An Introduction, Fourth Edition. Alister E. McGrath.
© 2012 John Wiley & Sons, Ltd. Published 2012 by John Wiley & Sons, Ltd.

polemical senses of the term on this era. We must learn to use the word in the sense of this age, which is the practice of this volume.

One important terminological point must also be made before beginning our discussion of humanism and the Renaissance as they relate to the Reformation. The reader is likely to encounter reference, even in English-language works, to the Italian terms *trecènto*, *quattrocènto*, and *cinquecènto* (often with the accent omitted). These refer, respectively, to the 1300s, the 1400s, and the 1500s – in other words, to the *fourteenth*, *fifteenth*, and *sixteenth* centuries. Similarly, a *quattrocentísta* is a fifteenth-century figure, and a *cinquecentísta* a sixteenth-century figure. Many English-speaking readers wrongly assume that the *quattrocènto* is the *fourteenth* century, and find themselves hopelessly confused as a result.

The Concept of "Renaissance"

Although the French term "Renaissance" is now universally used to designate the literary and artistic revival in fourteenth- and fifteenth-century Italy, contemporary writers tended to refer to the movement by means of other terms: "restoration," "revival," "awakening," and "reflowering." ("Italy," of course, here designates a geographical rather than a political entity.)

In 1546 Paolo Giovio referred to the fourteenth century as "that happy century in which Latin letters are conceived to have been reborn [*renatae*]," anticipating this development. Certain historians, most notably Jacob Burckhardt, have argued that the Renaissance gave birth to the modern era. It was in this era, Burckhardt argued, that human beings first began to think of themselves as *individuals*. The communal consciousness of the medieval period gave way to the individual consciousness of the Renaissance. Florence became the new Athens, the intellectual capital of a brave new world, with the river Arno separating the old and the new worlds.

In many ways, Burckhardt's definition of the Renaissance in purely individualist terms is highly questionable, in view of powerful evidence for the strongly collective values of aspects of Italian Renaissance humanism – from, for example, a collective approach to city life (seen in Florentine civic humanism), to politics (for example, the *parte Guelfa*), to commerce (seen in the wool guild), and to family life. But in one sense Burckhardt is unquestionably correct: *something* novel and exciting developed in Renaissance Italy, which proved capable of exercising a fascination over generations of thinkers.

It is not entirely clear why Italy in general, or Florence in particular, became the cradle of this brilliant new movement in the history of ideas. A number of factors have been identified as having some bearing on the question:

1   Italy was saturated with visible and tangible reminders of the greatness of antiquity. The ruins of ancient Roman buildings and monuments were scattered throughout the land. As Roberto Weiss points out in his *Renaissance*

Discovery of Classical Antiquity, these ruins represented vital links with a great past. They appear to have kindled interest in the civilization of ancient Rome at the time of the Renaissance, and acted as a vital stimulus to its thinkers to recover the vitality of classical Roman culture at a time which they regarded as being culturally arid and barren.

2   Scholastic theology – the major intellectual force of the medieval period – was never particularly influential in Italy. Although many Italians achieved fame as theologians (such as Thomas Aquinas and Gregory of Rimini), they were generally active in the universities of northern Europe. There was thus an intellectual vacuum in Italy during the fourteenth century. Vacuums tend to be filled – and it was Renaissance humanism which filled this particular gap.

3   The political stability of Florence depended upon the maintenance of her republican government. It was thus natural to turn to the study of the Roman Republic, including its literature and culture, as a model for Florence.

4   The economic prosperity of Florence created leisure, and hence a demand for literature and the arts. Patronage of culture and the arts was seen as a suitable use for surplus wealth.

5   As Byzantium began to crumble – Constantinople finally fell in 1453 – there was an exodus of Greek-speaking intellectuals westward. Italy happened to be conveniently close to Constantinople, with the result that many such émigrés settled in her cities. A revival of the Greek language was thus inevitable, and with it a revival of interest in the Greek classics.

The Concept of "Humanism"

The term "humanism" is actually a nineteenth-century invention. It is important to appreciate that the term "humanism" was not used at the time of the Renaissance itself, although we find frequent use of the Italian word *umanista*. This word refers to a university teacher of *studia humanitatis* – "human studies," or "liberal arts," such as poetry, grammar, and rhetoric. (The English word "humanist," which first appears in 1589, has the sense of "a literary scholar, especially someone versed in Latin studies.")

The observation that the word "humanism" dates from so late suggests that Renaissance writers themselves did not recognize the existence of a common outlook or worldview known by this name. Modern readers tend to assume that "humanists" were individuals who subscribed to a common body of beliefs, attitudes, and values known as "humanism," in much the same way as Marxists are individuals who subscribe to Marxism. Yet there is little historical evidence for this assumption. As we shall see, it proves remarkably difficult to define what this common body of beliefs, attitudes, and values was.

This present section is chiefly concerned with the problem of defining humanism. The term is still used widely in Renaissance and Reformation studies, often with an irritating degree of fluidity. What is meant by the term "humanism"? In the recent past, two major lines of interpretation of the movement were predominant. First, humanism was viewed as a movement devoted to classical scholarship and philology. Second, humanism was the new philosophy of the Renaissance. As will become clear, both these interpretations of humanism have serious shortcomings.

Classical Scholarship and Philology

It is beyond doubt that the Renaissance witnessed the rise of classical scholarship. The Greek and Latin classics were widely studied in their original languages. Although some early studies suggested that humanism originated outside a university context, the evidence now available points unquestionably to a close link between humanism and the universities of northern Italy. It might therefore seem that humanism was essentially a scholarly movement devoted to the study of the classical period. This, however, would be to overlook the question of *why* the humanists wished to study the classics in the first place. The evidence available makes it clear that such study was regarded as *a means to an end*, rather than *an end in itself*. That end was the promotion of contemporary written and spoken eloquence. In other words, the humanists studied the classics as models of written eloquence, in order to gain inspiration and instruction. Classical learning and philological competence were simply the tools used to exploit the resources of antiquity. As has often been pointed out, the writings of the humanists devoted to the promotion of eloquence, written or spoken, far exceed those devoted to classical scholarship or philology.

The New Philosophy of the Renaissance

According to some interpreters of humanism, the movement embodied the new philosophy of the Renaissance, which arose as a reaction to scholasticism. Thus it was argued that the Renaissance was an age of Platonism, whereas scholasticism was a period of Aristotelianism. Others argued that the Renaissance was essentially an anti-religious phenomenon, foreshadowing the secularism of the eighteenth-century Enlightenment. Hans Baron has argued that humanism was basically a republican movement, which studied Cicero in order to benefit from his political ideas.

Two major difficulties confronted these rather ambitious interpretations of humanism. First, as we have seen, humanists appear to have been primarily concerned with the promotion of eloquence. While it is not true to say that humanists made no significant contribution to philosophy, the fact remains that they were primarily interested in the world of letters. Thus, in comparison with those devoted to the "pursuit of eloquence," there are remarkably few humanist writings devoted to philosophy – and these are generally somewhat amateurish. Baron's theory concerning the humanist use of Cicero was weakened through the observation that most humanists read Cicero to learn from his style of writing, rather than from his political ideas.

Second, intensive study of humanist writings uncovered the disquieting fact that "humanism" was remarkably heterogeneous. For example, many humanist writers did indeed favor Platonism – but others favored Aristotelianism. The stubborn persistence of Aristotelianism (for example, at the University of Padua) throughout the Renaissance is a serious obstacle to those who regard humanism as philosophically homogeneous. Some Italian humanists did indeed display what seem to be anti-religious attitudes – but other Italian humanists were profoundly pious. Some humanists were indeed republicans – but others adopted different political attitudes.

Recent studies have also drawn attention to a less attractive side of human- ism – the obsession of some humanists with magic and superstition – which is difficult to harmonize with the conventional view of the movement. In short, it has become increasingly clear that "humanism" lacked any coherent philosophy. No single philosophical or political idea dominated or characterized the move- ment. Indeed, it seemed to many that the term "humanism" would have to be dropped from the vocabulary of historians, because it had no meaningful content. Designating a writer a "humanist" conveys no essential information concerning his philosophical, political, or religious views.

In fact, it is clear that the Italian Renaissance is so multifaceted that just about every generalization concerning its "characteristic ideas" tends to be a distortion. It is for this reason that the view of humanism developed by Paul Oskar Kristeller (1905–99) is of decisive importance. Kristeller's view of humanism has gained wide acceptance within North American and European scholarship, and has yet to be discredited.

Kristeller's View of Humanism

Kristeller envisages humanism as a cultural and educational movement, primarily concerned with the promotion of eloquence in its various forms. Its interest in morals, philosophy, and politics is of secondary importance. To be a humanist is to be concerned with eloquence first and foremost, and with other matters inci- dentally. Humanism was essentially a cultural program, which appealed to clas- sical antiquity as a model of eloquence. In art and architecture, as in the written and spoken word, antiquity was seen as a cultural resource, which could be appropriated by the Renaissance. Petrarch referred to Cicero as his father and Virgil as his brother. The architects of the quattrocento studiously ignored the Gothic style of northern Europe, in order to return to the classical styles of antiquity. Cicero was studied as an orator, rather than a political or moral writer.

In short, humanism was concerned with *how ideas were obtained and expressed*, rather than with *the actual substance of those ideas*. A humanist might be a Platonist or an Aristotelian – but in either case, the ideas involved derived from antiquity. A humanist might be a skeptic or a religious believer – but both attitudes could be defended from antiquity. The enormous attractiveness of Kristeller's view of humanism derives from the fact that it accounts brilliantly for the remarkable diversity of the Renaissance. Where Baron identifies one set of ideas as central and Burckhardt another, Kristeller points to the way in which ideas were generated and handled as being central. The diversity of *ideas* which is so characteristic of Renaissance humanism is based upon a general consensus concerning *how to derive and express those ideas.*

It will be obvious that any discussion of the relation of humanism to the Reformation will be totally dependent upon the definition of humanism employed. Kristeller's definition of humanism allows the most reliable assessment of the relation of these two movements now available.

Ad Fontes – Back to the Fountainhead

The literary and cultural program of humanism can be summarized in the slogan *ad fontes* – "back to the fountainhead." This slogan sums up the retrospective admiration for antiquity that is so characteristic of this age. Humanist writers invented the term "Middle Ages" as a way of dismissing the cultural and intellectual merits of the period between the glories of antiquity and the present day. For Petrarch (1304–74), the centuries between the fall of Rome and his own age were little more than an extended period of darkness. The perceived squalor of the medieval period should, and could, be bypassed in order to recover the intellectual and artistic glories of the classical period. The slogan *ad fontes* demanded that the "filter" of medieval commentaries on classical texts – whether literary, legal, religious, or philosophical – should be abandoned, in favor of a direct engagement with these original texts themselves. Applied to the Christian church, the slogan *ad fontes* meant a direct return to the title deeds of Christianity: the **patristic** writers and, supremely, the New Testament.

patristic Adjective referring to the first few centuries in the history of the church, following the writing of the New Testament.

The slogan, however, does more than specify the sources to be used in the rebirth of civilization. It also specifies the attitude to be adopted toward those sources. It is necessary to remember that the Renaissance was an era of discovery, both geographical and scientific. The discovery of the Americas fired the imagination of the late Renaissance, as did new insights into the functioning of the human body and the natural world. Likewise, the classical sources were read with a view to rediscovering the experiences they reflected.

In his *Aeneid*, Virgil described the discovery of new and strange lands; so late Renaissance readers approached Virgil with a sense of expectation, for they too were in the process of discovering *terrae incognitae*. Galen was read in a new light: he described the gaining of physiological insights to a generation engaged in a similar search in their own day and age. And so it was also with Scripture.

The New Testament described the encounters of believers with the risen Christ – and late Renaissance readers approached the text of Scripture with the expectation that they too could meet the risen Christ, a meeting which seemed to be denied to them by the church of their day.

This point is often overlooked, but holds the key to the humanist reverence for ancient texts. For the humanists, classical texts mediated an experience to posterity – an experience which could be regained by handling the text in the right way. The new philological and literary methods developed by the thinkers of the Renaissance were thus seen as a way of recapturing the vitality of the classical period. For the Christian church, this opened up a new, exciting, and challenging possibility – that the experience of the first Christians, described in the New Testament, could be regained and transferred to a much later point in history.

It is this factor, perhaps more than any other, which helps to explain the remarkably high regard in which humanists were held in Reforming circles throughout Europe. It seemed to many that the sterile form of Christianity associated with the Middle Ages could be replaced with a new, vital, and dynamic form, through the study of Scripture. *Ad fontes* was more than a slogan: it was a lifeline to those who despaired of the state of the late medieval church. The **apostolic era**, the Golden Age of the church, could once more become a present reality.

> **apostolic era** Definitive period of the Christian church, bounded by the resurrection of Jesus Christ (c.35) and the death of the last apostle (c.90?).

It is perhaps difficult for some modern readers to empathize with this sense of excitement and anticipation, yet to enter into the thought-world of Europe on the eve of the Reformation, we must try to recapture this sense of expectation. To many individuals and groups throughout Europe, it seemed that a new day in the history of the church was about to dawn, in which the risen Christ would be restored to the church. It seemed to many, such as Luther, that God in his providence had given the church the key (in the new humanist textual and philological tools) by which the New Testament experience of Christ could be unlocked and made available.

Northern European Humanism

At this point, we must pause to clarify one important point. The "humanism" which affected the Reformation is primarily *northern European* humanism, rather than *Italian* humanism. We must therefore consider what form this northern European movement took.

The Northern European Reception of the Italian Renaissance

It is becoming increasingly clear that northern European humanism was decisively influenced by Italian humanism at every stage of its development. If there

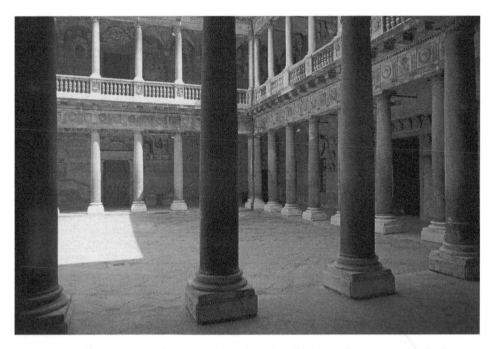

Figure 3.1 A scene from the medieval University of Padua. Veneto region: Padua, Bo Palace, university cloister. © De Agostini/SuperStock

were indigenous humanist movements in northern Europe which originated independently of their Italian counterpart (which is very doubtful), the evidence unambiguously points to those movements having subsequently been decisively influenced by Italian humanism. This does not mean that northern humanists simply took over Italian ideals in their totality; rather, these ideals were adopted and adapted as they seemed to relate to the northern situation. Thus the civic humanism associated with, for example, the city of Florence was not adopted extensively in northern Europe, except in a few German and Swiss cities.

Three main channels for the diffusion of the methods and ideals of the Italian Renaissance into northern Europe have been identified:

1 *Northern European scholars moving south to Italy*, perhaps to study at an Italian university or as part of a diplomatic mission (Figure 3.1). On returning to their homeland, they brought the spirit of the Renaissance back with them. An excellent example of this is provided by Christoph Scheurl, who studied law at Bologna before returning to the newly founded University of Wittenberg with a doctorate of law and a love of letters. This latter soon expressed itself in major reforms of the curriculum at Wittenberg, which may have been of importance in attracting Martin Luther to teach there.

2 *The foreign correspondence of the Italian humanists.* Humanism was concerned with the promotion of written eloquence, and the writing of letters

was seen as a means of embodying and spreading the ideals of the Renaissance. The foreign correspondence of Italian humanists was considerable, extending to most parts of northern Europe.

3   *Printed books, originating from sources such as the Aldine Press in Venice.* These works were often reprinted by northern European presses, particularly those at Basle in Switzerland. Italian humanists often dedicated their works to northern European patrons, thus ensuring that they were taken notice of in potentially influential quarters. The university library at Wittenberg is known to have possessed significant holdings of humanist writings, many personally dedicated to Frederick the Wise.

The Ideals of Northern European Humanism

Although there were major variations within northern European humanism, three ideals seem to have achieved widespread acceptance throughout the movement:

1   A concern for *bonae litterae* – written and spoken eloquence, after the fashion of the classical period – similar to that so characteristic of the Italian Reformation.
2   A religious program specifically directed toward the corporate revival of the Christian church. The Latin slogan *Christianismus renascens,* "Christianity being born again," summarizes the aims of this program (see p. 20), and indicates its relation to the "rebirth" of letters associated with the Renaissance. Although Burckhardt is unquestionably right to state that the Renaissance led to a new emphasis on the subjective consciousness of the individual, northern European humanists supplemented this new emphasis on the individual with a recognition of the need to reform the communities (both church and state) to which the individual belonged. It is worth noting at this point that the Renaissance emphasis upon the subjective consciousness of the individual is specifically linked with the doctrine of justification by faith, to which we shall return in Chapter 7.
3   Some sections of northern European humanism adopted strongly pacifist attitudes during the early sixteenth century, largely in reaction to the tragedy of the Franco-Italian war. The quest for international peace and mutual understanding was espoused by most humanists at the time, particularly in Switzerland. Distaste for papal political maneuvering was also an important element in the background to the Swiss Reformation.

Eastern Swiss Humanism

Perhaps on account of its geographical position, eastern Switzerland proved especially receptive to the ideas of the Italian Renaissance. The University of Vienna attracted large numbers of students from this region. A palace revolution within the faculty of arts, engineered largely through the influence of Konrad Celtis, ensured that Vienna became a center of humanist learning in the final years of the fifteenth century, attracting individuals such as the great humanist writer Joachim von Watt (1484–1551), alias Vadian. Vadian, having gained every academic honor possible at Vienna, returned to his native town of St Gallen, becoming its leading citizen (*Burgomeister*) in 1529. The University of Basle achieved a similar reputation in the 1510s, and became the center of a humanist group (usually known as a "**sodality**") that gathered around such individuals as Thomas Wyttenbach.

Eastern Swiss humanism has been the subject of intensive study, and its basic ethos is fairly well understood. For its leading representatives – Vadian, Xylotectus, Beatus Rhenanus, Glarean, and Myconius – Christianity was primarily a way of life, rather than a set of doctrines. They saw reform as indeed needed – but reform related primarily to the morality of the church and to personal moral renewal of individual believers. There was no pressure for a reform of church doctrine.

The ethos of Swiss humanism was strongly moralistic. The Bible was regarded as prescribing correct moral behavior for Christians, rather than narrating the promises of God. This ethos has a number of significant implications, especially in relation to the doctrine of justification (see pp. 128–30). In the first place, the questions which stimulated Luther's concern for the doctrine were quite absent from Swiss circles, in which justification was something of a non-issue. Second, as it became an issue in Germany, a certain degree of anxiety developed within Swiss humanist circles in the 1520s about Luther's doctrine of justification. To the Swiss humanists, Luther seemed to be developing ideas which were a radical threat to morality, and thus to the distinctive ethos of their movement.

These observations are important in relation to Huldrych Zwingli, educated at the universities of Vienna (1498–1502) and Basle (1502–6). Zwingli's program of reform at Zurich, initiated in 1519, bears the hallmark of Swiss humanist moralism. Augustine, the "doctor of grace," does not appear to figure prominently in Zwingli's thought until the 1520s (and even then, his influence relates primarily to Zwingli's sacramental thinking). Eventually Zwingli broke with the moralism of Swiss humanism (probably around 1523, certainly by 1525), but until this point his program of reform was based upon the moralist educational outlook so characteristic of Swiss humanist sodalities of the period.

French Legal Humanism

In early sixteenth-century France, the study of law was in the process of radical revision. The absolutist French monarchy under Francis I, with its increasing trend toward administrative centralization, regarded legal reform as essential to the modernization of France. In order to speed up the process of legal reform, which eventually led to the formulation of a legal system universally valid throughout France, it patronized a group of scholars, centered on the universities of Bourges and Orléans, engaged in studying the theoretical aspects of general codes of law founded on universal principles.

A pioneer among these was Guillaume Budé, who argued for a direct return to Roman law, which was both eloquent and economic, as a means of meeting the new legal needs of France. In contrast with the Italian custom (*mos italicus*) of reading classical legal texts in the light of the glosses (annotations to the text) and commentaries of medieval jurists such as Bartholis and Accursius, the French developed the procedure (*mos gallicus*) of appealing directly to the original classical legal sources in their original languages.

One direct result of the humanist program of proceeding directly *ad fontes* was a marked impatience with glosses and commentaries. Far from being viewed as useful study tools, these increasingly became regarded as obstacles to engagement with the original text. The interpretations of classical Roman legal texts by writers like Bartholis and Accursius came to be seen as irrelevant. They were like distorting filters, placed between the reader and the text. As humanist scholarship became more confident in its assertions, the reliability of Accursius and others was increasingly called into question by legal humanists. The great Spanish scholar Antonio Nebrija published a detailed account of errors he had detected in Accursius's glosses, while the French novelist and wit François Rabelais wrote scornfully of "the inept opinions of Accursius." The foundations of French legal humanism had been well and truly laid.

The importance of this development to the Reformation must be noted. One student at Bourges and Orléans during the heyday of French legal humanism was the future reformer John Calvin, who probably arrived at Orléans in 1528. Through studying civil law at Orléans and Bourges, Calvin came into first-hand contact with a major constituent element of the humanist movement. This encounter turned Calvin into a competent lawyer; when he was subsequently called upon to assist with the codification of the "laws and edicts" of Geneva, he was able to draw on his knowledge of the *Corpus iuris civilis* for models of contract, property law, and judicial procedure. But Calvin learned more than this from French legal humanism.

Budé's literary output points to his conviction not merely that the classical heritage, including its legal institutions and codes, was laden with importance for the present, but also that the study of antiquity was a proper preparation for the gospel of Jesus Christ. Calvin would adopt a similar approach in the great 1559 edition of the *Institutes of the Christian Religion*, allowing Cicero to guide the reader from the natural religion of antiquity toward the superior gospel of Jesus Christ.

The origins of the methods of Calvin, who was perhaps the greatest biblical commentator and preacher of his age, may be argued to lie in his study of law in the advanced atmosphere of Orléans and Bourges. There is every indication that Calvin learned from Budé the need to be a competent philologist, to approach a foundational text directly, to interpret it within the linguistic and historical parameters of its context, and to apply it to the situation of his own day. It is precisely this attitude which undergirds Calvin's exposition of Scripture, especially in his sermons, in which he aims to fuse the horizons of Scripture and the context of his audience. French legal humanism gave Calvin both the incentive and the tools to allow the documents of yesteryear to interact with the circumstances of the city of Geneva in the 1550s.

Erasmus of Rotterdam

If any figure stands head and shoulders above other northern European humanists, not least in terms of his influence upon both the German and the Swiss reformations, it was Erasmus of Rotterdam (Figure 3.2). Although the direct influence of Erasmus upon Luther and Calvin is less than might be expected, many other reformers (such as Zwingli and Bucer) were heavily influenced by him. It is therefore essential that his considerable contribution to the thought of the Reformation be considered in some detail.

Erasmus is often presented as reflecting northern European humanism at its best. While there is much that could be said in support of this suggestion, certain tensions within northern European humanism must be recognized. Two are of

Figure 3.2 Erasmus von Rotterdam, humanist, philologist, and church critic. Copperplate engraving, 1526, by Albrecht Dürer (1471–1528), 24.9 × 19.3 cm. Photo: akg-images

particular interest: one concerning the question of national languages, the other concerning the question of national boundaries.

Erasmus regarded himself as a "citizen of the world" and Ciceronian Latin as the language of that world. National languages were an obstacle to his vision of a cosmopolitan Europe united by the Latin language. To other humanists, especially in Germany and Switzerland, national languages were to be encouraged as promoting a sense of national identity.

For Erasmus, the vision of a cosmopolitan Europe was threatened by political and cultural nationalism, which only served to reinforce outdated concepts such as a "sense of national identity" and associated ideas such as national boundaries. Other humanists, by contrast, saw themselves as engaged in a struggle to *promote* national identity. Where Erasmus would have preferred to concentrate upon *eliminating* nationalist ideas and values, the Swiss humanists Glarean, Myconius, and Xylotectus saw themselves as having a sacred duty to defend Swiss national identity and culture by literary means. This tension between the "cosmopolitan" and "nationalist" humanist visions, between those wishing to *abolish* and those wishing to *consolidate* national identities, reflects the conflicting views current within humanism. It also demonstrates that Erasmus cannot be regarded as a totally representative spokesman for humanism, as some scholars suggest.

The most influential humanist work to circulate in Europe during the first decades of the sixteenth century was Erasmus's *Enchiridion militis Christiani* (Handbook of the Christian Soldier). Although the work was first published in 1503, and was then reprinted in 1509, the real impact of the work dates from its third printing in 1515. From that moment onward, it became a cult work, apparently going through 23 editions in the next six years.

Its appeal was to educated lay men and women, whom Erasmus regarded as the most important resource that the church possessed. Its amazing popularity in the years after 1515 suggests that a radical alteration in lay self-perception may have taken place as a result – and it can hardly be overlooked that the reforming rumbles at Zurich and Wittenberg date from soon after the *Enchiridion* became a bestseller. Erasmus's success also highlighted the importance of printing as a means of disseminating radical new ideas – a point which neither Zwingli nor Luther overlooked, when their turn came to propagate such ideas.

The *Enchiridion* developed the attractive thesis that the church of the day could be reformed by a collective return to the writings of the Fathers and to Scripture. The regular reading of Scripture is put forward as the key to a new lay piety, on the basis of which the church may be renewed and reformed. Erasmus conceived of his work as a layperson's guide to Scripture: it provided a simple yet learned exposition of the "philosophy of Christ." This "philosophy" was really a form of practical morality rather than an academic philosophy; the New Testament concerns the knowledge of good and evil, in order that its readers may eschew the latter and love the former.

The New Testament, according to Erasmus, is the *lex Christi*, "the law of Christ," which Christians are called to obey. Christ is the example whom Christians are called to imitate. Yet Erasmus does not understand Christian faith to be mere external observance of some kind of morality. His characteristically humanist emphasis upon inner religion leads him to suggest that reading of Scripture *transforms* its readers, giving them a new motivation to love God and their neighbors.

A number of features of this book are of particular importance. First, Erasmus understands the future vitality of Christianity to lie with the laity, not the clergy. The clergy are seen as educators, whose function is to allow the laity to achieve the same level of understanding as themselves. There is no room for any superstitions which give the clergy a permanent status superior to that of their lay charges. Second, Erasmus's strong emphasis on inner religion results in an understanding of Christianity which makes no reference to the church – its rites, its priests, or its institutions. Why bother confessing sins to another human being, asks Erasmus, just because he's a priest, when you can confess them directly to God himself? Religion is a matter of the individual's heart and mind; it is an inward state. Erasmus pointedly avoids any significant reference to the sacraments in his exposition of Christian living. Similarly, he discounts the view that the "religious life" (in other words, that of a monk or a nun) is the highest form of the Christian life: the layperson who reads Scripture is just as faithful to his or her calling as any monk.

The revolutionary character of Erasmus's *Enchiridion* lies in its daring new suggestion that the recognition of the Christian vocation of the layperson holds the key to the revival of the church. Clerical and ecclesiastical authority is discounted. Scripture should and must be made available to all, in order that all may return *ad fontes,* to drink of the fresh and living waters of the Christian faith, rather than the stagnant ponds of late medieval religion.

Erasmus came to recognize, however, that there were serious obstacles in the path of the course he proposed, and he was responsible for a number of major developments to remove them. First, there was a need to be able to study the New Testament in its original language, rather than in the inaccurate Vulgate translation. This required two tools, neither of which was then available: the necessary philological competence to handle the Greek text of the New Testament, and direct access to that text itself.

The Critique of the Vulgate Text

The first tool became available through Erasmus's discovery of Lorenzo Valla's fifteenth-century notes on the Greek text of the New Testament. These notes, which had languished in the archives of a local monastery, were discovered and published by Erasmus in 1505. The second was made available through the publication by Erasmus of the first printed Greek New Testament, the *Novum Instrumentum omne,* which rolled off Froben's presses at Basle in 1516. Although a superior version of the same text had been set up in type at Alcalá in Spain two years earlier, publication of this version (the so-called Complutensian Polyglot) was delayed, probably for political reasons, until 1520.

Important though it was, Erasmus's text was not as reliable as it ought to have been: Erasmus had access to a mere four manuscripts for most of the New Testament and only one for its final part, the Book of Revelation. As it happened, that manuscript left out five verses, which Erasmus himself had to translate into Greek from the Latin of the Vulgate. Nevertheless, it proved to be a literary milestone. For the first time, theologians had the opportunity to compare the original Greek text of the New Testament with the later Vulgate translation into Latin.

Drawing on Lorenzo Valla's work, Erasmus showed that the Vulgate translation of several major New Testament texts could not be justified. As a number of medieval church practices and beliefs were based upon these texts, Erasmus's allegations were viewed with consternation by many conservative Catholics (who wanted to retain these practices and beliefs) and with equally great delight by the reformers (who wanted to eliminate them). Some examples will indicate the relevance of Erasmus's biblical scholarship.

The Christian church has always attached particular importance to certain rites, or forms of worship, which are referred to as *sacraments* (see pp. 163–4). Two such sacraments were recognized by the early church as "dominical" (in other words, as having been authorized by Jesus Christ himself). These were baptism and the sacrament now known by a variety of names, such as "the Mass," "the Lord's supper," the "breaking of the bread," or "the Eucharist." In his exposition of the parable of the Good Samaritan (Luke 10:25–37), the great patristic theologian Augustine argued that the two silver coins given by the Samaritan to the innkeeper (10:35) were an allegory of the two sacraments of the gospel given by Christ to his church.

By the end of the twelfth century, however, this number had increased to seven. The development and consolidation of the sacramental system of the church is one of the most important aspects of medieval theology, and is due in part to a major work of medieval theology – Peter Lombard's *Four Books of the Sentences*. The seven sacraments now recognized by the church were Eucharist, baptism, penance, confirmation, marriage, ordination, extreme unction.

Erasmus's new translation of the New Testament seemed to many to call this entire system into question. The noted English scholar Thomas Linacre, who gave up the practice of medicine in order to become a priest, is reported to have spoken the following words after reading the gospels for the first time in their original Greek: "Either this is not the gospel, or we are not Christians." It will be helpful to consider some of the things which may have moved Linacre to make such a statement.

Much medieval theology justified the inclusion of matrimony in the list of sacraments on the basis of a New Testament text which – at least in the Vulgate translation – spoke of marriage being a *sacramentum* (Ephesians 5:31–32). Erasmus followed Valla in pointing out that the Greek word (*musterion*) here translated as "sacrament" simply meant "mystery." There was no reference whatsoever to marriage being a "sacrament." One of the classic proof texts used by medieval theologians to justify the inclusion of matrimony in the list of sacraments was thus rendered virtually useless.

Similarly, the Vulgate translated the opening words of Jesus's ministry (Matthew 4:17) as "*Do penance*, for the Kingdom of heaven is at hand." This translation suggested that the coming of the kingdom of heaven had a direct connection with the sacrament of penance. Erasmus, again following Valla, pointed out that the Greek should be translated as "*Repent*, for the Kingdom of heaven is at hand." In other words, where the Vulgate seemed to refer to an outward practice (the sacrament of penance), Erasmus insisted that the reference was to an inward psychological attitude – that of "being repentant." Once more, an important justification of the sacramental system of the church was challenged.

Another area of theology which medieval theologians had developed far beyond the modest views of the early church relates to Mary, the mother of Jesus. For many later medieval theologians, Mary was compared to a reservoir of grace, which could be drawn upon when needed. In part, this view rested on the medieval understanding of grace as a kind of substance – an understanding that was abandoned at the time of the Reformation (see pp. 115–16). It also rested upon the Vulgate translation of Gabriel's words to Mary (Luke 1:28) as "the one who is full of grace [*gratia plena*]," thus suggesting the image of a reservoir full of a liquid (grace). But, as Erasmus and Valla both pointed out, the Greek simply meant "favored one," or "one who has found favor." Once more, an important feature of medieval theology seemed to be contradicted by humanist New Testament scholarship.

There was thus a general loss of confidence in the reliability of the Vulgate, the "official" Latin translation of the Bible. No longer could "Scripture" and "the Vulgate text" be regarded as one and the same thing. For the reformers, however, these developments were nothing less than providential. As we have seen, the reformers wanted to return to the beliefs and practices of the early church – and if Erasmus's new translation of the New Testament helped demolish medieval additions to those beliefs and practices, then so much the better. Humanist biblical scholarship was therefore regarded as an ally in the struggle for the return to the simplicity of the apostolic church. Much of the complex network of religious ideas and customs of the late Middle Ages could thus be set to one side, as distortions of (or additions to) an earlier and simpler form of Christianity.

Editions of Patristic Writers

Erasmus's program of reform also required ready access to the writings of the Fathers. This necessitated the production of reliable editions of the writings of theologians such as Ambrose, Augustine, and Jerome (Erasmus's favorite patristic writer). Erasmus was responsible for a remarkable feat of editorial work, producing a series of patristic editions which were the marvel of the age. Although Erasmus's edition of the writings of Augustine compares unfavorably with the great 11-volume Amerbach edition of 1506, his edition of the works of Jerome was widely regarded as an intellectual wonder of the world.

It must not be thought that the theologians of the medieval period ignored the views of patristic writers such as Augustine. They revered such writings, but did not have access to full and accurate editions. Thus medieval writers tended to quote very short extracts, usually referred to as "sentences," from the Fathers. These sentences were quoted without reference to their context. Since the full versions of the works from which they were quoted were to be found only in a few manuscripts locked away in monastic libraries, it was virtually impossible to check that a Father's viewpoint was being accurately presented. Augustine in particular was often misunderstood through being quoted out of context. The production of printed editions of these works allowed the context of these sentences to be studied, so it now became possible to gain an understanding of the Fathers at a depth denied to the earlier medieval writers.

Furthermore, a large number of works ascribed to Augustine in circulation in the Middle Ages were found to have been written by somebody else. These "pseudo-Augustinian" works frequently developed views opposed to those of Augustine, making it remarkably difficult for readers to make sense of his apparently contradictory statements. The arrival of the textual-critical methods of humanist scholarship led to these pseudo-Augustinian works being recognized for what they were, and hence being excluded from definitive editions of Augustine's writings. The way was thus opened to more reliable interpretation of the Fathers, by eliminating spurious "patristic" writings. The scholarly techniques for identifying spurious writings had been developed by Lorenzo Valla (c.1406–57) in the fifteenth century, and these were used to demonstrate the inauthenticity of the famous *Donation of Constantine* (a document allegedly drawn up by the emperor Constantine giving certain privileges to the western church).

The editions of patristic writers prepared by humanist scholars such as Erasmus and the Amerbach brothers thus made the theology of this important age available in a fuller, more reliable form than had ever been possible before. As a result, it became possible to discern major differences of emphasis and substance between the views of writers such as Augustine and those of the theologians of the later Middle Ages. In Luther's view, it was necessary to reform the ideas of the medieval church by returning to the authentic teachings of Augustine, especially in relation to the doctrine of grace. The new editions of the patristic writers thus added further fuel to the demands for reform of the church.

Humanism and the Reformation – An Evaluation

What impact did humanism have upon the Reformation? In order to give a reliable answer to this question, it is necessary to draw a distinction between two wings of the Reformation: the Reformation as it developed at Wittenberg under

Martin Luther, and the Reformation as it developed at Zurich under Huldrych Zwingli. These two wings had very different characters, and generalizations about "the Reformation" tend to confuse them. The assumption that underlies some writing about the Reformation – that it was intellectually and culturally homogeneous – is seriously flawed. As we emphasized earlier, although the Wittenberg and Swiss reformations (which ultimately led to the establishment of the Lutheran and the Reformed churches) appealed to much the same theological sources (Scripture and the Fathers) as the basis of their reforming programs, they did so using very different methods and with correspondingly different results. One of the most striking differences between these wings of the Reformation concerns their very different relation to humanism. We shall consider them individually before returning to some more general points.

Humanism and the Swiss Reformation

The origins of the Swiss Reformation may be traced back to the rise of humanist groups (usually known as "sodalities") at the universities of Vienna and Basle in the early 1500s. Swiss students, who in the fifteenth century had tended to study at universities noted for their links with scholastic theology, now showed a marked preference for universities with strongly humanist associations. Switzerland was geographically close to Italy, and appears to have become a clearing-house for the northern European dissemination of the ideas of the Renaissance by the beginning of the sixteenth century. Many of the leading printing houses of Europe – for example, Froschauer in Zurich and Froben and Cratander in Basle – were Swiss. At a time when Swiss national identity appeared to be threatened by the Franco-Italian war, many Swiss humanists appear to have been inspired by the vision of establishing the literary and cultural identity of Switzerland.

The overall impression gained of early sixteenth-century Swiss intellectual life is that of groups of intellectuals based in the Swiss university cities beginning to develop the vision of *Christianismus renascens*. The turning point for this movement came when one member of a humanist sodality, Huldrych Zwingli, was called to Zurich as a preacher in January 1519. Exploiting his position, Zwingli initiated a program of reform based on broadly humanist principles, especially the vision of the corporate renewal of church and society on the basis of Scripture and the Fathers.

Zwingli had earlier studied at the humanist universities of Vienna and Basle, and his early works reflect the particular concerns of Swiss humanism. He had met Erasmus while the latter was at Basle in 1516 seeing his Greek New Testament through Froben's presses, and was deeply influenced by his ideas and methods. Erasmus's influence upon Zwingli is evident in the following:

1 Religion is seen as something spiritual and internal; external matters cannot be allowed to become of vital importance. The primary purpose of religion

is to inculcate in the believer a set of inner attitudes, such as humility and willing obedience to God. Although Zwingli would argue that any program of reform worthy of the name would extend to external matters (such as the nature of worship and the manner in which the church should be governed), his primary emphasis appears to fall firmly on the need for inner renewal.

2   Considerable importance is attached to moral and ethical regeneration and reform. To many scholars, the early Swiss Reformation appears to be primarily a *moral* reformation, with emphasis upon the need to regenerate both individual and society.

3   The relevance of Jesus Christ to the Christian is primarily as a moral example. Erasmus developed the idea of Christian faith as an *imitatio Christi*, an "imitation of Christ," and Zwingli follows him in this respect.

4   Certain of the early church Fathers are singled out as being of particular importance. For both Erasmus and Zwingli, Jerome and Origen are particularly valued. Although Zwingli would later begin to recognize the importance of Augustine, this development dates from the 1520s: the *origins* of Zwingli's reforming program seem to owe nothing to Augustine.

5   Reformation concerns primarily the life and morals of the church, rather than its doctrine. For most humanists, "philosophy" was about the process of living, rather than a set of philosophical doctrines (see, for example, Erasmus's concept of the *philosophia Christi*, the "philosophy of Christ," which is essentially a code of life). Initially, Zwingli does not seem to have regarded reformation of the church as extending to its doctrine – merely to its life. Thus his first reforming actions concerned the practices of the Zurich church, such as the way in which services were ordered and the manner in which churches were decorated.

6   Reformation is viewed as a pedagogical or educational process. It is an essentially human process, based upon the insights contained in the New Testament and the early church Fathers. It was only in the early 1520s that we find Zwingli breaking away from this idea, to embrace the idea of Reformation as a divine action overruling human weakness.

To summarize, then: the Swiss Reformation was dominated by humanism, which was the only intellectual force of any significance in the region at the time. Zwingli's early program of reform is thoroughly humanist, drawing on both the characteristic insights of Swiss humanism and those of Erasmus. The influence of humanism upon the Swiss Reformation was nothing less than decisive. This makes the contrast with the Reformation at Wittenberg, to which we now turn, all the more obvious.

Humanism and the Wittenberg Reformation

Although humanism was a fairly important intellectual force in Germany by the early 1500s, its impact on Martin Luther appears to have been limited. Luther was an academic theologian, whose world was dominated by the thought-patterns of scholastic theology. Through a careful reading of the writings of Augustine, Luther became convinced that the form of scholastic theology with which he was familiar was wrong. It failed to do justice to the grace of God, and tended to suggest that the individual could earn his or her own salvation. His task was to oppose this theology. Whereas Zwingli regarded the *morals* of the church as what needed reforming, Luther saw the church's theology as what was in need of reform. Luther's reforming theology is set in an academic context (the University of Wittenberg), and is aimed at an academic target (the theology of "**nominalism**," or the *via moderna*, which we shall consider in more detail in the following chapter). Furthermore, Luther's quarrel with scholastic theology centered on the doctrine of justification – a concern which finds no real echo in the Swiss Reformation.

Equally, Luther's concern with *doctrine* as such is without any real parallel in either humanism or the early Swiss Reformation. Humanism saw reformation as concerning the *life and morals* of the church – but not doctrine. Indeed, most humanists seem to have regarded an interest in doctrine as equivalent to an obsession with scholastic theology. With Luther, however, we find a determination to inquire into the teaching of the church, with a view to reforming that teaching in the light of Scripture. It is true, of course, that the later Swiss Reformation – especially under the leadership of Bullinger and Calvin – became much more concerned with matters of doctrine. But at this early stage, under Zwingli's leadership, doctrine was marginalized.

In order to combat scholasticism, Luther drew heavily upon Scripture and the Fathers, supremely Augustine. In doing so, he used the new editions of the Greek New Testament and the writings of Augustine which had been prepared by humanist editors. Luther regarded it as nothing less than providential that these new sources should be available to support his program of reform. His knowledge of Hebrew, his editions of Augustine, his Greek text of the New Testament – all were provided by humanist editors and educationalists. In many ways, the theological program developed by Luther and Karlstadt at Wittenberg could be seen as humanist. Luther and the humanists were strongly opposed to scholasticism (although for different reasons, as we shall see below).

Indeed, the impression that Luther was sympathetic to humanism gained ground in the late 1510s, perhaps supremely as a result of the Leipzig Disputation of 1519, in which Luther debated a series of issues with the Catholic controversialist Johann Eck. Much of what Luther said during that debate seemed to echo the concerns of humanists. Not surprisingly, reports began to circulate in humanist circles concerning this previously obscure figure who had publicly defended humanist ideals with such bravado. The Leipzig Disputation might have remained an obscure academic debate had not humanists taken up Luther's cause with enthusiasm, convinced that he was one of their number.

There is no real evidence, however, that Luther had any interest in humanism as such, or any sympathy for its goals; he seems simply to have exploited its products for his own ends. The superficial similarities between the two programs mask profound differences. Luther and his colleagues used only the textual and philological skills of humanism, while remaining hostile to humanist attitudes. In the final section of this chapter we shall develop this point further.

Tensions between the Reformation and Humanism

Although humanism made decisive contributions to the development of the Reformation, as we have just seen, there were, nevertheless, tensions between humanism and both wings of the Reformation. Five areas may be singled out for comment:

1 *Their attitude to scholastic theology.* The humanists, the Swiss reformers, and the Wittenberg reformers all had no hesitation in rejecting scholasticism; yet their reasons for doing so were different. The humanists rejected scholasticism because of its unintelligibility and inelegance of expression; they wanted a simpler and more eloquent theology. Similar attitudes are evident within the Swiss Reformation. The Wittenberg reformers, by contrast (especially Luther and Karlstadt), had no difficulty in *understanding* scholastic theology; their rejection of scholasticism was based on their conviction that its theology was fundamentally wrong. Where the humanists and Zwingli dismissed scholasticism as an irrelevance, the Wittenberg reformers regarded it as the major obstacle in the path of a reforming theology.

2 *Their attitude to Scripture.* All three groups believed that Scripture held the key to reform of the church, in that it bore witness to Christian belief and practice in its original form. For the humanists, the authority of Scripture rested in its eloquence, simplicity, and antiquity. The Swiss and Wittenberg reformers, by contrast, grounded the authority of Scripture in the concept of the "word of God." Scripture was seen as embodying the commands and promises of God, thus giving it a status over and above any purely human document. The phrase *sola scriptura*, "by Scripture alone," expresses the basic Reformation belief that no source other than Scripture need be consulted in matters of Christian faith and practice. A further tension exists between the Swiss and the Wittenberg reformers: the former regarded Scripture primarily as a source of moral guidance, whereas the latter regarded it primarily as a record of God's gracious promises of salvation to those who believed.

3 *Their attitudes to patristic writers.* For the humanists the writings of the patristic period represented a simple, comprehensible form of Christianity, lent authority by their antiquity and eloquence. In general, humanists appear to have regarded the Fathers as being of more or less equal value, in that all

dated from roughly the same period. Erasmus, however, regarded certain Fathers as of particular importance; in the early 1500s, he singled out Origen (a Greek Father from the third century, noted as much for the unorthodoxy as for the elegance of his writings) for special mention, while by 1515 he had decided to opt for Jerome. His new preference for Jerome is to be explained on the basis of his textual studies of the New Testament, leading to the publication of the Greek edition of the New Testament in 1516. Jerome had earlier undertaken extensive work on the scriptural texts, and Erasmus appears to have regarded Jerome with new interest for this reason. This Erasmian attitude toward the Fathers is also evident within the Swiss Reformation.

The Wittenberg reformers Luther and Karlstadt, by contrast, regarded Augustine as preeminent among the Fathers. The humanists employed two criteria in evaluating the Fathers: antiquity and eloquence – hence Erasmus's preference for both Origen and Jerome. The Wittenberg reformers, however, used an explicitly *theological* criterion in evaluating the Fathers: how reliable were they as interpreters of the New Testament? On the basis of this criterion, Augustine was to be preferred, and Origen to be treated with some suspicion. The humanists were not prepared to use such an explicitly theological criterion in evaluating the relative merits of the Fathers, thus heightening the tension between these two movements.

4   *Their attitudes to education.* In that the Reformation witnessed the birth of a series of new religious ideas (or, at least, ideas which were new to most people in the sixteenth century, even if the reformers argued that they represented the recovery of older ideas), it was essential to the success of both the Wittenberg and the Swiss Reformations that a major program of religious education be undertaken.

Humanism was essentially an educational and cultural movement based upon reform of the liberal arts, with the result that most early sixteenth-century humanists were professional educators. It is therefore interesting to note that most northern European humanists joined the cause of the Reformation not necessarily because they approved of its *religious* ideas, but because they were attracted strongly by its *educational ideals.* The reformers were concerned with the religious ideas being taught, viewing educational methods as the means to that end, whereas the professional humanist educators were primarily concerned with the development of educational techniques, rather than the ideas being taught.

5   *Their attitude to rhetoric.* As we have seen, humanism was concerned with eloquence, both written and spoken. Rhetoric was thus studied as a means to this end. The reformers, in both Germany and Switzerland, were concerned with the promotion of their religious ideas through the written word (for example, in books such as Calvin's famous *Institutes of the Christian Religion*) and the spoken word (for example, in sermons, Luther's eight Wittenberg sermons of 1522 being an excellent example). Rhetoric was

therefore the means to the end of the propagation of the ideas of the Reformation. Recent studies, for example, have emphasized how Calvin's style is heavily influenced by rhetoric. Both humanist and reformer, therefore, regarded rhetoric highly – but for different reasons. For the humanists, rhetoric promoted eloquence; for the reformers, it promoted the Reformation. Once more, we encounter superficial similarities between the two groups which mask profound differences.

On the basis of our discussion so far, it will be clear that the Swiss wing of the Reformation was influenced by humanism to a far greater extent than its counterpart at Wittenberg. Even at Wittenberg, however, the new program of study of the Bible and Augustine appeared to many to be thoroughly humanist in inspiration. With the benefit of hindsight, it is very easy for us to distinguish Luther and Karlstadt from the humanists – yet *at the time*, this distinction was virtually impossible to make. To most observers, Luther and Erasmus were engaged in precisely the same struggle.

A famous illustration of this misunderstanding of Luther by humanists may be noted. In 1518 Luther delivered the famous Heidelberg Disputation, in which he developed a radically anti-humanist and anti-scholastic theology. Among his audience was the young humanist Martin Bucer, later to become a leading reformer in the city of Strasbourg. Bucer wrote with enthusiasm to his humanist correspondent Beatus Rhenanus, declaring that Luther merely stated Erasmus's views, but did so more forcefully. Yet a close comparison of that letter and Luther's own text makes it clear that Bucer seems to have misunderstood Luther on virtually every point.

Again, Luther's stance in the Leipzig Disputation in 1519 – as reflected, for example, in his critique of papal authority – was widely regarded as humanist, and led to his becoming something of a cult figure in humanist circles. Yet Luther's position at Leipzig was not distinctively "humanist" in any meaningful sense of the word; it echoed reforming ideas which were beginning to gain a widespread hearing in evangelical circles throughout Europe at the time.

The full extent of the tension between humanism and the Reformation only became fully apparent perhaps in 1525. In this year, both Zwingli and Luther composed public attacks on Erasmus, both concentrating their attention on the concept of the "freedom of the will." For both reformers, Erasmus's teaching of the total freedom of the human will led to a grossly overoptimistic conception of human nature. With the publication of Zwingli's *Commentary on True and False Religion* and Luther's *On the Bondage of the Will*, the tensions that had always been in existence between humanism and the Reformation became obvious to all.

Yet humanism was only one of two significant intellectual and cultural movements of importance to the Reformation. We must now turn to consider the second such movement – scholasticism.

Further Reading

Baron, H., *The Crisis of the Early Italian Renaissance: Civic Humanism and Republican Liberty in an Age of Classicism and Tyranny* (Princeton, NJ, 1966).

Bouwsma, W. J., *The Waning of the Renaissance, 1550–1640* (New Haven, CN, 2002).

Boyle, M. O., *Rhetoric and Reform: Erasmus' Civil Dispute with Luther* (Cambridge, MA, 1983).

Burckhardt, J., *The Civilization of the Renaissance* (London, 1944).

Burke, P., *The Italian Renaissance: Culture and Society in Italy*, rev. edn (Oxford, 1986).

Dowling, M., *Humanism in the Age of Henry VIII* (London, 1986).

Furey, C. M., *Erasmus, Contarini, and the Religious Republic of Letters* (Cambridge, 2005).

Grassi, E., *Rhetoric as Philosophy: The Humanist Tradition* (University Park, PA, 1980).

Grossmann, M., *Humanism at Wittenberg 1485–1517* (Nieuwkoop, 1975).

McConica, J. K., *Erasmus* (Oxford, 1991).

McGrath, A. E., *The Intellectual Origins of the European Reformation*, 2nd edn (Oxford, 2003).

Monfasani, J., ed., *Kristeller Reconsidered: Essays on His Life and Scholarship* (New York, 2006).

Overfeld, J. H., *Humanism and Scholasticism in Late Medieval Germany* (Princeton, NJ, 1984).

Rabil, A., ed., *Renaissance Humanism: Foundations, Forms, and Legacy*, 3 vols (Philadelphia, PA, 1988).

Rummel, E., *The Humanist–Scholastic Debate in the Renaissance and Reformation* (Cambridge, MA, 1995).

Schoeck, R. J., *Erasmus of Europe: The Making of a Humanist 1467–1500* (Edinburgh, 1990).

Spitz, L. W., *The Religious Renaissance of the German Humanists* (Cambridge, MA, 1963).

Trinkaus, C., *The Scope of Renaissance Humanism* (Ann Arbor, MI, 1983).

van Liere, K. E., "Humanism and Scholasticism in Sixteenth-Century Academe: Five Student Orations from the University of Salamanca," *Renaissance Quarterly* 53 (2000), 57–107.

Weiss, R., *The Renaissance Discovery of Classical Antiquity* (Oxford, 1988).

Witt, R. G., *In the Footsteps of the Ancients: The Origins of Humanism from Lovato to Bruni* (Boston, MA, 2000).

4

Scholasticism and the Reformation

Scholasticism is probably one of the most despised intellectual movements in human history. Thus the English word "dunce" (fool) derives from the name of one of the greatest scholastic writers, John Duns Scotus. Scholastic thinkers – the "schoolmen," as they were called – are often represented as debating earnestly, if pointlessly, how many angels could dance on the head of a pin. This particular debate never actually took place, intriguing though its outcome would unquestionably have been, but it summarizes precisely the way in which scholasticism was regarded by most people, especially the humanists, at the beginning of the sixteenth century: as pointless, arid, intellectual speculation over trivia.

Erasmus of Rotterdam spent some time toward the end of the fifteenth century at the scholasticism-dominated University of Paris. He wrote at length of the many things he detested about Paris: the lice, the poor food, the stinking latrines, and the utterly tedious debates which vexed the schoolmen. Could God have become a cucumber instead of a human being? Could he undo the past, by making a prostitute into a virgin? Although serious questions lay behind these debates, Erasmus's waspish wit diverted attention from those questions themselves to the frivolous and ridiculous way in which they were debated.

Most textbooks dealing with the Reformation therefore feel justified in dismissing scholasticism without actually explaining what it is and why it was of fundamental importance to the Wittenberg Reformation. This chapter seeks to explain these two things, and we begin by attempting to offer a working definition of the term "scholasticism."

Reformation Thought: An Introduction, Fourth Edition. Alister E. McGrath.
© 2012 John Wiley & Sons, Ltd. Published 2012 by John Wiley & Sons, Ltd.

"Scholasticism" Defined

The very word "scholasticism" could be argued to be the invention of humanist writers, anxious to discredit the movement which it represented. The phrase "the Middle Ages" was certainly largely a humanist invention, coined by sixteenth-century humanist writers such as Vadian and Beatus Rhenanus to refer disparagingly to an uninteresting period of stagnation between antiquity (the classical period) and modernity (the Renaissance). The "Middle Ages" was seen as little more than an intermezzo between the cultural magnificence of antiquity and its revival during the Renaissance.

Similarly, the term "scholastics" (*scholastici*) was used by humanists to refer, equally disparagingly, to the ideas of the Middle Ages. In their concern to discredit the ideas of the medieval period, in order to lend enhanced attraction to their appeal to the classical period, the humanists had little interest in drawing distinctions between the various types of "scholastics" – such as Thomists and Scotists. The word "scholasticism" is thus both pejorative and imprecise; yet the historian cannot avoid using it.

How may scholasticism be defined? Like humanism, it is difficult to offer a precise definition that is capable of doing justice to the distinctive positions of all the major schools within the Middle Ages. Perhaps the following working definition may be helpful: scholasticism is best regarded as the medieval movement, flourishing in the period 1200–1500, which placed emphasis upon the rational justification of religious beliefs and the systematic presentation of those beliefs. Thus "scholasticism" does not refer to a *specific system of beliefs*, but to a *particular way of organizing theology* – a highly developed method of presenting material, making fine distinctions, and attempting to achieve a comprehensive view of theology. It is perhaps understandable why, to its humanist critics, scholasticism seemed to degenerate into little more than logical nit-picking.

When the so-called Dark Ages finally lifted from over western Europe, the scene was set for revival in every field of academic work. The restoration of some degree of political stability in France in the late eleventh century encouraged the reemergence of the University of Paris, which rapidly became recognized as the intellectual center of Europe. A number of theological "schools" were established on the Left Bank of the Seine, and on the Île de la Cité, in the shadow of the newly built cathedral of Notre Dame de Paris. Two themes began to dominate theological debate: the need to *systematize* and *expand* Christian theology, and the need to *demonstrate the inherent rationality* of that theology. Although most early medieval theology was little more than a replay of the views of Augustine, there was growing pressure to systematize Augustine's ideas and take them further. But how could this be done? By what method? And on the basis of what philosophical system could the rationality of Christian theology be demonstrated?

Figure 4.1 Thomas Aquinas. Detail in Fra Angelico's *Crucifixion* with the Virgin and Saints John the Evangelist, Dominic, and Thomas Aquinas. Florence, Museo di San Marco. Early Renaissance fresco. © 2011 Photo Scala, Florence – courtesy of the Ministero Beni e Att. Culturali

The answer to these questions came through the rediscovery of Aristotle, in the late twelfth and early thirteenth centuries. By about 1270, Aristotle had become established as "the Philosopher." His ideas came to dominate theological thinking, despite fierce opposition from more conservative quarters. Through the influence of writers such as Thomas Aquinas (Figure 4.1) and Duns Scotus, Aristotle's ideas became established as the best means of establishing and developing Christian theology. The ideas of Christian theology were thus arranged and correlated systematically, on the basis of Aristotelian presuppositions. Equally, the rationality of Christian faith was demonstrated on the basis of Aristotelian ideas. Thus some of Thomas Aquinas's famous "proofs" for the existence of God actually rely on principles of Aristotelian physics, rather than any distinctively Christian insights.

For example, consider his argument from motion. Aquinas argues, on the basis of an Aristotelian axiom, that everything which moves is moved by something else. For every motion, there is a cause. Things don't just move – they are moved. (Duns Scotus disagreed here; angels, he argued, had access to independent means of motion.) Now each cause of motion must itself have a cause. And *that* cause must have a cause as well.

Aquinas therefore argues that there are a whole series of causes of motion underlying the world as we know it. Now unless there are an infinite number of these causes, Aquinas argues, there must be a single cause right at the origin of the series. From this original cause of motion, all other motion is ultimately derived. This is the origin of the great chain of causality, which we see reflected in the way the world behaves. From the fact that things are in motion, Aquinas thus argues for the existence of a single original cause of all this motion – and this Prime Unmoved Mover, he concludes, is God himself. Yet, as his later critics pointed out, this rested on the dangerous and unproved assumption that the Prime Unmoved Mover and the God of Christianity were identical. It seemed to those critics, among whose number we must include Martin Luther, that the gods of Aristotle and Christianity were actually radically different.

This, then, is the essence of scholasticism: the demonstration of the inherent rationality of Christian theology by an appeal to philosophy, and the demonstration of the complete harmony of that theology by the minute examination of the relationship of its various elements. Scholastic writings tended to be long and argumentative, frequently relying upon closely argued distinctions. Thus Duns Scotus, generally known as the "subtle doctor," is obliged to distinguish as many as 15 senses of the Latin word *ratio*, "reason," in order to justify his views on its role in theology.

The noted medieval historian Etienne Gilson once described the great scholastic systems as "cathedrals of the mind." Each scholastic system tried to embrace reality in its totality, dealing with matters of logic, metaphysics, and theology. Everything was shown to have its logical place in a totally comprehensive intellectual system. In what follows, we shall look briefly at the main types of scholasticism encountered in the Middle Ages. But first, we shall consider the milieu in which scholasticism flourished.

Scholasticism and the Universities

For obvious reasons, the influence of scholasticism was at its greatest in the medieval universities. Unlike **quattrocento** humanism, which both flourished in the universities and enjoyed enormous influence in society, scholasticism had a very limited sphere of influence. Humanism made its appeal to the world of education, art, and culture, whereas scholasticism could at best make a limited appeal (in bad Latin) to those who enjoyed dialectics. In an age in which rhetoric and dialectic were seen as mutually incompatible, the superior appeal of the former virtually guaranteed the decline of the latter.

quattrocento The 1400s, i.e., the fifteenth century.

In the late fifteenth century, a confrontation between humanism and scholasticism developed in many universities. The University of Vienna, of fundamental importance to the development of the Swiss Reformation, witnessed precisely such a humanist revolt against scholasticism in the final decade of the fifteenth century. In the early sixteenth century, many students seem to have begun avoiding universities traditionally dominated by scholasticism in favor of those with humanist educational programs. Thus the influence of scholasticism was gradually being eroded even in its academic strongholds as the sixteenth century dawned.

Although on the wane as an academic force, however, the fact remains that Martin Luther's theological development took place in reaction against scholastic theology. Whereas scholasticism was a negligible intellectual force in Switzerland, it was still of major importance in Germany, particularly at the University of Erfurt, at which Luther was educated. Luther's early work as a theological reformer was carried out in a university context, fighting against an academic opponent. In marked contrast, the Swiss reformers were, as we have seen, humanists, bent on reforming the life and morals of the church of their day; they had no need to pay any attention to scholasticism. Luther, by contrast, was forced to enter into dialogue with the major force on his intellectual horizon, scholasticism. The Swiss reformers could afford to ridicule scholasticism, for it posed no threat to them – but Luther had to engage with it directly.

This serves to emphasize the differences between the Swiss and the Wittenberg reformations, whose totally different contexts are too often overlooked. Zwingli began by reforming a city (Zurich); Luther began by reforming a university faculty of theology (Wittenberg). Zwingli began by opposing the life and morals of the pre-Reformation Zurich church; Luther began by opposing a particular form of scholastic theology. Initially Zwingli had no need to propose a reformation of the doctrine of the church, whereas for Luther, doctrinal reformation was the essential springboard of his program of reform. In a later chapter, we shall consider Luther's reaction against scholastic theology. Our attention now turns to the types of scholasticism encountered in the later Middle Ages.

Types of Scholasticism

The reader must accept an apology before proceeding any further. I have found it impossible to simplify any further the material that follows. My experience of teaching Reformation theology suggests that many readers will probably find their attention wandering as I try to explain some of the leading ideas of scholasticism. (This, incidentally, goes some considerable way toward explaining why humanism proved so attractive at the time of the Reformation.) To understand Luther's theological development, however, it is necessary to become acquainted with at least the basics of two major movements in late medieval scholasticism.

Realism versus Nominalism

In order to comprehend the complexities of medieval scholasticism, it is necessary to grasp the distinction between "realism" and "nominalism." The early part of the scholastic period (c.1200–c.1350) was dominated by realism, the later part (c.1350–c.1500) by nominalism. The difference between the two systems may be summarized as follows. Consider two white stones. Realism affirms that there is a universal concept of "whiteness" which these two stones embody. These particular stones possess the universal characteristic of "whiteness." But whereas the white stones exist in time and space, the universal of "whiteness" exists on a different metaphysical plane. Nominalism, by contrast, asserts that the universal concept of "whiteness" is unnecessary, and instead argues that we should concentrate on particulars. There are these two white stones – and there is no need to start talking about "a universal concept of whiteness."

The idea of a "universal," used here without definition, needs to be explored further. Consider Socrates. He is a human being, and is an example of humanity. Now consider Plato and Aristotle. They are also human beings and examples of humanity. We could go on doing this for some time, naming as many individuals as we liked, but the same basic pattern would emerge: individual named people are examples of humanity. Realism argues that the abstract idea of "humanity" has an existence of its own. It is a universal; and particular people – such as Socrates, Plato, and Aristotle – are individual examples of this universal. The common feature of humanity which unites these three individuals has a real existence of its own.

This debate may strike many readers as typical of scholasticism: pointless and pedantic. Nevertheless, it is important for the reader to appreciate that the term "nominalism" refers to a debate concerning universals. *It has no direct theological relevance, and defines no specific theological opinion.* We shall return to this point shortly.

Two major scholastic "schools" influenced by realism dominated the earlier medieval period. These were **Thomism** and **Scotism**, derived from the writings of Thomas Aquinas and Duns Scotus respectively. Neither of these schools had any major influence upon the Reformation, and need not, therefore, be discussed any further. Two later forms of scholasticism, however, appear to have had a major influence upon the Reformation, and thus merit careful attention. These are the *via moderna* (the "modern way") and the *schola Augustiniana moderna* (the "modern Augustinian school").

Many textbooks dealing with the Reformation refer to a confrontation between "nominalism" and **"Augustinianism"** on the eve of the Reformation, and interpret the Reformation as the victory of the latter over the former. In recent years, however, considerable progress has been made in understanding the nature of late medieval scholasticism, leading to a rewriting of the intellectual history of the early Reformation. In what follows, I shall indicate the situations as established by most recent scholarship.

An earlier generation of scholars writing in the period 1920–65 regarded "nominalism" as a religious school of thought which captured most northern European university faculties of theology in the later Middle Ages. It proved remarkably difficult, however, to identify the exact features of this theology. Some "nominalist" theologians (such as William of Ockham and Gabriel Biel) seemed to be very optimistic about human abilities, suggesting that it was possible for a human being to do everything that was necessary to enter into a relationship with God. Other "nominalist" theologians (such as Gregory of Rimini and Hugolino of Orvieto) appeared to be profoundly pessimistic about those same abilities, suggesting that without the grace of God, humanity was totally unable to enter into such a relationship. In desperation, scholars began to speak of "nominalistic diversity." Eventually, however, the real solution to the problem emerged: namely, that there were actually *two* different schools of thought, whose sole common feature was anti-realism. Both schools adopted a nominalist position in matters of logic and the theory of knowledge – but their theological positions differed radically. Earlier, we noted that the term "nominalism" referred strictly to the question of universals and did not designate any particular theological position. Thus both schools rejected the necessity of universals – but thereafter could agree on virtually nothing. One was highly optimistic concerning human abilities, the other considerably more pessimistic. These two schools are now generally known as the *via moderna*, "the modern way," and the *schola Augustiniana moderna*, "the modern Augustinian school." We shall consider these two schools presently. But first, attention is claimed by the terms "Pelagian" and "Augustinian," which are invariably encountered in any discussion of late medieval scholasticism. In what follows, I shall explain what is meant by these terms.

"Pelagianism" and "Augustinianism"

The doctrine of justification, which assumed particular importance within the Lutheran Reformation, concerns the question of how an individual enters into a relationship with God. How can a sinner be accepted by a righteous God? What must the individual do in order to be acceptable to God? This question was debated with some intensity in the early fifth century during the debate between Augustine and Pelagius. This controversy is known as the "Pelagian controversy," and Augustine's writings concerning the doctrines of grace and justification which arose out of it are known as the "anti-Pelagian writings." In many ways, this controversy was replayed in the fourteenth and fifteenth centuries, with the *via moderna* tending toward the position of Pelagius and the *schola Augustiniana moderna* toward that of Augustine. In what follows, I shall give a brief outline of each position.

A central theme of Augustine's thought is the *fallenness* of human nature. The imagery of "the Fall" derives from Genesis 3, and expresses the idea that human nature has "fallen" from its original pristine state. The present state of human nature is thus not what it was intended to be by God. The created order no longer corresponds directly to the "goodness" of its original integrity. It has lapsed. It has been spoiled or ruined – but not irredeemably, as the doctrines of salvation and justification affirm. The image of a "Fall" conveys the idea that creation now exists at a lower level than that intended for it by God.

According to Augustine, it follows that all human beings are now contaminated by sin from the moment of their birth. In contrast to many twentieth-century existentialist philosophies (such as that of Martin Heidegger), which affirm that "fallenness" (*Verfallenheit*) is an option which we choose (rather than something which is chosen for us), Augustine portrays sin as inherent to human nature. It is an integral, not an optional, aspect of our being. This insight, which is given more rigorous expression in Augustine's doctrine of original sin, is of central importance to his doctrines of sin and salvation. In that all are sinners, all require redemption. In that all have fallen short of the glory of God, all require to be redeemed.

For Augustine, humanity, left to its own devices and resources, could never enter into a relationship with God. Nothing that a man or woman could do could ever be sufficient to break the stranglehold of sin. To use an image which Augustine was fortunate enough never to have encountered, it is like a narcotic addict trying to break free from the grip of heroin or cocaine. The situation cannot be transformed from within; hence, if transformation is to take place, it must come from outside the human situation. According to Augustine, God has intervened in the human dilemma in the person of Jesus Christ in order to redeem it.

Augustine lays such emphasis on "grace" that he is often referred to as *doctor gratiae*, "the doctor of grace." "Grace" is the unmerited or undeserved gift of God, by which God voluntarily breaks the hold of sin on humanity. Redemption is possible only as a divine gift. It is not something which we can achieve ourselves, but is something which must be done for us. Augustine thus emphasizes that the resources of salvation are located outside humanity, in God himself. It is God who initiates the process of salvation, not men or women.

For Pelagius, however, the situation looked very different. Pelagius taught that the resources of salvation are located within humanity. Individual human beings have the capacity to save themselves. They are not trapped by sin, but have the ability to do all that is necessary to be saved. Salvation is something which is earned through good works, which place God under an obligation to humanity. Pelagius marginalizes the idea of grace, understanding it in terms of demands made of humanity by God in order that salvation may be achieved – such as the Ten Commandments or the moral example of Christ. The ethos of Pelagianism could be summed up as "salvation by merit," whereas Augustine taught "salvation by grace."

It is obvious that the two different theologies have very different understandings of human nature. For Augustine, human nature is weak, fallen, and powerless; for Pelagius, it is autonomous and self-sufficient. For Augustine, it is necessary to depend upon God for salvation; for Pelagius, God merely indicates what has to be done if salvation is to be attained, and then leaves men and women to meet those conditions unaided. For Augustine, salvation is an unmerited gift; for Pelagius, salvation is a justly earned reward.

One aspect of Augustine's understanding of grace needs further comment. Since human beings are incapable of saving themselves, and since God has given the gift of grace to some (but not all), it follows that God has "preselected" those who are to be saved. Using hints of this idea to be found in the New Testament, Augustine developed a doctrine of predestination. The term "predestination" refers to God's original or eternal decision to save some, and not others. It was this aspect of Augustine's thought which many of his contemporaries, not to mention his successors, found unacceptable. It need hardly be said that there is no direct equivalent in Pelagius's thought.

In the ensuing controversy within the western church, Augustine's position was recognized as authentically Christian, and Pelagius's views were censured as heretical. Two important councils established Augustine's views as normative: the Council of Carthage (418) and the Second Council of Orange (529). Interestingly, Augustine's views on predestination were diluted somewhat, even though the remainder of his system was enthusiastically endorsed. The term "Pelagian" hence came to be pejorative as well as descriptive, meaning "placing excessive reliance upon human abilities, and insufficient trust in the grace of God." At the time of the Reformation, Luther was convinced that most of the western church had lost sight of the idea of the "grace of God" and had come to rely upon human self-sufficiency. He therefore regarded it as his duty to recall the church to the views of Augustine, as we shall see in Chapter 7.

We must now consider the fourteenth- and fifteenth-century replay of this controversy between the *via moderna* and *schola Augustiniana moderna*, the former assuming broadly the role of Pelagius, the latter that of Augustine.

The *Via Moderna*

The term *via moderna* is now becoming generally accepted as the best way of referring to the movement once known as "nominalism," which included among its adherents such fourteenth- and fifteenth-century thinkers as William of Ockham, Pierre d'Ailly, Robert Holcot, and Gabriel Biel. During the fifteenth century, the *via moderna* began to make significant inroads into many northern European universities – for example, at Paris, Heidelberg, and Erfurt. In addition to its philosophical nominalism, the movement adopted a doctrine of justification which many of its critics branded as "Pelagian." In view of the importance of this form of scholasticism to Luther's theological breakthrough, we need to consider its understanding of justification in some detail.

The central feature of the soteriology, or doctrine of salvation, of the *via moderna* is a convenant between God and humanity. The later Middle Ages saw the development of political and economic theories based upon the concept of a covenant (for example, between a king and his people), and the theologians of the *via moderna* were quick to realize the theological potential of this idea. Just as a *political* convenant between a king and his people defined the obligations of king to people and people to king, so a *religious* covenant between God and his people defined God's obligations to his people and their obligation to God. This covenant was not negotiated, of course, but was unilaterally imposed by God. The theologians of the *via moderna* were able to develop this theme – already familiar to readers of the Old Testament – using ideas borrowed from their own political and economic world.

According to the theologians of the *via moderna*, the covenant between God and human beings established the conditions necessary for justification. God has ordained that he will accept an individual on condition that this individual first fulfills certain demands. These demands were summarized using the Latin tag *facere quod in se est*, literally "doing what lies within you," or "doing your best." When individuals met this precondition, God was obliged, by the terms of the covenant, to accept them. A Latin maxim was often used to express this point: *facienti quod in se est Deus non denegat gratiam*, "God will not deny grace to anyone who does what lies within them." The noted late medieval theologian Gabriel Biel, who is known to have influenced Luther through his writings, explained that "doing your best" meant rejecting evil and trying to do good.

At this point, the parallels between the *via moderna* and Pelagius become obvious. Both assert that men and women are accepted on the basis of their own efforts and achievements. Both assert that human works place God under an obligation to reward them. It would seem that the writers of the *via moderna* were simply reproducing the ideas of Pelagius, using a more sophisticated covenantal framework. At this point, however, the theologians of the *via moderna* drew upon contemporary economic theory to argue that they were doing nothing of the sort. Their use of late medieval economic theory is fascinating, in that it illustrates the extent to which medieval theologians were prepared to exploit ideas drawn from their social context.

The classic example invariably cited by these theologians to illustrate the relation between good works and justification is that of the king and a small lead coin. Most medieval coinage systems used gold and silver coins. This had the advantage of guaranteeing the value of the coins, even if it also encouraged the practice of "clipping" precious metal from the coins' sides. The introduction of milled edges to coins represented an attempt to prevent removal of gold or silver in this way.

Occasionally, however, kings found themselves in a financial crisis – typically as a result of the outbreak of war. A standard way of raising funds was to recall gold and silver coins and melt them down. The gold and silver thus retrieved could be used to finance a war. In the meantime, however, currency of some sort was still required. To meet this need, small leaden coins were issued, which bore the same face value as the gold and silver coins. Although their *inherent* value was negligible, their *ascribed* or *imposed* value was considerable. The king would promise to replace the lead coins with their gold or silver equivalents once the financial crisis was past. The value of the lead coins thus resided in the king's promise to redeem them at their full ascribed value at a later date. The value of a gold coin derives from the gold; but the value of a lead coin derives from the royal covenant to treat that coin *as if it were gold*. A similar situation exists, of course, in most modern economies. For example, paper money is of negligible inherent value. Its value derives from the promise of the issuing bank to honor its notes to their full face value.

The theologians of the *via moderna* used this economic analogy to counter the charge of Pelagianism. To the suggestion that they were exaggerating the value of human works (in that they seemed to be making them capable of meriting salvation), they replied that they were doing nothing of the sort. Human works were like lead coins, they argued – of little inherent value. But God had promised, through the covenant, to treat them as if they were of much greater value, in just the same way as a king could treat a lead coin as if it were gold. Pelagius, they conceded, certainly treated human works as if they were gold, capable of purchasing salvation. But *they* were arguing that human works were like lead and that the only reason why they were of any value was that God had graciously undertaken to treat them as if they were much more valuable. The theological exploitation of the difference between the inherent and the imposed value of coins thus served to get the theologians of the *via moderna* out of a potentially awkward situation, even if it did not satisfy their more severe critics, such as Martin Luther.

It is this "covenantal" understanding of justification which underlies Martin Luther's theological breakthrough, to which we shall return in a later chapter. Our attention now turns to the late medieval scholastic theology which re-embraced the ideas of Augustine, in deliberate opposition to the *via moderna*.

The *Schola Augustiniana Moderna*

One of the strongholds of the *via moderna* in the early fourteenth century was the University of Oxford. A group of thinkers, largely associated with Merton College, developed the ideas on justification noted above, characteristic of the *via moderna*. And it was at Oxford that the first backlash against the *via moderna* occurred. The individual responsible for this backlash was Thomas Bradwardine, later to become archbishop of Canterbury. Bradwardine wrote a furious attack on the ideas of the Oxford *via moderna*, entitled *De causa Dei contra Pelagium*, "The case of God against Pelagius." In this book he charged his Merton colleagues with being "modern Pelagians," and developed a theory of justification which represents a return to the views of Augustine, as they are found in the anti-Pelagian writings.

Although Bradwardine's ideas would be developed in England by John Wycliffe, they were taken up on the mainland of Europe by Gregory of Rimini at the University of Paris. Gregory had one particularly significant advantage over Bradwardine: he was a member of a religious order (the Order of the Hermits of St Augustine, generally referred to as the "Augustinian Order"). And just as the Dominicans propagated the views of Thomas Aquinas and the Franciscans those of Duns Scotus, so the Augustinians promoted the ideas of Gregory of

Rimini. It is this transmission of an Augustinian tradition, deriving from Gregory of Rimini, within the Augustinian Order which is increasingly referred to as the *schola Augustiniana moderna*, "the modern Augustinian school." What were these ideas?

First, Gregory adopted a nominalist view on the question of universals. Like many thinkers of his time, he had little time for the realism of Thomas Aquinas or Duns Scotus. In this respect, he had much in common with thinkers of the *via moderna*, such as Robert Holcot and Gabriel Biel.

Second, Gregory developed a soteriology, or doctrine of salvation, which strongly reflected the influence of Augustine's anti-Pelagian writings. He places an emphasis on the need for grace, on the fallenness and sinfulness of humanity, on the divine initiative in justification, and on the divine sovereignty expressed in predestination. Salvation is understood to be *totally* a work of God, from its beginning to its end. Where the *via moderna* held that humans could initiate their justification by "doing their best," Gregory insisted that only God could initiate justification.

In contrast, the *via moderna* held that most (but not all) necessary soteriological resources were located *within* human nature. The merits of Christ were an example of a resource lying outside humanity; the ability to desist from sin and turn to righteousness was, for a writer such as Biel, an example of a vital soteriological resource located within humanity. Gregory of Rimini rejected such approaches and argued that such resources were located exclusively *outside* human nature. Even the ability to desist from sin and turn to righteousness arose through the action of God, not a human action. It is obvious that these represent two totally different ways of understanding the human and divine roles in justification.

Although this academic Augustinianism was particularly associated with the Augustinian Order, not every Augustinian monastery or university school seems to have adopted its ideas. Nevertheless, it seems that a school of thought which was strongly Augustinian in cast was in existence in the late Middle Ages on the eve of the Reformation. In many ways, the Wittenberg reformers, with their particular emphasis on the anti-Pelagian writings of Augustine, may be regarded as having rediscovered and revitalized this tradition. As the views of some leading reformers, such as Luther or Calvin, seem to parallel those of this academic Augustinianism, the question has often been asked: were the reformers influenced, directly or indirectly, by this Augustinian tradition? We shall explore this question in the following section.

The Impact of Medieval Scholasticism upon the Reformation

It is beyond doubt that the two leading lights of the Reformation were Martin Luther and John Calvin. In what follows, we shall consider the possible influences of forms of scholastic theology upon them, noting how their educational environments exposed them to central ideas of late medieval scholasticism.

Luther's Relation to Late Medieval Scholasticism

There can be no doubt that Luther was well versed in scholastic philosophy and theology. During his period at the University of Erfurt (1501–5), the faculty of arts was dominated by representatives of the *via moderna*. He would have gained a deep appreciation of the basic features of this nominalist philosophy during his time there. After his decision to enter an Augustinian monastery (1505), he is known to have become immersed in the theology of the *via moderna*, devouring the writings of leading representatives of the movement such as William of Ockham, Pierre d'Ailly, and Gabriel Biel. Biel's *Commentary on the Canon of the Mass* was a standard theological textbook for those preparing for ordination, and there is ample evidence that Luther studied this work and absorbed its contents.

In the autumn of 1508 Luther went to teach philosophical ethics at the newly founded University of Wittenberg. Earlier that year important changes had been introduced in the university statutes, especially those relating to the faculty of arts. Up to that point, members of that faculty were permitted to teach only according to the *via Thomae* and *via Scoti* – in other words, only Thomist and Scotist ideas were allowed, not those of the *via moderna*. According to the new statutes, however, they were now also permitted to teach according to the *via Gregorii*. The evidence suggests that this was simply another way of referring to the *via moderna*, thus bringing Wittenberg into line with other German universities of the period.

Recent Luther scholarship has emphasized the continuity between the theology of the *via moderna* and that of the young Luther, especially in relation to his philosophy of knowledge and his doctrine of justification. Luther's theology of justification during the years 1513–14 is clearly that of the *via moderna*. God, according to Luther, has entered into a covenant with humanity, whereby those who do *quod in se est* are rewarded with divine grace.

God has established a covenant (*pactum*) with humanity, by which God has promised to justify anyone who meets a certain minimum precondition (*quod in se est*). In effect, Luther teaches that God gives grace to the humble, so that all who humble themselves before God can expect to be justified as a matter of course. Two passages from Luther's *Dictata super Psalterium*, dating from this period, make this point particularly clearly:[1]

> It is for this reason that we are saved: God has made a testament and a covenant with us, so that whoever believes and is baptized will be saved. In this covenant God is truthful and faithful, and is bound by what he has promised.

> "Ask and you will receive; seek and you will find; knock and it shall be opened to you. For everyone who asks, receives, etc." (Matthew 7.7–8) Hence the doctors of theology rightly say that God gives grace without fail to whoever does what lies within them [*quod is se est*].

Because sinners recognize their need for grace and call upon God to bestow it, this places God under an obligation to do so, thereby justifying the sinner. In

Figure 4.2 Seal of the University of Paris, fourteenth century. Woodcut with a watercolor wash. Photo: akg-images/North Wind Picture Archives

other words, the sinner takes the initiative, by calling upon God: the sinner is able to do something which ensures that God responds by justifying him or her.

Luther would eventually break away from this approach to justification, emphasizing God's willingness to give justifying righteousness, rather than the human obligation to earn this through appropriate acts of disposition or preparation. Yet it is important to appreciate that Luther's theological starting point was strongly shaped by a certain school of late medieval scholasticism.

Calvin's Relation to Late Medieval Scholasticism

Calvin began his academic career at the University of Paris in the 1520s. As study after study has made clear, the University of Paris – and especially Calvin's college, the Collège de Montaigu – was a stronghold of the *via moderna* (Figure 4.2). During his four or five years' studying at the faculty of arts at Paris, Calvin could not have avoided encountering the leading ideas of this movement.

One especially obvious point of affinity between Calvin and late medieval theology concerns voluntarism: the doctrine that the ultimate grounds of merit lie in the will of God, not in the intrinsic goodness of an action. To explore this doctrine, let us consider a human moral action – for example, giving money to a charity. What is the meritorious value of this action? What is it worth in the sight of God? The relation between the moral (that is, the human) and the meritorious (that is, the divine) value of actions was of major concern to late medieval theologians. Two distinctive approaches developed: the *intellectualist* and the *voluntarist*.

The intellectualist approach argued that the divine intellect recognized the inherent moral value of an act and rewarded it accordingly. There was a direct connection between the moral and the meritorious. The voluntarist approach rejected this, arguing that it made God dependent on his creatures. The meritorious value of a human action could not be allowed to be predetermined; God had to be free to choose whatever value he liked. There was thus no necessary connection between the moral and the meritorious. So the meritorious value of a human action does not rest upon its inherent value, but is grounded solely in the worth which God chooses to ascribe to it.

This principle is summarized in the maxim of Duns Scotus (usually, though not entirely correctly, regarded as the originator of the trend toward voluntarism in later medieval thought) to the effect that the value of an offering is determined solely by the divine will, rather than by its inherent goodness. The divine will imposed whatever value it chose upon human actions, thereby preserving the freedom of God. In the later Middle Ages, the voluntarist position gained increasing sympathy, especially within radical Augustinian circles. Most theologians of the *via moderna* and *schola Augustiniana moderna* adopted it.

In the *Institutes*, Calvin adopts precisely this voluntarist position in relation to the merit of Christ. Although this is implicit in earlier editions of the work, it is only explicitly stated in the 1559 edition, in the aftermath of Calvin's correspondence with Laelius Socinus on the subject. In 1555, Calvin responded to questions raised by Socinus concerning the merit of Christ and the assurance of faith, and appears to have incorporated these replies directly into the text of the 1559 edition of the *Institutes*.

The death of Christ on the cross is a central focus of Christian thought and worship. But why should the death of Christ have such enormous importance? What justification can be given for its centrality? Why is the death of *Christ* – rather than of any other individual – declared to be of unique significance? In the course of this correspondence, Calvin considers this question, known technically as the *ratio meriti Christi* (the basis of the merit of Christ). Why is Christ's death on the cross sufficient to purchase the redemption of humanity? Is it something intrinsic to the person of Christ, as Luther had argued? For Luther, the divinity of Christ was adequate grounds for declaring that his death was uniquely important. Or was it that God chose to accept his death as sufficient to merit the redemption of humanity? Was this value *inherent* in Christ's death, or was it *imposed* upon it by God?

Calvin makes clear his view that the basis of Christ's merit is not located in Christ's offering of himself (which would correspond to an intellectualist approach to the *ratio meriti Christi*), but in the divine decision to accept such an offering as of sufficient merit for the redemption of mankind (which corresponds to the voluntarist approach). For Calvin, "apart from God's good pleasure, Christ could not merit anything." The continuity between Calvin and the late medieval voluntarist tradition at this point will be evident.

In the past, this similarity between Calvin and Scotus has been taken to imply the direct influence of Scotus on Calvin. In fact, however, Calvin's continuity appears to be with the late medieval voluntarist tradition, deriving from William of Ockham and Gregory of Rimini, in relation to which Scotus marks a point of transition. No reason may be given for the meritorious nature of Christ's sacrifice save that God benevolently ordained to accept it as such. The continuity of Calvin with this later tradition will be clear.

In the present chapter we have considered the phenomenon of medieval scholasticism, and indicated its potential relevance to the Reformation. As will become clear, each of the major reformers has their own distinct relationship to humanism and scholasticism, with Martin Luther perhaps being the most "scholastic" of the reformers, and Huldrych Zwingli perhaps the most "humanist." In the next chapter we shall provide biographical sketches of the major reformers, to help readers place them on a theological map.

Notes

1   WA 3.289; WA 4.262.

Further Reading

Bauerschmidt, F. C., ed. and trans., *Holy Teaching: Introducing the Summa Theologiae of St. Thomas Aquinas* (Grand Rapids, MI, 2005).

Colish, M. L., *The Medieval Foundations of the Western Intellectual Tradition, 400–1400* (New Haven, CN, 1997).

Coplestone, F., A *History of Christian Philosophy in the Middle Ages* (London, 1978).

Evans, G. R., ed., *The Medieval Theologians: An Introduction to Theology in the Medieval Period* (Oxford, 2001).

Gilson, E., *The Spirit of Medieval Philosophy* (London, 1936).

Janz, D. R., *Luther and Late Medieval Thomism* (Waterloo, ON, 1983).

Levi, A. H. T., "The Breakdown of Scholasticism and the Significance of Evangelical Humanism," in *The Philosophical Assessment of Theology*, ed. G. R. Hughes (Georgetown, 1987), pp. 101–28.

McGrade, A. S., ed., *The Cambridge Companion to Medieval Philosophy* (Cambridge, 2003).

McGrath, A. E., *The Intellectual Origins of the European Reformation*, 2nd edn (Oxford, 2003).

Nauert, C. G., "The Clash of Humanists and Scholastics: An Approach to Pre-Reformation Controversies," *Sixteenth Century Journal* 4 (1973), 1–18.

Oberman, H. A., *The Harvest of Medieval Theology* (Cambridge, MA, 1963).

Oberman, H. A., *Masters of the Reformation* (Cambridge, 1981).

Overfeld, J., "Scholastic Opposition to Humanism in Pre-Reformation Germany," *Viator* 7 (1976), 391–420.

Rummel, E., *The Humanist–Scholastic Debate in the Renaissance and Reformation* (Cambridge, MA, 1995).

Southern, R. W., *Scholastic Humanism and the Unification of Europe*, 2 vols (Oxford, 1997–2000).

Steinmetz, D. C., *Misericordia Dei: The Theology of Johannes von Staupitz in Its Late Medieval Setting* (Leiden, 1968).

5

The Reformers:
A Biographical Introduction

It is perhaps too easy to overlook the fact that the Reformation was not simply about social forces (a weakness which seriously reduces the value of the model of the Reformation offered by social historians), nor simply about religious ideas (a weakness which can often be detected in more explicitly theological accounts of the Reformation). The thought of the Reformation was generated and developed by a group of highly significant individuals. While there is no doubt that social factors were deeply involved in the manner in which these ideas were received, and the impact which they had upon society at large, this does not permit us to overlook the individuals who contributed so significantly to the genesis and development of the thought of the Reformation.

It is generally agreed that the Protestant Reformation had two leading luminaries: Martin Luther and John Calvin. The Swiss reformer Huldrych Zwingli, although widely agreed to have been of major importance in relation to the origins and early development of the Reformation in Switzerland, is commonly regarded as the "third man" of the Reformation. This generally low estimation of Zwingli has often been challenged by scholars anxious to point out the originality of his thought, and his major role in laying the ground for the consolidation of the Reformation within the political sphere of influence of certain leading Swiss cantons. Nevertheless, the general perception remains that Zwingli, rightly or wrongly, has had considerably less influence on the shaping of western Christian thought than Luther or Calvin.

The present chapter offers a biographical overview of five leading reformers. The three figures just noted are supplemented by brief accounts of Luther's

Reformation Thought: An Introduction, Fourth Edition. Alister E. McGrath.
© 2012 John Wiley & Sons, Ltd. Published 2012 by John Wiley & Sons, Ltd.

colleague Philipp Melanchthon, and the reformer of the great city of Strasbourg, Martin Bucer. Although women played a significant role at many levels in this age – for example, Margarette of Navarre (1492–1549) – the leading shapers of the intellectual mood of that age were male. It is strongly recommended that you read this chapter before proceeding to engage with the more specifically theological ideas of the Reformation, to be discussed in later chapters. This chapter provides important historical and biographical information which is essential background material to these ideas. We begin by considering the greatest of the first wave of reformers – Martin Luther.

Martin Luther (1483–1546)

Martin Luther (Figure 5.1) is widely regarded as one of the most significant of the reformers. Luther was born on November 10, 1483 in the German town of Eisleben, and named after Martin of Tours, whose festival fell on November 11, the day of Luther's baptism. His father, Hans Luder (as the name was spelled at this stage), moved the following year to the neighboring town of Mansfeld, where he established a small copper mining business. Luther's university education began at Erfurt in 1501. His father clearly intended him to become a lawyer, not

Figure 5.1 Martin Luther, color lithograph, English School, twentieth century, after a nineteenth-century lithograph. Private collection/Ken Welsh/The Bridgeman Art Library

unaware of the financial benefits that this would bring the family. In 1505, Luther completed the general arts course at Erfurt, and was in a position to move on to study law.

As events turned out, the study of law never got very far. At some point around June 30, 1505, Luther was returning to Erfurt from a visit to Mansfeld. As he neared the village of Storterheim, a severe thunderstorm gathered around him. Suddenly, a bolt of lightning struck the ground next to him, throwing him off his horse. Terrified, Luther cried out, "St Anne, help me! I will become a monk!" (St Anne was the patron saint of miners.) On July 17, 1505, he entered the most rigorous of the seven major monasteries at Erfurt – the Augustinian priory. Luther's father was outraged at the decision, and remained alienated from his son for some considerable time.

The Erfurt Augustinian monastery had close links with the University of Erfurt, which allowed Luther to wrestle with the great names of late medieval religious thought – such as William of Ockham, Pierre d'Ailly, and Gabriel Biel – in the course of his preparation for ordination. He was ordained priest in 1507. By 1509, he had gained his first major theological qualification. Finally, on October 18, 1512, he was awarded the degree of Doctor of Divinity, the culmination of his academic studies. By then, however, he had moved from Erfurt and established himself at the nearby town of Wittenberg, which was the home of one of the newer German universities.

The University of Wittenberg was founded in 1502 by Frederick the Wise. His motives in establishing this seat of learning were not entirely educational: he probably wanted to overshadow the reputation of the neighboring university of Leipzig. Luther took up a chair of biblical studies at Wittenberg immediately after gaining his doctorate, and remained there (apart from occasional periods of absence) for the rest of his life. He owed this position to Johann von Staupitz, vicar general of the German Observant Augustinian friars, who had held the position before him.

Luther's lectures at Wittenberg are widely regarded as laying the foundations for his subsequent theological development. It is of considerable significance that Luther's emerging theology was forged against the backdrop of a sustained engagement with certain biblical texts. Over the critical period 1513–19, Luther lectured as follows:

1513–15	Psalms (*Dictata super Psalterium*)
1515–16	Romans
1516–17	Galatians
1517–18	Hebrews

At some point during this period, Luther radically changed his theological views. There is intense scholarly debate over both the nature and the date of this breakthrough, and we shall consider this in more detail in the following chapter.

Luther was propelled to fame through a series of controversies. The first such controversy centered on the sale of indulgences. Archbishop Albert of Mainz had given permission for the sale of indulgences in his territories. Johann Tetzel, who was responsible for the sale of these indulgences in the Wittenberg region, irritated Luther considerably, and moved him to write to Archbishop Albert, protesting against the practice and offering 95 Latin theses which he proposed to dispute at the University of Wittenberg. Luther's colleague Philipp Melanchthon subsequently reported that these 95 theses were also "posted" (that is, nailed for public display) on the door of the castle church at Wittenberg on October 31, 1517. This date has subsequently been observed by some as marking the beginning of the Reformation. In fact, the theses drew little attention until later, when Luther circulated them more widely and had them translated into German.

The archbishop regarded the theses as a direct challenge to his authority, and forwarded them with a letter of complaint to Rome. However, this had less impact than might have been expected. The papacy needed the support of Frederick the Wise to secure the election of its favored candidate to succeed the Holy Roman Emperor Maximilian. As a result, Luther was not summoned to Rome to answer the charges laid against him, but was examined locally in 1518 by the papal legate Cajetan. Luther refused to withdraw his criticisms of the practice of selling indulgences.

Luther's profile was raised considerably in 1519 at the Leipzig Disputation. This disputation pitted Luther and his Wittenberg colleague Andreas Bodenstein von Karlstadt against Johann Eck, a highly regarded theologian from Ingolstadt. During the course of a complicated debate over the nature of authority, Eck managed to get Luther to admit that, in his view, both popes and general councils could err. Even more, Luther indicated a degree of support for Jan Huss, the Bohemian reformer who had been condemned as a heretic some time previously. Eck clearly considered himself to have won the debate, in that he had forced Luther to state views on papal authority which were unorthodox by the standards of the day.

Others, however, were delighted by Luther's criticisms. Of particular importance was the reaction of many humanists, who saw Luther's criticisms as indicating that he was one of their number. In fact, this was not the case. Nevertheless, this "constructive misunderstanding" led Luther to be lionized by humanists around this time, and given a high profile within humanist circles. Although Luther's controversy with Erasmus over the period 1524–5 finally ended any notion that Luther was sympathetic to a humanist agenda, he enjoyed at least the tacit support of many humanists (including Erasmus and Bucer) for several years after the Leipzig Disputation.

Luther's brief flirtation with humanism around 1519 can be illustrated from the way in which he styled himself. One of the conceits of the age was that humanist writers would insist on being known by the Latin or Greek versions of their personal names, perhaps in order to lend themselves a little more dignity. Thus Philipp Schwarzerd became "Melanchthon" (literally, "black earth"); Johann Hauschein became "Oecolampadius" (literally, "house light"). At some point around 1519, Luther himself fell victim to this trend of the age. By then, Luther was gaining a reputation as a critic of the medieval church. His emphasis upon Christian freedom – evident in the 1520 writing *On the Freedom of a Christian* – led him to play around with the original spelling of his family name "Luder." He altered this to "Eleutherius" – literally, "liberator." Within what seems to have been a very short period of time, he tired of this pretension. But the new way of spelling his family name remained. Luder had become Luther.

In 1520, Luther published three major works which immediately established his reputation as a major popular reformer. Shrewdly, Luther wrote in German, making his ideas accessible to a wide public: where Latin was the language of the intellectual and ecclesiastical elite of Europe, German was the language of the common people. In the *Appeal to the German Nobility*, Luther argued passionately for the need for reform of the church. In both its doctrine and its practices, the church of the early sixteenth century had cast itself adrift from the New Testament. His pithy and witty German gave added popular appeal to some intensely serious theological ideas.

Encouraged by the remarkable success of this work, Luther followed it up with *The Babylonian Captivity of the Christian Church*. In this powerful piece of writing, Luther argued that the gospel had become captive to the institutional church. The medieval church, he argued, had imprisoned the gospel in a complex system of priests and sacraments. The church had become the master of the gospel, where it should be its servant. This point was further developed in *The Liberty of a Christian*, in which Luther stressed both the freedom and obligations of the believer.

By now, Luther was at the center of both controversy and condemnation. On June 15, 1520, Luther was censured by a papal bull and ordered to retract his views. He refused, adding insult to injury by publicly burning the bull. He was excommunicated in January of the following year, and summoned to appear before the Diet of Worms. Again, he refused to withdraw his views. Luther's position became increasingly serious. Realizing this, a friendly German prince arranged for him to be "kidnapped," and took him off to the safety of the Wartburg, a castle near Eisenach. During his eight months of isolation, Luther had time to think through the implications of many of his ideas, and to test the genuineness of his motives. By the time he returned to Wittenberg in 1522 to take charge of the Reformation in that town, his ideas were gaining considerable support throughout Europe. By this stage, the Reformation may be said to have begun. In its early phase, it was decisively shaped by Luther.

Luther's influence on the Reformation at this early stage was fundamental. His period of isolation at the Wartburg allowed him to work on a number of major reforming projects, including liturgical revision, biblical translation, and other reforming treatises. The New Testament appeared in German in 1522, although it was not until 1534 that the entire Bible was translated and published. In 1524, Luther argued for the need to establish schools in German towns, and to extend education to women. The two Catechisms of 1529 broke new ground in religious education (see Chapter 12).

Serious controversy, however, was not slow to break out. In 1524, Erasmus published a work that was severely critical of his views on human free will. Luther's reply of 1525 was not the most diplomatic of documents, and led to a final break with Erasmus. More seriously, the Peasants' War of 1525 caused Luther's reputation to suffer severely. Luther argued that the feudal lords had every right to end the peasants' revolt, by force where necessary. Luther's writings on this matter – such as his *Against the Thieving and Murderous Hordes of Peasants* – had virtually no impact on the revolt itself, but tarnished his image severely.

Perhaps the most significant controversy erupted over the very different views on the nature of the real presence held by Luther and Huldrych Zwingli (see Chapter 9). Luther's strong commitment to the real presence of Christ in the Eucharist contrasted sharply with Zwingli's metaphorical or symbolic approach. Although many sought to reconcile the two views, or at least to limit the damage caused by the differences – these eventually came to nothing. The Colloquy of Marburg (1529), arranged by Philip of Hesse, was of particular importance. Its failure can be argued to have led to the permanent alienation of the German and Swiss reforming factions at a time when increasingly adverse political and military considerations made collaboration imperative.

By 1527, it was clear that Luther was not a healthy man. What can now be recognized as Ménière's disease had established itself. Convinced that he had not long to live, Luther married a former nun, Katharina von Bora. Although Luther went on to produce a number of major theological works in his later period (most notably, a commentary on Galatians), his attention was increasingly taken up with his personal health and the politics of the Reformation struggles. He died in 1546 while attempting to mediate in a somewhat minor quarrel which had broken out between some members of the German nobility in the city of Mansfeld.

Luther's influence on virtually every aspect of Reformation thought is immense. His approaches to biblical interpretation, the doctrine of justification, the church, and the sacraments remain theological landmarks, and will be discussed in detail in this work. His views on the relation of church and state, however, are perhaps not as fully thought through as one might like, and bear the impression of having been forged under the pressure of conflict. Nevertheless, Luther must be considered to be one of the two most significant representatives of the Reformation, and it is imperative that his ideas are examined in some detail.

We now move on to consider the career of a lesser, though still significant figure – the Swiss reformer Huldrych Zwingli.

Huldrych Zwingli (1484–1531)

It is impossible to understand the career and strategy of the Swiss reformer Huldrych (or "Ulrich") Zwingli (Figure 5.2) without considering his background within the Swiss Confederation. The name "Switzerland" derives from one of the three original cantons – Schwyz, Uri, and Unterwalden – which signed a treaty of mutual defense against the Austrians in 1291. This confederation – known as the "Helvetic Confederation" (*Confederatio Helvetica*) – was gradually enlarged in the following years. In 1332, Lucerne joined the confederation, followed by Zurich (1351), Glarus and Zug (1352), and Berne (1353). The strength of this confederation was demonstrated at the battle of Nähenfels (1388), at which an historic victory ensured its survival. The great legend of William Tell — a Swiss patriot who fought against the Austrian oppressors – has its origins in the events of this period. In 1481, the cantons of Solothurn and Fribourg joined the confederation, bringing the total membership to 10. In 1501, Basel and Schaffhausen joined, followed by Appenzell in 1513. No further cantons joined the confederation until the aftermath of the French Revolution.

Figure 5.2 Ulrich Zwingli, Swiss Reformation divine. Chaplain to Swiss forces during Second War of Kappel when he was killed in battle. Copperplate engraving by Konrad Meyer (1618–89) from series of 90 portraits of fellow citizens of Zurich, c.1618–c.1689. © The Print Collector/ Alamy

Zwingli was born on New Year's Day, 1484 in the Toggenburg valley in the canton of St Gallen, in the eastern part of modern-day Switzerland. Strictly speaking, St Gallen was not part of the Swiss Confederation. However, in the treaty of 1451, St Gallen had allied itself to some of the Swiss cantons, and Zwingli always appears to have regarded himself as Swiss. After an initial period of education at Berne, Zwingli attended the University of Vienna (1498–1502). Vienna was widely regarded as one of the most exciting universities close to Switzerland, on account of the university reforms then taking place. Under the guidance of leading humanists, such as Conrad Celtis, the university was adopting humanist reforms. He then moved to the University of Basle (1502–6), where he strengthened his humanist position. In 1506, he was ordained priest, and served in this capacity at Glarus for the next 10 years, before moving to serve as "people's priest" at the Benedictine monastery at Einsiedeln in 1516.

During his time as parish priest of Glarus, Zwingli served as a chaplain to Swiss soldiers serving as mercenaries in the Franco-Italian war. He was present at the disaster of Marignano (1515), in which large numbers of Swiss soldiers died. This event confirmed Zwingli's opposition to the mercenary trade, and was also of fundamental importance in the development of Swiss isolationism. In the light of Marignano, it was decided that the Swiss would take no part in other people's wars again.

By 1516, Zwingli had become convinced of the need for reform of the church, along the lines suggested by biblical humanists such as Erasmus. He purchased Erasmus's edition of the Greek New Testament, and studied the writings of both the Greek and Latin patristic authors. By the time he left Einsiedeln for Zurich, Zwingli had become convinced of the need to base Christian belief and practice on Scripture, not human traditions.

On January 1, 1519, Zwingli took up his new position as "people's priest" at the Great Minster in Zurich. From the outset, his commitment to a program of reform was obvious. He began to preach a course of sermons on Matthew's gospel, ignoring the conventional lectionary altogether. Zwingli's career at Zurich came close to being ended abruptly; he nearly died during an outbreak of the plague at Zurich in the summer of 1519. The influence of his escape on his thinking on providence is well established, and will be considered later in this work (see Chapter 10).

It was not long before Zwingli's reforms became more radical. In 1522, he was actively preaching against virtually every aspect of traditional Catholic religion, including the cult of the saints, the practice of fasting, and the worship of Mary. His preaching caused controversy within the city, and alarmed the city council. Anxious at the unrest which was growing within the city, the city council determined to settle the matter. In January 1523, a great public disputation was arranged between Zwingli and his Catholic opponents. The city council sat in judgment, as Zwingli debated his program of reform with some local Catholic clergy. It soon became clear that Zwingli was gaining the upper hand. Able to translate without difficulty from Hebrew, Greek, or Latin into the local Zurich dialect, Zwingli displayed a mastery of Scripture which his opponents simply could not match. There could only be one outcome. The city council decided that a program of reform based on Scripture, such as that outlined by Zwingli, would become official city policy.

In 1525, Zurich city council finally abolished the Mass, and substituted Zwingli's version of the Last Supper. Zwingli's views on precisely what took place at the Eucharist would prove to be immensely controversial (see Chapter 9); indeed, Zwingli is perhaps best remembered for his radical "memorialist" view of the Lord's Supper, which he regards as a remembrance of Christ's death in his absence.

Encouraged by his reforming successes, Zwingli persuaded other city councils to have public debates along the same lines. A major breakthrough took place in 1528, when the city of Berne decided to adopt the Reformation after a similar public disputation. Berne was a major center of political and military power in the region. Its political and military support for beleaguered Geneva in 1536 would prove to be decisive in establishing Calvin's influence over the second phase of the Reformation. Calvin's success as a reformer thus owes more to Zwingli than is generally realized. Zwingli was killed in battle on October 11, 1531, defending his reformation.

Philipp Melanchthon (1497–1560)

One of Luther's closest associates at Wittenberg, Melanchthon was born on February 16, 1497, and went on to attend university at Heidelberg (1509–12) and Tübingen (1512–18). He then moved to a newly established position at the University of Wittenberg in 1518.

Although Melanchthon's speciality was Greek, he soon developed an interest in theology, encouraged to no small extent by Luther, under whose influence he soon fell. One of Melanchthon's earliest theological emphases related to the authority of Scripture. This is particularly clear from a series of theses which he presented for the degree of Bachelor of Theology in 1519. However, it is generally agreed that this emphasis upon the authority of Scripture is seen at its clearest in a work for which Melanchthon is particularly remembered – the *Loci Communes* ("Commonplaces"), which appeared in its first edition in 1521.

We shall consider the influence of the *Loci Communes* in Chapter 10. However, at this stage we may note how Melanchthon constructed the work around a series of biblical themes, particularly relating to the doctrine of justification. The basic intention was to offer a system of Christian theology which was both generated and governed by Scripture. Melanchthon clearly regarded Peter Lombard's *Four Books of the Sentences* – the standard medieval textbook of theology – as deficient in this respect, and wished to move toward an approach which took central themes from Romans as normative. His role as an educationalist was also particularly clear with his finalizing of the text of both the Augsburg Confession and its Apology, both of which were published in 1530.

Luther's condemnation by Rome placed severe limitations on his travel. It therefore often fell to Melanchthon to undertake speaking engagements outside electoral Saxony. As a result, the development and diffusion of the Lutheran Reformation often reflected the particular emphases associated with him. In particular, Melanchthon placed an emphasis upon *adiaphora* ("matters of indifference"), believing that it was possible to tolerate disagreement over certain matters. The issue became of particular importance after Luther's death in 1546, when a series of political and military reverses meant that Lutheranism found itself having to adapt to an increasingly unsympathetic situation. Melanchthon's attempt to develop a pragmatic approach, intended to safeguard as much of the Lutheran heritage as possible under the new circumstances, was regarded as tantamount to betrayal by many. The rise of the Gnesio-Lutheran movement can be seen as a reaction against Melanchthon's accommodations.

We now turn to consider another reformer who achieved much at the time, but has generally been neglected subsequently – Martin Bucer.

Martin Bucer (1491–1551)

Martin Bucer was born in Alsace, a territory bordering both France and Germany. He joined the Dominican Order at an early age, perhaps wishing to take advantage of the educational opportunities this offered. Bucer (also known as "Butzer") went on to study theology at Heidelberg in 1517. He began to develop an admiration for Erasmus; this was both confirmed and significantly redirected in 1518, when he heard Luther speak at the Heidelberg Disputation. Bucer gained the impression that Luther merely stated explicitly what Erasmus hinted at implicitly, and thus came to the view that Luther and Erasmus could be seen as fighting for reform on the basis of a common set of assumptions.

In May 1523, Bucer moved to the imperial city of Strasbourg. The Reformation was underway in the city at this time, although in a somewhat attenuated and uncertain form. Bucer became involved in the movement, and became one of its most important apologists and theoreticians. He was heavily involved in intra-evangelical dialogues, in which he sought to maintain unity within the reforming movement. Although Bucer personally sided with Zwingli in the debate over the real presence, he actively campaigned for reconciliation on this issue, sensing the serious threat that it posed to unity. The "Wittenberg Concord" (1536) is generally regarded as his greatest achievement in this respect, in that it developed the notion of a common **evangelical** foundation, on the basis of which variations of emphasis or accentuation might be accepted.

evangelical   Term used to refer to the nascent reforming movements in the 1510s and 1520s.

Bucer's greatest impact was on the city of Strasbourg itself. During the 1530s, Bucer was able to establish a viable reformed church, which became a model for others seeking to achieve something similar in other cities. The sojourn of John Calvin in Strasbourg (1538–41) is of particular importance, as we shall note presently. However, Bucer chose to leave Strasbourg in 1549, following the political difficulties that arose through the defeat of the Schmalkaldic League by imperial forces over the period 1546–7. The same events which caused such difficulty for Melanchthon now caused related problems for Bucer.

Bucer emigrated to England at the invitation of Thomas Cranmer, archbishop of Canterbury. He was appointed Regius Professor of Divinity at Cambridge University by Edward VI, and devoted himself primarily to writing a major treatise on the ideal Christian society. *De regno Christi* ("On the reign of Christ") was published in 1550; it can be regarded as a model of Reformed theology, in that it sought to reform both church and society on the basis of the gospel. Bucer died in 1551, without having achieved the reforms which he had sought.

Theologically, Bucer may be regarded as a complex amalgam. His emphasis upon divine sovereignty, expressed particularly in his doctrine of election, may be argued to lie behind many of Calvin's statements on the matter. Although he embraced Luther's reformation with enthusiasm, he preferred the Swiss position on the real presence in the Eucharist. He also seemed to suggest that Luther's understanding of justification failed to give a due place to good works. In some ways, Bucer's own approach – which rested on a distinction between the "justification of the ungodly" through faith and the "justification of the godly" through works – can be seen as representing an Erasmian position, in which emphasis is placed upon the moral implications of justification.

We shall consider aspects of Bucer's thought at several points during this work. Our attention now turns to the second of the two leading theologians of the Reformation – John Calvin.

John Calvin (1509–64)

For many, the name of John Calvin (Figure 5.3) is virtually synonymous with that of Geneva. Although Geneva is now part of Switzerland, in the sixteenth century it was a small independent city state. Calvin, however, was a Frenchman. He was born on July 10, 1509, in the cathedral city of Noyon, about 70 miles northeast of Paris. His father was involved in the financial administration of the local diocese, and could rely on the patronage of the bishop to ensure support for his son. At some point in the early 1520s (probably 1523), the young Calvin was sent up to the University of Paris.

After a thorough grounding in Latin grammar at the hands of Mathurin Cordier, Calvin entered the Collège de Montaigu. Following completion of his rigorous education in the arts, Calvin moved to Orléans to study civil law,

Figure 5.3 John Calvin, engraving by Clement de Jonghe (fl.1640–70). Bibliotheque Nationale, Paris, France/Giraudon/ The Bridgeman Art Library

probably at some point in 1528. Although Calvin's father had originally intended that his son should study theology, he appears to have changed his mind. His father seemed to have realized that the study of law, Calvin later remarked, generally makes people rich. It is also possible that Calvin's father had lost the patronage of the local bishop on account of a financial wrangle back at Noyon.

It is generally thought that Calvin's detailed study of civil law gave him access to methods and ideas that he would later exploit in his career as a reformer. It was at Orléans that he learned Greek. At some point in 1529 Calvin moved to Bourges, attracted by the fame of the great Italian lawyer Andrea Alciati. Most Calvin scholars consider that Calvin's great clarity of expression is due to the influence of Alciati. Calvin's encounter with French legal humanism is generally thought to have been of fundamental importance in shaping his understanding of the way in which a classical text (such as the Bible or Roman legal texts) could be applied to modern situations.

Soon after graduating in law, Calvin had to return to Noyon. His father was ill, and died in May 1531. He had been excommunicated by the local cathedral chapter. Freed from family obligations (his mother had died while he was a child), Calvin returned to Paris to continue his studies, and became increasingly sympathetic to the reforming ideas then gaining an excited hearing in that city. The university and city authorities, however, were intensely hostile to Luther's ideas. On November 2, 1533, Calvin was obliged to leave Paris suddenly. The rector of the university of Paris, Nicolas Cop, had delivered a university address in which he openly supported Luther's doctrine of justification by faith. The parliament at Paris immediately took action against Cop. A copy of Cop's address exists in Calvin's handwriting, suggesting that he may have composed the address. At any rate, Calvin fled Paris, fearful for his safety.

By 1534 Calvin had become an enthusiastic supporter of the principles of the Reformation. During the following year he settled down in the Swiss city of Basle, safe from any French threat. Making the best use of his enforced leisure, he published a book destined to exercise a decisive effect upon the Reformation: the *Institutes of the Christian Religion*. First published in May 1536, this work was a systematic and lucid exposition of the main points of the Christian faith. It attracted considerable attention to its author, who revised and expanded the work considerably during the remainder of his life. The first edition of the book had six chapters; the final edition, published in 1559 (and translated by Calvin into his native French in 1560), had 80. It is generally regarded as one of the greatest works to emerge from the Reformation. We shall consider its development and influence in more detail in Chapter 13.

After winding up his affairs in Noyon early in 1536, Calvin decided to settle down to a life of private study in the city of Strasbourg. Unfortunately, the direct route from Noyon to Strasbourg was impassable, due to the outbreak of war between Francis I of France and the Emperor Charles V. Calvin had to make an extended detour, passing through the city of Geneva, which had recently gained its independence from the neighboring territory of Savoy. Geneva was then in a state of confusion, having just evicted its local bishop and begun a controversial program of reform under the Frenchmen Guillaume Farel and Pierre Viret. On hearing that Calvin was in the city, they demanded that he stay and help the cause of the Reformation. Calvin reluctantly agreed.

His attempts to provide the Genevan church with a solid basis of doctrine and discipline met intense resistance. Having just thrown out their local bishop, the last thing that many Genevans wanted was the imposition of new religious obligations. Calvin's attempts to reform the doctrine and discipline of the Genevan church were fiercely resisted by a well-organized opposition. After a series of quarrels, matters reached a head on Easter Day, 1538: Calvin was expelled from the city, and sought refuge in Strasbourg.

Having arrived in Strasbourg two years later than he had anticipated, Calvin began to make up for lost time. In quick succession he produced a series of major theological works. He revised and expanded his *Institutes* (1539), and produced the first French translation of this work (1541); he produced a major defense of Reformation principles in his famous *Reply to Sadoleto* (Cardinal Sadoleto had written to the Genevans, inviting them to return to the Catholic church); and his skills as a biblical exegete were demonstrated in his *Commentary on the Epistle to the Romans.* As pastor to the French-speaking congregation in the city, Calvin was able to gain experience of the practical problems facing Reformed pastors. Through his friendship with Martin Bucer, the Strasbourg reformer, Calvin was able to develop his thinking on the relation between the city and church.

In September 1541, Calvin was asked to return to Geneva. In his absence, the religious and political situation had deteriorated. The city appealed to him to return and restore order and confidence within the city. The Calvin who returned to Geneva was a wiser and more experienced young man, far better equipped for the massive tasks awaiting him than he had been three years earlier. Although Calvin would still find himself quarreling with the city authorities for more than a decade, it was from a position of strength. Finally, opposition to his program of reform died out. For the last decade of his life, he had virtually a free hand in the religious affairs of the city.

During this second period in Geneva, Calvin was able to develop both his own theology and the organization of the Genevan Reformed church. He established the Consistory as a means of enforcing church discipline, and founded the Genevan Academy to educate pastors in Reformed churches. Calvin also produced expanded editions of the *Institutes of the Christian Religion*, which became one of the most significant religious works of the sixteenth century. We shall consider the importance of this work later in this study (see pp. 247–9).

This final period in Geneva was not without its controversies. Calvin found himself embroiled in serious theological debate with Sebastien Castellion over the correct interpretation of Christ's descent into hell, and whether the Song of Songs was canonical. A furious and very public debate broke out between himself and Jerome Bolsec over the doctrine of predestination. Both Castellion and Bolsec ended up having to leave Geneva. A more serious controversy concerned Michael Servetus, accused by Calvin of heresy, who was finally burned at the stake in 1553. Although Calvin's role in this matter was less significant than some of his critics have implied, the Servetus affair continues to stain Calvin's reputation as a Christian leader.

By the early spring of 1564, it was obvious that Calvin was seriously ill. He preached for the last time from the pulpit of Saint-Pierre on the morning of Sunday, February 6. By April, it was clear that Calvin had not much longer to live. He found breathing difficult and was chronically short of breath. Calvin died at eight o'clock on the evening of May 27, 1564. At his own request, he was buried in a common grave, with no stone to mark his grave.

Calvin's theology remains of considerable interest, particularly in relation to his views on predestination and the doctrine of the church. We shall be examining some of those ideas in more detail later in this work.

Having considered something of the background to the leading contributors to the development of Reformation thought, we are now in a position to engage with those ideas in more detail. We begin with a theme which was of central importance to the great theological debates of the Reformation age – the question of the authority and interpretation of the Bible.

Further Reading

1   Martin Luther

Althaus, P., *The Theology of Martin Luther* (Philadelphia, PA, 1966).

Bainton, R. H., *Here I Stand: A Life of Martin Luther* (New York, 1959).

Bayer, O. *Martin Luther's Theology: A Contemporary Interpretation* (Grand Rapids, MI, 2008).

Brendler, G., *Martin Luther: Theology and Revolution* (New York, 1991).

Ebeling, G., *Luther: An Introduction to His Thought* (Philadelphia, PA, 1970).

Hendrix, S. H., *Luther and the Papacy* (Philadelphia, PA, 1981).

Kittelson, J. M., *Luther the Reformer: The Story of the Man and His Career* (Leicester, 1989).

Loewenich, W. von, *Martin Luther: The Man and His Work* (Minneapolis, MN, 1986).

Lohse, B., *Martin Luther: An Introduction to His Life and Writings* (Philadelphia, PA, 1986).

McGrath, A. E., *Luther's Theology of the Cross*, 2nd edn (Oxford, 2011).

McSorley, H. J., *Luther – Right or Wrong?* (New York, 1969).

Oberman, H. A., *Luther: Man Between God and the Devil* (New Haven, CN, 1989).

Rupp, E. G., *The Righteousness of God* (London, 1953).

Steinmetz, D. C., *Luther in Context* (Bloomington, IN, 1986).

2   Zwingli

Courvoisier, J., *Zwingli: A Reformed Theologian* (Richmond, VA, 1963).

Farner, O., *Zwingli the Reformer* (New York, 1952).

Furcha, E. J., and H. W. Pipkin, eds, *Prophet, Pastor, Protestant: The Work of Huldrych Zwingli* (Allison Park, PA, 1984).

Gäbler, U., *Huldrych Zwingli: His Life and Work* (Philadelphia, PA, 1986).

Potter, G. R., *Zwingli* (Cambridge, 1976).

Stephens, W. P., *The Theology of Huldrych Zwingli* (Oxford, 1986).

3   Calvin

Bouwsma, W. J., *John Calvin: A Sixteenth Century Portrait* (Oxford, 1989).

Cholakian, P. F., and R. C. Cholakian, *Marguerite de Navarre: Mother of the Renaissance* (New York, 2006).

Ganoczy, A., *The Young Calvin* (Edinburgh, 1988).

George, T., ed., *John Calvin and the Church: A Prism of Reform* (Louisville, KY, 1990).

Gordon, B., *Calvin* (New Haven, CN, 2009).

McGrath, A. E., *A Life of John Calvin* (Oxford, 1990).

Parker, T. H. L., *John Calvin* (London, 1976).

Reid, W. S., *John Calvin: His Influence in the Western World* (Grand Rapids, MI, 1982).

Reist, B. A., *A Reading of Calvin's Institutes* (Louisville, KY, 1991).

Selinger, S., *Calvin against Himself: An Inquiry in Intellectual History* (Hamden, CN, 1984).

Stauffer, R., "Calvin," in *International Calvinism 1541–1715*, ed. M. Prestwich (Oxford, 1985), pp. 15–38.

Wallace, R. S., *Calvin, Geneva and the Reformation* (Edinburgh, 1988).

Wendel, F., *Calvin: The Origins and Development of His Religious Thought* (London, 1963).

Zachman, R. C., *John Calvin as Teacher, Pastor, and Theologian: The Shape of His Writings and Thought* (Grand Rapids, MI, 2006).

4   Others

Baker, J. W., *Heinrich Bullinger and the Covenant: The Other Reformed Tradition* (Athens, OH, 1980).

Fraenkel, P., *Testimonia Patrum: The Function of the Patristic Argument in the Theology of Philip Melanchthon* (Geneva, 1961).

Fraenkel, P., "Bucer's *Memorandum* of 1541 and a 'lettera nicodemitica' of Capito's," *BHR* 36 (1974), pp. 575–87.

Hobbs, G., "Martin Bucer on Psalm 22: A Study in the Application of Rabbinical Exegesis by a Christian Hebraist," in *Etudes de l'exégèse au XVIe siècle*, ed. O. Fatio and P. Fraenkel (Geneva, 1978), pp. 144–63.

Kittelson, J. M., *Wolfgang Capito: From Humanist to Reformer* (Leiden, 1975).

Lugioyo, B., *Martin Bucer's Doctrine of Justification: Reformation Theology and Early Modern Irenicism* (New York, 2010).

Maag, K., ed., *Melanchthon in Europe: His Work and Influence Beyond Wittenberg* (Grand Rapids, MI, 1999).

Maxcey, C. E., *Bona Opera: A Study in the Development of the Doctrine in Philip Melanchthon* (Nieuwkoop, 1980).

Quere, R. W., *Melanchthon's Christum Cognoscere: Christ's Efficacious Presence in the Eucharistic Theology of Melanchthon* (Nieuwkoop, 1977).

Steinmetz, D. C., *Reformers in the Wings: From Geiler von Kaysersberg to Theodore Beza*, 2nd edn (New York, 2000).

Stephens, W. P., *The Holy Spirit in the Theology of Martin Bucer* (Cambridge, 1970).

6

The Return to the Bible

At the heart of most religious systems lies a core of written texts which are regarded as being "authoritative" – in other words, as having some permanent significance in defining the "shape" of that religion. In the case of Christianity, the written texts in question are those gathered together as the Bible and often referred to simply as "Scripture." (Throughout this book, terms such as "the Bible" and "Scripture" and "biblical" and "scriptural" are treated as equivalent.) The Bible is a central document of western civilization, not only as the source of Christian ideas but also as an influence upon education and culture.

The Reformation saw a new importance being attached to Scripture – or, perhaps, an ancient view of the importance of Scripture being recovered. The idea of *scriptura sola*, "by Scripture alone," became one of the great slogans of the reformers as they sought to bring the practices and beliefs of the church back into line with those of the Golden Age of Christianity. If the doctrine of justification by faith alone was the material principle of the Reformation, the principle of *scriptura sola* was its formal principle. If the reformers dethroned the pope, they enthroned Scripture.

Every strand of the Reformation movement regarded Scripture as the quarry from which its ideas and practices were hewn – yet, as we shall see, Scripture proved to be much more difficult to use in this way than might be expected. In this present chapter, we shall consider the Reformation understanding of Scripture in some detail, contextualizing it in the world of thought of the late medieval and Renaissance periods.

Reformation Thought: An Introduction, Fourth Edition. Alister E. McGrath.
© 2012 John Wiley & Sons, Ltd. Published 2012 by John Wiley & Sons, Ltd.

Scripture in the Middle Ages

To understand the importance of humanism in relation to the development of the ideas of the Reformation, as well as those ideas themselves, it is necessary to appreciate the way in which Scripture was understood and handled in the medieval period. In this section, I shall sketch an outline of the medieval understanding of the importance of Scripture.

The Concept of "Tradition"

For most medieval theologians, Scripture was the materially sufficient source of Christian doctrine. In other words, everything that was of essential importance to the Christian faith was contained in Scripture. There was no need to look anywhere else for material relevant to Christian theology. There were certainly matters on which Scripture had nothing to say: for example, who wrote the Apostles' Creed, at what precise moment during the celebration of the Eucharist the bread and wine became the body and blood of Christ, or whether the practice of baptism was intended solely for adult believers. On these matters, the church felt at liberty to attempt to work out what Scripture implied, although its judgments were regarded as subordinate to Scripture itself.

During the Middle Ages, the concept of "tradition" had come to be of major importance in relation to the interpretation and authority of Scripture. The word "tradition" derives from the Latin term *traditio* which means "handing over," "handing down," or "handing on." It is a thoroughly biblical idea, in that Paul reminded his readers that he was handing on to them core teachings of the Christian faith which he had himself received from other people (1 Corinthians 15:1–4).

The term "tradition" can refer to both the action of passing teachings on to others – something which Paul insists must be done within the church – and to the body of teachings which are passed on in this manner. Tradition can thus be understood as a *process* as well as a *body of teaching*. The Pastoral Epistles (three New Testament letters that are particularly concerned with questions of church structure and the passing on of Christian teaching: 1 Timothy, 2 Timothy, and Titus), in particular, stress the importance of "guarding the good deposit which was entrusted to you" (2 Timothy 1:14).

The importance of the idea of tradition first became obvious in a controversy which broke out during the second century. The "Gnostic controversy" centered on a number of questions, including how salvation was to be achieved. (The word "Gnostic" derives from the Greek word *gnosis*, "knowledge," and refers to the movement's belief in certain secret ideas that had to be known in order to secure salvation.) Christian writers found themselves having to deal with some highly unusual and creative interpretations of the Bible. How were they to deal with these? If the Bible was to be regarded as authoritative, was every interpretation of the Bible to be regarded as of equal value?

Irenaeus of Lyons (c.130–c.200), one of the church's greatest theologians, did not think so. The question of how the Bible was to be interpreted was of the greatest importance. Heretics, he argued, interpreted the Bible according to their own taste. Orthodox believers, in contrast, interpreted the Bible in ways that their apostolic authors would have approved. What had been handed down from the apostles through the church was not merely the biblical texts themselves, but a certain way of reading and understanding those texts.

Irenaeus's point was that a continuous stream of Christian teaching, life, and interpretation can be traced from the time of the apostles to his own period. The church is able to point to those who have maintained the teaching of the church, and to certain public standard creeds which set out the main lines of Christian belief. Tradition is thus the guarantor of faithfulness to the original apostolic teaching, a safeguard against the innovations and misrepresentations of biblical texts on the part of the Gnostics.

Irenaeus thus understands "tradition" as an authorized way of interpreting certain texts of Scripture, which went back to the time of the apostles themselves. Scripture must be interpreted within the context of the historical continuity of the Christian church. This idea of tradition as a traditional interpretation of the Bible is deeply embedded within early medieval theology.

In the fourteenth and fifteenth centuries, however, a somewhat different understanding of tradition developed. "Tradition" was now understood to be a separate, distinct source of revelation, *in addition to Scripture*. Scripture, it was argued, was silent on a number of points. But God had providentially arranged for a second source of revelation to supplement this deficiency: a stream of unwritten tradition, going back to the apostles themselves. This "unwritten tradition" was passed down from one generation to the next within the church.

As we shall see, the mainstream reformers had no difficulty with the notion of a "traditional interpretation of the Bible." Mainline Protestantism was emphatic that it was not a new church, brought into existence by the happenstances of the sixteenth century. Rather, it represented a reform and renewal of Christianity, implying and affirming continuity with the great historic tradition of Christian faith, stretching back through the patristic era to the apostles themselves. Both Luther and Calvin strongly affirmed the traditional practice of infant baptism, which they regarded as justified by biblical texts. Yet they directed considerable criticism against the notion of an "unwritten tradition," which was not accessible to every Christian believer. The "democratization of faith," which is so characteristic of the early Reformation, did not sit easily with the apparently elitist notion of an "unwritten tradition."

Anabaptism, however, was critical of the notion of tradition – not necessarily on account of a disregard for the wisdom of the past, but because of a more fundamental belief that the true Christian church had ceased to exist at an early stage (typically, following the conversion of Constantine in the fourth century). Why pay attention to the theological past, when it was not truly Christian?

The Vulgate Translation of the Bible

When a medieval theologian refers to "Scripture," he almost invariably means the *textus vulgatus*, the "common text," drawn up by the great patristic biblical scholar Jerome in the late fourth and early fifth centuries. Although the term "Vulgate" did not come into general use until the sixteenth century, it is perfectly acceptable to use the term to refer to the specific Latin translation of the Bible prepared by Jerome in the late fourth and early fifth centuries. This text was passed down to the Middle Ages in a number of forms, with considerable variations between them. For example, Theodulf and Alcuin, noted scholars of the Dark Ages, used quite different versions of the Vulgate text.

A new period of intellectual activity opened up in the later eleventh century, as the Dark Ages lifted, eventually leading to a renaissance in the twelfth century. It was clear that a standard version of this text was required to service the new interest in theology which developed as part of this intellectual renaissance. If theologians were to base their theology on different versions of the Vulgate, an equally great, if not greater, variation in their conclusions would be the inevitable result.

The need for standardization was met by what appears to have been a joint speculative venture by some Paris theologians and stationers in 1226, resulting in the "Paris version" of the Vulgate text. By then, Paris was recognized as the leading center of theology in Europe, with the inevitable result that – despite its many obvious imperfections – the "Paris version" of the Vulgate became established as normative. This version, it must be emphasized, was not commissioned or sponsored by any ecclesiastical figure; it appears to have been a purely commercial venture. History, however, concerns the fate of accidents, and it is necessary to note that medieval theologians, attempting to base their theology on Scripture, were obliged to equate Scripture with a rather bad commercial edition of an already faulty Latin translation of the Bible.

As we noted earlier (p. 48), the rise of humanist textual and philological techniques would expose the distressing discrepancies between the Vulgate and the texts it purported to translate – and thus open the way to doctrinal reformation as a consequence. Erasmus's 1516 edition of the Greek text of the New Testament is widely seen as a landmark in this development.

The Medieval Vernacular Versions of Scripture

During the Middle Ages a number of vernacular versions of Scripture were produced. Although it was once thought that the medieval church condemned this process of translation, it is now known that neither the production of such translations nor their use by clergy or laity was ever explicitly forbidden. An important example of such translations is provided by the Wycliffite versions, produced by a group of scholars who gathered around John Wycliffe at Lutterworth.

The motivation for the translation of the Bible into English was partly spiritual, partly political. It was spiritual in that the laity could now have access to "Goddis lawe" and political in that an implicit challenge was posed to the teaching authority of the church. The laity were enabled to detect the obvious differences between the scriptural vision of the church and its somewhat corrupt English successor, thus setting the agenda for a program of reform.

Important though such vernacular versions were, their importance must not be exaggerated. All these versions, it must be remembered, were simply *translations of the Vulgate*. They were not based on the best manuscripts of Scripture, in their original languages, but on the Vulgate version, with all its weaknesses and errors. The agenda for the Reformation would be set through the application of textual and philological techniques of a sophistication far beyond that of Wycliffe's circle at Lutterworth. It is to those methods, developed by humanist scholars such as Lorenzo Valla and Erasmus of Rotterdam, that we now turn.

The Humanists and the Bible

We have already seen how important the humanist movement was in relation to the study of Scripture (pp. 95–7). It may be helpful if we bring together the main elements of the humanist contribution to this important question.

1   The great humanist emphasis on the need to return *ad fontes* established the priority of Scripture over later commentaries on its text, particularly those of the Middle Ages. The text of Scripture was to be approached directly, rather than through a complicated system of glosses and commentaries.

2   Scripture was to be read directly in its original languages, rather than in Latin translation. Thus the Old Testament was to be studied in Hebrew (except for those few sections written in Aramaic), and the New Testament was to be read in Greek. The growing humanist interest in the Greek language (which many humanists held to be supreme in its capacity to mediate philosophical concepts) further consolidated the importance attached to the New Testament documents. The late Renaissance scholarly ideal was to be *trium linguarum gnarus*, "expert in three languages" (Hebrew, Greek, and Latin). Trilingual colleges were established at Alcalá in Spain, at Paris, and at Wittenberg. The new interest in, and availability of, Scripture in its original languages soon brought to light a number of serious mistakes in translation in the Vulgate, some of them of considerable importance (see pp. 95–7).

3   The humanist movement made available two essential tools for the new method of study of the Bible. First, it made available the printed text of Scripture in its original languages. For example, Erasmus's *Novum*

Instrumentum omne of 1516 allowed scholars direct access to the printed text of the Greek New Testament, and Lefèvre d'Etaples provided the Hebrew text of a group of important Psalms in 1509. Second, it made available manuals of classical languages, allowing scholars to learn languages which they otherwise could not have acquired. Reuchlin's Hebrew primer, *De rudimentis hebraicis* (1506), is an excellent example of this type of material. Greek primers were more common: the Aldine Press produced an edition of Lascaris's Greek grammar in 1495; Erasmus's translation of the famous Greek grammar of Theodore of Gaza appeared in 1516; and Melanchthon produced a masterly Greek primer in 1518.

4   The humanist movement developed textual techniques capable of establishing accurately the best text of Scripture. These techniques had been used, for example, by Lorenzo Valla to demonstrate the inauthenticity of the famous *Donation of Constantine* (see p. 51). It was now possible to eliminate many of the textual errors that had crept into the Parisian edition of the Vulgate. Erasmus shocked his contemporaries by excluding a significant part of one verse of the Bible (1 John 5:7), which he could not find in any Greek manuscript, as a later addition. The Vulgate version reads as follows: "For there are three that testify in heaven: the Father, the Word and the Holy Spirit, and these three are one. And there are three that testify on earth: the Spirit, the water and the blood." The capitalized section of the verse, omitted by Erasmus, was certainly there in the Vulgate – but not in the Greek texts which it purported to translate. As this text had become an important proof text for the doctrine of the Trinity, many were outraged at his action. In the end, Erasmus recanted, and restored this verse in later printings of his text.

5   The humanists tended to regard ancient texts as mediating an experience which could be recaptured through appropriate literary methods. Included in the theme *ad fontes* is the notion of recapturing the experience mediated by the text. In the case of the New Testament, the experience in question was that of the presence and power of the risen Christ. Scripture was thus read with a sense of anticipation; it was believed that the vitality and excitement of the apostolic era could be regained in the sixteenth century, by reading and studying Scripture in the right manner.

6   In his *Enchiridion*, which became enormously influential in 1515, Erasmus argued that a biblically literate laity held the key to the renewal of the church. In his work, both clergy and church were marginalized: the lay reader of Scripture had therein a more than adequate guide to the essentials of Christian belief and especially practice. These views, which achieved wide circulation among the lay intelligentsia of Europe, unquestionably prepared the way for the scriptural reforming program of Luther and Zwingli in the period 1519–25. Even if Luther adopted a theological approach to Scripture which contrasted with Erasmus's undoctrinaire attitude, he was widely regarded as building on a solidly Erasmian foundation.

The Bible and the Protestant Reformation

"The Bible," wrote William Chillingworth, "I say, the Bible only, is the religion of Protestants." These famous words of this seventeenth-century English Protestant summarize the Reformation attitude to Scripture. Calvin stated the same principle less memorably, if more fully, thus: "Let this then be a sure axiom: that nothing ought to be admitted in the church as the Word of God, save that which is contained, first in the Law of the Prophets, and secondly in the writings of the Apostles; and that there is no other method of teaching in the church than according to the prescription and rule of his Word."

For Calvin, as we shall see, the institutions and regulations of both church and society were required to be grounded in Scripture: "I approve only of those human institutions which are founded upon the authority of God and derived from Scripture." Zwingli entitled his 1522 tract on Scripture *On the Clarity and Certainty of the Word of God*, stating that "The foundation of our religion is the written word, the Scriptures of God." Such views indicate the consistently high view of Scripture adopted by the reformers. This view, as we have seen, is not a novelty; it represents a major point of continuity with medieval theology, which – certain later Franciscan writers excepted – regarded Scripture as the most important source of Christian doctrine. The difference between the reformers and medieval theology at this point concerns how Scripture is *defined* and *interpreted*, rather than the *status* that it is given. We shall explore these points further in what follows.

The Canon of Scripture

Central to any program which treats Scripture as normative is the delimitation of Scripture. In other words, what *is* Scripture? The term "canon" (a Greek word meaning "rule" or "norm") came to be used to refer to those Scriptures recognized as authentic by the church. For medieval theologians, "Scripture" meant "those works included in the Vulgate." The reformers, however, felt able to call this judgment into question. While all the New Testament works were accepted as canonical – Luther's misgivings concerning four of them gaining little support – doubts were raised concerning the canonicity of a group of Old Testament works. A comparison of the contents of the Old Testament in the Hebrew Bible on the one hand and the Greek and Latin versions (such as the Vulgate) on the other shows that the latter contain a number of books not found in the former.

The reformers argued that the only Old Testament writings which could be regarded as belonging to the canon of Scripture were those originally included in the Hebrew Bible. A distinction was thus drawn between the "Old Testament" and the "Apocrypha": the former consisted of books found in the Hebrew Bible, the latter of books found in the Greek and Latin Bibles (such as the Vulgate), but *not* in the Hebrew Bible. While some reformers allowed that the apocryphal works were edifying reading, there was general agreement that these works could not be used as the basis of doctrine. Medieval theologians, however, to be followed by the Council of Trent in 1546, defined the "Old Testament" as "those Old Testament works contained in the Greek and Latin bibles," thus eliminating any distinction between "Old Testament" and "Apocrypha."

A fundamental distinction thus developed between Catholic and Protestant understandings of what the term "Scripture" actually meant. This distinction persists to the present day. A comparison of Protestant versions of the Bible – the two most important being the *New Revised Standard Version* (NRSV) and the *New International Version* (NIV) – with Catholic versions, such as the Jerusalem Bible, will reveal these differences. For the reformers, *scriptura sola* thus implied not merely one, but *two*, differences from their Catholic opponents: not only did they attach a different status to Scripture, but they disagreed over what Scripture actually was. But what is the relevance of this dispute?

One Catholic practice to which the reformers took particular exception was that of praying for the dead. To the reformers, this practice rested on a nonbiblical foundation (the doctrine of purgatory), and encouraged popular superstition and ecclesiastical exploitation. Their Catholic opponents were able to meet this objection, however, by pointing out that the practice of praying for the dead is explicitly mentioned in Scripture, at 2 Maccabees 12:40–46. The reformers, on the other hand, having declared that this book was apocryphal (and hence not part of the Bible), were able to respond that, in their view at least, the practice was not scriptural. This merited the obvious riposte from the Catholic side: that the reformers based their theology on Scripture, but only after having excluded from the canon of Scripture any works which happened to contradict this theology.

One outcome of this debate was the production and circulation of authorized lists of books which were to be regarded as "scriptural." The Fourth Session of the Council of Trent (1546) produced a detailed list which included the works of the Apocrypha as authentically scriptural, while the Protestant congregations in Switzerland, France, and elsewhere produced lists which deliberately omitted reference to these works or else indicated that they were of no importance in matters of doctrine.

The Authority of Scripture

The reformers grounded the authority of Scripture in its relation to the Word of God. For some, that relation was an absolute identity: Scripture *was* the Word of God. For others, the relation was slightly more nuanced: Scripture *contained* the Word of God. Nevertheless, there was a consensus that Scripture was to be received as if it were God himself speaking. For Calvin, the authority of Scripture was grounded in the fact that the biblical writers were "secretaries [*notaires authentiques* in the French version of the *Institutes*] of the Holy Spirit."

As Heinrich Bullinger stated it, the authority of Scripture was absolute and autonomous: "Because it is the Word of God, the holy biblical Scripture has adequate standing and credibility in itself and of itself." Here was the gospel itself, able to speak for itself and challenge and correct its inadequate and inaccurate representation in the sixteenth century. Scripture was able both to pass judgment upon the late medieval church (and find it wanting) and to provide the model for the new Reformed church which would arise in its wake.

The importance of the *sola scriptura* principle can be seen in a number of ways. First, the reformers insisted that the authority of popes, councils, and theologians is subordinate to that of Scripture. This is not necessarily to say that they have *no* authority; as we shall see later, the reformers allowed certain councils and theologians of the patristic era a genuine authority in matters of doctrine. It *is* to say, however, that such authority is *derived from Scripture*, and is thus subordinate to Scripture. The Bible, as the Word of God, must be regarded as superior to both the **Fathers** and councils. Luther tends to defend the *sola scriptura* principle by emphasizing the confusion and incoherence of medieval theology, whereas Calvin and Melanchthon argue that the best Catholic theology (such as that of Augustine) supports their views on the priority of Scripture.

> **Fathers** Alternative term for "patristic writers."

Second, the reformers argued that authority within the church does not derive from the status of the office bearer, but from the Word of God which the office bearer serves. Traditional Catholic theology tended to ground the authority of the office bearer in the office itself – for example, the authority of a bishop resides in the fact that he is a bishop – and emphasized the historical continuity of the office of bishop with the apostolic era. The reformers grounded the authority of bishops (or their Protestant equivalent) in their faithfulness to the Word of God.

Historical continuity is of little importance in relation to the faithful proclamation of the Word of God. The breakaway churches of the Reformation were obviously denied historical continuity with the institutions of the Catholic church: no Catholic bishop would ordain their clergy, for example. Yet the reformers argued that the authority and functions of a bishop derived ultimately from faithfulness to the Word of God. Similarly, the decisions of bishops (and also of councils and popes) are authoritative and binding to the extent that they are faithful to Scripture.

Where Catholics stressed the importance of *historical* continuity, the reformers emphasized equally the importance of *doctrinal* continuity. While the Protestant churches could not generally provide historical continuity with the episcopacy (except, as in the case of the English or the Swedish reformations, through defections of Catholic bishops), they could supply the necessary fidelity to Scripture – thus, in their view, legitimating the Protestant ecclesiastical offices. There might not be an unbroken historical link between the leaders of the Reformation and the bishops of the early church, but, the reformers argued, since they believed and taught the same faith as those early church bishops (rather than the distorted gospel of the medieval church), the necessary continuity was there none the less.

The *sola scriptura* principle thus involved the claim that the authority of the church was grounded in its fidelity to Scripture. The opponents of the Reformation, however, were able to draw on a dictum of Augustine: "I should not have believed the gospel, unless I was moved by the authority of the Catholic church." Did not the very existence of the canon of Scripture point to the church having authority over Scripture? After all, it was the church which defined what "Scripture" was – and this would seem to suggest that the church had an authority over, and independent of, Scripture. Thus Johann Eck, Luther's opponent at the famous Leipzig Disputation of 1519, argued that "Scripture is not authentic without the authority of the church." This clearly raises the question of the relation between Scripture and tradition, to which we may now conveniently return.

The Role of Tradition

The *scriptura sola* principle of the reformers would seem to eliminate any reference to tradition in the formation of Christian doctrine. In fact, however, the magisterial reformers had a very positive understanding of tradition, as we shall see. Three major approaches to the question of "Bible and tradition" emerged during the sixteenth century, which we can summarize as follows:

1   There is no place for tradition in the interpretation of the Bible. Every individual or community is free to interpret the Bible without reference to the Christian past. This view is characteristic of the **radical Reformation**, and partly reflects their view that the true church ceased to exist shortly after the period of the apostles. Why appeal to the views of past writers, when these either had tarnished credentials, or were not even proper Christians?

radical Reformation   Term used to refer to the Anabaptist movement.

2   Tradition designates a traditional way of interpreting the biblical text, which does not displace the text. This view emerged during the patristic period, and played an important role in the theological renaissance of the early medieval period.
3   Tradition refers to an additional mode of divine revelation, in which information that was not committed to writing in the Bible was passed down from one generation of authorized and privileged persons within the church to another.

At first sight, the *scriptura sola* principle might seem to refer to an understanding of theology which allocates no role whatsoever to tradition. This was certainly the view of Anabaptist writers, who insisted that this principle demanded that beliefs and practices which were not specifically stated or endorsed in the Bible were to be uprooted. As Balthasar Hubmaier put this point in his Dialogue with Zwingli (November 1525): "Christ does not say, 'All plants which my heavenly Father has forbidden should be uprooted.' Rather he says, 'All plants which my heavenly Father has not planted should be uprooted.'"

Yet mainline reformers took a different view, arguing that the *sola scriptura* principle endorsed two sets of beliefs and practices:

1 Those that are explicitly stated in the Bible.
2 Those that, though not stated explicitly in the Bible, may reasonably be inferred from those that are thus stated.

As we have already noted, the idea of a "traditional interpretation of Scripture" was perfectly acceptable to the magisterial reformers, *provided that this traditional interpretation could be justified*.

The only wing of the Reformation to apply the *scriptura sola* principle consistently was the radical Reformation, or "Anabaptism." For the radicals (or "fanatics," as Luther dubbed them), such as Thomas Müntzer and Caspar Schwenkfeld, every individual had the right to interpret Scripture as he pleased, subject to the guidance of the Holy Spirit. For the radical Sebastian Franck, the Bible "is a book sealed with seven seals which none can open unless he has the key of David, which is the illumination of the Spirit." The way was thus opened, at least in theory, for individualism, with the private judgment of the individual raised above the corporate judgment of the church. Thus the radicals rejected the practice of infant baptism (to which the magisterial Reformation remained committed) as non-scriptural. (There is no explicit reference to the practice in the New Testament.) Similarly, doctrines such as the Trinity and the divinity of Christ were rejected as resting on inadequate scriptural foundations.

As has been noted, the magisterial Reformation was theologically conservative. It retained most traditional doctrines of the church – such as the divinity of Christ and the doctrine of the Trinity – on account of the reformers' conviction that these traditional interpretations of Scripture were correct. Equally, many traditional practices (such as infant baptism) were retained, on account of the reformers' belief that they were consistent with Scripture.

The magisterial Reformation was painfully aware of the threat of individualism, and attempted to avoid this threat by stressing the church's traditional interpretation of Scripture where this traditional interpretation was regarded as correct. Doctrinal criticism was directed against those areas in which Catholic theology or practice appeared to have gone far beyond, or to have contradicted, Scripture. As most of these developments had taken place in the Middle Ages, it is not surprising that the reformers spoke of the period 1200–1500 as an "era of decay" or a "period of corruption" which they had a mission to reform. Equally, it is hardly surprising that we find the reformers appealing to the Fathers as generally reliable interpreters of Scripture.

This point is of particular importance, and has not received the attention it merits. One of the reasons why the reformers valued the writings of the Fathers, especially Augustine, was that they regarded them as exponents of a biblical theology. In other words, the reformers believed that the Fathers were attempting to develop a theology based upon Scripture alone – which was, of course, precisely what they were also trying to do in the sixteenth century. Of course, the new textual and philological methods available to the reformers meant that they could correct the Fathers on points of detail; but the reformers were prepared to accept the "patristic testimony" as generally reliable. Since that testimony included such doctrines as the Trinity and the divinity of Christ and such practices as infant baptism, the reformers were predisposed to accept these as authentically scriptural. It will thus be obvious that this high regard for a traditional interpretation of Scripture gave the magisterial Reformation a strong bias toward doctrinal conservatism.

This understanding of the *sola scriptura* principle allowed the reformers to criticize their opponents on both sides – on the one side the radicals, on the other the Catholics. The Catholics argued that the reformers elevated private judgment above the corporate judgment of the church. The reformers replied that they were doing nothing of the sort: they were simply restoring that corporate judgment to what it once was, by combating the doctrinal degeneration of the Middle Ages by an appeal to the corporate judgment of the patristic era. The radicals, however, had no place whatsoever for the "testimony of the Fathers." As Sebastian Franck wrote in 1530: "Foolish Ambrose, Augustine, Jerome, Gregory – of whom not one even knew the Lord, so help me God, nor was sent by God to teach. Rather, they were all apostles of Antichrist." The magisterial reformers, however, dismissed this radical understanding of the role of Scripture as pure individualism, a recipe for theological chaos.

It will therefore be clear that it is totally wrong to suggest that the magisterial reformers elevated private judgment above the corporate judgment of the church or that they degenerated into some form of individualism. No leading mainstream reformer was prepared to abandon the concept of a traditional interpretation of Scripture in favor of the radical alternative. As Luther observed, the inevitable result of such an approach was chaos, a "new Babel."

The Council of Trent, meeting in 1546, responded to the threat of the Reformation by affirming a two-source theory of tradition, which recognized the existence of an "unwritten tradition" alongside the public text of the Bible (see pp. 112–14). According to Trent, the Christian faith reaches every generation through two sources: Scripture and an unwritten tradition. This extra-scriptural tradition is to be treated as having equal authority with Scripture.

Methods of Interpreting Scripture

Texts need to be interpreted. There is little point in treating a certain text as authoritative or normative if there is serious disagreement concerning what that text means. During the later Middle Ages, increasing emphasis came to be placed upon the role of the church as interpreter of Scripture. The authority of Scripture was guaranteed by the authority of its interpreter – the church, under the divine guidance of the Holy Spirit. As we have seen (pp. 27–9), however, there was such doctrinal confusion and disagreement over the nature and location of theological authority in the later medieval period that it was far from clear who had

Figure 6.1   The four-horse chariot (Latin: *Quadriga*) on the Brandenburg Gate, Unter den Linden, Berlin. Medieval theological writers likened the four senses of Scripture to four horses pulling a chariot. © Danita Delimont/Alamy

the ultimate authority to interpret Scripture. The pope? A council? Or maybe even a pious individual who knew his Bible well, as Panormitanus (Nicolo de Tudeschi) suggested, perhaps with his tongue firmly in his cheek.

In practice, it seemed to be the pope of the day who held such authority; but there was sufficient confusion concerning this question to allow pluralism to develop virtually unchecked in the later fifteenth century, partly through new approaches to biblical interpretation which laid down a significant challenge to existing views.

The standard method of biblical interpretation used during the Middle Ages is usually known as the *Quadriga*, or the "fourfold sense of Scripture," as we have seen (Figure 6.1). The origins of this method lie in the patristic period, although its systematic formulation was part and parcel of the new trend toward theological systematization which accompanied the cultural renaissance of the twelfth century.

The basic principle underlying this approach is as follows. Scripture possesses a number of different senses. In addition to the literal sense, three non-literal senses could be distinguished: the allegorical, regarding what Christians are to believe; the tropological or moral, regarding what Christians are to do; and the anagogical, regarding what Christians were to hope for. The four senses of Scripture were thus the following:

1   The *literal* sense, whereby the text was taken at face value.
2   The *allegorical* sense, whereby certain passages of Scripture were interpreted so as to produce statements of doctrine. Those passages tended to be either obscure, or to have a literal meaning which was unacceptable, for theological reasons, to their readers.
3   The *tropological or moral* sense, whereby certain passages were interpreted to produce ethical guidance for Christian conduct.
4   The *anagogical* sense, whereby certain passages were interpreted to indicate the grounds of Christian hope, pointing toward the future fulfillment of the divine promises in the New Jerusalem.

A potential weakness in this approach was avoided by insisting that nothing should be believed on the basis of a non-literal sense of Scripture unless it could first be established on the basis of the literal sense. This insistence on the priority of the literal sense may be seen as an implied criticism of the allegorical approach adopted by Origen, which virtually allowed interpreters of Scripture to read into any passage whatever "spiritual" interpretations they liked. As Luther states this principle in 1515: "In the Scriptures no allegory, tropology, or anagogy is valid, unless that same truth is explicitly stated literally somewhere else. Otherwise, Scripture would become a laughing matter."

Yet the idea of a "literal" sense of Scripture was regarded by many humanist writers to be imprecise and ill defined, especially in relation to many passages in the Old Testament. Jacques Lefèvre d'Etaples (c.1455–1536), writing in the first decade of the sixteenth century, argued that a basic distinction had to be made between two different senses of the term "literal." The "literal historical" sense of Scripture designates the obvious historical sense of a passage. Luther refers to this approach as "referring to ancient history, rather than to Christ." The "literal prophetic" sense of Scripture designates the prophetic sense of a passage – in other words, where a passage points ahead to its fulfillment in the coming of Jesus Christ.

As Luther puts it, "Christ has opened the mind of those who are his, in order that they might understand the Scriptures." Thus an Old Testament passage could be taken either as a literal historical reference to a series of events in the ancient Near East or as a literal prophetic reference to the coming of Christ. This Christological scheme of interpretation would prove especially important in relation to the Psalter, the Old Testament book which figured so prominently in medieval Christian spirituality and theology, and upon which Luther lectured from 1513 to 1515.

Luther was fully aware of these distinctions, and had no hesitation in using them to the full in his biblical exposition. In his analysis of the Psalter, he distinguished eight senses of the Old Testament. This amazing precision (which may impress some readers as typical of scholasticism) resulted from combining the four senses of Scripture with the insight that each of these senses could be interpreted historically or prophetically.

Luther developed this distinction by arguing that a distinction had to be made between what he termed "the killing letter" (*litera occidens*) – in other words, a crudely literal or historical reading of the Old Testament – and "the life-giving spirit" (*spiritus vivificans*) – in other words, a reading of the Old Testament which is sensitive to its spiritual nuances and prophetic overtones. As a worked example, we may consider Luther's analysis of an Old Testament image using this eightfold scheme of interpretation.

The image in question is Mount Zion, which can be interpreted either in a woodenly historical and literal sense as a reference to ancient Israel or as a prophetic reference to the New Testament church. Luther explores the possibilities (perhaps tongue in cheek?) as follows:

1   Historically, according to "the killing letter":
    (a)   literally: the land of Canaan;
    (b)   allegorically: the synagogue, or a prominent person within it;
    (c)   tropologically: the righteousness of the Pharisees and the Law;
    (d)   anagogically: a future glory on earth.
2   Prophetically, according to "the life-giving spirit":
    (a)   literally: the people of Zion;
    (b)   allegorically: the church, or a prominent person within it;
    (c)   tropologically: the righteousness of faith;
    (d)   anagogically: the eternal glory of the heavens.

The *Quadriga* was a major component of academic study of the Bible within scholastic theological faculties of universities. But it was not the only option available to biblical interpreters in the first two decades of the sixteenth century. Indeed, it may be argued that Luther was the only reformer to make significant use of this scholastic approach to biblical interpretation. By far the most influential approach to the subject within reforming and humanist circles employed the methods associated with Erasmus of Rotterdam, to which we now turn.

Erasmus's *Enchiridion* made much of the distinction between the "letter" and the "spirit" – that is, between the words of Scripture and their real meaning. Especially in the Old Testament, the words of the text are like a shell, containing – but not identical with – the kernel of the meaning. The surface meaning of the text often conceals a deeper, hidden meaning, which it is the task of the enlightened and responsible exegete to uncover. Biblical interpretation, according to Erasmus, is concerned with establishing the underlying sense, not the letter, of Scripture.

Zwingli's basic concern echoes that of Erasmus. The interpreter of the Bible is required to establish the "natural sense of Scripture" – which is not necessarily identical with the literal sense of Scripture. Zwingli's humanist background allowed him to distinguish various figures of speech, especially *alloiosis, catachresis*, and *synecdoche*. An example will make this point clear. Take the statement of Christ at the Last Supper, in which, when breaking the bread, he spoke the words "this is my body" (Matthew 26:26). The literal sense of these words would be "this piece of bread is my body," but the natural sense is "this piece of bread signifies my body."

Zwingli's search for the deeper meaning of Scripture (as contrasted with the superficial meaning) is well illustrated by the story of Abraham and Isaac (Genesis 22). The historical details of the story are too easily assumed to constitute its *real* meaning. In fact, Zwingli argues, the real meaning of that story can only be understood when it is seen as a prophetic anticipation of the story of Christ, in which Abraham represents God and Isaac is a figure (or, more technically, "type") of Christ.

Most important, perhaps, is the stress placed by Erasmus, Bucer, and Zwingli upon the moral or tropological sense of Scripture. Humanist approaches to Christianity never entirely managed to escape from the notion that the gospel primarily designates a way of life, whose moral contours are mapped out by Scripture. It is the task of the exegete to uncover these contours, and thus to allow Scripture to act as an ethical *vade mecum*, guiding believers through the moral maze of life.

Whereas Luther tended to treat Scripture as primarily concerned with proclaiming the gracious promises of God to believers, there is a perceptibly more moralist cast to the writings of his three more humanist colleagues, who often portray Scripture as laying down a "new law." Similarly, whereas Erasmus and Bucer regard the tropological sense of Scripture as defining what believers must *do*, Luther, in his moment of theological breakthrough (p. 120), interprets that same sense as defining what God *has done* for believers in Christ.

A number of options were thus available for the interpretation of Scripture in the early sixteenth century. The Reformation, however, was not primarily an academic movement, based in universities, but a popular movement which increasingly made its appeal directly to an educated laity. Such academic methods of interpretation were difficult to explain and use at the popular level. It may be argued that the Reformation got under way only with the emphatic declaration that all had the right to interpret Scripture and to call into question existing teachings and practices of the church. In what follows, we shall explore how this development occurred and examine the weaknesses and inconsistencies which arose in its wake.

The Right to Interpret Scripture

The general consensus of the magisterial Reformation was that Scripture was the container of the Word of God. This Word, although uniquely given at a definite point in the past, could be recovered and appropriated by every generation through the guidance of the Holy Spirit. The early Reformation was characterized by the optimistic belief that it was possible to establish exactly what the Bible said on everything of importance and make this the basis of a reformed Christianity. The archetypal statement of this exegetical optimism may be found in Erasmus's *Enchiridion*: in Erasmus's view, the ploughman may read Scripture and understand it without any great difficulty. Scripture was clear and persuasive, and could serve as the manifesto of the reforming parties within Christendom.

In his great reforming treatise of 1520, *To the Christian Nobility of the German Nation*, Luther declared that the "Romanists" had eliminated any threat of reform to the church by constructing three defensive walls around themselves:

> In the first place, when pressed by the temporal power, they have made decrees and declared that the temporal power had no jurisdiction over them, but that, on the contrary, the spiritual power is above the temporal. In the second place, when the attempt is made to reprove them with the Scriptures, they raise the objection that only the pope may interpret the Scriptures. In the third place, if threatened with a council, their story is that no one may summon a council except the pope.[1]

Luther thus seems to have seen himself as a Joshua with a mission to cast down the three walls of this new Jericho (see Joshua 6:1–20). With three blasts of his reforming trumpet, Luther delineates the broad features of his reforming program. First, the distinction between "spiritual" and "temporal" powers is abolished. Second, every believing Christian has the right to interpret Scripture. Third, any Christian (but especially a German prince) has the right to summon a reforming council. Luther's program of reform is initially founded on these three principles, of which the second is of particular interest to us:

> Their claim that only the pope may interpret Scripture is an outrageous fancied fable . . . The Romanists must admit that there are among us good Christians who have the true faith, spirit, understanding, word, and mind of Christ. Why, then, should we reject the word and understanding of good Christians and follow the pope, who has neither faith nor the Spirit?

Luther appears to suggest that the ordinary pious Christian believer is perfectly capable of reading Scripture and making sense of what he finds within its pages. A similar position is defended by Zwingli in his important treatise of 1522, *On the Clarity and Certainty of the Word of God*. For Zwingli, Scripture is perfectly clear. "The Word of God, as soon as it shines upon an individual's understanding, illuminates it in such a way that he understands it."

Yet, by the end of the 1520s, this exegetical optimism had been discredited to a significant degree, largely through the serious disagreement between Luther and Zwingli over the interpretation of one particular biblical text: *hoc est corpus meum*, "this is my body" (Matthew 26:26), which was central to the Eucharist, and hence of enormous theological importance to reformer and Catholic alike. For Luther, this text meant what it said: in other words, the bread in the Eucharist *is* the body of Christ. For Zwingli, however, its interpretation was somewhat different: for him, it meant "this *signifies* my body" – in other words, the bread in the Eucharist *represents* the body of Christ.

As we shall see in a later chapter, the seriousness of this disagreement between the reformers over the Eucharist did more than divide the **magisterial Reformation** permanently into two movements; it demonstrated how difficult it was to

> **magisterial Reformation** Term used to refer to the Lutheran and Reformed wings of the Reformation.

reach agreement over the interpretation of even those passages of Scripture which Luther regarded as most straightforward. The exegetical optimism of the late 1510s and early 1520s was also evident in the suggestion that the ordinary Christian could understand Scripture – but by the 1530s, it was considered that ordinary Christians could be relied upon to understand Scripture only if they were fluent in Hebrew, Greek, and Latin and were familiar with the complexities of linguistic theories.

For the Catholic, Scripture was difficult to interpret – and God had providentially supplied a reliable and authoritative interpreter in the form of the Catholic church. The radical reformers rejected this totally, as we have seen: every individual believer had the right and the ability to interpret Scripture as seemed right to him. The magisterial reformers found themselves in something of a quandary at this point. They had conceded that Scripture is obscure at certain points, and thus requires interpretation. Yet how could an authoritative communal *Protestant* interpretation of Scripture be given, without implying that there was some authority higher than the Bible, by which its interpretation was to be determined?

So how can any Protestant claim to speak with "authority," when Protestantism subverts that claim by insisting that there is no "spiritual elite" who are placed above others? The Protestant understanding of the place of the Bible in the Christian life is utterly and irreconcilably opposed to placing any human figure, agency, or institution above it. This would seem to lead to the conclusion that Protestantism is a democratic faith, in which the views of every believer are of equal value, making it impossible for authority figures to emerge.

We shall examine two means by which the Reformation attempted to overcome this difficulty. The first might be designated the "catechetical" approach. Protestant readers of Scripture were provided with a filter by means of which they might interpret Scripture. One example of such a "filter" is Luther's *Lesser Catechism* (1529), which provided its readers with a framework by which they could make sense of Scripture. The most famous guide to Scripture, however, was Calvin's *Institutes*, especially the definitive version of 1559. Calvin is known to have initially modeled this work on Luther's catechism. In the preface to the French edition of 1541, he states that the *Institutes* "could be like a key and an entrance to give access to all the children of God, in order that they might really understand Holy Scripture." In other words, the reader is expected to use Calvin's *Institutes* as a means to interpret Scripture.

As the history of the development of the Reformed church in France and the Lowlands indicates, Calvin's approach was remarkably successful. The reader need only have two books – the Bible and Calvin's *Institutes* – to gain full access to the Reformed faith. Calvin's use of Scripture in the *Institutes* was so persuasive that it seemed to many that this book held the key to the proper interpretation of Scripture. The complex medieval hermeneutical schemes could be dispensed with, in favor of this elegantly written, lucid work.

The second means of dealing with the problem of the interpretation of Scripture might be designated "the political hermeneutic," and was specifically associated with Zwingli's Reformation at Zurich. This method is of particular importance in relation to the political history of the Reformation. At some point in 1520, the Zurich city council required all clergy in the city to preach according to Scripture, avoiding "human innovations and explanations." In effect, the decree committed Zurich to the *scriptura sola* principle. By 1522, however, it had become clear that this decree had little meaning: for how was Scripture to be interpreted?

A minor crisis arose in Lent 1522, when some of Zwingli's followers broke the fast traditionally observed at this time of year. During a period in which it was traditional to eat only vegetables or fish, it seems that some of Zwingli's supporters succumbed to the forbidden pleasures of some sort of sausage. A few weeks later, on April 9, the city council reaffirmed its commitment to the observance of the Lenten fast, and fined Froschauer a trivial amount for allowing it to be broken in his house. There the matter might have rested, had not Zwingli, seven days later, published (on Froschauer's presses) a treatise arguing that nowhere in Scripture was it said that believers should abstain from meat during Lent. A similar debate developed the same year concerning clerical marriage. As tension began to grow in Zurich, it became clear that some means of resolving such ambiguities was needed.

The central difficulty concerned how Scripture was to be interpreted. On January 3, 1523 the city council announced that, as the body entrusted with control of public preaching, it had arranged a public disputation for later that same month to determine whether Zwingli's 67 *Schlussreden*, or "key theses," were in accordance with Scripture. This debate is now known as the "First Zurich Disputation." The debate, apparently modeled on academic disputations, took place at Zurich town hall on January 29. It was a personal triumph for Zwingli. More significant, however, was the outcome for the city council, which emerged from the debate as the body entitled to determine what was in accordance with Scripture and what was not.

For Zwingli, the city and the church at Zurich were effectively one and the same body – a point which is of particular importance in relation to his theology of the church and the sacraments, as we shall see in the following chapter. The city council, therefore, had a right to be involved in theological and religious matters. No longer was the Zurich Reformation to be detained by questions concerning the proper interpretation of Scripture. The city council effectively declared that *it* – not the pope or an ecumenical council – had the right to interpret Scripture for the citizens of Zurich, and gave notice that it intended to exercise that right. Scripture might indeed be ambiguous, but the political success of the Reformation at Zurich was virtually guaranteed by the unilateral decision of the city council to act as its interpreter. Similar decisions reached at Basle and Berne on the basis of the Zurich model consolidated the Reformation in Switzerland, and, by allowing Geneva political stability in the mid-1530s, indirectly led to the success of Calvin's Reformation.

It will be obvious that the power struggles within early Protestantism concerned the question of who had the authority to interpret Scripture. Whoever was recognized as possessing that authority was de facto in control of the ideology – and hence the social and political views – of the various factions of the Reformation. The pope's secular authority was linked with his role as the authoritative interpreter of Scripture for Catholics in much the same way. This observation allows us some important insights concerning the social and political dimensions of the Reformation. For example, the radical Reformation axiom, that the enlightened individual had full authority to interpret Scripture for himself, is linked with the communism often associated with the movement. All individuals must be regarded as equal. Similarly, the failure of the radical Reformation to produce any first-class theologians – a factor of some importance in relation to the movement's premature degeneration into ideological chaos – reflects a reluctance to allow that any one individual has a right to lay down what others should think or how they should interpret Scripture.

The **magisterial Reformation** initially seems to have allowed that every individual had the right to interpret Scripture; but subsequently it became anxious concerning the social and political consequences of this idea. The Peasants' Revolt of 1525 appears to have convinced some, such as Luther, that individual believers (especially German peasants) were simply not capable of interpreting Scripture. It is one of the ironies of the Lutheran Reformation that a movement which laid such stress upon the importance of Scripture should subsequently deny its less educated members direct access to that same Scripture, for fear that they might misinterpret it (in other words, reach a different interpretation from that of the magisterial reformers).

For example, the school regulations of the duchy of Württemberg laid down that only the most able schoolchildren were to be allowed to study the New Testament in their final years – and even then, only if they studied it in Greek or Latin. The remainder – presumably the vast bulk – were required to read Luther's *Lesser Catechism* instead. The direct interpretation of Scripture was thus effectively reserved for a small, privileged group of people. To put it crudely, it became a question of whether you looked to the pope, to Luther, or to Calvin as an interpreter of Scripture. The principle of the "clarity of Scripture" appears to have been quietly marginalized, in the light of the use made of the Bible by the more radical elements within the Reformation. Similarly, the idea that everyone had the right and the ability to interpret Scripture faithfully became the sole possession of the radicals.

The Translation of Scripture

One of the most distinctive themes of the Protestant Reformation was its insistence on the priority of vernacular languages. Worship and preaching were to be in the language of the ordinary people, not the Latin of the church and universities. Yet most significantly of all, the Bible was to be translated into everyday language, so that all might benefit from its spiritual riches and theological wisdom.

Luther demanded that all Christians should be able to read the Bible for themselves. The agenda here was both political and theological. Lay access to the Bible was about power as much as it was about encouraging personal spirituality. Pressure for the Bible to be placed in the hands of the ordinary person was an implicit demand for the emancipation of the laity from clerical domination. Luther found that he had time on his hands when he was placed in safe custody in the Wartburg for 11 weeks. He used this time to translate the New Testament into German. It was published in 1522, and created a sensation.

Others were inspired by this action, and longed to do the same. The English reformer William Tyndale traveled to Wittenberg, to benefit from both Luther's personal example, as well as his translation of the New Testament. Tyndale translated the New Testament directly from Greek into English. The work was smuggled into England, where its arrival caused consternation amongst the church authorities (Figure 6.2). The Bishop of London ordered that every available copy should be seized and burned.

Figure 6.2 Title page of William Tyndale's New Testament, printed in the 1530s, from *The National and Domestic History of England* by William Hickman Smith Aubrey (1858–1916) published London, c.1890 (litho), English School, nineteenth century. Private Collection/Ken Welsh/The Bridgeman Art Library

Why was this translation regarded as so dangerous? Tyndale's translation used vocabulary that threatened to undermine traditional authority structures within the church. For example, Tyndale's New Testament rendered the Greek word *presbyteros*, traditionally translated as "priest," as "senior." The English word "priest" should, he argued, be reserved solely for translating the Greek term *hiereus*, used in the New Testament exclusively to refer to Jewish or pagan priests, or to Christ himself. The Greek term *ekklesia*, traditionally translated as "church," was now translated as "congregation." Bible translation was a potentially subversive activity. It was little wonder that the English church authorities aimed to ensure that only "authorized" translations were permitted.

The Catholic Response: Trent on Scripture and Tradition

The Council of Trent reacted forcefully to what it regarded as Protestant irresponsibility in relation to the questions of the authority and interpretation of Scripture. The Fourth Session of the Council, which concluded its deliberations on April 8, 1546, laid down five fundamental challenges to the Protestant position, as follows.

1   Scripture could not be regarded as the only source of revelation; tradition was a vital supplement, which Protestants irresponsibly denied. "All saving truths and rules of conduct . . . are contained in the written books and in the unwritten traditions, received from the mouth of Christ himself or from the apostles themselves." As we noted earlier, this can be seen as a reassertion of the idea of tradition as "unwritten traditions," passed down from one generation to another within the church.
2   Trent ruled that Protestant lists of canonical books were deficient, and published a full list of works which it accepted as authoritative. This included all the books rejected as apocryphal by Protestant writers.
3   The Vulgate edition of Scripture was affirmed to be reliable and authoritative. The council declared that "the old Latin Vulgate edition, which has been used for many centuries, has been approved by the Church, and should be defended as authentic in public lectures, disputations, sermons or expositions, and that no one should dare or presume, under any circumstances, to reject it."
4   The authority of the church to interpret Scripture was defended, against what the Council of Trent clearly regarded as the rampant individualism of Protestant interpreters, thus:

> To check reckless spirits, this council decrees that no one, relying on his or her own judgment, in matters of faith and morals relating to Christian doctrine (distorting the Holy Scriptures in accordance with their own ideas), shall

presume to interpret Scripture contrary to that sense which Holy Mother Church, to whom it belongs to judge of their true sense and interpretation, has held and now holds.[2]

5   No Catholic was to be allowed to publish any work relating to the interpretation of Scripture, unless it had first been vetted by his or her superiors and declared that publication had been approved. In particular, the writing, reading, circulation, or possession of anonymous books (such as the remarkably successful and influential *Beneficio di Cristo*, which propagated reforming views in the early 1540s) was totally forbidden:

> It shall not be lawful for anyone to print, or have published, any books whatsoever, dealing with sacred doctrinal matters without the name of the author, or in future to sell them, or even to have them in one's possession, unless they have first been examined and approved . . . The approval of such books shall be given in writing, and shall appear properly at the beginning of the book.[3]

On the basis of these five measures, the Council of Trent was able to restore order within its own ranks. Once more, the Catholic church was able to speak with a single voice on matters of doctrine and biblical interpretation. The price paid, however, was high. It would be centuries before Catholic biblical scholarship recovered from this setback. One of the major contributing causes to the superiority of Protestant biblical scholarship in the nineteenth and early twentieth centuries was that their Catholic counterparts were virtually forbidden to express any views about Scripture unless they had received prior approval from the authorities. That situation has now, happily, changed for the better, not least through the wisdom of the Second Vatican Council.

On the basis of the material presented in this chapter, it will be clear that the Reformation program of a return to Scripture ended up being considerably more complex than at first had seemed to be the case. The slogan *scriptura sola* turned out to mean something rather different from what might have been expected, with the radical Reformation alone conforming to the popular stereotype of the Reformation on this point.

We now turn to consider one of the most important theological debates of the Reformation period – the controversy over how individuals are accepted in the sight of God, focusing on the doctrine of justification by faith.

Notes

1 WA 6.406–8.
2 Council of Trent, Fourth Session, Decree on the Holy Scriptures.
3 Council of Trent, Fourth Session, Decree on the Editions and Use of Sacred Books.

Further Reading

Ackroyd, P. R., *et al.*, eds, *The Cambridge History of the Bible*, 3 vols (Cambridge, 1963–9).

Bennett, M. J., "Erasmus and the Hermeneutics of Biblical Practice," *Renaissance Quarterly* 49 (1996), 542–72.

Bentley, J. H., *Humanists and Holy Writ: New Testament Scholarship in the Renaissance* (Princeton, NJ, 1983).

Boyle, L. E., "Innocent III and Vernacular Versions of Scripture," in *The Bible in the Medieval World*, ed. K. Walsh and D. Wood (Oxford, 1985), pp. 131–55.

Bradshaw, B. "The Christian Humanism of Erasmus," *Journal of Theological Studies* 33 (1982), 411–47.

Celenza, C. S., "Renaissance Humanism and the New Testament: Lorenzo Valla's Annotations to the Vulgate," *Journal of Medieval and Renaissance Studies* 24 (1994), 33–52.

Coolman, B. T., "Pulchrum esse: the Beauty of Scripture, the Beauty of the Soul, and the Art of Exegesis in Hugh of St. Victor," *Traditio* 58 (2003), 175–200.

de Lubac, H., *Medieval Exegesis*, 3 vols (Grand Rapids, MI, 1998–2009).

Evans, G. R., *The Language and Logic of the Bible: The Road to Reformation* (Cambridge, 1985).

Forstman, H. J., *Word and Spirit; Calvin's Doctrine of Biblical Authority* (Stanford, CA, 1962).

Gerrish, B. A., "The Word of God and the Word of Scripture: Luther and Calvin on Biblical Authority," in *The Old Protestantism and the New: Essays on the Reformation Heritage* (Edinburgh, 1982), pp. 51–68.

Gibson, M. T., *The Bible in the Latin West* (Notre Dame, IN, 1993).

Hale Williams, M., *The Monk and the Book: Jerome and the Making of Christian Scholarship* (Chicago, IL, 2006).

Jenkins, A. K., and P. Preston, *Biblical Scholarship and the Church: A Sixteenth-Century Crisis of Authority* (Aldershot, 2007).

Muller, R. A., and J. L. Thompson, eds, *Biblical Interpretation in the Era of the Reformation: Essays Presented to David C. Steinmetz in Honor of his Sixtieth Birthday* (Grand Rapids, MI, 1996).

Oberman, H. O., "Quo vadis, Petre? Tradition from Irenaeus to *Humani Generis*," in *The Dawn of the Reformation: Essays in Late Medieval and Early Reformation Thought* (Edinburgh, 1986), pp. 269–96.

Old, H. O., *The Reading and Preaching of the Scriptures in the Worship of the Church: The Age of the Reformation* (Grand Rapids, MI, 2002).

Ratzinger, J., "On the Interpretation of the Tridentine Decree on Tradition," in *Revelation and Tradition*, ed. K. Rahner and J. Ratzinger (New York, 1966), pp. 50–68.

Smalley, B., *The Study of the Bible in the Middle Ages*, 3rd edn (Oxford, 1983).

Smith, S., *Masters of the Sacred Page: Manuscripts of Theology in the Latin West to 1274* (Notre Dame, IN, 2001).

Tavard, G. H., *Holy Writ or Holy Church? The Crisis of the Protestant Reformation* (London, 1959).

Tracy, J. D., "*Ad Fontes*: The Humanist Understanding of Scripture as Nourishment for the Soul," in *Christian Spirituality II: High Middle Ages and Reformation*, ed. Jill Raitt (New York, 1988), pp. 252–67.

Worth, R. H., *Church, Monarch and Bible in Sixteenth-Century England: The Political Context of Biblical Translation* (Jefferson, NC, 2000).

7

The Doctrine of Justification by Faith

A major theme of Reformation thought is the doctrine of justification by faith, which played an especially important role in the thought of Martin Luther. Yet it is impossible to discuss this doctrine – or related issues, such as the theology of grace, predestination, or the sacraments – without some understanding of the complex notion of "redemption through Christ" in Christian thought, and how these matters were discussed during the sixteenth century. The section which follows introduces this theme, and indicates its importance for Reformation thought in general.

A Foundational Theme: Redemption through Christ

The theme of "redemption through Christ" resonates throughout the New Testament, Christian worship, and Christian theology. The basic idea is that God has achieved the redemption of sinful humanity through the death of Christ on the cross. This redemption could be achieved in no other way. The term "soteriology" (from the Greek word *sōteria*, "salvation") is used in works of Christian theology to refer to the network of ideas and images which centers on the redemption achieved through the death and resurrection of Christ. Five broad components to this network of ideas can be discerned:

1   *Images of victory.* Christ has gained a victory over sin, death, and evil through his cross and resurrection. Through faith, believers may share in that victory, and claim it as their own.

Reformation Thought: An Introduction, Fourth Edition. Alister E. McGrath.
© 2012 John Wiley & Sons, Ltd. Published 2012 by John Wiley & Sons, Ltd.

2   *Images of a changed legal status.* Through his obedience on the cross, Christ has obtained forgiveness and pardon for sinners. Those who are guilty can be washed clean of their sin and be justified in the sight of God. They are acquitted of punishment, and given the status of being righteous before God. "Justification" belongs to this category of images.

3   *Images of changed personal relationships.* Human sin entails alienation from God. "God was in Christ reconciling the world to himself" (2 Corinthians 5:19), thus making a renewed relationship between himself and humanity possible and available. Just as humans who are alienated from one another can draw together again through the process of forgiveness and reconciliation, so those who are far from God can draw close to God through the death of Christ.

4   *Images of liberation.* Those who are imprisoned by the oppressive forces of evil, sin, and the fear of death can be liberated through the death of Christ. Just as Christ broke free from the prison of death, so believers can, by faith, break free from the bonds of sin, and come to life in all its fullness. "Redemption" belongs to this category of images.

5   *Images of restoration to wholeness.* Those who are ill on account of sin can be made whole again through the cross of Christ. Through his cross and resurrection, Christ is able to bind up wounds of sinful humanity and heal them, restoring people to wholeness and spiritual health. "Salvation" belongs to this category of images.

"Justification" is thus an element of this network of terms used to describe the Christian experience of redemption through Christ. It came to assume a position of special importance at the time of the Reformation partly on account of the new interest in the writings of St Paul, in which this idea features prominently (especially in the letters to the Romans and the Galatians).

It needs to be understood that the noun "justification" and the verb "to justify" are used with a specifically theological meaning, which is quite distinct from the everyday use of the term. In everyday English, the word "justification" usually means either "a defense of an idea or a person," or "the process of alignment of margins in word processing or typesetting." This meaning can be seen clearly in the following statements:

1   She offered a justification of her late arrival for an important meeting.
2   The journal editor asked his authors not to justify their right-hand margins.

But how does this everyday use of the term help us understand this theological use of the word?

3   "Therefore, since we are justified by faith, we have peace with God through our Lord Jesus Christ" (Romans 5:1).

The word is here being used in a specifically theological sense, which bears little relation to its everyday use. It refers to the "rectification" of the relationship between humanity and God – the "putting right" of something that has become fractured, damaged, or distorted.

The English word "justification" is an attempt to denote the complex Old Testament idea of being "right before God." Through a contorted and complex tradition of translation and interpretation – from Hebrew to Greek, from Greek to Latin, and finally from Latin to English – "justification" has come to refer to the status of being righteous in the sight of God. It is helpful to paraphrase the word "justification" as "being right with God." Similarly, "to be justified" could be paraphrased as "to be put in a right relationship with God." The question of how sinners are justified lay at the heart of Luther's program of theological reform and renewal.

So how did Luther's emphasis on this doctrine come about? What brought him to this point? In what follows, we shall consider what is often referred to as Luther's "theological breakthrough."

Justification and Martin Luther's Theological Breakthrough

As we noted earlier in this chapter, the idea that human beings, finite and frail though they are, can enter into a relationship with the living God lies at the heart of the Christian faith. This idea is articulated in a number of metaphors and images, such as "salvation" and "redemption," initially in the writings of the New Testament (especially the Pauline letters) and subsequently in Christian theological reflection based upon these texts. By the late Middle Ages, one image had come to be seen as especially significant: that of justification. The term "justification" and the verb "to justify" came to signify "entering into a right relationship with God," or perhaps "being made righteous in the sight of God." The doctrine of justification came to be seen as dealing with the question of what an individual had to do in order to be saved. As contemporary sources indicate, this question came to be asked with increasing frequency as the sixteenth century dawned.

We have already seen (p. 36) how the rise of humanism brought with it a new emphasis upon individual consciousness and a new awareness of human individuality. In the wake of this dawn of the individual consciousness came a new concern with the doctrine of justification – the question of how human beings, *as individuals*, could enter into a relationship with God. A new interest developed in the writings of both Paul and Augustine, reflecting this concern with individual subjectivity. This interest is particularly evident in the writings of Petrarch (1304–74).

But what was the church's answer to the crucial question, "What must I do to be saved?" In fact, there was considerable confusion over this issue. A number of factors contributed to this confusion.

First, there had been no authoritative pronouncement from the church on the matter for over a thousand years. In 418, the Council of Carthage discussed the question, and more detailed proposals were set forth by the Second Council of Orange in 529. But for reasons which are still not fully understood, this latter council and its decrees were unknown to the theologians of the Middle Ages. The decisions of this council appear to have been "rediscovered" in 1546 – by which time the Reformation had been under way for decades.

Second, the doctrine of justification appears to have been a favorite topic of debate among later medieval theologians, with the result that a disproportionately large number of opinions on the question passed into circulation. But which of these opinions were *right*? Which had the authority of the church, and which were merely the private opinions of individuals? The reluctance or inability of the church to evaluate these opinions ensured that discussion of an already difficult question became even further confused. The central question forced upon the church by the rise of humanism – "What must I, *as an individual*, do to be saved?" – could not be answered with any degree of confidence. Humanism had forced a question upon a church which, as events would demonstrate, was unable to answer it.

Luther's Early Views on Justification

Luther was educated at the University of Erfurt (1501–5), then dominated by the *via moderna*. After a period in which he performed various functions for his Order, Luther was appointed to the chair of biblical studies at Wittenberg, in 1511. In accordance with his job specification, he lectured on various books of the Bible: the Psalms (1513–15), Romans (1515–16), Galatians (1516–17), and Hebrews (1517–18), before returning to the Psalms for a second time (1519–21). We possess the text of Luther's lectures (in various forms) in every case, allowing us to follow the development of his ideas over the period leading up to the Ninety-Five Theses (1517) and the famous Leipzig Disputation (1519).

Our interest especially concerns the first course of lectures on the Psalms, universally known as the *Dictata super Psalterium*. For two or three hours every week over a period of two years, Luther explained the meaning of each Psalm, as he understood it, to an audience which, by all accounts, was entranced by his style. Luther frequently discusses the doctrine of justification in the course of these lectures, allowing us to determine precisely what his early views on this matter were. It turns out that, initially, Luther was a remarkably faithful follower of the views of the *via moderna*.

As we saw in an earlier chapter (pp. 67–8), the covenant between God and humanity established a framework within which a relatively small human effort results in a disproportionately large divine reward. Nevertheless, a definite human effort is required to place God under an obligation to reward the sinner with grace. Luther's argument is that the covenantal understanding of justification proposed by theologians of the *via moderna* – such as Gabriel Biel – allows a small human effort to resist evil and seek good as being sufficient to "merit" (in a weak sense of the term) divine acceptance and justification. God's righteousness was demonstrated in that God faithfully granted forgiveness to those who did *quod in se est*, and condemned those who did not.

Luther's Discovery of the "Righteousness of God"

Yet Luther increasingly found himself facing serious difficulties over this idea of the "righteousness of God." What happens if sinners cannot meet this basic precondition? What happens if sinners are so damaged and trapped by sin that they cannot fulfill the demand which is made of them? Pelagius and Gabriel Biel, both of whom worked with this idea of the "righteousness of God," assumed that humans were capable of meeting this precondition without any undue difficulty – but Luther increasingly believed that humanity was so trapped in its sinfulness that it could not extricate itself from its own situation except through special divine intervention.

In a passage written toward the end of his career, Luther relates how he tried with all his might to do what was necessary to achieve salvation, but found himself more and more convinced that he could not be saved. If ever a monk could get to heaven through monastic discipline, Luther remarked, he was that monk. Yet he kept doubting: "'You didn't do that right. You weren't contrite enough. You left that out of your confession.'" It seemed to Luther that he simply could not meet the precondition for salvation. He did not have the resources needed to be saved. There was no way that God could justly reward him with salvation – only with condemnation.

The idea of the "righteousness of God" thus became a threat to Luther. It could only mean condemnation and punishment. The promise of justification was real – but the precondition attached to the promise made its fulfillment impossible. It was as if God had promised a blind man a million dollars, provided that he could see. Luther's growing pessimism concerning the abilities of sinful humanity led him to despair of his own salvation, which increasingly seemed an impossibility. "How can I find a gracious God?," he asked. By the end of 1514, it seems that Luther had failed to find an answer to his own question.

This was no mere theological problem of purely academic interest. Luther's growing anxiety regarding it shows a strongly existential dimension. It concerned him, personally; it was no mere textbook difficulty. For Luther, as for so many others, the crucial question of human existence concerned how to clinch one's salvation. Some modern readers may understandably find it difficult to empathize with this concern. However, to enter into Luther's personal situation and hence to appreciate the importance of his "theological breakthrough," it is necessary to understand how crucial this question was to him. It was *the* central question on his personal agenda.

But then something happened. We shall probably never know exactly what it was or when it occurred. We do not even know where it happened: many scholars refer to the discovery by means of the German term **Turmerlebnis**, "the tower experience," on account of a later (and somewhat confused) personal recollection of Luther, which seems to imply that his breakthrough took place in a tower of the Augustinian monastery. But whatever it was, and whenever and wherever it happened, it changed Luther's outlook on life completely, and ultimately propelled him into the forefront of the Reformation struggle.

In 1545, the year before he died, Luther wrote a preface to the first volume of the complete edition of his Latin writings in which he described how he came to break with the church of his day. The preface is clearly written with the aim of introducing him to a readership which may not know how he came to hold the radical reforming views linked with his name. In this "autobiographical fragment" (as it is usually known), Luther aims to provide those readers with background information about the development of his vocation as a reformer. After dealing with some historical preliminaries, which take his narrative up to the year 1519, he turns to describe his personal difficulties with the problem of the "righteousness of God":

> I had certainly wanted to understand Paul in his letter to the Romans. But what prevented me from doing so was not so much cold feet as that one phrase in the first chapter: "the righteousness of God is revealed in it" (Romans 1:17). For I hated that phrase, "the righteousness of God," which I had been taught to understand as the righteousness by which God is righteous, and punishes unrighteous sinners. . . .
>
> At last, as I meditated day and night on the relation of the words "the righteousness of God is revealed in it, as it is written, the righteous person shall live by faith," I began to understand that "righteousness of God" as that by which the righteous person lives by the gift of God (faith); and this sentence, "the righteousness of God is revealed," to refer to a passive righteousness, by which the merciful God justifies us by faith, as it is written, "the righteous person lives by faith." This immediately made me feel as though I had been born again, and as though I had entered through open gates into paradise itself. From that moment, I saw the whole face of Scripture in a new light . . . And now, where I had once hated the phrase, "the righteousness of God," I began to love and extol it as the sweetest of phrases, so that this passage in Paul became the very gate of paradise to me.[1]

So just what is Luther describing in this famous passage, which vibrates with the excitement of discovery? It is obvious that his understanding of the phrase "the righteousness of God" has changed radically. Luther's critical insight is that the God of the Christian gospel is not a harsh and indifferent judge who rewards individuals according to their merits, but a merciful and gracious God who bestows righteousness upon sinners as a gift. True repentance is now to be seen as the result, rather than the precondition, of grace.

So when did this change take place? Although the evidence is difficult to interpret at points, it seems that the basic change described by Luther in 1545 took place at some point in 1515. The Luther who posted the Ninety-Five Theses in October 1517 was already in possession of the insights on which he would base his program of reform.

Central to these insights was the doctrine of "justification by faith alone (*sola fide*)," and it is important to understand what was meant by this term. We have already explored the idea of "justification" (see p. 117). But what about the phrase "by faith alone"? What is the nature of this "justifying faith"?

The Nature of Justifying Faith

"The reason why some people do not understand why faith alone justifies is that they do not know what faith is." In writing these words, Luther draws our attention to the need to inquire more closely concerning that deceptively simple word "faith." Three points relating to Luther's idea of faith may be singled out as having special importance to his doctrine of justification. Each of these points was taken up and developed by later writers, such as Calvin, indicating that Luther made a fundamental contribution to the development of Reformation thought at this point. These three points are:

1   Faith has a personal, rather than a purely historical, reference.
2   Faith concerns trust in the promises of God.
3   Faith unites the believer to Christ.

We shall consider each of these points individually.

First, faith is not simply historical knowledge. Luther argues that a faith which is content to believe in the historical reliability of the gospels is not a faith which justifies. Sinners are perfectly capable of trusting in the historical details of the gospels, but these facts of themselves are not adequate for true Christian faith.

Second, faith is essentially "trust" (*fiducia*). Faith is about being prepared to put one's trust in the promises of God and in the integrity and faithfulness of the God who made those promises. This trust is not, however, an occasional attitude toward God. For Luther, it is an undeviating trusting outlook upon life, a constant stance of conviction of the trustworthiness of the promises of God.

In the third place, faith unites the believer with Christ. Luther states this principle clearly in his 1520 writing, *The Liberty of a Christian*.

Faith unites the soul with Christ as a bride is united with her bridegroom. . . . So it follows that everything that they have is held in common, whether good or evil. So the believer can boast of and glory in whatever Christ possesses, as though it were his or her own; and whatever the believer has, Christ claims as his own. Let us see how this works and how it benefits us. Christ is full of grace, life and salvation. The human soul is full of sin, death and damnation. Now let faith come between them. Sin, death and damnation will then be Christ's; and grace, life and salvation will be the believer's.[2]

Faith, then, is not assent to an abstract set of doctrines. Rather, it is a "wedding ring" (Luther's phrase), pointing to mutual commitment and union between Christ and the believer. It is the response of the whole person of the believer to God, which leads in turn to the real and personal presence of Christ in the believer. Faith makes both Christ and his benefits – such as forgiveness, justification, and hope – available to the believer.

The doctrine of "justification by faith" thus does not mean that the sinner is justified *because* he or she believes, on account of his or her faith. Rather, it involves recognizing that God provides everything necessary for justification, so that all the sinner needs to do is to receive it. In justification, God is active, and humans are passive. The phrase "justification *by* grace *through* faith" brings out the meaning of the doctrine more clearly: the justification of the sinner is based upon the grace of God, and is received through faith. Or perhaps we could cite the somewhat rambling title of Heinrich Bullinger's 1554 work on this subject as a comprehensive, if not particularly eloquent, statement of Luther's ideas: *The grace of God that justifies us for the sake of Christ through faith alone, without good works, while faith meanwhile abounds in good works.*

Luther's critics suggested that this seemed to minimize the role of good works in the Christian life. Luther was branded as an "antinomian" by some – in other words, someone who has no place for the law (Greek, *nomos*) in the religious life. In fact, however, Luther was arguing that good works are not the *cause* of justification, but its *result*, a point captured somewhat laboriously in the title of Bullinger's book noted above. In other words, Luther treats good works as the *natural result of having been justified*, rather than the *cause of that justification*. Far from destroying morality, Luther simply saw himself as setting it in its proper context. The believer performs good works as an act of thankfulness to God for having forgiven him, rather than in an attempt to get God to forgive him in the first place.

Consequences of Luther's Doctrine of Justification

So why was this change of thinking so significant? Some might suggest that the question of how sinners find acceptance in the sight of God was a purely academic question, which could be relegated to the appropriate sections of theological textbooks. In fact, it was much more significant. Forgiveness could now be seen as a matter between the individual and God. Neither the church nor its sacraments nor priests were *necessarily* required if someone was to find acceptance with God.

In fact, Luther was less radical at this point than many expected. He retained a real role in his theology for priests, the sacraments, and the institution of the church. Yet the emphasis of his reforming theology fell on the individual. How can an individual find forgiveness and acceptance in the sight of God? This emphasis brought Luther into immediate and direct conflict with one important feature of late medieval religious life – the indulgence.

In the late medieval period, sin was regarded as a visible and social matter, something which had to be forgiven in a visible and social way. Forgiveness is not a private matter between the individual and God; it is a public matter involving that individual, the church, and society. In 1215 the Fourth Lateran Council declared that "All believers of both sexes who have reached the age of discretion must faithfully confess their sins in person to their own priest, and attempt to carry out the penance imposed." Both priest and penance were thus firmly established as part of the medieval process by which God was understood to forgive sins through appointed human representatives and means on earth.

Yet ecclesiastical vagueness concerning the precise role of both penitent and priest in penance inevitably led to the development of a number of highly questionable trends in popular belief. Salvation was widely regarded as something which could be earned or merited through good works. The confused and vague theology of forgiveness of the late medieval period lent weight to the suggestion that it was possible to purchase the forgiveness of sins and procure the remission of "purgatorial penalties" through the purchase of indulgences. In other words, the eternal penalties resulting from sinful actions could be reduced, if not eliminated, by payment of an appropriate sum of money to the appropriate ecclesiastical figure. Thus Cardinal Albrecht of Brandenburg managed to accumulate a remission of purgatorial penalties reckoned to total 39,245,120 years, give or take a few millennia.

If such beliefs were contrary to the teaching of the church, no attempt was made by that church to disabuse its members of such ideas. Indeed, there are reasons for thinking that they were tolerated to the point of being unofficially incorporated into the structures of the church. The power and the income of much of the ecclesiastical establishment and its patrons were actually linked with the continuance of such practices and beliefs.

What was an indulgence? Originally, an indulgence seems to have been a gift of money to charity as an expression of thankfulness for forgiveness. By the beginning of the sixteenth century, however, this innocent idea had been transformed into an important source of income for a papacy facing a financial crisis and prepared to be flexible in its theology in order to meet it. Luther's wrath was particularly kindled by the marketing techniques of Johannes Tetzel. For a mere three marks, a sinner could be released from all punishments that he would otherwise face in purgatory – and many found this an offer difficult to refuse at the price. In an age which knew how to enjoy its venial sins, the possibility of being able to do so without any fear of divine punishment was enormously tempting. Tetzel's suggestion that it would be possible to secure the immediate release of the soul of a loved one from its sufferings in purgatory for a reasonable sum (based on a sliding scale according to the individual's wealth) was calculated to make a powerful appeal to the guilt of the living concerning the dead.

In the early sixteenth century, indulgences were a major source of papal revenue; and, as the somewhat sordid trilateral deal between the pope, Albrecht of Brandenburg, and the banking house of Fuggers indicates, that income found

Figure 7.1 The Pope's selling of indulgences by Lucas Cranach the Elder (1472–1553). Illustration from Martin Luther (?), *Passional Christi und Antichristi,* 1521. Woodcut. Photo: akg-images

its way into a number of coffers (Figure 7.1). In a period when ecclesiastical offices were often purchased rather than earned, the buyers generally felt justified in looking for a return on their investment – and such practices as paying for masses for the dead were encouraged for this reason. As a result, there were a number of vested interests concerned to ensure that the early sixteenth-century vagueness concerning the doctrine of justification was maintained. The unique and indispensable role of the priest in **confession** and forgiveness was obviously open to corruption, and the evidence suggests that clerical venality was no small problem on the eve of the Reformation.

confession Term referring primarily to the admission of sin. Also, in the sixteenth century, a document embodying the principles of faith of a Protestant church.

Luther's doctrine of justification by faith, with its associated doctrine of the "priesthood of all believers," thus assumed an importance which far transcended the sphere of academic theology. It cut the ground from under the vested interests we have just noted. Forgiveness was a matter between the believer and God: no others were involved. No priest was required to pronounce that the person had been forgiven; the believer could read in Scripture the promises of forgiveness to those who confessed their sins, and needed no one to repeat them or execute them. No payment of any kind was required to receive divine forgiveness.

Luther's action in posting the Ninety-Five Theses on indulgences on October 31, 1517 (now celebrated as "Reformation Day" in Germany) was not merely a protest against Tetzel's claims for indulgences, which rivaled those of modern detergent manufacturers in terms of their optimistic claims. Nor was it merely a request that the church clarify its teaching on forgiveness. It marked the appearance of a new theology of forgiveness (or, more accurately, the *re*appearance of an old and apparently forgotten theology of forgiveness) which threatened to take away from the institutional church any role in forgiveness, thereby threatening the vested interests of the pope, many clergy, some princes, and one rather important banking house (the Fuggers of Augsburg, which replaced the Medicis as the official church bankers when Leo X, himself a Medici, became pope in 1513).

The doctrine of justification by faith alone reaffirmed that God's forgiveness was given, not bought, and was available to all, irrespective of their financial means or social condition. The related doctrine of the "priesthood of all believers" meant that the believer, with the gracious assistance of God, could do everything necessary to his or her own salvation without having to rely totally upon either priest or church (although Luther believed that both professional ministers and the institution of the church had a significant role to play in the Christian life). It is thus little wonder that Luther's views were regarded with such anxiety by the ecclesiastical establishment and were received with great interest by so many laity at the time.

The Concept of "Forensic Justification"

One of the central insights of Luther's doctrine of justification by faith alone is that the individual sinner is incapable of self-justification. It is God who takes the initiative in justification, providing all the resources necessary to justify the sinner. One of those resources is the "righteousness of God." In other words, the righteousness on the basis of which the sinner is justified is not his own righteousness, but a righteousness which is given to him by God. Augustine had made this point earlier; Luther, however, gives it a subtle new twist, which leads to the development of the concept of "forensic justification."

The point at issue is a little difficult to explain. It centers on the question of the *location of justifying righteousness*. Both Augustine and Luther are agreed that God graciously gives sinful humans a righteousness which justifies them. But where is that righteousness located? Augustine argued that it was to be found within believers; Luther insisted that it remained outside believers. That is, for Augustine, the righteousness in question is internal; for Luther, it is external.

In Augustine's view, God bestows justifying righteousness upon the sinner in such a way that it becomes part of his or her person. As a result, this righteousness, although originating *outside* the sinner, becomes part of him or her. In Luther's view, by contrast, the righteousness in question remains outside the sinner: it is an "alien righteousness" (*iustitia aliena*). God treats, or "reckons," this righteousness *as if* it is part of the sinner's person. In his lectures on Romans of 1515–16, Luther developed the idea of the "alien righteousness of Christ," imputed – not imparted – to the believer by faith, as the grounds of justification. His comments on Romans 4:7 are especially important: "we are righteous solely by the imputation of God and not of ourselves or of our own works."

Believers are thus, according to Luther, righteous on account of the alien righteousness of Christ which is imputed to them – that is, treated as if it were theirs through faith. Earlier, we noted that an essential element of Luther's concept of faith is that it unites the believer to Christ. Justifying faith thus allows the believer to link up with the righteousness of Christ, and be justified on the basis of it. Christians are thus "righteous by the imputation of a merciful God."

Through faith, the believer is clothed with the righteousness of Christ in much the same way, Luther suggests, as Ezekiel 16:8 speaks of God covering our nakedness with a garment. For Luther, faith is the right (or righteous) relationship to God. Sin and righteousness thus coexist: we remain sinners inwardly, but are righteous extrinsically, in the sight of God. By confessing our sins in faith, we stand in a right and righteous relationship with God. From our own perspective we are sinners; but in the perspective of God, we are righteous. Commenting on Romans 4:7, Luther declares:

> The saints are always aware of their sin and seek righteousness from God in accordance with God's mercy. And for this very reason, they are regarded as righteous by God. Thus in their own eyes (and in reality!) they are sinners; but in the eyes of God they are righteous, because God reckons them as such on account of their confession of their sin. In reality they are sinners; but they are righteous by the imputation of a merciful God. They are unknowingly righteous, and knowingly sinners. They are sinners in fact, but righteous in hope.[3]

Luther is not necessarily implying that this coexistence of sin and righteousness is a permanent condition. The Christian life is not static, as if – to use a very loose way of speaking – the relative amounts of sin and righteousness remain constant throughout. Luther is perfectly aware that the Christian life is dynamic, in that the believer (hopefully) grows in righteousness. Rather, his point is that the existence of sin does not negate our status as a Christian. In justification, we are given the status of righteousness while we work with God toward attaining the nature of righteousness. God shields our sin through Christ's righteousness.

This righteousness is like a protective covering, beneath which we may battle with our sin. In that God has promised to make us righteous one day, ultimately eliminating our sin, there is a sense in which we are *already* righteous in God's sight. Luther makes this point as follows:

It is just like a man who is sick, and who believes the doctor who promises his full recovery. In the meantime, he obeys the doctor's orders in the hope of the promised recovery, and abstains from those things which he has been told to lay off, so that he may in no way hinder the promised return to health . . . Now is this sick person well? In fact, he is both sick and well at the same time. He is sick in reality – but he is well on account of the sure promise of the doctor, whom he trusts, and who reckons him as already being cured.[4]

Luther then takes this medical analogy a stage further. Having established that illness is an analogue of sin and health of righteousness, he concludes: "So [the believer] is at one and the same time both a sinner and righteous – a sinner in reality, but righteous by the sure imputation and promise of God that God will continue to deliver this person from sin until God has completely cured him. So [the believer] is entirely healthy in hope, but a sinner in reality." This approach accounts for the persistence of sin in believers, while at the same time accounting for the gradual transformation of the believer and the future elimination of that sin. But it is not necessary to be perfectly righteous to be a Christian. Sin does not point to unbelief or a failure on the part of God; rather, it points to the continued need to entrust one's person to the gentle care of God. Luther thus declares that a believer is "at one and the same time righteous and a sinner" (*simul iustus et peccator*): righteous in hope, but a sinner in fact; righteous in the sight and through the promise of God, yet a sinner in reality.

These ideas were further developed by Luther's follower Philipp Melanchthon, resulting in an explicit statement of the doctrine now generally known as "forensic justification." Whereas Augustine taught that the sinner is *made righteous* in justification, Melanchthon taught that he is *counted as righteous* or *pronounced to be righteous*. For Augustine, "justifying righteousness" is *imparted*; for Melanchthon, it is *imputed* in the sense of being declared or pronounced to be righteous.

Melanchthon now drew a sharp distinction between the event of being *declared* righteous and the process of being *made* righteous, designating the former "justification" and the latter "sanctification" or "regeneration." For Augustine, these were simply different aspects of the same thing. According to Melanchthon, God pronounces the verdict that the sinner is righteous in the heavenly court (*in foro divino*). This legal approach to justification gave rise to the term "forensic justification," from the Latin word *forum* ("marketplace" or "courtyard"), the place traditionally associated with the dispensing of justice in classical Rome.

The importance of this development lies in the fact that it marks a complete break with the teaching of the church up to that point. From the time of Augustine onward, justification had always been understood to refer to both the event of being declared righteous and the process of being made righteous. Melanchthon's concept of forensic justification diverged radically from this. As it was taken up by virtually all the major reformers subsequently, it came to represent a standard difference between Protestant and Catholic from then on. In addition to differences regarding how the sinner was justified, there was now an additional disagreement on what the word "justification" designated in the first place. The Council of Trent, the Catholic church's definitive response to the Protestant challenge, reaffirmed the views of Augustine on the nature of justification, and censured the views of Melanchthon as woefully inadequate.

As suggested above, the concept of forensic justification actually represents a development of Luther's thought. This naturally leads us to ask what other developments and divergences in relation to the question of justification may be discerned within the Reformation.

Divergences among the Reformers on Justification

Popular accounts of the Reformation often create the impression of a monolithic uniformity within the movement in relation to the doctrine of justification. In fact, there are substantial differences of substance and emphasis between individual reformers on the doctrine. This section aims to explore some of those differences.

Justification and the Swiss Reformation

Especially in introductory textbooks, the European Reformation is often portrayed as a homogeneous phenomenon. In other words, it is presented as being consistent in terms of its underlying ideas and emphases. In fact, this is an inaccurate view, and the role played by the doctrine of justification by faith alone in the Swiss Reformation is a particularly important illustration of this point.

Over the period 1515–20, as we have seen, the doctrine of justification came to the fore in Luther's thought. In addition to becoming the center of his theology, it also became the focus of his program of reform. Luther's polemical writings, his liturgical innovations and reforms, and his sermons of the period all reveal the practical importance of the doctrine of justification by faith to his reforming program. As noted above, an essential component of Luther's doctrine of justification by faith concerns his understanding of justifying faith itself – a faith which unites the believer to Christ and brings about the real and personal presence of Christ within him or her.

Yet the Swiss reformer Huldrych Zwingli develops approaches that reflect the concerns of the eastern Swiss humanist sodalities during the same period. Ernst Ziegler, in a masterly survey of Reforming writings originating in this region of Switzerland around this time, makes the point that, for these writers, the word "Reformation" designates a reformation of life and morality. The term "justification by faith" is often conspicuous by its absence from such writings. The moralist ethos of eastern Swiss humanism contrasts sharply with Luther's emphasis upon the unmerited gift of grace, given in advance of and independent of any human moral action. This does not mean that writers such as Vadian or Zwingli defended a doctrine of justification by works, as if salvation came about as a result of human moral achievement. Rather, these reformers chose to place their emphasis on the *moral consequences* of the gospel, with a resulting tendency to play down issues which were of great importance to Luther.

Similar views are found within Anabaptism. Writers such as Kaspar Schwenkfeld preferred to speak of the moral regeneration of believers. The believer is required to imitate Christ at the moral and spiritual levels, rather than merely to trust in God's promises. Once more, we find a suspicion of Luther's doctrine of justification by faith alone on the grounds of its possible moral implications. For Schwenkfeld, the believer is justified actively through moral actions, not through passive reception of divine virtues.

As we saw earlier, Luther's doctrine of justification was directed toward the individual believer, clarifying his relationship with both God and the church, in order that his troubled conscience might be relieved. In many ways, it illustrates Luther's concern with the individual and his subjective consciousness, reflecting the rise of individualism associated with the Renaissance. But what of the Swiss Reformation, where more attention was paid to reformation of the *community*?

Zwingli saw the Reformation as affecting church and society, rather than just the individual. That Reformation, according to Zwingli, was primarily *moral* in character, affecting attitudes and actions, rather than ensuring correct beliefs. Zwingli was concerned with the moral and spiritual regeneration of Zurich (Figure 7.2) along New Testament lines, rather than with any doctrine of justification. He was not concerned with questions about how individuals found a gracious God. Luther's emphasis upon justification by faith was thus absent from Zwingli.

Yet the differences between the two on this doctrine in fact extend to matters of substance, as well as of emphasis. For example, Zwingli tends to treat Christ as an external moral example, rather than a personal presence within the believer. It would not be true to say that Zwingli teaches justification by works in his early period – that is to say, that human achievements have a purchasing power capable of attaining salvation. The emphasis in Zwingli's early writings is that of the priority of human moral renewal over divine forgiveness. For writers such as Vadian, the gospel is concerned primarily with the moral renewal and regeneration of individuals and institutions, with justification (although the term, interestingly, is used but rarely by Vadian) following in the wake of these processes.

During the 1520s, Zwingli's ideas about justification began to become closer to those of Luther, perhaps on account of Zwingli's increased familiarity with the latter's writings. Yet the reader can still discern a fundamental difference between the two writers, reflecting different approaches to justification. For Luther, Scripture declares the promises of God, which reassure and console the believer; it is primarily concerned with narrating and proclaiming what God has done for sinful humanity in Christ. For Zwingli, Scripture sets out the moral demands which God makes of believers; it is primarily concerned with indicating what humanity must do in response to the example provided by Christ.

Figure 7.2 View of Zurich, from *Cosmographie Universelle* by Sebastien Munster (1488–1552), Basle, published 1559. Woodcut, German School, sixteenth century. Bibliotheque des Arts Decoratifs, Paris, France/Archives Charmet/The Bridgeman Art Library

Even in the 1520s, then, diverging views on justification were evident within the Reformation. The widely differing views of Luther and Zwingli perhaps illustrate two extreme positions. Attempts to mediate between them were eventually forthcoming, and our attention now turns to those associated with Bucer and Calvin.

Later Developments: Bucer and Calvin on Justification

The divergences between Luther and Zwingli may be said to set the scene for extended discussion of the proper understanding of the doctrine of justification in the later Reformation. Two matters required resolution: the role of Christ in justification and the relationship between God's gracious act of justification and human obedience to the divine will. Luther himself, largely through occasional overstatement on the one hand and confusion on the other, managed to convey the impression to many (such as the humanist Georg Spalatin, 1484–1545) that once a sinner was justified, he or she was under no obligation at all to perform moral actions. In fact, Luther's basic position was that good works were an entirely appropriate response to God's gracious act of justification, but that they could not – and *must* not – be considered as a cause of that justification. Yet a significant section of his public in the 1520s understood Luther to imply that Christians were dispensed from moral obligation.

Perhaps the most significant attempt to redress the apparent faults in this approach were due to the Strasbourg reformer Martin Bucer. In a series of writings, especially during the 1530s, Bucer developed a doctrine of *double justification*, which seemed to him to get round the difficulty raised by Luther's one-sided stress on the grace of God. Bucer argued that there were two stages in justification. The first stage, which he termed "justification of the ungodly" (*iustificatio impii*), consisted of God's gracious forgiveness of human sin. (Later Protestant theology simply referred to this stage as "justification.") The second stage, which he termed "justification of the godly" (*iustificatio pii*), consisted of an obedient human response to the moral demands of the gospel. (Later Protestant theology would refer to this process as "regeneration" or "sanctification.") Christ was regarded as an external moral example, graciously provided by God, which justified sinners were required, through the assistance of the Holy Spirit, to imitate.

A causal link was thus established between justification and moral regeneration. Unless both took place, the sinner could not be said to be justified. Since the "justification of the ungodly" caused the "justification of the godly," it followed that the absence of moral regeneration in an individual implied that he or she had not been justified in the first place. Bucer thus believed that he had successfully safeguarded both the reality of grace and the necessity of human obedience. Others were not so sure. The theory seemed somewhat artificial, and reduced Christ to an external moral example. What had happened to Luther's emphasis on the real personal presence of Christ within believers?

The model of justification which eventually gained the ascendancy in the later Reformation was formulated by Calvin in the 1540s and 1550s. Calvin's approach avoids the deficiencies both of an external understanding of the role of Christ in justification and the view that justification causes moral renewal. The basic elements of his approach may be summarized as follows. Faith unites the believer to Christ in a "mystic union." (Here, Calvin reclaims Luther's emphasis on the real and personal presence of Christ within believers, established through faith.) This union with Christ has a twofold effect, which Calvin refers to as "a double grace."

First, the believer's union with Christ leads directly to his or her *justification*. Through Christ, the believer is declared to be righteous in the sight of God. Second, on account of the believer's union with Christ – and *not* on account of his or her justification – the believer begins the process of becoming like Christ through regeneration. Where Bucer argued that justification causes regeneration, Calvin asserts that both justification and regeneration are the results of the believer's union with Christ through faith.

This brief survey of understandings of justification current within the Reformation indicates that the movement was far from uniform on this matter. If space had permitted the views of other significant reformers – such as Wolfgang Capito, Andreas Bodenstein von Karlstadt, and Johann Oecolampadius – to be considered, still further differences would have emerged. If the reformers were united in rejecting the view that human beings could achieve their own salvation, this unity did not extend to the precise manner in which God achieved this salvation through Christ. A spectrum of opinions existed in the first generation of the Reformation, with those of Calvin and Melanchthon gradually gaining the ascendancy, through a long process of debate, within the Reformed and Lutheran churches respectively.

Theological Diplomacy: "Double Justification"

During the 1530s, there was considerable optimism in some circles that an accommodation might be reached between Protestants and Catholics over the divisive issue of justification. Although Luther himself had adopted what might be called a "sanative" or "transformative" model of justification in the late 1510s (obvious in his analogy, borrowed from Augustine, of a sick person who is recovering), the 1520s saw a crystallization of the view that justification was a declarative concept. To be justified was to be declared righteous in the sight of God, on the basis of the external righteousness of Christ – not some internal righteousness, located within the human soul.

Catholicism, however, remained committed to Augustine's view that justification was an essentially transformative process, in which the believer was "made righteous." Believers were reckoned as righteous because they were righteous – even though that righteousness could be understood as a divine gift, rather than a human achievement.

So could the gap between these two positions be bridged? Martin Bucer, widely regarded as one of the most irenic reformers, certainly thought so. His own approach to justification, as already noted (p. 131), brings together these two "justifying righteousnesses" and holds that both are involved – although in different ways – in the justification of the believer. The approach Bucer developed is often loosely designated "double justification." This is not a helpful term, as it is open to multiple interpretations. In fact, all that Bucer seems to have intended to do was to forge a secure theological link between the totally gratuitous justification of sinners and the moral obligations which this subsequently placed upon them. Yet his approach seemed to many to hold the key to resolving the increasing tensions between Protestant and Catholic theologians over the question of how sinners find acceptance with God.

Theologically, the real issue concerned the following question: can the gratuity of justification be maintained, independent of the location of justifying righteousness? Calvin, for example, held that any notion that a righteousness within humanity was implicated in justification might be tantamount to Pelagianism, or a doctrine of justification by works. His Catholic opponents argued that Augustine had successfully defended the gratuity of justification against Pelagius, without relying on the notion of an "external" justifying righteousness.

In the 1530s, a number of writers – including the Dutch Catholic Albert Pighius (1490–1542) and the German Catholic Johann Gropper (1503–59) – argued that it was possible to safeguard the concerns of both Protestant and Catholic by developing a doctrine of justification based upon a "double right-eousness" – the righteousness which God imputes to the believer, and the righteousness within the believer, which results from renewal and regeneration. Although the term "double justification" is often used to refer to the position of Gropper and Pighius, this is not correct. There is no question of a "double formal cause of justification"; simply the recognition that both notions of right-eousness are involved in justification.

The Colloquy of Regensburg (1541), which brought together both Catholic and Protestant representatives, included an article which attempted to bridge the gap between the two confessional positions by allowing both an imputed external righteousness and an imparted inherent righteousness to be involved in human justification. Yet this approach to justification failed to find support on either side. In the end, the Council of Trent formulated its own approach to the doc-trine of justification which failed to endorse the approach commended at Regensburg.

The Catholic Response: Trent on Justification

It was obvious that the Catholic church needed to make an official and definitive response to Luther. By 1540, Luther had become something of a household name throughout Europe. His writings were being read and digested with various degrees of enthusiasm, even in the highest ecclesiastical circles in Italy. Something had to be done. The Council of Trent – named after the northern Italian city in which it met (known in Italian as "Trentino") – was summoned in 1545, and began the long process of formulating a comprehensive response to Luther. High on its agenda was the doctrine of justification.

It must be appreciated that there were significant disagreements within Catholicism over the doctrine of justification by the 1540s. Scholars are generally agreed that two major positions can be discerned among those who gathered in Trent to debate the question. The Dominicans and Franciscans had relatively well-developed approaches to the question, with the Franciscans placing greater emphasis on the positive contributions that human beings can make toward their own justification. Yet perhaps the most significant development concerned the abandoning of the language of early medieval writers concerning justification (for example, their references to "created habits of grace"). Trent tends to use pre-dominantly biblical and Augustinian language in setting out its ideas.

The Sixth Session of the Council of Trent was brought to a close on January 13, 1547. The Tridentine Decree on Justification, as the substantial product of this session has generally come to be known, probably represents the most significant achievement of this council. Its 16 chapters set out the Catholic teaching on justification with a considerable degree of clarity. A series of 33 canons condemn specific opinions attributed to opponents of the Catholic church, including Luther. Interestingly, the council seems unaware of the threat posed by Calvin, and directs the vast bulk of its criticisms against views which were known to be held by Luther himself.

Trent's critique of Luther's doctrine of justification can be broken down into four main sections:

1   The nature of justification.
2   The nature of justifying righteousness.
3   The nature of justifying faith.
4   The assurance of salvation.

We shall consider each of these four matters individually.

The Nature of Justification

In his earlier phase, around the years 1515–19, Luther tended to understand justification as a process of *becoming*, in which the sinner was gradually conformed to the likeness of Jesus Christ through a process of internal renewal. Luther's analogy of a sick person under competent medical care points to this understanding of justification, as does his famous declaration in the 1515–16 lectures on Romans: *fieri est iustificatio*, "justification is about becoming." In his later writings, however, dating from the mid-1530s and beyond, perhaps under the influence of Melanchthon's more forensic approach to justification (see pp. 125–7), Luther tended to treat justification as a matter of being declared to be righteous, rather than a process of becoming righteous. Increasingly, he came to see justification as an event, which was complemented by the distinct process of regeneration and interior renewal through the action of the Holy Spirit. Justification altered the outer status of the sinner in the sight of God (*coram Deo*), while regeneration altered the sinner's inner nature.

Trent strongly opposed this view, and vigorously defended the idea, originally associated with Augustine, that justification is the process of regeneration and renewal within human nature, which brings about a change in both the outer status and the inner nature of the sinner. Its fourth chapter provided the following precise definition of justification:

> The justification of the sinner may be briefly defined as a translation from that state in which a human being is born a child of the first Adam, to the state of grace and of the adoption of the sons of God through the second Adam, Jesus Christ our

Saviour. According to the gospel, this translation cannot come about except through the cleansing of regeneration, or a desire for this, as it is written, "Unless someone is born again of water and the Holy Spirit, he or she cannot enter into the Kingdom of God" (John 3:5).[5]

Justification thus included the idea of regeneration. This brief statement was amplified in the seventh chapter, which stressed that justification "is not only a remission of sins but also the sanctification and renewal of the inner person through the voluntary reception of the grace and gifts by which an unrighteous person becomes a righteous person." This point was given further emphasis through canon 11, which condemned anyone who taught that justification takes place "either by the sole imputation of the righteousness of Christ or by the sole remission of sins, to the exclusion of grace and charity . . . or that the grace by which we are justified is only the good will of God."

Trent insists that justification is closely linked with the sacraments of baptism and penance. The sinner is initially justified through baptism; however, on account of sin, that justification may be forfeited. It can be renewed, however, by penance, as the fourteenth chapter makes clear:

> Those who through sin have forfeited the received grace of justification can be justi-fied again when, moved by God, they exert themselves to obtain through the sacra-ment of penance the recovery, by the merits of Christ, of the grace which was lost. Now this manner of justification is restoration for those who have lapsed into sin. The holy fathers have properly called this a "second plank after the shipwreck of lost grace." For Christ Jesus instituted the sacrament of penance, on behalf of those who lapse into sin after baptism . . . The repentance of a Christian after a lapse into sin is thus very different from that at baptism.[6]

In brief, then, Trent maintained the medieval tradition, stretching back to Augustine, which saw justification as comprising both an event and a process – the event of being declared to be righteous through the work of Christ and the process of being made righteous through the internal work of the Holy Spirit. Reformers such as Melanchthon and Calvin distinguished these two matters, treating the word "justification" as referring only to the event of being declared to be righteous; the accompanying process of internal renewal, which they termed "sanctification" or "regeneration," they regarded as theologically distinct.

Serious confusion thus resulted: Catholics and Protestants used the same word "justification" to mean very different things. Trent used it to mean what, accord-ing to Protestants, was *both* justification *and* sanctification.

The Nature of Justifying Righteousness

Luther stressed the fact that sinners possess no righteousness in themselves. They have nothing within them which could ever be regarded as the basis of God's gracious decision to justify them. Luther's doctrine of the "alien righteousness of Christ" (*iustitia Christi aliena*) made it clear that the righteousness which justified sinners was outside them. It was imputed, not imparted; external, not internal.

Early critics of the Reformation argued, following Augustine, that sinners were justified on the basis of an internal righteousness, graciously infused or implanted within their persons by God. This righteousness was itself given as an act of grace; it was not something merited. But, they argued, there had to be something within individuals which could allow God to justify them. Luther dismissed this idea. If God had decided to justify someone, he might as well do it directly, rather than through an intermediate gift of righteousness.

Trent, in marked contrast, strongly defended the Augustinian idea of justification on the basis of an internal righteousness. The seventh chapter makes this point crystal clear:

> The single formal cause (of justification) is the righteousness of God – not the righteousness by which God is righteous, but the righteousness by which God makes us righteous, so that, when we are endowed with it, we are "renewed in the spirit of our mind" (Ephesians 4:23), and are not only counted as righteous, but are called, and are in reality, righteous . . . Nobody can be righteous except God communicates the merits of the passion of our Lord Jesus Christ to him or her, and this takes place in the justification of the sinner.[7]

The technical phrase "single formal cause" needs explanation. A "formal" cause is the *direct*, or most immediate, cause of something. Trent is thus stating that the direct cause of justification is the righteousness which God graciously imparts to us – as opposed to more distant causes of justification, such as the "efficient cause" (God) or the "meritorious cause" (Jesus Christ). But the use of the word "single" should also be noted.

One proposal for reaching agreement between Catholic and Protestant, which gained especial prominence at the Colloquy of Regensburg (also known as Ratisbon) in 1541, was that *two* causes of justification should be recognized: an external righteousness (the Protestant position) and an internal righteousness (the Catholic position). This compromise seemed to hold some potential. Trent, however, had no time for it. The use of the word "single" was deliberate, intended to eliminate the idea that there could be more than one such cause. The *only* direct cause of justification was the interior gift of righteousness.

The Nature of Justifying Faith

Luther's doctrine of justification by faith alone came in for severe criticism. Canon 12 condemned a central aspect of Luther's notion of justifying faith when it rejected the idea that "justifying faith is nothing other than confidence in the mercy of God, which remits sin for the sake of Christ." In part, this rejection of Luther's doctrine of justification reflects the ambiguity, noted above (p. 135), concerning the meaning of the term "justification." Trent was alarmed that anyone should believe that they could be justified – in the Tridentine sense of the term – by faith, without any need for obedience or spiritual renewal. Trent, interpreting "justification" to mean *both* the beginning of the Christian life *and* its continuation and growth, believed that Luther was suggesting that simply trusting in God (without any requirement that the sinner be changed and renewed by God) was the basis of the entire Christian life.

In fact, Luther meant nothing of the sort. He was affirming that the Christian life was begun through faith, and faith alone; good works followed justification, but did not cause that justification in the first place. Trent itself was perfectly prepared to concede that the Christian life was begun through faith, thus coming very close indeed to Luther's position. As chapter 8 of the Decree on Justification declares, "We are said to be justified by faith, because faith is the beginning of human salvation, the foundation and root of all justification, without which it is impossible to please God." This is perhaps a classic case of a theological misunderstanding resting upon the disputed meaning of a major theological term.

The Assurance of Salvation

For Luther, as for the reformers in general, one could rest assured of one's salvation. Salvation was grounded in the faithfulness of God to God's promises of mercy; to fail to have confidence in salvation was, in effect, to doubt the reliability and trustworthiness of God. Yet this must not be seen as a supreme confidence in God, untroubled by doubt. Faith is not the same as certainty; although the theological foundation of Christian faith may be secure, the human perception of and commitment to this foundation may waver.

This point is brought out clearly by Calvin, often thought to be the most confident of all the reformers in relation to matters of faith. His definition of faith certainly seems to point in this direction:

> Now we shall have a right definition of faith if we say that it is a steady and certain knowledge of the divine benevolence towards us, which is founded upon the truth of the gracious promise of God in Christ, and is both revealed to our minds and sealed in our hearts by the Holy Spirit.[8]

Yet the *theological* certainty of this statement does not, according to Calvin, necessarily lead to *psychological* security. It is perfectly consistent with a sustained wrestling with doubt and anxiety on the part of the believer:

> When we stress that faith ought to be certain and secure, we do not have in mind a certainty without doubt, or a security without any anxiety. Rather, we affirm that

believers have a perpetual struggle with their own lack of faith, and are far from possessing a peaceful conscience, never interrupted by any disturbance. On the other hand, we want to deny that they may fall out of, or depart from, their confidence in the divine mercy, no matter how much they may be troubled.[9]

The Council of Trent regarded the reformers' doctrine of assurance with considerable skepticism. Chapter 9 of the Decree on Justification, entitled "Against the vain confidence of heretics," criticized the "ungodly confidence" of the reformers. While no one should doubt God's goodness and generosity, the reformers erred seriously when they taught that "nobody is absolved from sins and justified unless they believe with certainty that they are absolved and justified, and that absolution and justification are effected by this faith alone." Trent insisted that "nobody can know with a certainty of faith which is not subject to error, whether they have obtained the grace of God."

Trent's point seems to be that the reformers seemed to be making human confidence or boldness the grounds for justification, so that justification rested upon a fallible human conviction, rather than on the grace of God. The reformers, however, saw themselves as stressing that justification rested upon the promises of God; a failure to believe boldly in such promises was tantamount to calling the reliability of God into question.

In the present chapter, we have considered the importance of the doctrine of justification to the Reformation. However, important though this doctrine was to the development of the reforming movement, it may be argued that a related doctrine came to have even greater significance in the later phases of that movement. If the doctrine of justification captured the imagination of the first wave of the Reformation, the second wave was forced to think through the consequences of this for the nature of the church. We shall consider this development in the next chapter, as we consider the theologies of the church associated with the sixteenth century.

Notes

1 WA 54.185–6. For the full Latin text and an English translation, see McGrath, *Luther's Theology of the Cross*, pp. 128–31. In this "quotation" in the text, I have paraphrased Luther a little, and omitted some of his more technical phrases for the sake of clarity.

2 WA 7.25–6.

3 WA 56.269.

4 WA 56.272.

5 Council of Trent, Sixth Session, Decree on Justification, chapter 4.

6 Council of Trent, Sixth Session, Decree on Justification, chapter 14.

7 Council of Trent, Sixth Session, Decree on Justification, chapter 7.

8 John Calvin, *Institutes of the Christian Religion*, III.ii.7.

9 John Calvin, *Institutes of the Christian Religion*, III.ii.17.

Further Reading

Bagchi, D. V. N., *Luther's Earliest Opponents: Catholic Controversialists, 1518–1525* (Minneapolis, MN, 1991).

Beachy, A. J., *The Concept of Grace in the Radical Reformation* (Nieuwkoop, 1977).

Boehme, A. J., "Justification by Grace through Faith: Do Wittenberg and Geneva See Eye to Eye?" *Logia: A Journal of Lutheran Theology* 11 (2002), 17–27.

Courtenay, W. J., "The King and the Leaden Coin: The Economic Background of Sine Qua Non Causality," *Traditio* 28 (1972), 185–209.

Donnelly, J. P., *Calvinism and Scholasticism in Vermigli's Doctrine of Man and Grace* (Leiden, 1976).

Douglass, E. J. D., *Justification in Late Medieval Preaching* (Leiden, 1966).

Harran, M. J., *Luther on Conversion: The Early Years* (Ithaca, NY, 1983).

Lane, A. N. S., "Cardinal Contarini and Article 5 of the Regensburg Colloquy (1541)," in *Grenzgänge der Theologie: Alexandre Ganoczy zum 75. Geburtstag*, ed. O. Meuffels and J. Bründl (Münster, 2004), pp. 163–90.

McGrath, A. E., *Iustitia Dei: A History of the Christian Doctrine of Justification*, 3rd edn (Cambridge, 2005).

McGrath, A. E., *Luther's Theology of the Cross*, 2nd edn (Oxford, 2011).

Santmire, P. H., "Justification in Calvin's 1540 Romans Commentary," *Church History* 33 (1964), 294–313.

Steinmetz, D. C., *Misericordia Dei: The Theology of Johannes von Staupitz in Its Late Medieval Setting* (Leiden, 1968).

Tentler, T. N., *Sin and Confession on the Eve of the Reformation* (Princeton, NJ, 1977).

Yarnold, E. J., "*Duplex Iustitia*: The Sixteenth Century and the Twentieth," in *Christian Authority: Essays in Honour of Henry Chadwick*, ed. G. R. Evans (Oxford, 1988), pp. 204–23.

8

The Doctrine of the Church

The medieval church in western Europe offered a strongly institutionalized account of how salvation was effected. There was no salvation outside the institution of the church; it was by membership of the sacral community and observation of its rites that the individual secured salvation. Continuity with the apostles was safeguarded by historical institutional continuity, transmitted by the laying on of hands, passed down from one generation of the successors of the apostles to the next. This strongly institutionalized vision of the church was often defended by citing a maxim of the third-century martyr Cyprian of Carthage: "outside the church, there is no salvation." If you wanted to be saved, you had to belong to the Catholic church.

The forced detachment of the fledgling Protestant churches from this body, which began in the 1520s, was thus fraught with theological peril. Were these breakaway communities *really* Christian churches? Could they really offer the same assurance of salvation and spiritual security as the Catholic church? These were no academic questions, but matters of ultimate significance. Salvation was a serious matter in the sixteenth century.

The Protestant response to these entirely proper questions was to offer a new vision of what it meant to be a "Christian church" that removed any necessity for institutional continuity with the medieval church. While tokens of historical continuity with the apostolic church were to be welcomed, the all-important thing was continuity with the apostolic teaching. Yet this emphasis on theological, rather than institutional, continuity with the apostolic church raised some important difficulties – one of which was how the Reformation related to the

Reformation Thought: An Introduction, Fourth Edition. Alister E. McGrath.
© 2012 John Wiley & Sons, Ltd. Published 2012 by John Wiley & Sons, Ltd.

Figure 8.1 Saint Augustine of Hippo (354–430), bishop and doctor of the Church, presiding over community of monks. From *Altar of Saint Augustine*, 1480 (detail), by Master of Uttenheim or Neustift, late fifteenth century, Austrian. © The Art Archive/Alamy

ideas of the leading theologian of the western church, Augustine of Hippo (354–430) (Figure 8.1).

The Princeton theologian Benjamin B. Warfield (1851–1921) had no doubt about the theological tensions which arose from the rediscovery of Augustine's doctrine of grace by writers such as Luther in the early sixteenth century. "The Reformation," he declared, was "the ultimate triumph of Augustine's doctrine of grace over Augustine's doctrine of the church."[1] Warfield's comment shows considerable historical and theological insight. His basic point is that the ecclesiastical situation of that age made it impossible to hold to both Augustine's doctrine of grace and his doctrine of the church in their totality. Something had to give – or be modified.

We have already seen how both wings of the magisterial Reformation laid claim to the insights of Augustine of Hippo concerning grace. Both Luther's doctrine of justification by faith alone, and the emphasis placed by Zwingli and Calvin upon divine predestination, represent slightly different ways of reading Augustine's **anti-Pelagian writings**. As we have seen, the Reformation arose within an intellectual context which placed new emphasis upon the importance of this great Christian writer of the late fourth and early fifth centuries, reflected in the publication of the Amerbach edition of Augustine's works in 1506.

anti-Pelagian writings Augustine's defense of his views on grace and justification.

In many ways, the reformers' views on the church represent their Achilles heel. The reformers were confronted with two consistent rival views of the church whose logic they could not match – those of their Catholic and radical opponents. For the former, the church was a visible, historic institution, possessing historical continuity with the apostolic church; for the latter, the true church was in heaven, and no institution of any kind on earth merited the name "church of God." The magisterial reformers attempted to claim the middle ground somewhere between these two rival views, and found themselves involved in serious inconsistencies as a result.

The reformers were convinced that the church of their day and age had lost sight of the doctrine of grace, which Luther regarded as the center of the Christian gospel. Thus Luther declared that his doctrine of justification by faith alone was the *articulus stantis et cadentis ecclesiae*, "the article by which the church stands or falls." Convinced that the Catholic church had lost sight of this doctrine, he concluded (with some reluctance, it would seem) that it had lost its claim to be considered as the authentic Christian church.

The Catholic church responded to this suggestion with a certain degree of derision: Luther was simply creating a breakaway faction which had no connection with the church. In other words, he was a schismatic – and had not Augustine himself condemned **schism**? Had not he placed enormous emphasis upon the unity of the church, which Luther now threatened to disrupt? Luther, it seemed, could only uphold Augustine's doctrine of grace by rejecting Augustine's doctrine of the church. It is in the context of this tension between two aspects of Augustine's thought, which proved to be incompatible in the sixteenth century, that the Reformation understandings of the nature of the church are to be seen.

> **schism** A deliberate break with the unity of the church.

The Reformation debates over the nature of the church allow us to appreciate the major differences that existed within the Reformation itself, as well as between the Reformation and its Catholic opponents. While both the magisterial and radical Reformations rejected the institutional definition of the church offered by Catholicism, the magisterial Reformation found itself defending a more "institutional" definition of the church against their radical opponents. In an earlier chapter, we explored the differences between the radical Reformation, the magisterial Reformation, and Catholicism over the role of tradition; related differences can be observed over the doctrine of the church.

The Background to the Reformation Debates: The Donatist Controversy

We must begin our discussion by returning to the question of the legacy of Augustine. The Reformation, at least in part, can be seen as an endorsement of Augustine's theology of grace. But what were Augustine's views on the church – views with which the reformers allegedly found themselves in conflict? To understand the complexities of the sixteenth-century debates, we need to examine the Donatist controversy, in which very similar issues were debated a thousand years before the Reformation. There are remarkable parallels between the Reformation debates over the identity and function of the church and those associated with the Donatist controversy.

The "Donatist controversy" had its origins in North Africa in the third century. In part, the controversy reflected tensions between native north African Christians (the Berbers) and Roman colonials who had settled in the region. The real issue, however, was the status of Christian believers and congregations who had lapsed under the threat of persecution.

Under the Roman emperor Diocletian (284–313), the Christian church was subject to various degrees of persecution. The beginnings of the persecution date from 303; it finally ended with the conversion of Constantine, and the issuing of the Edict of Milan in 313. Under an edict of February 303, Christian books were ordered to be burned and churches demolished. Those Christian leaders who handed over their books to be burned came to be known as *traditores* – "those who handed over." The modern word "traitor" derives from the same root. One such *traditor* was Felix of Aptunga, who later consecrated Caecilian as bishop of Carthage in 311.

Many local Christians were outraged that such a person should have been allowed to be involved in this consecration, and declared that they could not accept the authority of Caecilian as a result. The hierarchy of the Catholic church was tainted as a result of this development. The church ought to be pure, and should not be permitted to include such people. By the time Augustine returned to Africa from Italy in 388, a breakaway faction had established itself as the leading Christian body in the region, with especially strong support from the local African population. Sociological issues clouded theological debate; the Donatists (so named after the breakaway African church leader Donatus) tended to draw their support from the indigenous population, whereas the Catholics drew theirs from Roman colonists.

The theological issues involved are of considerable importance, and relate directly to a serious tension within the theology of a leading figure of the African church in the third century – Cyprian of Carthage. In his *Unity of the Catholic Church* (251), Cyprian had defended two major related beliefs. First, schism is totally and absolutely unjustified. The unity of the church cannot be broken, on any pretext whatsoever. To step outside the bounds of the church is to forfeit any possibility of salvation. Second, it therefore follows that lapsed or schismatic bishops are deprived of all ability to administer the sacraments or act as a minister of the Christian church. By passing outside the sphere of the church, they have lost their spiritual gifts and authority. They should therefore not be permitted to ordain priests or bishops. Any whom they have ordained must be regarded as invalidly ordained; any whom they have baptized must be regarded as invalidly baptized.

But what happens if a bishop lapses under persecution, and subsequently repents? Cyprian's theory is profoundly ambiguous at this important point, and is open to two very different lines of interpretation:

1   By lapsing, the bishop has committed the sin of apostasy (literally, "falling away"). He has therefore placed himself outside the bounds of the church, and can no longer be regarded as administering the sacraments validly.
2   By his repentance, the bishop has been restored to grace, and is able to continue administering the sacraments validly.

The Donatists advocated the first such position, and the Catholics (as their opponents came to be universally known) the second.

The Donatists believed that the entire sacramental system of the Catholic church had become corrupted. It was therefore necessary to replace *traditores* with people who had remained firm in their faith under persecution. It was also necessary to rebaptize and reordain all those who had been baptized and ordained by *traditores*. Inevitably, this resulted in the formation of a breakaway faction. By the time Augustine returned to Africa, the breakaway faction was larger than the church it had broken away from.

Yet Cyprian had totally forbidden schism of any kind. One of the greatest paradoxes of the Donatist schism is that it resulted from principles which were due to Cyprian – yet contradicted those very same principles. As a result, both Donatists and Catholics appealed to Cyprian as an authority – but to very different aspects of his teaching. The Donatists stressed the outrageous character of apostasy; the Catholics equally emphasized the impossibility of schism. A stalemate resulted – that is, until Augustine arrived, and became bishop of Hippo in the region. Augustine was able to resolve the tensions within the legacy of Cyprian, and put forward an "Augustinian" view of the church, which has remained enormously influential ever since.

First, Augustine emphasizes the *sinfulness of Christians*. The church is not meant to be a society of saints, but a "mixed body" (*corpus permixtum*) of saints and sinners. Augustine finds this image in two biblical parables: the parable of the net that catches many fishes, and the parable of the wheat and the tares. It is this latter parable (Matthew 13:24–31) which is of especial importance, and requires further discussion.

The parable tells of a farmer who sowed seed, and discovered that the resulting crop included both wheat and tares – grain and weeds. What could be done about it? To attempt to separate the wheat and the weeds while both were still growing would be to court disaster, probably involving damaging the wheat while trying to get rid of the weeds. But at the harvest, all the plants – wheat and tares – are cut down and sorted out without any danger of damaging the wheat. The separation of the good and the evil thus takes place at the end of time, not in history.

For Augustine, this parable refers to the church in the world. It must expect to find itself including both saints and sinners. To attempt a separation in this world is premature and improper. That separation will take place in God's own time, at the end of history. No human can make that judgment or separation in God's place. So in what sense is the church holy? For Augustine, the holiness in question is not that of its members, but of Christ. The church cannot be a congregation of saints in this world, in that its members are contaminated with original sin. However, the church is sanctified and made holy by Christ – a holiness which will be perfected and finally realized at the Last Judgment.

In addition to this theological analysis, Augustine makes the practical observation that the Donatists failed to live up to their own high standards of morality. The Donatists, Augustine suggests, were just as capable as Catholics of getting drunk or beating people up.

Second, Augustine argues that schism and *traditio* (the handing over of Christian books, or any form of lapse from faith) are indeed both sinful – but that, for Cyprian, schism is by far the more serious sin. The Donatists are thus guilty of serious misrepresentation of the teaching of the great North African martyr bishop.

On the basis of these considerations, Augustine argues that Donatism is fatally flawed. The church is, and is meant to be, a mixed body. Sin is an inevitable aspect of the life of the church in the present age, and is neither the occasion nor the justification for schism. Yet precisely the schism which Augustine feared and detested so much would eventually come about in the sixteenth century, with the formation of breakaway Protestant churches in western Europe as a result of the Reformation. It is to these major developments that we now turn.

The Context of the Reformation Views on the Church

In his period as an academic reformer, Luther shared a profound distaste for schism. Even the row over the Ninety-Five Theses on indulgences of October 31, 1517 did not persuade Luther to break away from the church. In the twentieth century, we have become used to the phenomenon of "denominationalism" – but the very idea of the western church breaking up into smaller parts was completely alien to the medieval period. Schism, to put it bluntly, was unthinkable. As Luther himself wrote in early 1519: "If, unfortunately, there are things in Rome which cannot be improved, there is not – and cannot be – any reason for tearing oneself away from the church in schism. Rather, the worse things become, the more one should help her and stand by her, for by schism and contempt nothing can be mended." Luther's views here parallel those of other reforming groups throughout Europe: the church must be reformed from within.

The assumption that the growing alienation of the Wittenberg Reformation from the Catholic church was purely temporary seems to underlie much of the thinking of Lutheran writers in the period 1520–41. It seems that the evangelical faction at Wittenberg believed that the Catholic church would indeed reform itself, perhaps through convening a reforming council, within a matter of years, thus allowing the Lutherans to rejoin a renewed and reformed church. Thus the Augsburg Confession (1530), setting out the main lines of Lutheran belief, is actually remarkably conciliatory toward Catholicism. Such hopes of reunion were, however, dashed in the 1540s. In 1541, the Colloquy of Regensburg seemed to offer the hope of reconciliation, as a group of Protestant and Catholic theologians met to discuss their differences. Those discussions ended in failure.

In 1545, the Council of Trent finally met to hammer out the response of the Catholic church to the Reformation, and institute a major program of reform within that church. Some present at that Council, such as Cardinal Reginald Pole, had hoped that it would prove to be conciliatory toward the Protestants: in the event, however, the Council identified and condemned the leading ideas of Protestantism. Any hopes of reconciliation had been dashed. The Protestant churches now had to recognize that their existence as separate entities was permanent, rather than temporary. They had to justify their existence as Christian churches alongside a body which seemed to have a much stronger claim to that title – the Catholic church itself.

On the basis of this historical preamble, it will be obvious that the reformers' particular concern with the theory of the church dates from the 1540s. It was in the aftermath of Regensburg – and especially as it became clear that the evangelical groupings would be permanently excluded from the Catholic church – that the question of the true identity of the church became of critical importance. This was thus a question which preoccupied the second, rather than the first, generation of reformers. If Luther was concerned with the question, "How may I find a gracious God?," his successors were obliged to deal with the question that arose out of this: "Where can I find the true church?" Theoretical justification had to be given to the separate existence of the evangelical churches. Most influential among second-generation reformers, of course, is John Calvin, and it is in his writings that we find perhaps the most important contributions to this debate. Our attention initially focuses on Luther.

Luther on the Nature of the Church

The early reformers were convinced that the medieval church had become corrupted and its doctrine distorted through a departure from Scripture on the one hand and through human additions to Scripture on the other. Luther's early views on the nature of the church reflect his emphasis on the Word of God: the Word of God goes forth conquering, and wherever it conquers and gains true obedience to God is the church. "Now, anywhere you hear or see [the Word of

God] preached, believed, confessed, and acted upon, do not doubt that the true *ecclesia sancta catholica*, a 'holy Christian people' must be there, even though there are very few of them."[2] An episcopally ordained ministry is therefore not *necessary* – though it might, if properly constituted, be *beneficial* – to safeguard the existence of the church, whereas the preaching of the gospel is essential to the identity of that church: "Where the word is, there is faith; and where faith is, there is the true church." The visible church is constituted by the preaching of the Word of God: no human assembly may claim to be the "church of God" unless it is founded on this gospel.

We have already seen (p. 143) how this understanding of the church is functional, rather than historical: what legitimates a church or its office bearers is not historical continuity with the apostolic church, but theological continuity. It is more important to preach the same gospel as the apostles than to be a member of an institution that is historically derived from them. A similar understanding of the church was shared by Philipp Melanchthon, Luther's colleague at Wittenberg, who conceived of the church primarily in terms of its function of administering the means of grace.

Alongside this view of the nature of the church, Luther set a new understanding of the role of individual Christians. Whereas the medieval church argued for an absolute distinction between priests and laity, Luther insisted that the distinction in question was functional, not ontological. All Christians are priests by virtue of their baptism, faith, and the gospel – a doctrine which is often referred to as the "priesthood of all believers." The only distinction that can be recognized between them relates to the different "office" or "function" (*Amt*) and "work" or "responsibility" (*Werk*) with which they are entrusted. Priests are to be reckoned as "office holders," whose privileges and functions can only continue for as long as they are accepted by those who appointed or elected them. Luther was thus quite clear that, once priests retire or are dismissed, they revert to the role of lay people:

It is an invention that the Pope, bishop, priests and monks are called "the spiritual estate" [*geistliche Stand*], while princes, lords, craftsmen and farmers are called "the secular estate" [*weltliche Stand*]. This is a spurious idea, and nobody should fear it for the following reason. All Christians truly belong to the spiritual estate, and there is no difference among them apart from their office [*Amt*] . . . We all have one baptism, one gospel, one faith, and are all alike Christians, in that it is baptism, gospel and faith which alone make us spiritual and a Christian people. . . . We are all consecrated priests through baptism, as St Peter says: "You are a royal priesthood and a priestly kingdom" (1 Peter 2:9) . . . Therefore someone who bears the status of a priest is nothing other than an officeholder. He takes priority for as long as he holds this office; when he is deposed, he becomes a peasant or citizen like all the others . . . It follows from this that there is no basic true difference between lay people, priests, princes and bishops, between the spiritual and the secular, except for their office and work (and not their status).[3]

Luther's vision of the church possessed the great virtue of simplicity. Simplicity, however, frequently amounts to inadequacy. As it became increasingly clear that Luther and Zwingli could not agree over what the gospel was (their Eucharistic disagreement highlighting this point), the credibility of Luther's vision of the church became undermined. In part, Luther's difficulties related to the challenge posed by the radical Reformation, to which we may now turn.

The Radical View of the Church

It is important to note the implications of the term "Reformation." For the magisterial reformers, such as Luther and Calvin, the task of the Reformation was to reform a church which had become corrupted or disfigured as a result of developments in the Middle Ages. The essential presupposition underlying this program should be noted carefully: *to reform a church is to presuppose that a church already exists.* Luther and Calvin were both clear that the medieval church was indeed a Christian church. The difficulty was that it had lost its way and required to be reformed.

The theologians of the radical wing of the Reformation, however, did not share this basic assumption. For them, the church had simply ceased to exist. How could the church be reformed, when there was no longer a church? It needed restoration, not reformation. By "reforming" the medieval church, Luther had merely altered the external appearance of a corrupt institution that had no right to call itself a Christian church. As Menno Simons stressed in his 1552 treatise, *The Confession of Distressed Christians*:

> The brightness of the sun has not shone for many years . . . However, in these latter days, the gracious, great God by the rich treasures of his love has again opened the windows of heaven and let drop the dew of his divine word, so that the earth once more as of yore produces its green branches and plants of righteousness which bear fruit unto the Lord and glorify his great and adorable name. The holy word and sacraments of the Lord rise up again from the ashes.[4]

Similarly, Sebastian Franck argued that the apostolic church had been totally compromised through its close links with the state, dating back to the conversion of the Emperor Constantine. As an institution, the church was corrupted by human power struggles and ambition. Just as most of the radicals were utterly consistent in their application of the *scriptura sola* principle, so they were equally consistent in their views on the institutional church. The true church was in heaven, and its institutional parodies were on earth.

It will therefore be clear that the radical view of the church is much closer to the Donatist than the Augustinian view. For Menno Simons (Figure 8.2), the church is a society of saints, a pure body which is not contaminated by sin in any

Figure 8.2 Menno Simons, theologian, founder of the Mennonites (1496–1561), historical illustration, portrait, 1880. © Historical image collection by Bildagentur-online/Alamy

way. In contrast to those false churches which are recognized by the state, and enjoy its privileges, the true church is totally pure and regenerate:

> They are the true congregation of Christ who are truly converted, who are born from above of God, who are of a regenerate mind by the operation of the Holy Spirit through the hearing of the divine word, and have become the children of God, have entered into obedience to him, and live unblamably in his holy commandments, and according to his holy will all their days, or from the moment of their call.[5]

It is therefore important to note that the issue of church discipline is highly significant to radical church leaders. Discipline is the means by which doctrinal and moral purity may be enforced within the church. The "ban" (p. 208) serves to ensure the purity of the church, and remove any who might contaminate or compromise the congregation at this point. If the church is defined by its purity, that purity must be safeguarded by appropriate institutional measures – of which discipline was the most effective.

ecclesiology Section of Christian theology dealing with the theory of the church.

The radical view of the church was highly coherent, and posed a serious challenge to mainline reformers, such as Luther, who worked with a "mixed body" **ecclesiology** – that is to say, they followed Augustine's view that the church, as a matter of fact, included both saints and sinners. We shall consider some of those difficulties in the following section.

Tensions within Luther's Doctrine of the Church

As we have seen, Luther was forced to deal with two difficulties relating to his understanding of the church. If the church was not defined institutionally, but by the preaching of the gospel, how could he distinguish his views from those of the radicals? He himself had conceded that "the church is holy even where the fanatics [Luther's term for the radicals] are dominant, so long as they do not deny the word and the sacraments."

Alert to the political realities of his situation, Luther countered his radical critics at this point by asserting the need for an institutional church. Just as he tempered the radical implications of the *scriptura sola* principle by an appeal to tradition (see pp. 98–102), so he tempered his potentially radical views on the nature of the true church by insisting that it had to be viewed as an historical institution. The institution of the church is the divinely ordained means of grace. But in countering the radicals by asserting that the church was indeed visible and institutional, Luther found himself having difficulty in distinguishing his views from those of his Catholic opponents. He himself fully appreciated this problem:

> We on our part confess that there is much that is Christian and good under the papacy; indeed, everything that is Christian and is good is to be found there and has come to us from this source. For instance, we confess that in the papal church there are the true Holy Scriptures, true baptism, the true sacrament of the altar, the true keys to the forgiveness of sins, the true office of the ministry, the true catechism in the form of the Lord's Prayer, the Ten Commandments and the articles of the Creed.[6]

Luther is thus obliged to assert that "the false church has only the appearance, although it also possesses the Christian offices." In other words, the medieval church may have looked like the real thing, but it was really something rather different.

The logic of the situation became increasingly difficult, for a number of reasons. Perhaps most obviously, Paul's New Testament letters to the Corinthians and Galatians accuse them of having departed from the gospel at critical points. Yet Paul still addresses these as Christian churches, and refers to their wayward members as Christians. Surely Luther ought to follow Paul at this point? At worst, Luther's critics argued, the Catholic church was like the Galatian church. It might indeed have departed from the gospel at certain points, yet it could and should still be treated as a Christian church.

A second difficulty arose from an aspect of Augustine's theory of the church, going back to the Donatist controversy of the early fifth century, which we noted earlier. The Donatists were a breakaway movement in the North African church, who insisted that the Catholic church of their day had become compromised through its attitude to the Roman authorities during a period of persecution. Only those who had not compromised their personal religious integrity could be recognized as members of the true church. It can be seen that this corresponds closely to the radical view of the church.

Augustine argued the Catholic case: the church must be recognized as having a mixed membership, both saints and sinners. The righteous and the wicked coexisted within the same church, and no human had the authority to weed out the wicked from the church. Augustine drew upon what is often known as "the parable of the tares" (Matthew 13:24–31) to support this point. Most biblical interpreters see this parable as offering an explanation of the persistence of evil in the world.

According to Augustine, however, this parable applies to the church. Like the field in the parable, the church contains both wheat and weeds, the just and the wicked, which coexist until the Day of Judgment. On that day, God will judge between them – and no human is permitted to preempt God's judgment. The church will thus contain both good and evil until the end of time. Augustine argues that the term "catholic" (which literally means "whole"), as applied to the church, describes its mixed membership of saints and sinners.

Luther followed Augustine in adopting a "mixed body" ecclesiology. But this raised a serious problem. Luther had argued that the moral failings of the medieval church called into question its credentials. Yet his acceptance of the Augustinian church seemed to many to necessarily imply that there will *always* be corruption in the true church, on account of the fact that it is a mixed body of saints and sinners. On the basis of Augustine's theory, corruption in the Catholic church does not necessarily mean that it is a "false church."

In practice, the force of this second point was reduced by Luther's insistence on the priority of theology over morals. Luther tended to see his criticisms of the morals of the medieval church as being secondary to its theological deficiencies. Yet the considerations set out in this section will make it clear that the magisterial Reformation at times found itself experiencing difficulties with its concept of the church. The Catholic and radical views of the church possessed a considerable degree of internal consistency and coherence which, at times, seemed absent from Luther's viewpoint.

It is in the writings of John Calvin that we find a more considered and rigorous approach to this important doctrine, and we shall now turn to consider his influential ideas.

Calvin on the Nature of the Church

If any reformer wrestled with the problem posed by the doctrine of the church, it was Calvin. The first major discussion of the theory of the church is to be found in the second edition of his *Institutes of the Christian Religion*, published in 1539. Although Calvin deals with the subject in the first edition of the *Institutes* (1536), he was then quite innocent of any experience of ecclesiastical management or responsibility, which accounts for the curiously unfocused nature of his discussion. By the time of the second edition of this work, Calvin had gained more experience of the problems presented to the new evangelical churches.

The Two Marks of the Church

For Calvin, the marks of the true church were that the Word of God should be preached, and that the sacraments be rightly administered. Since the Catholic church did not conform even to this minimalist definition of the church, the evangelicals were perfectly justified in leaving it. And as the evangelical churches conform to this definition of a church, there was no justification for further division within them. This point is of particular importance, reflecting Calvin's political judgment that further fragmentation of the evangelical congregations would be disastrous to the cause of the Reformation. The text in which Calvin sets out these principles merits careful study:

> Wherever we see the Word of God purely preached and listened to, and the sacraments administered according to Christ's institution, it is in no way to be doubted that a church of God exists. For his promise cannot fail: "Wherever two or three are gathered in my name, there I am in the midst of them" (Matthew 18:20). . . . If the ministry has the Word and honours it, if it has the administration of the sacraments, it deserves without doubt to be held and considered a church.[7]

Calvin's definition is significant as much for what it does *not* say as for what it does explicitly affirm. There is no reference to the necessity of any historical or institutional continuity with the apostles, or with any institutionalized conception of the church – most notably, the medieval church. For Calvin, institutional continuity was not sufficient to guarantee intellectual and spiritual fidelity. It was more important to teach what the apostles taught than to be able to show an unbroken line of institutional continuity with them. (It should be remembered here that Calvin himself was never really "ordained"; he was simply licensed as a pastor by the city council of Geneva.)

This radical new understanding of the church in effect envisaged the church as a community which gathered around the preaching of the word of God, and celebrated and proclaimed the gospel through the sacraments. Where the gospel is truly preached, there a church will gather. Protestant theologians, sensitive to the charge that this new approach represented a distortion of a proper theology of the church, pointed to a classic statement of the first-century martyr-bishop Ignatius of Antioch: "wherever Christ is, there is also the church" (*ubi Christus ibi ecclesia*). Gathering together in the name of Christ ensures his presence – and with that presence, a church comes into being. Preaching and the sacraments were the two means of grace by which Christ was made present to the faithful.

The Structures of the Church

Calvin thus lays a theological foundation for his doctrine of the church, grounded in the presence of Christ within the Christian community. But what of the *organization* of that church? By 1543, Calvin had gained considerably more experience of ecclesiastical responsibility, particularly during his period at Strasbourg. Bucer, the intellectual force behind the Reformation at Strasbourg, had a considerable reputation as an ecclesiastical administrator, and it is probable that Calvin's later theory of the church reflects his personal influence. The four-fold office of pastor, doctor (or teacher), elder, and deacon owes its origins to Bucer, as does the distinction between the visible and the invisible church (explored below).

Nevertheless, Bucer's suggestion that ecclesiastical discipline was an essential feature (technically, a "note" [*nota*] or "mark") of the church is not endorsed by Calvin. It may be good for the church, but it is not necessary for a true church to exist. Although Calvin includes "example of life" among the "certain sure marks" of the church in the 1536 edition of the *Institutes*, later editions lay stress upon the proper preaching of the word of God and the administration of the sacraments. Discipline strengthens the nerve of the church – but the saving doctrine of Christ establishes its heart and soul.

Calvin argues that there are specific scriptural directions regarding the right order of ministry in the visible church, so that a specific form of ecclesiastical order now becomes an item of doctrine. In other words, he includes a specific form of ecclesiastical administration (and he here borrows the term *administratio* from the field of secular government) in "the gospel purely preached."

The importance of the external administration of the church had been recognized for some time within Reformed circles. The First Helvetic Confession (1536), drawn up at Zurich, stressed that the church was distinguished by certain external signs:

> It is the fellowship and congregation of all saints which is Christ's bride and spouse, and which He washes with His blood and finally presents to the Father without blemish or any stain. And although this Church and congregation of Christ is only open and known to God's eyes, yet it is not only known but also gathered and built up by visible signs, rites and ordinances, which Christ Himself has instituted and appointed by the Word of God as a universal, public and orderly discipline. Without these marks (speaking generally and without a special permission revealed by God) no one is numbered with this Church.[8]

Calvin's minimalist definition of the church now takes on a new significance. The true church is to be found where the gospel is rightly preached, and the sacraments rightly administered – and understood to be included within this definition is a specific form of ecclesiastical institution and administration. Calvin refers to the "order by which the Lord willed his church to be governed," and develops a detailed theory of church government based upon his **exegesis** of the New Testament, drawing extensively upon the terminology of the imperial Roman administration.

> **exegesis** Science of textual interpretation, usually referring specifically to the Bible.

Contrary to what the radicals asserted, Calvin insists that a specific form of church structure and administration is laid down by Scripture. Thus Calvin held that the ministerial government of the church is divinely ordained, as is the distinction between "minister," "elder," "deacon," and "people."

Whereas Luther regarded the organization of the church as a matter of historical contingency, not requiring theological prescription, Calvin held that a definite pattern of church government was prescribed by Scripture. So what is the importance of this new development in the theory of the church? It will be recalled that Luther had defined the church in terms of the ministry of the Word of God, which was of little help in distinguishing the magisterial Reformation from the Catholic position on the one hand, and the position of the radicals on the other. Calvin, while retaining an emphasis on the importance of the ministry of the Word of God, now insisted that this same Word of God specified one particular form of church government.

This was a bold new step in the interpretation of Scripture; it also gave Calvin a criterion by which to judge (and find wanting) his Catholic and radical opponents. Where Luther was vague, Calvin was precise. By the time of Calvin's death (1564), the Reformed church was as institutionalized as its Catholic rival, and had become its most formidable opponent. No small part of that success was due to the role of the Consistory, perhaps the most distinctive and innovative aspect of Calvin's plan for structuring his church.

Calvin on the Church and Consistory

The most distinctive and controversial aspect of Calvin's system of church government was the Consistory. This institution came into being in 1542, with 12 lay elders (selected annually by the magistrates), and all the members of the Venerable Company of Pastors (nine in 1542, 19 in 1564). The body was intended to meet weekly on a Thursday, with the purpose of maintaining ecclesiastical discipline. The origins of this institution are unclear; it seems that existing matrimonial courts may have served as a model, and that a prototype had actually been established in Geneva during Calvin's exile in Strasbourg. It is certainly significant that one of the early activities of the Consistory centered on marital problems, viewed as a pastoral, as much as a legal, difficulty; this may well reflect the role of already existing matrimonial courts (which were predominantly lay in character).

If the *Institutes of the Christian Religion* were the muscles of Calvin's reformation, his ecclesiastical organization was its backbone. The *Ecclesiastical Ordinances* (1541), which gave the Genevan church its characteristic shape and identity, were drawn up by Calvin virtually immediately on his return to Geneva from his period of exile in Strasbourg. Convinced of the need for a disciplined, well-ordered, and structured church, Calvin proceeded to lay down detailed guidelines governing every aspect of its existence. The establishment of an ecclesiastical apparatus appropriate to Calvin's goals must be regarded as one of the most significant aspects of his ministry, and lends added weight to the case for comparing Calvin to Lenin; both were admirably aware of the importance of institutions for the propagation of their respective revolutions, and lost no time in organizing what was required.

Calvin conceived of the Consistory primarily as an instrument for the "policing" of religious orthodoxy. It was the guarantor of the discipline which Calvin's experience at Strasbourg had led him to recognize as essential to the survival of reformed Christendom. Its primary function was to deal with those whose religious views were sufficiently devious to pose a threat to the established religious order at Geneva. Persons whose behavior was regarded as unacceptable for other reasons, pastoral or moral, were to be treated in the same way. Such individuals were, in the first instance, to be shown the error of their ways; should this fail, the penalty of excommunication was available as a deterrent.

This, however, was an ecclesiastical rather than a civil penalty; the miscreant might be denied access to one of the four annual communion services at Geneva, but he could not be subjected to any civil penalty by the Consistory itself. The city council, perennially jealous of its authority, had insisted that "all this is to take place in such a manner that the ministers have no civil jurisdiction, nor use anything but the spiritual sword of the Word of God . . . nor is the Consistory to detract from the authority of the Seigneurie or ordinary justice. Civil power is to remain unimpeded."

The importance of church structures, such as the Consistory, to the international development of **Calvinism** can perhaps be appreciated best by comparing the very different situations within which Lutheranism and Calvinism came to be established in western Europe and North America. Lutheranism generally advanced through the sympathy of monarchs and princes, perhaps not totally unaware of the important ecclesiastical role allotted to them by Luther's doctrine of the "Two Kingdoms."

Although Calvin was aware of the potential of winning over monarchs to his ideas (his particular ambition being to gain a sympathetic hearing within the French court), Calvinism generally had to survive and advance in distinctly hostile situations (such as France in the 1550s), in which both monarch and the existing church establishment were opposed to its development. Under such conditions, the very survival of Calvinist groups was dependent upon a strong and well-disciplined church, capable of surviving the hostility of its milieu. The more sophisticated Calvinist church structures proved capable of withstanding considerably more difficult situations than their Lutheran equivalents, providing Calvinism with a vital resource for gaining ground in what might at first sight seem thoroughly unpromising political situations.

Calvin on the Role of the Church

Why is there any need for a church – understood, that is, as an institution, rather than a building – in the first place? Just as God redeemed human beings within the historical process through the incarnation, so he sanctifies them within that same process by founding an institution dedicated to that goal. God uses certain definite earthly means to work out the salvation of his elect; although he is not absolutely bound by these means, he normally works within them. The church is thus identified as a divinely founded body, within which God effects the sanctification of his people. As Calvin puts it:

> I shall begin then, with the church, into the bosom of which God is pleased to gather his children, not only so that they may be nourished by her assistance and ministry while they are infants and children, but also so that they may be guided by her motherly care until they mature and reach the goal of faith. "For what God has joined together, no one shall divide" (Mark 10:9). For those to whom God is Father, the church shall also be their mother.[9]

Calvin confirms this high doctrine of the church by citing the two great ecclesiological maxims of Cyprian of Carthage: "You cannot have God as your father unless you have the church for your mother," used above, and "Outside the church there is no hope of remission of sins nor any salvation."

Calvin's doctrine of the church reminds us that it is seriously inadequate to portray the reformers as rampant radical individualists, with no place for corporate conceptions of the Christian life. We have already seen (pp. 100–1) how mainline Reformation biblical interpretation lacks the individualism often projected onto it by its critics; the same is true of the Reformation understanding of the Christian life. The image of the "church as mother" (which Calvin gladly borrows from Cyprian of Carthage) underscores the corporate dimensions of Christian faith. The institution of the church is a necessary, helpful, God-given and God-ordained means of spiritual growth and development.

Calvin draws an important distinction between the visible and invisible church. At one level, the church is the community of Christian believers, a visible group. It is also, however, the fellowship of saints and the company of the elect – an invisible entity. In its invisible aspect, the church is the invisible assembly of the elect, known only to God; in its visible aspect, it is the community of believers on earth. The former consists only of the elect; the latter includes both good and evil, elect and reprobate. The former is an object of faith and hope, the latter of present experience. Calvin stresses that all believers are obliged to honor and to remain committed to the visible church, despite its weaknesses, on account of the invisible church, the true body of Christ. Despite this, there is only one church, a single entity with Jesus Christ as its head.

The distinction between the visible and invisible churches has two important consequences. In the first place, it is to be expected that the visible church will include both the elect and the reprobate. Augustine of Hippo had made this point against the Donatists, using the parable of the tares (Matthew 13:24–31) as his basis. It lies beyond human competence to discern their difference, correlating human qualities with divine favor (in any case, Calvin's doctrine of predestination precludes such grounds of election). In the second, however, it is necessary to ask which of the various visible churches corresponds to the invisible church.

Calvin thus recognizes the need to articulate objective criteria by which the authenticity of a given church may be judged. Two such criteria are stipulated: "Wherever we see the Word of God preached purely and listened to, and the sacraments administered according to the institution of Christ, we cannot doubt that a church exists." It is thus not the quality of its members, but the presence of the authorized means of grace that constitutes a true church. Interestingly, Calvin does not follow Bucer, and make discipline a mark of the true church; although passionately concerned with the need for charitable discipline of church members, Calvin did not regard this as essential to the definition or evaluation of the credentials of a church.

The Debate over the Catholicity of the Church

The Nicene Creed affirms belief in "one holy, catholic and apostolic church." Each of these four characteristics (often referred to as the "four notes of the church") has been the subject of considerable discussion within Christian theology, with the Donatist controversy having given considerable impetus to the issues involved. At the time of the Reformation, particular attention was directed toward the meaning of the term "catholic." What did it mean to affirm belief in the catholicity of the church? And were Protestant churches able to affirm such a belief, when they had broken away from the mainstream medieval church?

In modern English, the term "Catholic" is often confused, especially in non-religious circles, with "Roman Catholic." Although this confusion is understandable, the distinction must be maintained. It is not only Roman Catholics who are catholic, just as it is by no means Eastern Orthodox writers who are orthodox in their theology. Indeed, many Protestant churches, embarrassed by the use of the term "catholic" in the creeds, have replaced it with "universal."

The word "catholic" comes from the Greek phrase *kath' holou* ("referring to the whole"). The Greek words subsequently found their way into the Latin word *catholicus*, which came to have the meaning "universal" or "general." This sense of the word is retained in the English phrase "catholic taste," meaning "a wide-ranging taste" rather than "a taste for things that are Roman Catholic." Older versions of the English Bible often refer to some of the New Testament letters (such as those of James and John) as "catholic epistles," meaning that they are directed to all Christians (rather than those of Paul, which are directed to the needs and situations of individual identified churches, such as those at Rome or Corinth).

At no point does the New Testament use the term "catholic" to refer to the church as a whole. The New Testament uses the Greek word *ekklesia* to refer to local churches or worshipping communities, which it nevertheless understands to represent or embody something which transcends that local body. While an individual church is not the church in its totality, it nevertheless shares in that totality. It is this notion of "totality" which is subsequently encapsulated in the term "catholic." The term is introduced in later centuries, in an attempt to bring together central New Testament insights, and attach them to a single term.

The first known use of the phrase "the catholic church" occurs in the writings of Ignatius of Antioch, who was martyred at Rome around 110: "Wherever Christ is, there is also the church." Other writings of the second century use the term to refer to the existence of a universal church alongside local congregations.

The meaning of the term changed fundamentally with the conversion of Constantine. By the end of the fourth century, the term "the catholic church" came to mean "the imperial church" – that is, the only legal religion within the Roman empire. Any other forms of belief, including Christian beliefs that diverged from the mainline, were declared to be illegal.

Further expansion of the church in this period contributed to a developing understanding of the term. By the beginning of the fifth century, Christianity was firmly established throughout the entire Mediterranean world. In response to this development, the term "catholic" came to be interpreted as "embracing the entire world." These general themes can be found in the writings of Thomas Aquinas, who set out the medieval consensus on "catholicity" as follows:

> The church is catholic, i.e., universal, first with respect to place, because it is throughout the entire world, against the Donatists. See Romans 1:8: "Your faith is proclaimed in all the world"; Mark 16:15: "Go into all the world and preach the gospel to the whole creation." In ancient times, God was known only in Judea, but now throughout the entire world. This church, moreover, has three parts. One is on earth, another is in heaven, and the third is in purgatory. Secondly, the Church is universal with respect to the condition of people, because no one is rejected, whether master or slave, male or female. See Galatians 3:28: "There is neither male nor female." Thirdly, it is universal with respect to time. For some have said that the church should last until a certain time, but this is false, because this church began from the time of Abel and will last to the end of the world. See Matthew 28:20: "And I am with you always, to the close of the age." And after the close of the age it will remain in heaven.[10]

On the basis of this understanding of catholicity, it was argued that continuity with the apostolic church could only be maintained *institutionally* – that is, through direct historical continuity with the early church. To break with the historic institution of the church, represented by its bishops, was to step outside the church. Cyprian of Carthage had argued that there was no salvation outside the church; to place oneself outside the institution of the church was therefore to forfeit any hope of salvation.

A fundamental reexamination of the notion of "catholicity" took place at the time of the Reformation. It seemed to many that the catholicity and unity of the church were destroyed simultaneously with the fragmentation of the western European church in the sixteenth century. Catholic opponents of the Reformation declared that Protestants had broken away from the Catholic church by introducing innovations (such as the doctrine of justification by faith alone) or by abandoning the traditional structures of the church (such as the papacy and the episcopacy). By breaking with the continuity of the church, the reformers had forfeited any right to call their churches "Christian." One of the essential hallmarks of an authentically Christian church was therefore *institutional continuity*. It was clear to the Catholic opponents of the Reformation that this continuity had been destroyed or disregarded by the reformers, with the result that Protestant congregations could not be regarded as Christian churches, in any meaningful sense of the word.

Protestant writers argued that the essence of catholicity lay not in church institutions, but in matters of doctrine. The fifth-century writer Vincent of Lérins had defined catholicity in terms of "that which is believed everywhere, at all times, and by all people." The reformers argued that they remained Catholic, despite having broken away from the medieval church, in that they retained the central and universally recognized elements of Christian doctrine. Historical or institutional continuity was secondary to doctrinal fidelity.

For this reason, the mainline Protestant churches insisted they were simultaneously Catholic and reformed – that is, maintaining continuity with the apostolic church at the level of teaching, having eliminated spurious non-biblical practices and beliefs. This approach is adopted by Philipp Melanchthon:

> Why is this term added in the article of the creed, so that the church is called catholic? Because it is an assembly dispersed throughout the whole world and because its members, wherever they are, and however separated in place, accept and externally profess one and the same utterance or true doctrine throughout all ages from the beginning until the very end . . . It is one thing to be called catholic, something else to be catholic in reality. Those are truly called catholic who accept the doctrine of the truly catholic church, i.e., that which is supported by the witness of all time, of all ages, which believes what the prophets and apostles taught, and which does not tolerate factions, heresies, and heretical assemblies.[11]

Note how Melanchthon insists that the essence of the "catholicity" of the church concerns the universal teaching of the true faith. The reformers may thus claim to teach the true faith without being appended to the institution of the medieval church. This doctrinal interpretation of catholicity led to the institutional connections of a congregation being regarded as having less than fundamental importance. The important thing was to teach what the apostles taught, rather than to have physical evidence of historical continuity (for example, through the laying on of hands).

It will also be clear at this point that the emphasis placed by Luther and Calvin on the preaching of the gospel as a mark of the church is of foundational significance. If the true gospel is preached, a true Christian church is present – irrespective of its historical pedigree. In this way, the reformers were able to blunt the force of the arguments brought against them by their Catholic opponents, while at the same time offering a theological interpretation of the notion of "catholicity" which allowed the church to be defined *functionally*. The implications of this development for western Christianity are substantial, in that denominational proliferation was given an important theological justification.

The Council of Trent on the Church

Curiously, the Council of Trent had relatively little to say concerning the doctrine of the church. In part, this may reflect the fact that ecclesiological issues began to emerge as significant for both Protestants and Catholics after the final failure of attempts to achieve reconciliation between them at the Colloquy of Regensburg (1541). After that date, Protestant writers began to realize the importance of consolidating their own distinct views on the church. Up to that point, many Protestant writers had hoped for recognition of the validity of their movement and ministries. Whereas the first generation of reformers focused on the doctrine of justification, it was the second generation that focused on ecclesiological issues. These therefore emerged too late to be considered by the Council of Trent.

Trent's contribution to the sixteenth-century debates over the church primarily concerned matters not of theory, but of practice. The Fifth Session of the Council (1546), for example, made provision for "Lectureships in Holy Scripture" at every major church, to deepen a general awareness of the contents of the Bible and their relevance for the life of faith. The Seventh Session of the Council (1547) focused on practical reforms, designed to reinvigorate the life of the church, and eliminate abuses and corruptions, particularly on the part of its clergy and bishops.

Yet there is little doubt that the fundamental ecclesiological assumptions underlying the Council of Trent are those developed by Augustine of Hippo during the Donatist controversy, which were extended during the early Middle Ages, especially in relation to the emerging emphasis upon the spiritual and temporal authority of the Pope.

As we noted earlier, the Catholic church was the only international agency to possess any significant credibility or influence throughout the Middle Ages. It played a decisive role in the settling of international disputes. Under Innocent III (pope from 1198 to 1216), the medieval papacy reached a hitherto unprecedented level of political authority in western Europe. This was given theological justification in the decree *Sicut universitatis conditor*, issued in October 1198, in which Innocent III set out the principle of the subordination of the state to the church. Just as God established "greater" and "lesser" lights in the heavens to rule the day and night – a reference to the sun and moon (Genesis 1:16) – so God ordained that the power of the pope exceeded that of any monarch. "Just as the moon derives her light from the sun, and is inferior to the sun in terms of its size and its quality, so the power of the king derives from the authority of the pope."

Such ideas are clearly assumed by Trent, but are neither explicitly reaffirmed nor defended in the face of criticism. The aspects of theology most directly related to the everyday life of the church to be addressed by Trent concern the theology of the sacraments, which became the subject of intense debate between leading reformers during the 1520s. In the next chapter, we shall consider these debates in some detail.

Notes

1   B. B. Warfield, *Calvin and Augustine* (Philadelphia, PA, 1956), p. 322.

2   WA 50.630.

3   WA 6.406–8.

4   *Complete Writings of Menno Simons*, ed. J. C. Wenger (Scottsdale, PA, 1956), p. 502.

5   *Complete Writings of Menno Simons*, p. 300.

6   WA 50.630.

7   John Calvin, *Institutes of the Christian Religion*, IV.i.9.

8   The First Helvetic Confession, 1536, article 14; in E. F. K. Müller (ed.), *Die Bekenntnisschriften der reformierten Kirche* (Leipzig, 1903), p. 101.

9   John Calvin, *Institutes of the Christian Religion*, IV.i.10.

10 Thomas Aquinas, *In Symbolum Apostolorum*, 9; in *S. Thomae Aquinitatis Opera Omnia*, vol. 6, ed. R. Busa (Holzboog, 1980), p. 20.

11 CR 24.397–9.

Further Reading

Avis, P. D. L., *The Church in the Theology of the Reformers* (Basingstoke, 1980).

Eire, C. M. N., *War against the Idols: The Reformation of Worship from Erasmus to Calvin* (Cambridge, 1986).

Gamble, R. C., ed., *Calvin's Ecclesiology: Sacraments and Deacons* (New York, 1992).

Little, F. H., *The Anabaptist View of the Church*, 2nd edn (Boston, 1958).

Mabry, E. L., *Balthasar Hubmaier's Doctrine of the Church* (Lanham, MD, 1994).

Maruyama, T., *The Ecclesiology of Theodore Beza: The Reform of the True Church* (Geneva, 1978).

McNeill, J. T., "The Church in Sixteenth-Century Reformed Theology," *Journal of Religion* 22 (1942), 251–69.

Stephens, W. P., *The Holy Spirit in the Theology of Martin Bucer* (Cambridge, 1970), pp. 156–66.

Stephens, W. P., *The Theology of Huldrych Zwingli* (Oxford, 1986), pp. 260–81.

Sunshine, G. S., *Reforming French Protestantism: The Development of Huguenot Ecclesiastical Institutions, 1557–1572* (Kirksville, MO, 2003).

9

The Doctrine of the Sacraments

The great sixteenth-century debates over the status, identity, and function of the church extended to its services or rites. Major debates developed over what Christians thought that they were doing when they baptized children, or met to obey Christ's command to eat bread and drink wine in his memory. The Protestant Reformation had a significant impact on Christian worship – most notably, in insisting that forms of service and preaching were to be conducted in a language that could be understood by ordinary people. Yet a particularly significant debate developed around the sacraments of baptism and the Eucharist, which we shall consider in this chapter.

The Background to the Sacramental Debates

The word term "sacrament" derives from the Latin term *sacramentum*, meaning "something which is consecrated," and has come to refer to a series of church rites or clerical actions which are regarded as having special spiritual qualities, such as the ability to convey the grace of God. Duns Scotus defined a sacrament as "a physical sign, instituted by God, which efficaciously signifies the grace of God, or the gracious action of God." Other definitions made much the same point, but more briefly. The basic idea was that sacraments were visible signs of invisible grace which somehow acted as "channels" of grace. The medieval period witnessed a consolidation of the theology of the sacraments, particularly in the

Reformation Thought: An Introduction, Fourth Edition. Alister E. McGrath.
© 2012 John Wiley & Sons, Ltd. Published 2012 by John Wiley & Sons, Ltd.

writings of Peter Lombard. Seven sacraments were recognized – baptism, the Eucharist, penance, confirmation, marriage, ordination, and extreme unction – and a complex theology developed to justify and explain their importance.

By the early 1520s, it was clear that the sacramental system of the medieval church was becoming the subject of considerable criticism from reforming factions. The reformers mounted a sustained attack on medieval understandings of the number, nature, and function of sacraments, and reduced the number of authentic sacraments from seven to two (baptism and the Eucharist). But why should the reformers have been so preoccupied with the theology of the sacraments? To many, it seems a remarkably obscure and irrelevant subject. However, reflection on the context in which the reformers operated will help explain why this question was so important for them.

Perhaps the most important point to make here is that the sacraments represented the *publicly visible face of the church*. For most laypersons the main point of contact with the church, as well as the wider world, was through church services on Sundays. The pulpit was one of the most important public platforms of the medieval period for this very reason – hence the desire of both reformers and city councils to control what was said from the pulpit. By attending Sunday services, the laity would thus be exposed to the ideas of the Reformation from two sources: the sermon and the liturgy.

To reform the theory or practice of the sacraments would thus be to make obvious changes to the public life of the church and the community. The main service of the medieval church was the Mass. This service was said according to a set form of words, in Latin, known as "the liturgy." The reformers objected to this specific liturgy, for two reasons. First, the Mass was said in Latin, which most laypersons could not understand. But second, and more seriously, the way in which the Mass was celebrated appeared to involve a number of assumptions that the reformers found unacceptable. They disliked the theory known as "transubstantiation," which held that the bread and wine in the Mass, when consecrated, retain their outward appearances but are in fact transformed into the substance of the body and blood of Jesus Christ. And they resented the implication that priests who celebrated the Mass were performing some kind of good work. To reform the liturgy was thus to help change the way people thought about the gospel.

One of the most effective ways of promoting the cause of the Reformation was therefore to rewrite the liturgy in the vernacular (so that all could understand what was going on), altering it where necessary to eliminate ideas which the reformers found unacceptable. Both the words and actions of services such as baptism articulated the *theology* which lay behind them.

Yet it soon became clear that the main representatives of the first period of the Reformation – especially Luther and Zwingli – were unable to agree on either the theory or practice of the sacraments. They agreed that there were two sacraments, not seven; and they agreed that the laity should be allowed to receive both the bread and the wine. Yet beyond this, they found themselves unable to reach anything even approaching a common mind on the theory and practice of the sacraments.

A number of factors combined to bring about this disagreement: for example, differences in the way in which Scripture was interpreted and the different social contexts of the Wittenberg and Zurich reformations. In what follows, I shall outline their different understandings of the sacraments, and indicate the importance of these differences for the history of the Reformation.

Among those differences, we must note a significant divergence in terminology. The Reformation gradually witnessed a rejection of the term "Mass" without any agreement being reached on what to call the evangelical equivalent. The Christian service at which bread and wine were consecrated and consumed came to be known by various names, including "Mass" (a term retained by Luther), "the bread," "communion," "the memorial" (or "remembrance"), "the Lord's Supper," or "Eucharist." In view of this disagreement, it is difficult to know which to pick. In the end, the word "Eucharist" has been selected to identify the Protestant equivalent of the Mass, on account of its recent use in major Protestant ecumenical documents; but the reader should note the variety of terms which could also be used.

The Sacraments and the Promises of Grace

A central theme to the Reformation emphasis upon the importance of the sacraments to an evangelical spirituality is that of *divine accommodation to human weakness*. The idea is especially associated with Calvin, who is usually regarded as its most lucid expositor. Calvin argues as follows. All good speakers know and understand the limitations of their audiences. And they adapt their way of speaking accordingly. They modify their language to suit the needs and limitations of their listeners, avoiding difficult words and ideas where necessary and using more appropriate ways of speaking in their place. This "principle of accommodation" also extends to the use of analogies and visual aids. Many people find ideas and concepts difficult to handle, forcing responsible public speakers to use stories and illustrations to make their point.

So it is with God, Calvin argues. God accommodates himself to our limitations. God comes down to our level, using powerful images and ways of speaking as means of self-disclosure. No one is excluded from learning about God on account of their educational abilities. That God chooses to be revealed in these ways reflects a weakness on our part, which God graciously acknowledges and takes into account. God is thus able to deploy a wide range of resources in creating and sustaining faith – words, concepts, analogies, models, signs, and symbols. The sacraments are to be seen as an important element in this arsenal of revelation and spiritual resources.

For the first generation of reformers, the sacraments were God's response to human weakness. Knowing our difficulty in receiving and responding to his promises, God has supplemented the Bible with visible and tangible signs of divine grace and favor. They are an accommodation to our limitations. The sacraments represent the promises of God, mediated through objects of the everyday world. In his *Propositions on the Mass* (1521), Philipp Melanchthon stressed that sacraments were primarily a gracious divine accommodation to human weakness. "Signs are the means by which we may be both reminded and reassured of the word of faith." Not every sign is a sacrament; a sacrament is an *instituted and authorized* sign of grace, the credentials of which rest upon a firm evangelical foundation. They are not signs of our own choosing; they have been chosen for us.

In an ideal world, Melanchthon suggests, human beings would be prepared to trust God on the basis of his Word alone. However, one of the weaknesses of fallen humanity is its need for signs (Melanchthon appeals to the story of Gideon as he makes this point). For Melanchthon, sacraments are signs: "What some call sacraments, we call signs – or, if you prefer, sacramental signs." These sacramental signs enhance our trust in God. "In order to mitigate this distrust in the human heart, God has added signs to the word." Sacraments are thus signs of the grace of God added to the promises of grace in order to reassure and strengthen the faith of fallen human beings. Where scholastic theories of the sacraments stressed their ability to convey grace, the reformers emphasized their ability to confirm and convey the promises of God.

Luther made a similar point, defining sacraments as "promises with signs attached to them" or "divinely instituted signs and the promise of forgiveness of sins." Interestingly, Luther used the term "pledge" (*Pfand*) to emphasize the security-giving character of the Eucharist. The bread and the wine reassure us of the reality of the divine promise of forgiveness, making it easier for us to accept, and, having accepted it, to hold firmly to it. "In order that we might be certain of this promise of Christ, and truly rely on it without any doubt, he has given us the most precious and costly seal and pledge – his true body and blood, given under the bread and wine." The bread and wine of the Mass (note that Luther continues to use this traditional term) thus simultaneously remind us of the reality and the cost of the grace of God on the one hand and our response to this grace in faith on the other.

God's promises are thus both real and costly. The death of Christ is a token of both the trustworthiness and the costliness of the grace of God. Luther develops this point by using the idea of a "testament," understood in the sense of a "last will and testament." This point is developed to its full in the 1520 writing *The Babylonian Captivity of the Christian Church*:

A testament is a promise made by someone who is about to die, in which a bequest is defined and heirs appointed. A testament thus involves, in the first place, the death of the testator, and in the second, the promise of an inheritance and the naming of heirs. . . . We see these things clearly in the words of Christ. Christ testifies concerning his death when he says, "This is my body, which is given" and "This is my blood, which is poured out." He names and designates the bequest when he says "for the forgiveness of sins." And he appoints the heirs when he says, "for you and for many," that is, for those who accept and believe the promise of the testator.[1]

Luther's insight here is that a testament involves promises which become operational only after the death of the person who made those promises in the first place. The liturgy – or the Mass or the communion service – thus makes three vitally important points:

1   It affirms the promises of grace and forgiveness.
2   It identifies those to whom those promises are made.
3   It declares the death of the one who made those promises.

The Mass thus dramatically proclaims that the promises of grace and forgiveness are now in effect. It is "a promise of the forgiveness of sins made to us by God, and such a promise as has been confirmed by the death of the Son of God."

By proclaiming the death of Christ, the community of faith affirms that the precious promises of forgiveness and eternal life are now effective for those with faith. As Luther himself put this point:

> So you see that what we call the Mass is a promise of the forgiveness of sins made to us by God, and such a promise that has been confirmed by the death of the Son of God. For the only difference between a promise and a testament is that the testament involves the death of the one who makes it . . . Now God made a testament. Therefore it was necessary that he should die. But God could not die unless he became a human being. Thus the incarnation and the death of Christ are both included explicitly in this one word "testament."[2]

As noted above, a central function of the sacraments is to reassure believers that they are truly members of the body of Christ and heirs of the kingdom of God. Luther developed this point at some length in his 1519 treatise *The Blessed Sacrament of the Holy and True Body of Christ*, stressing the psychological assurance that it makes available to believers:

> To receive this sacrament in bread and wine, then, is nothing else than to receive a sure sign of this fellowship and union with Christ and all the saints. It is as if a citizen were given a sign, a document, or some other token, to assure him that he is indeed a citizen of the city, and a member of that particular community. . . . In this sacrament, therefore, a person is given a sure sign from God himself that he or she is united with Christ and the saints, and has all things in common with them, and that Christ's suffering and life are his own.[3]

This emphasis upon the sacraments as tokens of belonging to the Christian community is perhaps more characteristic of Zwingli than Luther (see pp. 174–6); nevertheless, it is a significant element of Luther's thought at this point.

We have already begun to engage with Luther's views on the sacraments; we must now consider them in more detail.

Luther on the Sacraments

In his reforming treatise of 1520, *The Babylonian Captivity of the Church*, Luther launched a major attack on the Catholic understanding of the sacraments. Taking advantage of the latest humanist philological scholarship, he asserted that the Vulgate use of the term *sacramentum* was largely unjustified on the basis of the Greek text. Where the Catholic church recognized seven sacraments, Luther initially recognized three (baptism, Eucharist, and penance), but shortly afterwards only two (baptism and Eucharist). The transition between these two views can be seen in *The Babylonian Captivity* itself, and we may pause to examine this change and determine its basis. (Incidentally, at his own request, Henry VIII of England gained from the pope the title *Fidei Defensor*, "defender of the faith," through his anti-Lutheran work *Assertio septem sacramentorum*, "I assert that there are seven sacraments." This title, which still appears on British coins in the abbreviated form *F. D.*, represents a riposte to the views developed by Luther in *The Babylonian Captivity of the Church*.)

The work opens with a powerful statement of principle, which sets to one side the medieval consensus regarding the sacraments: "I deny that there are seven sacraments, and for the present maintain that there are only three: baptism, penance and the bread. All three have been subjected to a miserable captivity by the Roman authorities, and the church has been robbed of all her freedom."[4] By the end of the work, however, Luther has come to place considerable emphasis upon the importance of a visible physical sign. Luther signaled this significant change in his views with the following statement:

> Yet it has seemed right to restrict the name of sacrament to those promises of God which have signs attached to them. The remainder, not being connected to signs, are merely promises. Hence, strictly speaking, there are only two sacraments in the church of God – baptism and the bread. For only in these two do we find the divinely instituted sign and the promise of the forgiveness of sins.[5]

Penance thus ceased to have sacramental status, according to Luther, because the two essential characteristics of a sacrament were the Word of God and an outward sacramental sign (such as water in baptism and bread and wine in the Eucharist). The only true sacraments of the New Testament church were thus baptism and Eucharist; penance, having no external sign, could no longer be regarded as a sacrament.

Luther further argued that the medieval sacramental system gave a totally unjustified prominence to the role of the priest. In theory, this development should not have taken place, on account of the sacramental theology which developed in response to the Donatist controversy of the late fourth and early fifth centuries. The point at issue in this controversy concerned whether an immoral priest (such as one who had collaborated with the Roman authorities during a time of persecution) should be allowed to baptize or celebrate the Eucharist. Two rival theories of the role played by the priest developed.

1 Sacraments work *ex opere operantis* (literally, "through the work of the one who works"). Here, the efficacy of the sacrament is understood to be dependent on the personal moral and spiritual qualities of the priest. Believers will only benefit from the sacraments if they are administered by a faithful priest.
2 Sacraments work *ex opere operato* (literally, "through the work that is worked"). Here, the efficacy of the sacrament is understood to depend not on the personal qualities of the priest, but on the inherent quality of the sacrament itself. The ultimate grounds of sacramental efficacy lie in Christ, whose person and benefits are conveyed by the sacraments, not in the priest himself. An immoral priest can thus be permitted to celebrate the sacraments, as the grounds of their validity do not rest in him.

The first view corresponds to the rigorist Donatist position, the second to Augustine's position (and subsequently to that of the Catholic church). Luther and the magisterial reformers had no hesitation in following this majority opinion.

It might therefore be thought that the principle had been firmly established, that the priest does not play a major role in relation to the sacraments. In fact, Luther argued, a number of developments have taken place through which the sacraments were "held captive by the church." Luther listed three ways in which this unacceptable situation had arisen:

1 The practice of "communion in one kind" (in other words, giving the laity bread alone, and not bread and wine). Until the twelfth century, it was the general practice to allow all present at Mass to consume both the consecrated bread and the consecrated wine. However, it seems that during the eleventh century, increasing offense arose through some of the laity being careless with the wine and spilling what was, according to the emerging theology of transubstantiation, the blood of Christ over none too clean church floors. By the thirteenth century, the laity had effectively been banned from receiving the wine.

According to Luther, this was unjustifiable and without scriptural or patristic precedent. Luther declared that the clerical refusal to offer the chalice (the vessel containing the wine) to the laity was sinful. His main reason for taking this position concerned its theological implications: that the laity were prevented from having access to what the wine signified. Only if the laity were allowed access to both the bread and the wine could the symbolism of the sacrament be acceptable: all of Christ's benefits for all of Christ's people. So influential did Luther's attitude become that the practice of offering the laity the chalice (Figure 9.1) became a hallmark of a congregation's allegiance to the Reformation.

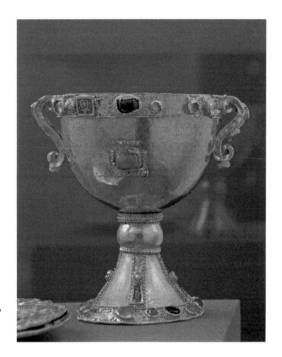

Figure 9.1 Chalice of S. Gauzelin, tenth century, Nancy cathedral. © 2011 Andrea Jemolo/Scala, Florence

2   The doctrine of transubstantiation (which we shall discuss below) seemed to Luther to be an absurdity, an attempt to rationalize a mystery. For Luther, the crucial point was that Christ was really present in the Eucharist – not some particular theory as to how he was present. If iron is placed in a fire and heated, it glows – and in that glowing iron, both the iron and heat are present. Why not use some simple everyday analogy such as this to illustrate the mystery of the presence of Christ in the Eucharist, instead of rationalizing it using some scholastic subtlety?

> For my part, if I cannot fathom how the bread is the body of Christ, yet I will take my reason captive to the obedience of Christ, and clinging simply to his words, firmly believe not only that the body of Christ is in the bread, but that the bread is the body of Christ. My warrant for this is the words which say: "He took bread, and when he had given thanks, he broke it and said, 'Take, eat, this (that is, this bread, which he had taken and broken) is my body'" (1 Corinthians 11:23–24).[6]

It is not the doctrine of transubstantiation which is to be believed, but simply that Christ really is present at the Eucharist. This fact is more important than any theory or explanation.

3   The idea that the priest made an offering or performed a good work or sacrifice on behalf of the people was equally unscriptural. For Luther, the sacrament

was primarily a promise of the forgiveness of sins, to be received through faith by the people.

> You see, therefore, that what we call the Mass is a promise of the forgiveness of sins made to us by God, and such a promise as has been confirmed by the death of the Son of God . . . If the Mass is a promise, as has been said, then access to it is to be gained, not with any works, or powers, or merits of one's own, but by faith alone. For where there is the word of the promising God, there must necessarily be the faith of the accepting believer. It is plain therefore, that the beginning of our salvation is a faith which clings to the word of the promising God who, without any effort on our part, in free and unmerited mercy takes the initiative and offers us the word of his promise.[7]

For Luther, sacraments were concerned with the generation and nourishment of the faith of the people of God, whereas the medieval church tended to treat them as some sort of marketable commodity, capable of earning merit.

We have now considered Luther's views concerning the sacraments in general. In the two sections that follow, we shall consider his views on specific sacraments. We begin by considering an aspect of his thought which subsequently proved to be controversial, eventually leading to a division within a hitherto more or less united reforming movement in Germany and Switzerland. The issue at stake concerns the "real presence" – that is, the question of whether, and in what manner, Christ can be thought of as being physically present in the Eucharist.

Luther on the Real Presence

Luther was ordained a priest in 1507, and celebrated his first Mass at Erfurt on May 2 of that year. In a recollection of this event shared around his dinner table on December 5, 1538, Luther recalled that his chief memories of this great occasion concerned his sense of self-importance and his anxiety in case he accidentally left anything out. We find no hint of any misgivings concerning the traditional Catholic understanding of the Mass in his writings, however, until 1519.

We have already noted his "theological breakthrough" of 1515, in which he made his celebrated discovery of the new meaning of the "righteousness of God" (see pp. 119–21). Although this discovery seems to have had no effect on his attitude to the sacraments initially, it appears that one aspect of his later critique of the medieval theology of the sacraments is foreshadowed in it. Linked with this discovery, significantly, was a new hostility to the use of Aristotelian ideas in theology. In his *Disputation against Scholastic Theology* of 1517, Luther made clear his total rejection of Aristotelianism in theology.

The importance of this anti-Aristotelian development lies in its relation to the medieval doctrine of transubstantiation. This doctrine had been defined by the

Fourth Lateran Council (1215), making use of Aristotle's famous distinction between "substance" and "accident." According to Aristotle, the *substance* of something is its essential nature, whereas its *accidents* are its outward appearances (for example, its color, shape, smell, and so forth). The theory of transubstantiation affirms that the accidents of the bread and wine (their outward appearance: taste, smell, and so forth) remain unchanged at the moment of consecration, while their substance changes from that of bread and wine to that of the body and blood of Jesus Christ.

Luther rejected this "pseudo-philosophy" as absurd, and urged the rejection of the use of such Aristotelian ideas. Aristotle had no place in Christian theology. Nevertheless, it is essential to appreciate that Luther did *not* criticize the underlying basic idea that the bread and wine became the body and blood of Christ: "No importance attaches to this error, if only the body and blood of Christ are left together with the Word." Luther's objection was not to the idea of the "real presence" as such, but to *one specific way of explaining that presence.* For Luther, God is not merely *behind* the sacraments: he is *in* them as well.

Luther's view that the bread and wine really did become the body and blood of Christ was not the result of sheer theological conservatism. Indeed, Luther pointed out that if he could have shown that this view was unbiblical, he would have been the first to abandon it. It seemed to him, however, that this was indeed the obvious meaning of biblical texts, such as Matthew 26:26: *hoc est corpus meum*, "this is my body." The verse was perfectly clear, and seemed to him to admit no other interpretation. It seemed to Luther that the whole principle of the clarity of Scripture (which he regarded as fundamental to his reforming program at this point) was at stake over the interpretation of this verse.

Andreas Karlstadt, his former colleague at Wittenberg – who eventually became his opponent in the 1520s – thought otherwise: it seemed to him that Christ pointed to himself when saying these words. Luther had little difficulty in dismissing this as a misreading of the text. He had considerably more difficulty in dealing with Zwingli's assertion that the word "is" was simply a rhetorical figure of speech (known as *alloiosis*), which really means "signifies" or "represents," and is not to be taken literally.

Luther on Infant Baptism

One important controversy of the Reformation era concerned whether it is legitimate to baptize infants – and if so, what theological justification may be provided for the practice. The New Testament includes no specific references to the baptism of infants. However, it does not explicitly forbid the practice, and there are also a number of passages (such as Acts 16:15, 33; 1 Corinthians 1:16) which could be interpreted as condoning or implying it – for example, references to the baptizing of entire households (which would probably have

Figure 9.2 Baptism of Charles VI of France in Saint-Paul in Paris, December 6, 1368. His mother, Joan of Bourbon, holds him over the baptism font. Book illumination, French, c.1380, from *Grandes Chroniques de France.* MS français 20350, fol. 472 v. Paris, Bibliothèque Nationale. Photo: akg-images/Jérôme da Cunha

included infants). Paul treats baptism as a spiritual counterpart to circumcision (Colossians 2:11–12), suggesting that the parallel may extend to its application to infants.

The practice of baptizing infants of Christian parents – often referred to as "paedobaptism" – appears to have been a response to a number of pressures. It is possible that the parallel with the Jewish rite of circumcision led Christians to devise an equivalent rite of passage for Christian infants. More generally, there seems to have been a pastoral need for Christian parents to celebrate the birth of a child within a believing household. Infant baptism may well have had its origins partly in response to this concern (Figure 9.2). However, it must be stressed that there is genuine uncertainty concerning both the historical origins and the social or theological causes of the practice. What can be said is that the practice had become normal, if not universal, by the second or third century. But is it a tradition that ought to be continued?

The Anabaptists argued that this practice represented a distortion of the Bible. At no point did the New Testament explicitly endorse or require infant baptism. If the church was to reform itself properly according to the Word of God, it ought to abandon this practice and only baptize consenting adults. Baptism presupposes faith on the part of an individual. How, then, can an infant be baptized? We shall consider Anabaptist concerns about this practice later in this chapter (pp. 183–4).

In common with all the magisterial reformers, Luther retained the traditional practice of infant baptism. Luther argued that the early church was right to baptize infants, in that this rests on a sound biblical foundation. Infant baptism is clearly consistent with the New Testament. But what about the argument that baptism requires faith? Luther insists that the emphasis in baptism falls not on the faith or worthiness of the one being baptized, but on the grace and generosity of the one who bestows grace, and commands that we are baptized.

> Everything depends upon the Word and command of God. This now is perhaps somewhat acute but it rests entirely upon what I have said, that Baptism is nothing else than water and the Word of God in and with each other – that is, when the Word is added to the water, Baptism is valid, even though faith be wanting.[8]

It might be thought that Luther's doctrine of justification by faith alone contradicts this practice. After all, infants could not meaningfully be said to have faith, if faith is understood as a conscious, deliberate response to the promises of God. It must be pointed out, however, that Luther's doctrine of justification by faith does not mean that the individual who has faith is justified for that reason: rather, as we saw earlier (pp. 121–2), it means that God graciously gives faith as a gift. In a paradoxical way, infant baptism is totally consistent with the doctrine of justification by faith, because it emphasizes that faith is not something we can achieve, but something which is given to us graciously.

For Luther, the sacraments do not merely strengthen the faith of believers – they are capable of generating that faith in the first place. The sacrament mediates the Word of God, which is capable of evoking faith. Thus Luther finds no difficulty with the practice of infant baptism. Baptism does not presuppose faith: rather, it generates faith. "A child becomes a believer if Christ in baptism speaks to him through the mouth of the one who baptizes, since it is his Word, his commandment, and his Word cannot be without fruit." Baptism effects what it signifies: "So we can see what a great and excellent thing Baptism is, in that it delivers us from the jaws of the devil and makes us God's own, suppresses and takes away sin, and then daily strengthens the new person, and is (and will always remain) efficacious until we pass from this state of misery to eternal glory."[9]

Zwingli on the Sacraments

Like Luther, Zwingli had grave misgivings about the word "sacrament" itself. He noted that the term had the basic sense of "oath," and initially treated the sacraments of baptism and Eucharist (the remaining five sacraments of the Catholic system having been rejected) as signs of God's faithfulness to his people and his gracious promise of forgiveness. Thus in 1523 he wrote that the word "sacrament" could be used to refer to those things which "God has instituted, commanded and ordained with his word, which is as firm and sure as if he had sworn an oath to this effect." Up to this point, there was a certain degree of similarity between the views of Luther and Zwingli on the functions of sacraments (although, as we shall see below, the question of the real presence of Christ in the Eucharist divided them radically).

This limited agreement, however, had evaporated by 1525. Zwingli retained the idea of a "sacrament" as an oath or a pledge; but whereas, earlier, he had understood this to be *God's pledge of faithfulness to us*, he now asserted that it refers to *our pledge of obedience and loyalty to one another*. It must be remembered that Zwingli was a chaplain to the army of the Swiss Confederacy (and was present at the disastrous defeat at Marignano in September 1515). Drawing on the military use of oaths, Zwingli argued that a "sacrament" was basically a declaration of allegiance of an individual to a community. Just as a soldier swears allegiance to his army (in the person of the general), so the Christian swears allegiance to his fellow Christians. Zwingli used the German term *Pflichtszeichen*, "a demonstration of allegiance," to designate the essence of a sacrament.

A sacrament is thus the means "by which someone proves to the church that he either intends to be, or already is, a soldier of Christ, and which informs the whole church, rather than himself, of his faith." In baptism, the believer pledges loyalty to the community of the church; in the Eucharist, he demonstrates that loyalty publicly.

Zwingli thus developed the idea that the sacraments are subordinate to the preaching of the Word of God. It is this preaching which brings faith into existence; the sacraments merely provide an occasion by which this faith may be publicly demonstrated. The preaching of the Word of God is of central importance, and the sacraments are like seals on a letter – they confirm its substance, without adding to it.

Zwingli developed the meaning of the Eucharist with a further military analogy drawn from his experience as a Swiss army chaplain:

> If someone sews on a white cross, he proclaims that he wishes to be a confederate. And if he makes the pilgrimage to Nähenfels and gives God praise and thanksgiving for the victory vouchsafed to our forefathers, he testifies that he is a confederate indeed. Similarly, whoever receives the mark of baptism is the one who is resolved to hear what God says to him, to learn the divine precepts, and to live his life in accordance with them. And whoever in the congregation gives thanks to God in the remembrance or supper testifies to the fact that he rejoices in the death of Christ from the depths of his heart, and thanks him for it.[10]

The reference here is to the victory of the Swiss over the Austrians in 1388 near Nähenfels, in the canton of Glarus. This victory is usually regarded as marking the beginning of the Swiss (or Helvetic) Confederation, and it was commemorated by a pilgrimage to the site of the battle on the first Thursday in April.

Zwingli makes two points. First, the Swiss soldier wears a white cross (now incorporated into the Swiss national flag, of course) as a *Pflichtszeichen*, demonstrating publicly his allegiance to the Confederacy. Similarly, the Christian publicly demonstrates his allegiance to the church, initially by baptism and subsequently by participating in the Eucharist. Baptism is the "visible entry and sealing into Christ."

Second, the historical event which brought the Confederacy into being is commemorated as a token of allegiance to that same Confederacy. Similarly, the Christian commemorates the historical event which brought the Christian church into being (the death of Jesus Christ) as a token of his commitment to that church. The Eucharist is thus a memorial of the historical event leading to the establishment of the Christian church and a public demonstration of the believer's allegiance to that church and its members.

This understanding of the nature of the Eucharist is confirmed by Zwingli's treatment of Matthew 26:26: in the Latin of the Vulgate, this reads *hoc est corpus meum*, "this is my body." These words were spoken by Christ during the Last Supper, on the day before his death, signifying the manner in which he wished to be remembered by his church. It is as if, Zwingli wrote, Christ had said: "I entrust to you a symbol of this my surrender and testament, to awaken in you the remembrance of me and of my goodness to you, so that when you see this bread and this cup, held forth in this memorial supper, you may remember me as delivered up for you, just as if you saw me before you as you see me now, eating with you."

For Zwingli, Christ's death has the same significance for the church as the battle of Nähenfels has for the Swiss Confederacy. It is the foundational event of the Christian church, central to its identity and self-understanding. Just as the commemoration of Nähenfels does not involve the reenactment of that battle, so the Eucharist involves neither the repetition of the sacrifice of Christ nor his presence at the commemoration. The Eucharist is "a memorial of the suffering of Christ, and not a sacrifice." For reasons which we shall explore below, Zwingli insisted that the words "this is my body" cannot be taken literally, thus eliminating any idea of the "real presence of Christ" in the Eucharist. Just as a man, on setting off on a long journey from home, might give his wife his ring to remember him by until his return, so Christ leaves his church a token to remember him by until the day on which he will return in glory.

Zwingli on the Real Presence

The background to Zwingli's views on the real presence of Christ can be traced back to some seemingly insignificant events of the year 1509. In November of that year, a change of personnel at a small library in the Lowlands took place, necessitating the cataloguing of its holdings. The work was entrusted to Cornelius Hoen, who discovered that the library contained a significant collection of the writings of the noted humanist Wessel Gansfort (c.1420–89). One of these was entitled *On the Sacrament of the Eucharist*. Although Gansfort did not actually deny the doctrine of transubstantiation, he developed the idea of a spiritual communion between Christ and the believer. Hoen, apparently attracted by this idea, reworked it into a radical critique of the doctrine of transubstantiation, which he wrote up in the form of a letter. It seems that this letter found its way to Luther at some point in 1521 (although the evidence is not entirely conclusive). By 1523 the letter had reached Zurich, where it was read by Zwingli.

In this letter, Hoen suggested that the word *est* in *hoc est corpus meum* should not be interpreted literally as "is" or "is identical with," but rather as *significat*, "signifies." For example, when Christ says "I am the bread of life" (John 6:48), he is clearly not identifying himself with a loaf of bread or bread in general. The word "is" here must be taken in a metaphorical, or non-literal, sense. The Old Testament prophets may indeed have foretold that Christ would "become flesh" (*incarnatus*) – but this was to happen once, and only once. At no point did the prophets foretell or the apostles preach that Christ would, so to speak, "become bread" (*impanatus*) every day through the actions of any priest offering the sacrifice of the Mass.

Hoen developed a number of ideas which eventually found their way into the Eucharistic thought of Zwingli. Two may be noted here. The first is the idea of the Eucharist being like a ring given by a groom to his bride to reassure her of his love. It is a *pledge* – an idea that resonates throughout Zwingli's writings on the subject. Zwingli deploys the imagery of a ring as a pledge of love with considerable skill at a number of points, and it is not impossible that it was Hoen who planted this powerful image in his mind. The second notion that Hoen employs is that of commemoration of Christ in his absence. Noting that Christ's phrase "this is my body" is immediately followed by the words "Do this in remembrance of me," Hoen argues that the second set of words clearly points to commemoration of "a person who is absent (at least, physically absent)."

Where Luther reacted with a notable lack of enthusiasm to Hoen's ideas, Zwingli was considerably more positive in his reaction. By November and December of 1524 he was promoting Hoen's ideas with some vigor, and the following year he arranged for the letter to be published. In the summer of 1525, the learned Oecolampadius of Basle joined in the discussion, producing a book in which he argued that the writers of the patristic period knew nothing of either transubstantiation or Luther's views on the real presence, but tended toward the view now increasingly being associated with Zwingli.

Zwingli argued that Scripture employed many figures of speech. Thus the word "is" might at one point mean "is absolutely identical with," and at another mean "represents" or "signifies." For example, in his treatise *On the Lord's Supper* (1526), he wrote:

> Throughout the Bible, we find figures of speech, called in the Greek *tropos*, that is, something that is metaphorical, or to be understood in another sense. For example, in John 15 Christ says "I am the vine." This means that Christ is like a vine when

considered in relation to us, who are sustained and grow in him in the same way as branches grow on a vine . . . Similarly, in John 1 we read "Behold the Lamb of God, who takes away the sin of the world." The first part of this verse is a trope, for Christ is not literally a lamb.[11]

After a rather wearisome exploration of relevant biblical texts, Zwingli concluded that "there are innumerable passages in Scripture where the word 'is' means 'signifies.'" The question that must therefore be addressed is whether Christ's words in Matthew 26, "this is my body" can also be taken metaphorically or *in tropice*. It has already become clear enough that in this context the word "is" cannot be taken literally. Hence it follows that it must be taken metaphorically or figuratively. In the words "this is my body," the word "this" means the bread, and the word "body" means the body which was put to death for us. Therefore the word "is" cannot be taken literally, for the bread is not the body.

This point was developed by Oecolampadius in 1527, who asserted that "in dealing with signs, sacraments, pictures, parables and interpretations, one should and one must understand the words figuratively and not understand the words literally." Zwingli developed this point concerning the relation between the sign and the thing which is signified. He uses this distinction to argue that it is inconceivable that the bread could be the body of Christ:

> A sacrament is the sign of a holy thing. When I say "the sacrament of the Lord's body," I am simply referring to that bread which is the symbol of the body of Christ who was put to death for our sakes . . . But the real body of Christ is the body which is seated at the right hand of God, and the sacrament of his body is the bread, and the sacrament of his blood is the wine, of which we partake with thanksgiving. Now the sign and the thing signified cannot be one and the same. Therefore the sacrament of the body of Christ cannot be that body itself.[12]

A further argument used by Zwingli against Luther, hinted at in the passage just cited, concerns the location of Christ. For Luther, Christ is present in the Eucharist. Whoever receives the bread and the wine receives Christ. Zwingli, however, pointed out that both Scripture and the creeds affirm that Christ is now "seated at the right hand of God." Now Zwingli had not the slightest idea where this might be, and wasted no time speculating on its location – but, he argued, it did mean that wherever Christ is now, he is not present in the Eucharist. He cannot be in two places at once. Luther argues that the phrase "the right hand of God" is actually a metaphorical expression, not to be taken literally. It really means "God's sphere of influence" or "God's rule." To say that "Christ is seated at the right hand of God" does not mean that Christ is now located at a definite location in the stratosphere, but simply that Christ is present wherever God rules. Once more, the question of which scriptural passages were to be interpreted literally and which metaphorically emerged as central to the debate on the real presence.

The same applies to the notion of "feeding on Christ," an image with a distinguished history of use in the Christian church, one traditionally linked with the doctrine of transubstantiation. Because the bread is the body of Christ, by eating the bread the believer may be said to feed on Christ. Zwingli insists that this biblical image must be interpreted figuratively as trusting in God through Christ.

So what is different about the communion bread? What makes the bread at a communion service different from any other bread? If it is not the body of Christ, what is it? Zwingli answers this question with an analogy. Consider a queen's ring, he suggests. Now consider that ring in two quite different contexts. In the first context, the ring is merely present. Perhaps you can imagine a ring lying on a table. It has no associations. Now imagine that ring transferred to a new context. It is placed on the finger of a queen, as a gift from her king. It now has personal associations, deriving from its connection with the king – such as his authority, power, and majesty. Its value is now far greater than that of the gold of which it is made. These associations arise through transfer from the original context to the new context: the ring itself remains completely unchanged. The ring thus gains its associations and its value through its new context; these associations and value are not *inherent*, but *acquired*.

So it is with the communion bread, Zwingli argues. The bread and the ring are both unchanged in themselves, but their signification alters dramatically. The signification – in other words, the associations of the object – can change, without there being any change in the nature of the object itself. Zwingli suggests that exactly the same process is at work in the case of the bread and the wine. In their ordinary everyday context, they are plain bread and plain wine, with no especial associations. But when they are moved into a new context, they take on new and important associations. When they are placed at the center of a worshipping community and when the story of the last night of the life of Christ is retold, they become powerful reminders of the foundational events of the Christian faith. It is their context that gives them this meaning; they remain unchanged in themselves.

Zwingli on Infant Baptism

Zwingli was obliged to face an obvious difficulty in relation to infant baptism. How, it was argued, could he justify baptizing infants, when these had no faith which they could publicly demonstrate? The traditional answer to this dilemma rested with original sin. Baptism purged the guilt of original sin. The argument in question went back to Augustine in the early fifth century, and was used by Luther in his defense of the practice of infant baptism.

Yet Zwingli had hesitations here. Following Erasmus, he had difficulty with the notion of original sin, and inclined toward the view that infants had no inherent original sinfulness which needed to be forgiven. As a result, infant baptism seemed to serve no purpose – unless another theoretical justification for the practice were forthcoming. Zwingli had no difficulty with the idea of individuals committing sins. His problem lay with the notion of a state of original sin, which he regarded as an unbiblical idea.

It is clear that Zwingli had misgivings in the late 1510s and early 1520s about continuing the practice of infant baptism in the light of his rejection of the notion of original sin. By 1524, however, he appears to have developed a theory of baptism which got round this difficulty altogether. Zwingli pointed out that in the Old Testament infant males were circumcised within days of their birth as a sign of their membership of the people of Israel. Circumcision was the rite laid down by the Old Testament covenant to demonstrate that the circumcised child belonged to the covenant community. The child had been born into a community, to which it now belonged – and circumcision was a sign of belonging to this community.

There had been a long-standing tradition within Christian theology of seeing baptism as the Christian equivalent of circumcision. Zwingli developed this idea, pointing out that baptism is gentler than circumcision, in that it involves no pain or shedding of blood, and more inclusive, in that it embraces both male and female infants. It too was a sign of belonging to a community – in this case, the Christian church. The fact that the child was not conscious of this belonging was irrelevant: it *was* a member of the Christian community, and baptism was the public demonstration of this membership. The contrast with Luther on this point will be obvious.

Zwingli subsequently took this argument a stage further. We noted earlier (pp. 16–18) how cities were seen as organic communities in the late Middle Ages, a factor which appears to have been significant for many cities as they considered whether to accept the Reformation. This same view appears in Zwingli, who treats "state" and "church" as virtually equivalent: "A Christian city is nothing other than a Christian church." The sacraments thus signified not merely loyalty to the church, but also loyalty to the city community, in this case Zurich. To refuse to allow one's child to be baptized, therefore, was an act of disloyalty to the Zurich city community. The magistrates were thus entitled to expel from Zurich all who refused to allow their children to be baptized.

The Anabaptists, as we have seen, regarded infant baptism as unjustifiable. As the radical Reformation posed a major threat to the Reformation at Zurich in the 1520s, on account of both its religious and political views, Zwingli's understanding of baptism as both an ecclesial and a civic event provided an excellent means of enforcing conformity.

Baptism thus became of central importance to Zwingli, in that it provided a criterion by which two totally different concepts of the church might be distinguished. Zwingli's concept of a state or city church was increasingly challenged by the Anabaptists, whose vision of the church involved a return to the simplicities of the apostolic church. For the radicals, the purity of that church had been totally destroyed through the conversion of the Roman emperor Constantine in the early fourth century, which had led to a close alliance of church and state.

The Anabaptists wished to sever this link, whereas Zwingli wished to continue it in the specific form found at Zurich. Thus Zwingli felt justified in declaring that "the issue is not baptism, but revolt, faction and heresy." Baptism represented the criterion which determined whether an individual was a loyal citizen of Zurich or a traitor to that city.

As Anabaptism became an increasing threat to the city in the 1520s, the magistrates at least appreciated the importance of Zwingli's theology on this point. But this merely emphasizes how closely theology and politics, church and city, were linked in the first era of the Reformation. The very term "magisterial Reformation" itself points to this close relationship between the magistrates and the Reformation.

Luther versus Zwingli: A Summary and Evaluation

The debate between Luther and Zwingli is somewhat technical, and the reader may have found it difficult to follow. It may be helpful, therefore, to summarize the main points of difference between them, both recapitulating and extending the above discussion.

1   Both reformers rejected the medieval sacramental scheme. Whereas the medieval theology had identified seven sacraments, the reformers insisted that only two sacraments – baptism and the Eucharist – were authorized by the New Testament. Luther was perhaps more conservative in this respect than Zwingli, initially allowing that penance might be considered sacramental, before withdrawing this view in 1520.

2   Luther understood the Word of God and the sacraments to be inseparably linked. Both bore witness to Jesus Christ, and both mediated his power and presence. The sacraments were thus capable of creating, as well as supporting or demonstrating, faith. For Zwingli, it was the Word of God which created faith and the sacraments which demonstrated that faith publicly. Word and sacrament were quite distinct, with the former being of greater importance.

3   Although both reformers retained the traditional practice of infant baptism, they did so for very different reasons. For Luther, sacraments could generate faith; and hence baptism could generate faith in an infant. For Zwingli, sacraments demonstrated allegiance to and membership of a community; hence baptism demonstrated that an infant belonged to a community.

4   Luther was considerably more traditional in his approach to the celebration of the Eucharist than Zwingli. In his major liturgical reforming work *Concerning the Order of Public Worship* (1523), Luther made it clear that he was prepared to retain the traditional title of "Mass," provided it was not misunderstood to imply a sacrifice, and to authorize it to be celebrated weekly, preferably in the vernacular, *as the main Sunday service*. Zwingli, however, abolished the title "Mass," and suggested that the equivalent

evangelical rite should be celebrated only three or four times a year. No longer was it the center of Christian worship. Where Luther included a new emphasis upon preaching within the context of the Eucharist, Zwingli insisted that preaching displace the Eucharist from its customary weekly Sunday celebration.

5   Luther and Zwingli could not agree on the meaning of the words *hoc est corpus meum* (Matthew 26:26), central to the Eucharist. For Luther, *est* meant "is"; for Zwingli, it meant "signifies." Two very different ways of interpreting Scripture underlay this disagreement.

6   Both reformers rejected the medieval doctrine of transubstantiation. Luther did so, however, on the basis of its Aristotelian foundations, and was prepared to accept the basic idea which underlay it – the real presence of Christ in the Eucharist. Zwingli rejected both the term and the idea. For him, Christ is remembered in his absence in the Eucharist.

7   Zwingli asserted that, since Christ now sits at the right hand of God, he cannot be present anywhere else. Luther dismissed Zwingli's assertion as philosophically unsophisticated, and defended the idea of Christ being present without any limits imposed by space or time. Luther's defense of the "ubiquity of Christ" rested upon some distinctions associated with William of Ockham, which further persuaded Luther's opponents that he had lapsed into some new form of scholasticism.

The dispute between Luther and Zwingli was important at both the theological and the political levels. At the theological level, it raised the gravest of doubts concerning the principle of the "clarity of Scripture." Luther and Zwingli were unable to agree on the meaning of such phrases as "this is my body" (which Luther interpreted literally and Zwingli metaphorically) and "at the right hand of God" (which – with apparent inconsistency on both sides – Luther interpreted metaphorically and Zwingli literally). The exegetical optimism of the early Reformation may be regarded as foundering on this rock: Scripture, it seemed, was far from easy to interpret.

At the political level, the dispute ensured the permanent separation of the two evangelical factions of the Reformation. An attempt to mediate between their rival views took place at the Colloquy of Marburg (1529), attended by such luminaries as Bucer, Luther, Melanchthon, Oecolampadius, and Zwingli. By this stage, it was becoming increasingly obvious that unless the Reformation could achieve a significant degree of internal unity, at least some of its gains would be reversed. The Catholics had been inhibited from taking military action against the cities of the Reformation as a result of the long-standing disputes between Emperor Charles V and Francis I of France on the one hand, and Pope Clement VII on the other. In 1529, these two disputes were resolved within weeks of each other. Suddenly, the two wings of the Reformation faced a powerful political and military threat.

The most obvious course of action in the face of this threat would have been to settle their differences – a procedure urged by Bucer, who suggested that differences should be tolerated among evangelicals provided they agreed to recognize the Bible alone as the normative source of faith. The local Protestant ruler Philip of Hesse, anxious at the implications of the new political situation, brought Luther and Zwingli together in the castle hall of Marburg in an attempt to resolve their differences. This attempt foundered on one point, and one point only. On 14 articles, Luther and Zwingli felt able to agree. The fifteenth contained six points, on which they were able to reach agreement on five. The sixth posed difficulties. Luther and Zwingli reluctantly were forced to declare that they had not "reached an agreement as to whether the true body and blood of Christ are bodily present in the bread and wine."

So this one point remained unresolved. For Luther, Christ was really present in the Eucharist, whereas for Zwingli he was present only in the hearts of believers. Philip of Hesse's hope of a united evangelical front against the newly regrouped Catholic forces was dashed, and the political credibility of the Reformation seriously compromised. By 1530, Charles V had begun to reassert his authority over the German Reformation, helped to no small extent by the political consequences of the differences between Luther and Zwingli concerning the Eucharist.

Aware of what was happening, Protestant leaders attempted to heal the resulting wounds as quickly as possible. One major attempt to define a common Protestant position on the sacraments should be noted: the *Consensus Tigurinus*, or "Consensus of Zurich," a formula of faith agreed on in May 1549. The document, drawn up by major leaders such as John Calvin and Heinrich Bullinger (Zwingli's successor as the leading reformer of the city of Zurich), managed to establish significant common ground within a Protestantism hitherto divided on this issue.

Yet the rifts within Protestantism went deeper than the disagreements between Luther and Zwingli. More radical elements within the evangelical movement were advocating more radical applications of the *sola scriptura* principle.

Anabaptist Views on the Sacraments

One of the most distinctive theological characteristics of the Anabaptist movement was its rejection of the traditional practice of infant baptism. The main reason for this was its lack of biblical warrant. Menno Simons (1496–1561) provided a detailed critique of the practice of infant baptism, arguing that it was a non-biblical tradition, which ought to be abandoned by all concerned with returning to a more authentic apostolic Christianity. "In all the New Testament there is not a word said or commanded about baptizing infants, by Christ nor by the apostles."

Yet the Anabaptist critique of the practice of infant baptism went beyond its lack of biblical warrant. As we noted earlier, Anabaptist writers argued that the New Testament clearly presupposed that those who were to be baptized possessed faith. As Simons argued, Christ "commanded that the gospel should be preached and that those who believe should be baptized." It was, he insisted, a distortion of the true faith to allow infants to be baptized, since these showed no signs of faith, knowledge of the truth, or inner regeneration.

Most Anabaptist writers held that baptism was a ceremony or rite which was performed in recognition that an individual showed clear signs of faith, repentance, and regeneration. This general principle, and its consequences for infant baptism, is clearly set out in the *Schleitheim Confession* (1527), one of the most important Anabaptist confessions of faith:

> Baptism shall be given to all those who have learned repentance and amendment of life, and who believe truly that their sins are taken away by Christ, and to all those who walk in the resurrection of Jesus Christ, and wish to be buried with Him in death, so that they may be raised with him . . . This excludes all infant baptism, the highest and chief abomination of the Pope.[13]

Baptism is thus clearly seen as an outward physical sign of an inward spiritual reality, which it signifies but does not cause. As Simons pointed out, "we are baptized because we are regenerated by faith in God's word, since regeneration is not the result of baptism, but baptism is the result of regeneration." Infant baptism was thus clearly inconsistent with this general theology of baptism. Simons, however, was clear that his rejection of infant baptism did not entail excluding children from the Kingdom of God. Baptism was a sign, not the cause, of such membership. "Christ has promised the kingdom to little children without baptism."

Donatism Donatism stressed the need for purity and holiness, and insisted that the church was a community of saints rather than a mixed body of the righteous and evil.

It is also important to consider how this theology of baptism relates to Anabaptist ecclesiology, which is generally **Donatist** in character (p. 144). The practice of believers' baptism defines and ensures a believers' church. As Balthasar Hubmaier put it, "no baptism, no church; no baptism, no discipleship." Baptism defined the point of entry to full membership of the church, representing a public declaration that an individual was considered to possess those characteristics deemed necessary for admittance.

The radical Reformation also took issue with the Eucharistic theology of Luther, tending toward – and occasionally surpassing – the views of Zwingli. The notion that the Eucharistic bread and wine were in any sense physically identical with the body and blood of Christ was rejected as contrary to reason, nature, and Scripture. As Menno Simons put it, this represented a confusion of the sacramental sign with the reality it represented. After all, Israel celebrated the festival of the Passover without in any way believing that it physically recreated the events of the Exodus from Egypt. Christ now stands at the right hand of God, and cannot be considered to be "present" in any physical sense in the bread or wine. The Lord's Supper was about recalling the past, and reaffirming the faith and mutual commitment of believers.

Calvin on the Sacraments

For Calvin, as for all the magisterial reformers, the sacraments were seen as identity-giving: without sacraments, there could be no Christian church. "Wherever we find the Word of God preached purely and listened to, and the sacraments administered according to the institution of Christ, we cannot doubt that a church exists." It is thus not the quality of its members, but the presence of the authorized means of grace that constitutes a true church. Having thus defined one of the "marks of the church" (*notae ecclesiae*) as the administration of the sacraments, Calvin was obliged to give a detailed consideration of what the true sacraments of the gospel might be and how they were to be understood. In doing so, Calvin was clearly aware of the divergences between Luther and Zwingli, and he attempted to steer a middle course between their rival viewpoints.

Calvin offered two definitions of a sacrament – as "an external symbol by which the Lord seals on our consciences his promises of good will towards us, in order to sustain the weakness of our faith," and as a "visible sign of a sacred thing, or a visible form of an invisible grace." The former was Calvin's own definition, whereas the latter was due to Augustine (although Calvin saw it as too brief to be of much use). Insisting that a sacrament must be based upon "a promise and a command of the Lord," he followed his colleagues in rejecting five of the seven sacraments traditionally accepted by the Catholic church, allowing only baptism and the Eucharist to remain.

For Calvin, sacraments are gracious accommodations to our weakness. God, knowing our weakness of faith, adapts to our limitations:

> A sacrament is never without a preceding promise, but is joined to it as a kind of appendix, in order to confirm and seal the promise itself, making it more clear to us, and in a sense ratifying it . . . As our faith is weak unless it is supported on every side and sustained by every means, it trembles, wavers, and finally collapses. Here our merciful Lord, according to his infinite kindness, so adjusts himself to our capacity that, since we are creatures who always cling to the earth and cleave to fleshly things, and do not think about or even conceive spiritual matters, he condescends to lead us to himself by just such earthly things, and to set before us in the flesh a mirror of spiritual blessings.[14]

The central debate between Luther and Zwingli concerned the relation between the sacramental sign and the spiritual gift which it signified. Calvin may be regarded as occupying a position roughly midway between the two extremes represented by them. In the sacraments, he argued, there is such a close connection between the symbol and the gift which it symbolizes that we can "easily pass from one to the other." The sign is visible and physical, whereas the thing signified is invisible and spiritual; yet, because the connection between the sign and the thing signified is so intimate, it is permissible to apply the one to the other. Thus the thing that is signified is effected by its sign. Calvin could thus maintain the difference between the sign and the thing signified, while insisting that the sign really points to the gift it signifies.

Calvin's understanding of baptism may be regarded as combining both Zwinglian and Lutheran elements. Nodding in Zwingli's direction, Calvin argued that baptism is a public demonstration of allegiance to God: "Baptism is the sign of the initiation by which we are received into the society of the church." Just as Zwingli had asserted that sacraments are primarily ecclesial events, serving to demonstrate the loyalty of believers to the church or civic community, so Calvin stressed the declaratory role of the sacrament of baptism. However, he also incorporated the characteristically Lutheran stress upon baptism as a sign of the remission of sins and the new life of believers in Jesus Christ: "Baptism also brings another benefit, for it shows us our being put to death in Christ, and our new life in him . . . Thus the free pardon of sins and the imputation of righteousness are first promised, and then the grace of the Holy Spirit to reform us to newness of life."

In common with all the magisterial reformers, Calvin upheld the validity of infant baptism. The practice, he argued, was an authentic tradition of the early church, and not a later medieval development. Zwingli had justified the practice by an appeal to the Jewish rite of circumcision. By this rite, he had argued, infant males were shown to be members of the covenant community. In a similar manner, baptism was the mark that an infant belonged to the church, the community of the new covenant. The rising influence of the Anabaptists, which Calvin had experienced at first hand during his Strasbourg period, demonstrated the importance of justifying the practice of infant baptism, which the Anabaptists vigorously rejected.

Calvin thus reiterated and extended Zwingli's covenantal justification of infant baptism: if Christian infants cannot be baptized, they are at a disadvantage in relation to Jewish infants, who are publicly and outwardly sealed into the covenant community through circumcision: "Otherwise, if the testimony by which the Jews were assured of the salvation of their posterity is taken away from us, the coming of Christ would have the effect of making God's grace more obscure and less well attested to us than it was to the Jews before us." Calvin thus argued that infants should be baptized, and not denied the benefits which this conveys.

In his discussion of the Eucharist, Calvin distinguished three aspects of the spiritual truth which is presented (*monstretur*) and offered through the visible elements of bread and wine. The *signification or meaning* is the divine promises, which are included or enclosed within the sign itself; believers are reassured, particularly through the words of institution, that the body and blood of Jesus

Christ have been broken and shed for them. The sacrament "confirms the promise in which Jesus Christ declares that his flesh is food indeed, and his blood drink indeed, and that they feed us with eternal life." The *substance or matter* of the Eucharist concerns our reception of the body of Christ: God communicates to us what he has promised us. In receiving the sign of the body of Christ (in other words, the bread), we are simultaneously receiving the body of Christ itself. Finally, the *virtue or effect* of the Eucharist is located in the *beneficia Christi* – the benefits won for the believer by Christ through his obedience. The believer participates by faith in all the benefits of Christ, such as redemption, righteousness, and eternal life.

Finally, the sacraments encourage Christians to value the creation. Material elements can signify the grace, generosity, and goodness of God. This insight is rigorously grounded in Calvin's doctrine of creation. For Calvin, the creation reflects its Creator at every point. Image after image is flashed in front of our eyes, as Calvin attempts to convey the multiplicity of ways in which the creation witnesses to its Creator: it is like a visible garment, which the invisible God dons in order to make himself known; it is like a book, in which the name of the Creator is written as its author; it is like a theater, in which the glory of God is publicly displayed; it is like a mirror, in which the works and wisdom of God are reflected.

This gives us a new motivation for *enjoying* nature. Although often portrayed as an ascetic killjoy, determined to stop believers from enjoying themselves at any cost, Calvin is genuinely concerned to stress that creation was fashioned in order that we might rejoice in it, rather than merely survive through it. Quoting Psalm 104:15, Calvin points out that God created wine that makes human hearts glad. Food does not merely allow us to survive; it tastes good.

Calvin developed this point at length in the *Institutes*, pointing out how we are able to appreciate and enjoy the good things of life. "All things are made for us, in order that we may know and acknowledge their author, and celebrate his goodness towards us by giving him thanks." The bread and wine of the Eucharist thus point not only to God's act of redeeming the world in Christ, but to his preceding act of creation, by which a world which we can enjoy was brought into being.

The Catholic Response: Trent on the Sacraments

Trent took some time to respond to the views on the sacraments associated with the Reformation. The Seventh Session of the Council of Trent reached its conclusion on March 3, 1547, and issued its "Decree on the Sacraments." In many ways, this is best seen as an interim measure, designed to counter Protestant views without providing a detailed Catholic rejoinder. The decree takes the form of a preface, followed by 13 general canons, each condemning some aspect of "the heresies that in our turbulent times are directed against the most holy sacraments." These were followed by specific canons relating to baptism and the Eucharist.

The following canons are of particular importance in that they explicitly condemn the reformers' views on the number of sacraments and the manner in which they operate. Criticism is in particular directed against the view that sacraments merely signify grace, which is to be received through faith. For Trent, sacraments *cause* what they signify.

1   If anyone says that the sacraments of the new law were not all instituted by our Lord Jesus Christ, or that there are more or less than seven, namely, baptism, confirmation, Eucharist, penance, extreme unction, ordination, and marriage, or that any one of these seven is not truly and intrinsically a sacrament, let them be condemned . . .

5   If anyone says that these sacraments have been instituted for the nourishment of faith alone, let them be condemned.

6   If anyone says that the sacraments of the new law do not contain the grace that they signify, or that they do not confer that grace upon those who do not place obstacles in its path (as though they were only outward signs of grace or righteousness, received through faith, and certain marks of Christian profession by which believers are, at the human level, distinguished from non-believers), let them be condemned . . .

8   If anyone says that the sacraments of the new law do not confer grace *ex opere operato* (see p. 169), but that faith alone in the divine promise is sufficient to obtain grace, let them be condemned.[15]

These 13 canons were then followed by a series of 14 canons relating to baptism and three relating to confirmation.

The Council of Trent strongly affirmed the validity of infant baptism, and criticized the Anabaptist view that baptism should be limited to consenting adults – or that those baptized as infants had to be baptized again on reaching spiritual maturity. The statement of canon 13 is particularly important, in that it condemned anyone who held the view that: Infants, not being able to make an act of faith, are not to be reckoned among the faithful after their baptism, and therefore when they come to the age of discretion they are to be rebaptized.[16]

It was not until the Thirteenth Session of the council, which concluded its deliberations on October 11, 1551, that Trent finally set forth the positive position of the Catholic church in the "Decree on the Most Holy Sacrament of the Eucharist." Up to this point, Trent had merely criticized the reformers without putting forth a coherent alternative position. This deficiency was now remedied.

The Decree opens with a vigorous attack on those who deny the real presence of Christ. Although neither Zwingli nor the Anabaptists are specifically mentioned, the council's allusions to Christ sitting at the right hand of God and the improper use of "tropes" makes it clear that their views are the object of its attack:

After the consecration of the bread and wine, our Lord Jesus Christ is truly, really and substantially contained in the venerable sacrament of the Holy Eucharist under the appearance of those physical things. For there is no repugnance in the fact that our Saviour sits at the right hand of the Father in heaven according to his natural mode of existing, while he is sacramentally present to us in his own substance in many other places . . . It is a most contemptible action on the part of some contentious and wicked people to twist them (the words of Christ) into fictitious and imaginary tropes by which the truth of the flesh and blood of Christ is denied.[17]

The Council vigorously defended both the doctrine and the terminology of transubstantiation: "By the consecration of the bread and wine a change is brought about of the whole substance of the bread into the substance of the body of Christ and of the whole substance of the wine into the blood of Christ. This change the Holy Catholic Church properly and appropriately calls transubstantiation."

The topics discussed in the present chapter represented issues of contention between Protestants and Catholics on the one hand, and between individual Protestants on the other. In the next chapter, we shall consider a theological issue that was not regarded as particularly significant by most Catholic writers of the time, but was debated intensely within Protestantism – namely, the question of predestination.

Notes

1 WA 6.513–14.

2 WA 6.513–14.

3 Martin Luther, *Ein Sermon von dem Hochwirdigen Sacrament*, 5–8; in *Luther's Works,* vol. 35 (Philadelphia, 1960), 51–2.

4 WA 6.509–12.

5 WA 6.512–13.

6 WA 6.509–12.

7 WA 6.513–14.

8 Martin Luther, *Greater Catechism*, On Infant Baptism, 53.

9 Martin Luther, *Greater Catechism*, On Infant Baptism, 83.

10 Huldrych Zwingli, *On Baptism*; CR 91.217.

11 Huldrych Zwingli, *On the Lord's Supper* (1526); CR 91.796–800.

12 Huldrych Zwingli, *On Baptism*; CR 91.218.

13 *The Schleitheim Confession of Faith* (1527), Article 1.

14 John Calvin, *Institutes of the Christian Religion,* IV.xiv.1–3.

15 Council of Trent, Seventh Session, Decree on the Sacraments, canons 1–8.

16 Council of Trent, Seventh Session, Decree on the Sacraments, canon 13.

17 Council of Trent, Thirteenth Session, Decree on the Most Holy Sacrament of the Eucharist, chapter 1.

Further Reading

Bierma, L. D., *The Doctrine of the Sacraments in the Heidelberg Catechism* (Princeton, NJ, 1999).

Brooks, P. N., *Thomas Cranmer's Doctrine of the Eucharist* (London, 1965).

Clark, F., *Eucharistic Sacrifice and the Reformation*, 2nd edn (Devon, 1981).

Elwood, C. *The Body Broken: The Calvinist Doctrine of the Eucharist and the Symbolization of Power* (New York, 1998).

George, T., "The Presuppositions of Zwingli's Baptismal Theology," in *Prophet, Pastor, Protestant: The Work of Huldrych Zwingli*, ed. E. J. Furcha and H. Pipkin (Allison Park, PA, 1984), pp. 71–87.

Gerrish, B. A., *Grace and Gratitude: The Eucharistic Theology of John Calvin* (Minneapolis, MN, 1993).

Hall, B., "*Hoc est corpus meum*: The Centrality of the Real Presence for Luther," in *Luther: Theologian for Catholics and Protestants*, ed. G. Yule (Edinburgh, 1985), pp. 112–44.

McClelland, J., *The Visible Words of God: An Exposition of the Sacramental Theology of Peter Martyr Vermigli* (London, 1957).

Rempel, J. D., *The Lord's Supper in Anabaptism: A Study in the Christology of Balthasar Hubmaier, Pilgram Marpeck, and Dirk Philips* (Scottdale, PA, 1993).

Steinmetz, D. C., "Scripture and the Lord's Supper in Luther's Theology," in *Luther in Context* (Bloomington, IN, 1986), pp. 72–84.

10

The Doctrine of Predestination

The doctrine of predestination is often thought of as being the central feature of Reformed theology. For many, the term "Calvinist" is virtually identical with "placing great emphasis upon the doctrine of predestination." For what reasons did the concept of grace, which for Luther was specifically linked with the justification of the sinner, came to refer to the sovereignty of God, especially as expressed in the doctrine of predestination? And how did this development take place? In this chapter, we shall be concerned with the various understandings of predestination that developed within the Reformation. In view of their complexity, we need to explore the background to them, in the theology both of Augustine of Hippo and the later Middle Ages.

The Background to the Reformation
Debates over Predestination

Grace is a gift, not a reward. This insight is fundamental to Augustine of Hippo's understanding of how salvation is secured. If grace were a reward, humans could purchase their salvation through good works. They could earn their redemption. Yet this, for Augustine, would be totally contrary to the New Testament proclamation of the doctrine of grace. Grace, according to Augustine, is nothing more and nothing less than a gift, reflecting the liberality of the one who gives. If grace were given in response to a human action or ability, it would be a reward, not a gift.

Reformation Thought: An Introduction, Fourth Edition. Alister E. McGrath.
© 2012 John Wiley & Sons, Ltd. Published 2012 by John Wiley & Sons, Ltd.

But God is not obliged to give the gift of grace to all people. Grace is only given to some. Augustine's defense of "the graciousness of God" partly rests on his belief that God must be free to give or withhold grace. If this insight is linked with Augustine's doctrine of sin, its full implications become clear. All of humanity is contaminated by sin, and unable to break free from its grasp. Only grace can set humanity free. Yet grace is not bestowed universally; it is only granted to some individuals. As a result, only some will be saved – those to whom grace is given. Predestination, for Augustine, involves the recognition that God withholds the means of salvation from those who are not elected.

"This is the predestination of the saints, and nothing else: the foreknowledge and preparation of the benefits of God, whereby whoever are set free are most certainly set free." Augustine emphasized that this did not mean that some were predestined to damnation. It meant that God had selected some from the mass of fallen humanity for salvation. The remainder were not, according to Augustine, actively condemned to damnation; they were merely not elected to salvation. Augustine tends (although he is not entirely consistent in this respect) to treat predestination as something that is *active* and *positive*. It is a deliberate decision to redeem on God's part. This can be described as a doctrine of "single predestination" in that God makes one electing decision – to redeem certain people. However, as his critics pointed out, this decision to redeem some was equally a decision *not* to redeem others.

This question surfaced with new force during the great predestinarian controversy of the ninth century, in which the Benedictine monk Godescalc of Orbais (c.804–c.869, also known as Gottschalk) developed a doctrine of double predestination similar to that later to be associated with Calvin and his followers. Pursuing with relentless logic the implications of his assertion that God has predestined some to eternal damnation, Godescalc pointed out that it was thus quite improper to speak of Christ dying for such individuals; if he had, he would have died in vain, for their fate would be unaffected.

Hesitant over the implications of this assertion, Godescalc proposed that Christ died *only for the elect*. The scope of his redeeming work was restricted, limited only to those who were predestined to benefit from his death. Most ninth-century writers reacted to this assertion critically. It was, however, to resurface in later Calvinism.

In the Middle Ages, predestination proved a controversial matter. The *via moderna* tended to interpret the idea as "foreknowledge." During the fourteenth century, however, the *schola Augustiniana moderna* reasserted a doctrine of double predestination. God was totally in control, and actively saved some and condemned others. This view was developed by Thomas Bradwardine at Oxford and Gregory of Rimini in Paris.

schola Augustiniana moderna Form of late medieval scholasticism which laid emphasis upon Augustine's doctrine of grace while adopting a nominalist position on the question of universals.

The Reformation debates over predestination take place against this background. Luther affirmed Augustine's emphasis on the "gratuity of grace'; however, he interpreted this primarily in terms of his doctrine of justification by faith. God gives justifying righteousness to people without the need for any merit on their part. Calvin, however, used the doctrine of predestination to affirm the graciousness of salvation, and developed a doctrine of "double predestination" similar to that of the "modern Augustinian school." It is possible that Calvin knew this approach to predestination, whether directly or indirectly.

We begin by considering Zwingli's views on predestination, which began to develop in the early 1520s.

Zwingli on the Divine Sovereignty

Zwingli began his ministry at Zurich on January 1, 1519. That ministry came close to extinction in August of that same year, when Zurich was struck by the plague. The fact that such outbreaks were commonplace in the early sixteenth century must not be allowed to obscure their seriousness. At least one in four, possibly as many as one in two, died from its effects at Zurich between August 1519 and February 1520. Zwingli's pastoral duties included the consolation of the dying, and it was perhaps inevitable that he himself should contract the disease. As death appeared to be drawing near, Zwingli seems to have been aware that whether he survived or not was a matter for God.

We possess a piece of poetry, generally referred to as the *Pestlied*, "Plague Song," dating from the autumn of 1519. In it, we find Zwingli reflecting on his destiny. We find him making no appeal to the saints for his recovery, and no suggestion that the church can in any way intercede for him. Instead, we find a rugged determination to accept whatever God has in store for him. Whatever God ordains as his lot, Zwingli is prepared to accept it: "I am your vessel, to be restored or destroyed."

It is impossible to read this poem without sensing Zwingli's self-surrender to the divine will. In fact, Zwingli survived his illness. It is probably out of this experience that his conviction arose that he was an instrument in the hand of God, to be used exclusively for God's purposes.

In an earlier chapter, we noted that Luther's difficulties concerning the "righteousness of God" were as much existential as theological (p. 119). It will be obvious that Zwingli's concern with divine providence also had a strong existentialist dimension. For Zwingli, the question of the omnipotence of God was no longer a textbook question, but an issue which had a direct bearing upon his existence. Whereas Luther's theology is, at least initially, largely shaped by his experience of God's justification of him, a sinner, Zwingli's is almost totally shaped by his sense of the absolute sovereignty of God and of humanity's total dependence upon him.

Zwingli's idea of the absolute sovereignty of God was developed in his doctrine of providence, especially in the famous sermon *De providentia*, "On Providence."

Many of Zwingli's more critical readers have noted the similarities between Zwingli's ideas and the fatalism of Seneca, and have suggested that Zwingli merely baptizes Senecan fatalism. This suggestion is lent some credence through Zwingli's interest in and reference to Seneca in *De providentia*. Whether an individual is saved or condemned is totally a matter for God, who freely makes his decision from eternity. However, it seems that Zwingli's emphasis upon the divine omnipotence and human impotence ultimately derives from his reading of St Paul, and is merely reinforced by his reading of Seneca and given existential importance through his close encounter with death in August 1519.

It is instructive to compare Luther's and Zwingli's attitudes to Scripture, which reflects their different approaches to the grace of God. For Luther, Scripture is concerned primarily with the gracious promises of God, culminating in the promise of the justification of the sinner by faith. For Zwingli, Scripture is concerned primarily with the law of God, with a code of conduct, with the demands made by a sovereign God of his people. Luther draws a sharp distinction between "law" and "gospel," whereas Zwingli regards the two as essentially the same.

It was Zwingli's growing concern with the sovereignty of God which eventually led to his break with humanism. It is notoriously difficult to say when Zwingli stopped being a humanist and started being a reformer: indeed, there are excellent reasons for suggesting that Zwingli remained a humanist throughout his life. As we saw earlier (pp. 39–40), Kristeller's definition of humanism has to do with its *methods* rather than its *doctrines*; if this definition of humanism is applied to Zwingli, he remained a humanist throughout his career. The same is true of Calvin. But, it may be objected, how can such people be thought of as humanists, when both develop such a rigorous doctrine of predestination?

It is certainly true that neither Zwingli nor Calvin could be thought of as "humanist" in the twentieth-century sense of the word – but that is irrelevant to the sixteenth century. When it is recalled that numerous writers of antiquity – such as Seneca and Lucretius – developed strongly fatalist philosophies, it can be seen that the case for treating both reformers as humanists is stronger than might have been thought. Nevertheless, it seems that at some point in his career, Zwingli changed his mind on one central presupposition shared by most of his Swiss humanist contemporaries. If Zwingli remained a humanist after this, he now embraced a somewhat different form of humanism, which many of his humanist colleagues regarded as slightly eccentric.

The program of reform initiated by Zwingli at Zurich in 1519 was essentially humanist. His use of Scripture was thoroughly Erasmian, as was his style of preaching, although his political views reflected the Swiss nationalism which Erasmus so detested. Most important for our purposes, he saw reformation as an educational process, thus echoing the views of both Erasmus and the Swiss humanist sodalities. Writing to his colleague Myconius on December 31, 1519, reviewing the achievements of his first year at Zurich, Zwingli announced that there were "more than two thousand more or less enlightened individuals in Zurich."

Yet things began to stall. In a letter of July 27, 1520, we find Zwingli apparently conceding the failure of this humanist conception of reformation: something more than the educational insights of Quintillian were needed if the Reformation was to succeed. The fate of humanity in general and the Reformation in particular is determined by divine providence. It is God, and not humanity, who is the chief actor in the reformation process. Humanist educational techniques are half-measures, incapable of dealing with the root of the problem.

This skepticism concerning the viability of the humanist reforming program was made public in March 1525, when Zwingli published his *Commentary on True and False Religion*. Zwingli attacked two presuppositions which were central to the Erasmian reforming program: the idea of "free will" (*liberum arbitrium*), which Erasmus had defended vigorously in 1524, and the suggestion that educational methods were capable of reforming corrupt, sinful humanity. What was required, according to Zwingli, was providential, divine intervention, without which true reformation was an impossibility.

The year 1525 also saw the publication of Luther's violently anti-Erasmian work *De servo arbitrio*, "On the Bondage of the Will," which also explicitly attacks Erasmus's doctrine of the "freedom of the will." Luther's work is permeated by an emphasis on the total sovereignty of God, linked with a doctrine of predestination similar to Zwingli's. Many humanists found this emphasis upon human sinfulness and divine omnipotence unacceptable, and this led to a certain alienation between Zwingli and many of his former supporters.

Some scholars have suggested that the influence of humanism may have led the Lutheran reformer Philip Melanchthon to weaken his initial commitment to a strong doctrine of predestination – a matter to which we now turn.

Melanchthon's Changing Views on Predestination

Although initially sympathetic to the idea of divine predestination developed by Luther in 1525, Philip Melanchthon (Figure 10.1) began to have hesitations about the notion in the later 1520s. His early commitment to the doctrine is evident from his comments in the 1521 edition of the *Loci Communes* ("Common Places"), in which Melanchthon declares that, in relation to spiritual matters, "since everything that happens takes place through divine predestination, the freedom of the human will is nothing." This position is restated in the 1525 edition of this work.

Yet from this point onward, a degree of hesitation becomes noticeable. One clear concern on Melanchthon's part was that the doctrine was perceived to be divisive. Melanchthon, who had a decisive role in drawing up the text of the *Augsburg Confession* (1530), omitted any discussion of this doctrine, clearly seeing it as a potential barrier to meaningful discussions with other Christian groups. Luther is known to have been unhappy with the irenic tone of this document, which is perhaps most obvious at this point.

NATVS ES ISLEBII DIVINE PROPHETA LVTHERE, IAPETI DE GENTE   PRIOR MAIORVE LVTHER
RELLIGIO FVLGET, TE DVCE PAPA IACET.   NEMO FVIT, TV PAR DOCTE MELANTHON ERAS

Figure 10.1 Double portrait of Martin Luther (1483–1546) (left) and Philip Melanchthon (1497–1560), by Lucas Cranach the Younger, oil on panel. © The Art Gallery Collection/Alamy

By 1532, it was clear that Melanchthon had moved away from Luther's view of predestination, as set out in *De servo arbitrio*. It is difficult to place Melanchthon's position on a theological map. Perhaps it is best understood as an attempt to navigate a "middle way" between **Pelagianism** on the one hand, and Luther's 1525 views on the other. Where Luther argued that God predestined people in such a way that they could not resist the divine will, Melanchthon increasingly came to see predestination in communal, rather than individual terms.

> **Pelagianism** Humans are able to merit their salvation through good works; plays down the idea of divine grace.

Where Luther held that God predestined individuals for salvation or damnation, Melanchthon came to the somewhat different view that God predestined a community for salvation – namely, the church. Whether individuals chose to respond to God's call by joining the church was up to them. Melanchthon located three causes of such a conversion: the Word, the Spirit, and the individual free will. An individual might indeed hear the Word proclaimed, and interpreted by the Holy Spirit. But the decision concerning whether they would embrace the salvation thus being offered remained theirs. In the 1535 edition of the *Loci Communes*, Melanchthon allows human beings the possibility of rejection of grace: "God precedes us, calls us, helps us, and moves us – but we must see that we do not fight against God."

The reasons for Melanchthon's change of mind remain disputed. Some see the influence of Erasmus at work; others see it as the outcome of his philosophical reflections on human freedom. Neither of these explanations is compelling.

Melanchthon appears to have come to the view that the faith that results through the Word and Spirit is *instrumental* for salvation rather than *causative* – in other words, that it does not bring about an individual's salvation, but places the individual in a position in which that individual may embrace this salvation through an informed choice.

The significance of this change of emphasis also remains disputed. Some argue that Melanchthon's development of the notion of justification in the 1530s is simply a reworking of Luther's position; others suggest that he is moving toward allowing humanity a say in whether they are justified or not. Yet there is no doubt that this matter became a hotly disputed topic after Luther's death in 1545, with Melanchthon being seen as "revisionist" by some of Luther's interpreters of the time. The later *Formula of Concord* (1577) appears to endorse a doctrine of single predestination, rather than the concept of double predestination found in the 1525 Luther, and in Calvin's *Institutes*. On this reading of things, predestination refers to "God's ordination to salvation, which does not extend simultaneously over both the godly and the wicked, but only extends over the children of God, who were elected and ordained."

Calvin on Predestination

The popular conception of Calvin's religious thought is that of a rigorously logical system centering on the doctrine of predestination. Influential though this popular image may be, it bears little relation to reality; important though the doctrine of predestination may be for later followers of Calvin (see pp. 202–4), this is not reflected in Calvin's exposition of the subject. Calvin's successors in the later sixteenth century, confronted with the need to impose method on his thought, found that his theology was eminently suited to recasting within the more rigorously logical structures suggested by the Aristotelian methodology favored by the later Italian Renaissance (p. 61). This has perhaps led to the too-easy conclusion that Calvin's thought itself possesses the systematic cast and logical rigor of later Reformed orthodoxy, and has allowed orthodoxy's preoccupation with the doctrine of predestination to be read back into the 1559 *Institutes*. Yet many would argue that there is a subtle difference between Calvin and Reformed thought as a whole at this point, marking and reflecting a significant turning point in intellectual history in general. If Calvin's followers developed Calvin's ideas, it was in response to a new spirit of the age, which regarded systematization and a concern for method as not only intellectually respectable but also highly desirable.

Calvin's thought reflects a concern with human sinfulness and divine omnipotence, a concern which finds its most complete expression in his doctrine of predestination. In his early period, Calvin appears to have held mildly humanist reforming views, perhaps similar to those of Lefèvre d'Etaples (Stapulensis). By 1533, however, he appears to have moved to a more radical position. On

November 2, 1533, Nicolas Cop, rector of the University of Paris, delivered an oration to mark the beginning of the new academic year. In the course of this, he alluded to several major themes which by then were associated with the Lutheran Reformation. Although the allusions were discreet and were mingled with substantial tracts of traditional Catholic theology, the address provoked an outcry. The rector and Calvin, who appears to have been involved in some way in drafting this oration, were obliged to flee Paris. But how and when did the young humanist become a reformer?

The question of the date and the nature of Calvin's conversion has intrigued generations of Calvin scholars, even if that intrigue has produced remarkably little in the way of concrete findings. It is generally agreed that Calvin switched from a mildly humanist reforming program to a more radical platform in late 1533 or early 1534. But we do not know why. Calvin appears to be describing his conversion at two points in his later writings, but we lack the wealth of autobiographical detail provided by Luther. It is clear, nevertheless, that Calvin understands his conversion to be due to divine providence. He asserts that he was so deeply devoted to the "superstitions of the papacy" that nothing less than an act of God could have freed him. He asserts that God "tamed his heart and reduced it to obedience." Once more, we find the emphasis characteristic of the Reformation: on the impotence of humanity and the omnipotence of God. It is these ideas which are linked and developed in Calvin's doctrine of predestination.

Although some scholars have suggested that predestination constitutes the center of Calvin's thought, it is clear that this is not the case. It is simply one aspect of his doctrine of salvation. Calvin's chief contribution to the development of the doctrine of grace is the logical rigor with which he approached it. This is best seen, perhaps, by comparing Augustine and Calvin on the doctrine.

For Augustine, humanity after the Fall is corrupt and impotent, requiring the grace of God to be redeemed. That grace is not given to all. Augustine uses the term "predestination" to refer to God's action in giving grace to some. It designates the special divine decision and action by which God grants his grace to those who are to be saved. But what, it may be asked, happens to everyone else? God passes them over, according to Augustine. He does not actively decide that they will be damned; he simply omits to save them. Predestination, for Augustine, refers only to the divine decision to redeem, not to the act of abandoning the remainder of fallen humanity.

For Calvin, logical rigor demands that God actively chooses to redeem or to damn. God cannot be thought of as doing something by default: he is active and sovereign in his actions. Therefore God actively wills the salvation of those who will be saved and the damnation of those who will not. Predestination is thus the "eternal decree of God, by which he determined what he wished to make of every individual. For he does not create all in the same condition, but ordains eternal life for some and eternal damnation for others." One of the central functions of the doctrine is to emphasize the graciousness of God. For Luther, God's graciousness is reflected in the fact that he justifies sinners, men and women who are totally unworthy of such a privilege. For Calvin, God's graciousness is demonstrated in his decision to redeem individuals irrespective of their merits: the decision to redeem an individual is made without reference to how worthy that individual might be. For Luther, God's graciousness is demonstrated in that he saves sinners *despite* their demerits; for Calvin, that graciousness is demonstrated in that he saves individuals *irrespective* of their merits. Although Luther and Calvin defend the graciousness of God in somewhat different manners, the same principle is affirmed by their respective views on justification and predestination.

Although the doctrine of predestination was not central to the thought of Calvin himself, it became the central nucleus of later Reformed theology through the influence of writers such as Peter Martyr Vermigli and Theodore Beza. From about 1570 onward, the theme of "election" came to dominate Reformed theology, and allowed an easy identification of the Reformed congregations with the people of Israel. Just as God had once chosen Israel, so he had now chosen the Reformed congregations as his people. From this moment onward, the doctrine of predestination began to assume a major social and political function – a function it did not possess under Calvin.

Calvin expounds his doctrine of predestination in Book 3 of the 1559 edition of the *Institutes of the Christian Religion*, as an aspect of the doctrine of redemption through Christ. In the earliest edition of the work (1536), it was treated as an aspect of the doctrine of providence. From the edition of 1539 onward, it is treated as a topic of importance in its own right.

Calvin's discussion of "the manner of obtaining the grace of Christ, the benefits which it confers, and the effects which result from it" presupposes that there is a possibility of redemption on account of what Christ achieved by his death on the cross. Having discussed how that death can be the basis of human redemption (see pp. 73–4), Calvin now goes on to discuss how humans can profit from the benefits which result from it. Thus the discussion shifts from the *grounds* of redemption to the manner in which it is *actualized*.

The order of the topics which follow has puzzled Calvin scholars for some time. Calvin discusses a series of matters in the following order: faith, regeneration, the Christian life, justification, predestination. On the basis of Calvin's discussion of the relation of these entities in the order of salvation, it might be expected that the order would be somewhat different, with predestination preceding justification and regeneration following justification. Calvin's ordering appears to reflect educational considerations rather than theological precision.

Calvin adopts a distinctly low-key approach to the doctrine of predestination, devoting a mere four chapters to its exposition (chapters 21–4 of Book 3). Predestination is defined as "the eternal decree of God, by which he determined what he wished to make of every person. For he does not create everyone in the same condition, but ordains eternal life for some and eternal damnation for others." Predestination is something which should induce a sense of awe within us. The *decretum horribile* is not a "horrible decree," as a crude translation, insensitive to the nuances of the Latin, might suggest; rather it is an "awe-inspiring" or "terrifying" decree.

The very location of Calvin's discussion of predestination in the 1559 edition of the *Institutes* is significant in itself. It follows his exposition of the doctrine of grace. It is only after the great themes of this doctrine – such as justification by faith – have been expounded that Calvin turns to consider the mysterious and perplexing subject of predestination. Logically, predestination ought to precede such an analysis; predestination, after all, establishes the grounds of an individual's election, and hence his or her subsequent justification and sanctification. Yet Calvin declines to be subservient to the canons of such logic. Why?

For Calvin, predestination must be considered in its proper context. It is not the product of human speculation, but a mystery of divine revelation. It has been revealed, however, in a specific *context* and in a specific *manner*. That manner relates to Jesus Christ himself, who is the "mirror in which we may behold the fact of our election." The context relates to the efficacy of the gospel proclamation. Why is it that some individuals respond to the Christian gospel and others do not? Is the failure of some to respond to be put down to some lack of efficacy, some inherent inadequacy, in that gospel? Or is there some other reason for this divergence in response? Calvin argues as follows:

> The covenant of life is not preached equally to all people, and amongst those to whom it is preached, it does not meet with the same acceptance either constantly or in equal degree . . . God does not indiscriminately adopt all to the hope of salvation, but gives to some what he denies to others.[1]

Far from being arid, abstract theological speculation, Calvin's analysis of predestination begins from observable facts. Some do, and some do not, believe the gospel. The primary function of the doctrine of predestination is to explain why some individuals respond to the gospel and others do not. It is an ex post facto explanation of the particularity of human responses to grace. Calvin's predestinarianism is to be regarded as a posteriori reflection upon the data of human experience, interpreted in the light of Scripture, rather than something which is deduced a priori on the basis of preconceived ideas concerning divine omnipotence. Belief in predestination is not an article of faith in its own right, but is the final outcome of scripturally informed reflection on the effects of grace upon individuals in the light of the enigmas of experience.

Experience, Calvin declares, indicates that God does not touch every human heart. Why not? Is this due to some failure on God's part? Or is there something wrong with the gospel, which prevents it from converting everyone? In the light of Scripture, Calvin feels able to deny the possibility of any weakness or inadequacy on the part of God or the gospel; the observable pattern of responses to the gospel reflects a mystery by which some are predestined to respond to, and others to reject, the promises of God. "Some have been allocated to eternal life, others to eternal damnation."

This, it must be stressed, is no theological innovation. Calvin is not introducing a hitherto unknown notion into the sphere of Christian theology. As we have seen the "modern Augustinian school" (*schola Augustiniana moderna*), exemplified by such leading medieval theologians as Gregory of Rimini, also taught a doctrine of absolute double predestination – that God allocates some to eternal life, others to eternal condemnation, without any reference to their merits or demerits. Their fate rests totally upon the will of God, rather than their individualities. Indeed, it is possible that Calvin has knowingly appropriated this aspect of late medieval Augustinianism, which certainly bears an uncanny resemblance to his own teaching.

Salvation thus lies outside the control of the individual, who is powerless to alter the situation. Calvin stresses that this selectivity is not in any way peculiar to the matter of salvation. In every area of life, he argues, we are forced to reckon with the mystery of the inexplicable. Why is it that some are more fortunate than others in life? Why does one person possess intellectual gifts denied to another? Even from the moment of birth, two infants may find themselves in totally different circumstances through no fault of their own: one may find a full breast of milk to suck and thus gain nourishment, while another may suffer malnutrition through having to suck a breast that is nearly dry. For Calvin, predestination is merely a further instance of a general mystery of human existence, in which some are inexplicably favored with material or intellectual gifts which are denied to others. It raises no difficulties which are not already presented by other areas of human existence.

Does not this idea of predestination imply that God is dispensed from common notions of goodness, justice, or rationality? Although Calvin specifically repudiates the conception of God as an absolute and *arbitrary* power, his discussion of predestination raises the specter of a God whose relationship to his creation is whimsical and capricious and whose conception and exercise of power are not bound to any law or order. At this point, Calvin clearly aligns himself with the late medieval discussion of this contentious issue, particularly within the *via moderna* and the *schola Augustiniana moderna*, concerning the relation of God to the established moral order. God is not subject in any sense to law; for this would place law above God, an aspect of creation – or even something outside God *prior* to creation – above the Creator. God is outside the law, in that God's will is the foundation of existing conceptions of morality. These terse statements reflect one of Calvin's clearest affinities with the late medieval voluntarist tradition.

In the end, Calvin argues that predestination must be recognized to rest in the inscrutable judgments of God. We cannot know why God elects some and condemns others. Some scholars have suggested that this position may reveal the influence of late medieval discussions of the "absolute power of God" (*potentia Dei absoluta*), by which a whimsical or arbitrary God is perfectly at liberty to do whatever God pleases, without being obliged to justify those actions.

This suggestion, however, rests on a serious misunderstanding of the role of the dialectic between the two powers – absolute and ordained – of God in late medieval thought. God must be free to choose whom God wills, otherwise God's freedom is compromised by external considerations and the Creator becomes subject to the creation. Nevertheless, God's decisions reflect God's wisdom and justice, which are upheld, rather than contradicted, by the fact of predestination.

Far from being a central premise of Calvin's theological "system" (a quite inappropriate term, in any case), predestination is thus an ancillary doctrine, concerned with explaining a puzzling aspect of the consequences of the proclamation of the gospel of grace. Yet, as Calvin's followers sought to develop and recast his thinking in the light of new intellectual developments, it was perhaps inevitable (if this lapse into a potentially predestinarian mode of speaking may be excused) that alterations to his structuring of Christian theology would occur.

Predestination in Later Reformed Theology

As noted earlier, it is not correct to speak of Calvin developing a "system" in the strict sense of the term. Calvin's religious ideas, as presented in the 1559 *Institutes*, are *systematically arranged* on the basis of pedagogical considerations; they are not, however, *systematically derived* on the basis of a leading speculative principle. Calvin regarded biblical exposition and systematic theology as virtually identical, and refused to make the distinction between them which became commonplace after his death.

From about the 1570s, a new concern for method – that is, the systematic organization and coherent deduction of ideas – gained momentum within Genevan theological circles. Reformed theologians, particularly in Germany, found themselves having to defend their ideas against both Lutheran and Catholic opponents. Aristotelianism, regarded with a certain degree of suspicion by Calvin himself, was now seized upon as an ally. It became increasingly important to demonstrate the internal consistency and coherence of the Reformed construal of the Christian faith. Above all, the rationality of faith became an increasingly important issue in the war of words between the Reformed churches on the one hand, and their Lutheran and Catholic rivals on the other. As a result, many Reformed writers turned to Aristotle, in the hope that his writings on method might provide hints as to how their theology might be placed upon a firmer rational foundation.

Four characteristics of the new approach to theology which began to emerge around this time may be noted:

1   Human reason was assigned a major role in the exploration and defense of Reformed theology.
2   Reformed theology was presented as a logically coherent and rationally defensible system, derived from syllogistic deductions based on known axioms. In other words, theology began from first principles, and proceeded to deduce its doctrines on their basis.
3   Theology was understood to be grounded in Aristotelian philosophy, particularly Aristotelian insights into the nature of method; some later Reformed writers are probably better described as philosophical, rather than biblical, theologians.
4   Theology was seen as being concerned with metaphysical and speculative questions, especially as these relate to the nature of God, the divine will for humanity and creation, and above all the doctrine of predestination.

The starting point of theology thus came to be general principles, not a specific historical event. The contrast with Calvin will be clear. For Calvin, theology centered on and derived from the event of Jesus Christ, as witnessed by Scripture. It is this new concern for establishing a logical starting point for theology which enables us to understand the new importance which came to be attached to the doctrine of predestination. Calvin focused on the specific historical phenomenon of Jesus Christ and then moved out to explore its implications (that is, to use the appropriate technical language, his method was analytic and inductive). By contrast, Theodore Beza began from general principles and proceeded to deduce their consequences for Christian theology (that is, his method was synthetic and deductive).

So what general principles did Beza use as a logical starting point for his theological systematization? The answer is that he based his system on the divine decrees of election – that is, the divine decision to elect certain people to salvation and others to damnation. The rest of theology was concerned with the exploration of the consequences of those decisions. The doctrine of predestination thus assumed the status of a controlling principle.

One major consequence of this development may be noted: the doctrine of "limited atonement" or "particular redemption." (The term "atonement" is often used to refer to "the benefits resulting from the death of Christ.") Consider the following question: For whom did Christ die? The traditional answer to this question took the following form: Christ died for everyone. Yet, although his death had the potential to redeem all, it was only effective for those who chose to allow it to have this effect.

In marked contrast, later Lutheranism marginalized Luther's 1525 insights into divine predestination, preferring to work within the framework of a free human response to God, rather than a sovereign divine election of specific individuals. For later sixteenth-century Lutheranism, "election" meant a human decision to love God, not God's decision to elect certain individuals. Indeed, disagreement over the doctrine of predestination was one of the two major controversies which occupied polemical writers of both confessions for centuries thereafter (the other controversy concerned the sacraments). Lutherans never had quite the same sense of being the "elect of God," and were correspondingly modest in their attempts to expand their sphere of influence as a result. The remarkable success of "international Calvinism," by contrast, reminds us of the power of an idea to transform both individuals and groups – and the Reformed doctrine of election and predestination was unquestionably the driving force behind the great expansion of the Reformed church in the seventeenth century.

Finally, it is important to reflect on the high profile of the doctrine of predestination in intra-Protestant disputes. The need for Lutheranism and Calvinism to distinguish themselves became of no small importance in the 1560s and 1570s, especially in Germany. They were, in many respects, very similar. Both claimed to be evangelical; that is, both argued that they were rooted in the gospel (Latin *evangelium*) itself, rather than in human traditions. Both rejected more or less the same central aspects of medieval Catholicism. But despite these obvious similarities, Lutheranism and Calvinism needed to be distinguished from one another. The political situation demanded some way of placing clear blue water between the two confessions, despite their obvious similarities. German politics demanded that some simple way of identifying Lutheranism and Calvinism be developed; and the doctrine of predestination proved to be the most reliable way of distinguishing these two otherwise very similar bodies.

On most points of doctrine, Lutherans and Calvinists were in broad agreement. Yet there was one matter – the doctrine of predestination – upon which they were radically opposed. The emphasis placed upon the doctrine of predestination by Calvinists in the period 1559–1622 partly reflects the fact that this doctrine distinguished them from their Lutheran colleagues. It is therefore important to realize that the high profile of the doctrine of predestination may reflect polemical considerations, rather than the internal dynamics of Reformed theology. Few would argue that predestination stands at the center of Calvin's thought. Yet the dynamics of church debates led to this doctrine being accentuated by both its critics and its supporters, precisely because it was a reliable way of distinguishing two otherwise very similar Protestant communities.

We now turn to consider a somewhat different aspect of the question of authority, debated intensely during the Reformation period – the foundation and limits of secular political authority.

Notes

1   John Calvin, Institutes of the Christian Religion, III.xxi.1, 5.

Further Reading

Graybill, G. B., *Evangelical Free Will: Philipp Melanchthon's Doctrinal Journey on the Origins of Faith* (Oxford, 2010).

Holtrop, P. C., *The Bolsec Controversy on Predestination from 1551 to 1555* (Lewiston, NY, 1993).

Kolb, R., *Bound Choice, Election, and Wittenberg Theological Method: From Martin Luther to the Formula of Concord* (Grand Rapids, MI, 2005).

McGrath, A. E., "John Calvin and Late Medieval Thought. A Study in Late Medieval Influences Upon Calvin's Theological Thought," *Archiv für Reformationsgeschichte* 77 (1986), 58–78.

Muller, R. A., *Christ and the Decree: Christology and Predestination from Calvin to Perkins* (Grand Rapids, MI, 1988).

Penny, D. A., *Freewill or Predestination? The Battle over Saving Grace in Mid-Tudor England* (London, 1990).

Stephens, W. P., *The Holy Spirit in the Theology of Martin Bucer* (Cambridge, 1970).

Wallace, D. D., *Puritans and Predestination: Grace in English Protestant Theology, 1525–1695* (Chapel Hill, NC, 1982).

White, P. O. G., *Predestination, Policy and Polemic: Conflict and Consensus in the English Church from the Reformation to the Civil War* (Cambridge, 1992).

11

The Political Thought
of the Reformation

In an earlier chapter we noted two distinct theological views of the church associated with the Reformation, each resulting in a different sociological role for that body: the Augustinian model, which corresponds sociologically to a "church," and the Donatist model, which corresponds sociologically to a "sect" (see pp. 143–5). The magisterial reformers adopted the former model, their radical opponents the latter model.

The Radical Reformation and Secular Authority

The radical Reformation conceived of the church as an "alternative society" within the mainstream of sixteenth-century European culture. Just as the pre-Constantinian church existed within the Roman empire, yet refused to conform to its standards, so the radical Reformation envisaged itself existing parallel to, but not within, its sixteenth-century environment. For Menno Simons, the church was "an assembly of the righteous," at odds with the world. This notion of the church as a faithful remnant in conflict with the world harmonized with the Anabaptist experience of persecution by the forces of Antichrist, personified in the magistracy.

The radical Reformation was generally hostile to the use of coercion, and advocated a policy of non-resistance. Exceptions to this rule may be noted: for example, Balthasar Hubmaier regarded the coercive powers of government (such as the prerogative to engage in warfare and capital punishment) as something of

Reformation Thought: An Introduction, Fourth Edition. Alister E. McGrath.
© 2012 John Wiley & Sons, Ltd. Published 2012 by John Wiley & Sons, Ltd.

a necessary evil, and held that Christians could hold office as magistrates without compromising their integrity. But this view was not typical of Anabaptism as a whole, which regarded the swearing of oaths, the use of coercive force, and the authority of the magistrate as Satanic. Jakob Hutter gave this apolitical stance a theological justification through an appeal to the example of Christ: "As all can see, we have no physical weapons, such as spears or muskets. We wish to show, by our words and deeds, that we are true followers of Christ." Hans Denck appealed to the meekness of Christ and his silence before his accusers in declaring that "force is not an attribute of God."

The clearest statement of the general Anabaptist attitude toward secular authority may be found in the Schleitheim Confession (1527), the sixth and seventh articles of which explain and justify the policy of non-involvement in secular affairs and non-resistance to secular authorities. Coercion has its place "outside the perfection of Christ" (that is, outside the radical community); inside that community, however, physical force has no place.

> The sword is ordained of God outside the perfection of Christ . . . It is not appropriate for a Christian to serve as a magistrate, for the following reasons. The government magistracy is according to the flesh, but the Christian's is according to the Spirit. Their houses and dwelling places are in this world, but the Christian's is in heaven; their citizenship is of this world, but the Christian's is in heaven; the weapons of their war and conflict are physical, and against the flesh, whereas the Christian's weapons are spiritual, against the fortification of the devil. The worldlings are armed with steel and iron, but the Christian is armed with the armour of God, with truth, righteousness, peace, faith, salvation and the word of God.[1]

Anabaptism maintained discipline within its communities through "the ban," a means by which church members could be excluded from Anabaptist congregations. This means of discipline was regarded as being essential to the identity of a true church. Part of the Anabaptist case for radical separation from the mainstream churches (a practice which continues to this day among the Amish of Lancaster County, Pennsylvania, and elsewhere) was the failure of those churches to maintain proper discipline within their ranks. The Schleitheim Confession grounded its doctrine of the ban on Christ's words, as they are recorded in Matthew 18:15–20:

> The ban shall be used in the case of all those who have given themselves to the Lord, to walk in his commandments, and with all those who are baptized into the one body of Christ and are called brothers or sisters, yet who lapse on occasion, and inadvertently fall into error and sin. Such people shall be admonished twice in secret, and on the third occasion, they shall be disciplined publicly, or banned according to the command of Christ (Matthew 18).[2]

The "ban" was seen as being both deterrent and remedial in its effects, providing both an incentive for banned individuals to amend their way of life and a disincentive for others to imitate them in their sin. The Polish *Racovian Catechism* (1605) lists five reasons for maintaining rigorous discipline within Anabaptist communities, most of which reflect its policy of radical separation:

1   So that the fallen church member may be healed, and brought back into fellowship with the church.
2   To deter others from committing the same offense.
3   To eliminate scandal and disorder from the church.
4   To prevent the Word of the Lord falling into disrepute outside the congregation.
5   To prevent the glory of the Lord being profaned.

Despite its pastoral intentions, the "ban" often came to be interpreted harshly, with congregation members often avoiding all social contact with both the banned individual and his or her family.

Where the majority of the radicals, with their rigorous views on church membership, had no time for compromises with the state or city authorities, however, the magisterial reformers depended on precisely such compromises. Indeed, as we have seen, the very phrase "magisterial Reformation" points to the close cooperation of reformer and magistrate in the propagation and defense of the Reformation.

We have already noted (pp. 31–2) the rise in power of secular governments throughout Europe in the early sixteenth century. The Concordat of Bologna, for example, had given to the king of France the right to appoint all the senior clergy of the French church. The ascendancy of the Catholic church in both France and Spain was maintained primarily through state interests. The political realities of the early sixteenth century demanded a similar liaison between the states or cities and the churches of the Protestant Reformation. So threatening and destabilizing were their social attitudes that radical congregations and thinkers were gradually excluded from the cities, forced into the countryside, and denied any political or social authority.

For example, the Thirty-Nine Articles (1571), which laid down the principles governing the reformed Church of England during the reign of Elizabeth I, explicitly stipulate that "the laws of the realm may punish Christians with death for heinous and grievous offences. It is lawful for Christians, at the command of the magistrate, to carry weapons and serve in wars" (Article 37). The Anabaptist position was thus rigorously excluded. In this, the English state church followed a pattern that was being established throughout Europe.

It must not be thought, however, that the magisterial reformers were political puppets: their understanding of the role of the city or state authorities in reforming the church reflects their theological presuppositions. In what follows, we shall examine the political views of the four major magisterial reformers: Luther, Zwingli, Bucer, and Calvin.

Luther's Doctrine of the Two Kingdoms

The medieval period witnessed the development of the "doctrine of the two estates": the *temporal* and the *spiritual*. According to this view, actively promoted by supporters of papal political maneuvering, the clergy belonged to the "spiritual estate" and the laity to the "temporal" estate. These two estates, or realms or spheres of authority, were quite distinct. Although the spiritual estate could (and did) intervene in the affairs of the temporal estate, the latter was not permitted to interfere with the former. Underlying this theory is a long history of conflict between papal and secular authority, particularly during the period of the Avignon papacy.

Viewed pragmatically, this understanding of the spheres of influence of the secular and ecclesiastical powers meant that the reformation of the church was a matter purely for that church itself: laity, whether peasants or secular rulers such as the emperor himself, did not possess the necessary authority to bring about the reform of the church. As we saw earlier (p. 107), this was the first of the "three walls" of the modern-day Jericho which Luther proposed to demolish. Convinced that the church had become entrenched in corrupted views of priesthood, Luther developed the doctrine of the "priesthood of all believers" in his famous reforming treatise of 1520, *To the Christian Nobility of the German Nation*:

> It is pure invention that pope, bishop, priests and monks are called the spiritual estate, while princes, lords, artisans and farmers are called the temporal estate . . . All Christians are truly of the spiritual estate, and there is no difference between them except that of office . . . We are all consecrated priests through baptism, as St Peter says in 1 Peter 2:9.[3]

While fully recognizing the need for administration within the church, Luther insists that the difference is purely one of office, not status.

Medieval Catholicism recognized a fundamental distinction between the "spiritual estate" (that is, the clergy, whether they were priests, bishops, or popes) and the "temporal estate" (that is, everyone else). Luther declared this distinction to be null and void, a human invention rather than an ordinance of God:

> All Christians are truly of the spiritual estate, and there is no difference among them except that of function [*Amt*]. Paul says in 1 Corinthians 12:12–13 that we are all one body, with every member having his or her own function by which he or she serves the others. This is because we have one baptism, one gospel and one faith, and are all Christians, just the same as each other; for baptism, gospel and faith alone make us spiritual and a Christian people. . . . And so it follows that there is no true fundamental difference between laypersons and priests, between princes and bishops, between those living in monasteries and those living in the world. The only difference has nothing to do with status, but with the function and work which they perform.[4]

There was no place in Christianity for any notion of a professional class within the church which is in a closer spiritual relationship to God than their fellows.

Nevertheless, not everyone could be allowed to *act* as a priest. Luther's doctrine of the priesthood of all believers did not entail the abolition of a professional ministry. His fundamental principle was that all Christians share the same priestly status (*Stand*) on account of their baptism; they may, however, exercise different functions (*Amt*) within the community of faith, reflecting their individual God-given gifts and abilities. To be a minister is to stand alongside one's fellow Christians, sharing their status before God; nevertheless, those fellow believers have recognized the gifts of that individual, and invited him or her, directly or indirectly, to exercise that ministerial function amongst them:

> Although we are all priests, this does not mean that all of us may preach, teach and exercise authority. Certain ones from within the community must be selected and set apart for such office. Anyone who holds such an office is not a priest by virtue of that office, but is a servant of all the others, who are just as much priests as he is.
>
> The recognition of the *equality* of all believers thus does not imply the *identity* of all believers.[5]

"Through baptism, we are all consecrated priests." All believers, by virtue of their baptism, belong to the spiritual estate. (Notice that Luther is able to assume that all Germans are baptized.) "Christ does not have two bodies, one temporal, the other spiritual. There is but one head and one body." Laity thus have a right to demand a general council to reform the church; and, tongue placed firmly in his cheek, Luther reminds his readers that it was the Roman emperor Constantine (a layperson if ever there was one) who was responsible for calling the most important council in the history of the church (the Council of Nicaea, which met in 325). Why should not the German nobility call for a council to reform the church in 1520?

Having thus abolished the medieval distinction between the "temporal" and "spiritual" estates, Luther proceeds to develop an alternative theory of spheres of authority, based upon a distinction between the "Two Kingdoms," or the "Two Governments." It is this doctrine of the "Two Kingdoms" which is central to Luther's social thought and with which we are concerned in the present section.

Luther draws a distinction between the "spiritual" and the "worldly" government of society. God's *spiritual* government is effected through the Word of God and the guidance of the Holy Spirit. The believer who "walks by the Spirit" needs no further guidance from anyone as to how he should act: he is perfectly in tune with the divine will, and acts accordingly. Just as a good tree needs no instructions to bear fruit, so the true believer needs no legislation to guide his conduct. Just as a tree bears fruit naturally, so the believer naturally acts morally and responsibly. Luther also emphasizes the difference between human and divine conceptions of "righteousness" or "justice," a theme characteristic of his "theology of the cross." God's standards of justice call those of the world into question.

God's *worldly* government is effected through kings, princes, and magistrates, through the use of the sword and the civil law. These have no authority in matters of doctrine. "When temporal princes and lords try to change and be master of the Word of God in such a high-handed manner – something which is as forbidden to them as it is to the meanest beggar – they are seeking to be God themselves." Their proper sphere of authority concerns the affairs of the world, the things of Caesar rather than of God. Although these temporal rulers are involved in the secular world, they are nevertheless performing the work of God. Whether these princes or magistrates are true believers or not, they still perform a divine role (Luther appeals to Romans 13:1–7 and 1 Peter 2:13–14 in support of this contention). God has ordained that order shall be imposed upon creation, for the maintenance of peace and the repression of sin. There are three hierarchies, or "orders," within a Christian society: the household or family, with the father as the head (reflecting the paternalism of Luther's age); the princes and magistrates, who exercise secular authority; and the clergy, who exercise spiritual authority. All these are founded on the Word of God, and reflect the divine will for the structuring and preservation of the worldly realm.

Luther recognizes that his Augustinian view of the relation between church and society implies that there are "mouse droppings among the peppercorns, tares among the grain": in other words, the good and the evil coexist within both church and society. This is not to say that "good" and "evil" cannot be *distinguished*: it is simply to recognize, with the pragmatism for which Luther is noted, that they cannot be *isolated*. The good can be ruled by the Spirit, but the evil must be ruled by the sword. Luther insisted that the great masses of baptized Germans were not true Christians. Thus Luther recognized that it was utterly unrealistic to hope that society could be governed by the precepts of the **Sermon on the Mount**. Perhaps everyone ought to be so governed – but not everyone would be. Spirit and sword must coexist in the government of a Christian society.

Sermon on the Mount Standard way of referring to Christ's moral and pastoral teaching in the specific form which it takes in Matthew 5–7.

Nevertheless, Luther's social ethic seems to suggest that two totally different moralities exist side by side: a private Christian ethic, reflecting the rule of love embodied in the Sermon on the Mount and challenging human conceptions of righteousness; and a public morality, based upon force, which endorses human conceptions of righteousness. Christian ethics is grounded in the doctrine of justification by faith alone, in which the believer gratefully responds to God's grace with good works; public morality is based upon coercion, in which the citizen obeys the law for fear of the consequences of failing to do so. The Sermon on the Mount is a splendid moral guide for the individual Christian, but its moral demands are not necessarily applicable to the public morality. It will therefore be obvious that Luther puts the Christian who is also a public figure (such as a prince or a magistrate) in the virtually impossible position of having to employ two different ethics, one for his private life, the other for his public life.

God thus governs the church by the Holy Spirit through the gospel in a manner from which all coercion is excluded; and governs the world by the sword of secular authority. The magistrates are entitled to use the sword to enforce the law, not because violence is inherently justified, but on account of the intractability of human sinfulness. Were there no human sin, no coercion would be necessary: all would recognize the wisdom of the gospel, and modify their behavior accordingly. God established political order in order to restrain human greed and wickedness, themselves the result of sinful inclinations.

The spiritual authority of the church is thus persuasive, not coercive, and concerns the individual's soul, rather than his body or goods. The temporal authority of the state is coercive, rather than persuasive, and concerns the individual's body and goods, rather than his soul. Luther's fundamental criticism of the medieval papacy was that it had confused these two separate realms of authority, especially through its system of canon law. Although Luther carefully distinguished these two realms of authority, in terms of both their scope and their source, he insisted that they are not in opposition to one another, but are merely different aspects of the same thing – God's rule over his fallen and sinful world.

Luther's political theology is thus pragmatic. Recognizing the political realities of his situation at Wittenberg and his reliance on the political support of the German princes, Luther reinforced their political authority by grounding it in divine providence. God governs the world, including the church, through the princes and magistrates. The church is in the world, and so must submit itself to the order of the world.

But what happens, it may reasonably be asked, if the state becomes tyrannical? Have Christians the right to intervene and actively oppose the state? Luther thought not, at least in the 1520s. As the Peasants' Revolt loomed on the horizon, however, it seems that the deficiencies of his political thought became obvious. Secular rulers possessed their office by divine right. Thus, in his *Admonition to Peace* (1525), Luther criticized the German lords for their tyranny over the peasants, but upbraided the peasants for even contemplating revolt against their masters. "The fact that the rulers are wicked and unjust does not excuse disorder and rebellion, for the punishing of wickedness is not the responsibility of everyone, but of the worldly rulers who bear the sword." The peasants, by assuming the role of judges and avenging what they regarded as wrong, were in effect assuming the place of God.

This understanding of the relation of church and state has been the object of intense criticism. Luther's social ethic has been described as "defeatist" and "quietist," encouraging the Christian to tolerate (or at least fail to oppose) unjust social structures. Luther preferred oppression to revolution. It also seemed to draw a cynical distinction between a private morality which is identifiably Christian

Figure 11.1 German Peasants' War (1524–26), armed peasants. Woodcut to a leaflet with the peasants' 12 articles, 1525. © INTERFOTO/Alamy

and a public morality which is not. The Peasants' War seemed to show up the tensions within Luther's social ethic: the peasants were supposed to live in accordance with the private ethic of the Sermon on the Mount, turning the other cheek to their oppressors – while the princes were justified in using violent coercive means to reestablish social order (Figure 11.1). And although Luther maintained that the magistrate had no authority in the church, except as a Christian believer, the technical distinction involved was so tenuous as to be unworkable. The way was opened to the eventual domination of the church by the state, which was to become a virtually universal feature of Lutheranism. The failure of the German church to oppose Hitler in the 1930s is widely seen as reflecting the inadequacies of Luther's political thought. Even Hitler, it appeared to some German Christians, was an instrument of God.

David C. Steinmetz has helpfully identified five central premises underlying Luther's confused political theology:

1 Christian ethics, but not human morality, is grounded in the doctrine of justification by faith alone.
2 All Christians have a civic and social responsibility to perform. Some Christians may discharge these responsibilities by holding public office.

3 The morality of the Sermon on the Mount applies to the life of every Christian, but not necessarily to every decision which Christians may make if they hold public office.
4 The state has been divinely ordained to achieve certain purposes, which the church cannot, and should not attempt to, achieve. In other words, their spheres of influence and authority are different, and must not be confused.
5 God rules the church through the gospel, but is obliged to rule the sinful world through law, wisdom, natural law, and coercion.[6]

Luther was no political thinker, and his limited and deficient experiments in this field are best regarded as an attempt to accommodate himself to the political realities of his time. For the consolidation of the German Reformation, the full support of the German princes and magistrates was essential. Luther appears to have been prepared to lend these rulers religious dignity in return for their continued support for the Reformation. The end justified the means.

Luther appealed to a specific power group; but had a different group held political power, he would almost certainly have appealed to that group instead and justified *its* existence. Thus Luther was clearly a monarchist, whereas Zwingli argued that all monarchs eventually degenerate into tyrants. For Zwingli, aristocracy (even when it degenerates into oligarchy) is to be preferred to monarchy. One wonders what would have happened if Luther had been a reformer in oligarchical Zurich and Zwingli in electoral Wittenberg. The "ifs" of history, even if unanswerable, are intriguing.

It is interesting to note the position of Martin Bucer on this point. Bucer's sphere of influence was twofold. The pioneer of the Reformation in the great imperial city of Strasbourg, he ended his days in Cambridge attempting to give a new sense of direction to the faltering English Reformation. Now Strasbourg was governed by a city council, and England by a monarch. Since Luther's theology reflected a monarchical and Zwingli's an oligarchical form of government, Bucer was obliged to tread warily, lest he offend either one of two governments. It is thus perhaps no cause for surprise that we find Bucer affirming that the precise form of temporal authority adopted is a matter of indifference. Temporal authority may be individual or corporate, based on a hereditary monarchy or an elected assembly: the essential point is that whoever exercises such authority should be godly, open to the guidance of the Holy Spirit.

A similar position was developed by John Calvin in the 1536 *Institutes*: any form of government whatever – whether it be a monarchy, an aristocracy, or a democracy – is equally legitimate and equally competent to perform its divinely appointed office. Perhaps aware of the impact his ideas were to have in a variety of different political contexts, Calvin affirmed (despite his obvious misgivings concerning monarchy) that a scripturally determined understanding of the nature of the church was consistent with whatever form of civil government happened to be established.

Zwingli on the State and Magistrate

We have already noted the strong link in Zwingli's thought between the church and state, evident in his baptismal views (see pp. 179–81). From the beginning of his reforming ministry at Zurich, Zwingli appears to have recognized the political realities of the situation: Zurich could not be reformed without the consent and active involvement of the city council. For Zwingli, "church" and "state" were simply different ways of looking at the city of Zurich, rather than separate entities. The life of the state does not differ from the life of the church, in that each demands what the other demands. Both the preacher and the ruler are under obligation to God, in that they have both been entrusted with establishing the rule of God over the city. Zwingli regarded Zurich as a theocracy, in the sense that the whole life of the city community was under the rule of God: minister and magistrate alike were charged with expounding and enforcing that rule.

There are obvious parallels between the theories of government associated with Luther and with Zwingli. It may be helpful to list them:

1 Both maintained that the need for such government is the result of sin. As Zwingli put it, "If everyone rendered to God what they owed him, we should need neither prince nor ruler – indeed, we should never have left paradise."

2 Both recognized that not all members of the community were Christians. While the proclamation of the gospel may convert some, there are those who will never be converted. (Both Luther and Zwingli, it must be remembered, were strongly predestinarian in their views: see pp. 191–5.) As government takes in the whole community, it is legitimate for the government to use force where necessary.

3 Those who exercise authority within the community do so with the authority of God. God exercises his authority through the magistrates.

4 Against the radicals, both Luther and Zwingli insisted that Christians could hold public office. For the radicals, holding such office involved political compromises which corrupted the Christian. For Luther and Zwingli, by contrast, a believer was more likely to exercise power responsibly and charitably than anyone else, and should therefore be encouraged to gain office for that reason. Zwingli insisted that, without the fear of God, a ruler would become a tyrant. Where Plato wished his kings to be philosophers, Zwingli wished his aristocrats to be Christians.

5 Both Luther and Zwingli drew a distinction between private and public morality. The commands of the Sermon on the Mount (for example, not to resist evil, or to turn the other cheek) apply to the Christian as a private individual, but not to the Christian as the holder of a public office. Thus Zwingli pointed out that Christ himself attacked the Pharisees, and did not turn his other cheek when brought before the high priest.

6 Both Luther and Zwingli distinguished the types of righteousness associated
   with the Christian and the state. Zwingli argued that the gospel is concerned
   with the promotion of inner righteousness, arising from the transformation
   of the individual through the hearing of the gospel, whereas the state is concerned with the promotion of outward righteousness, arising from the individual being constrained to keep the law. The gospel alters human nature,
   whereas the state merely restrains human greed and evil, having no positive
   power to alter human motivation. Luther emphasized the tension between
   human and divine righteousness; whereas Zwingli stated that divine righteousness is interior and human righteousness exterior, Luther suggested that
   they are also mutually contradictory. The righteousness which Christians are
   commanded to seek is diametrically opposed to the more cynical standards
   of righteousness employed by rulers.

For Zwingli, the city council derived its authority from God, whose Word it was
not in a position to judge or challenge. This insight appears to have been of
theoretical, rather than practical, importance. The First Zurich Disputation of
January 19, 1523 (see p. 109) effectively ensured that the city council was recognized as having the authority to interpret Scripture. While Zwingli clearly
understood the council to be *under* the Word of God, the city council appears
to have maneuvered itself into a position by which it was really *over* the Word of
God. Whoever interprets the Word of God in effect has authority over it –
whether that interpreter be the pope or a city council. This led to the complaint
that Zwingli allowed "matters which ought to belong to the whole church to be
dealt with by the Two Hundred (the city council) when the church of the whole
city and neighborhood is seven thousand, more or less."

But what form of government was to be preferred? Zwingli draws a distinction
between three political systems: monarchy, oligarchy, and democracy. In his
discussion of these systems, he displays a political realism which seems to owe
virtually nothing to any specifically Christian insight. In many ways, his discussion
of the question reflects similar discussions of antiquity, with an emphasis on
historical rather than theoretical analysis. Monarchy is an arbitrary form of government, in which the ruler is selected on the basis of inadequate criteria.
Monarchs are prone to degenerate into tyrants, and are difficult to replace when
inadequate. And, Zwingli points out, there are obvious shortcomings in entrust-
ing authority to one single individual. Democracy, by contrast, places authority
in the hands of the whole people, but can easily degenerate into chaos. When
this happens, individual interests are placed above those of the state, and the res
publica suffers as a result. Aristocracy, however, possesses both a representative
element and an accountability to the people, avoiding the shortcomings of both
monarchy and democracy. It is the *via media* between these two deficient forms
of government.

This position contrasts sharply with Luther's preference for a monarchical form
of government. It also allows us to understand Zwingli's more positive attitude

toward the resistance of tyranny. For Zwingli, tyranny was not to be tolerated. Although he occasionally denied that rulers may legitimately be killed, there are a number of passages which clearly imply that tyrannicide is acceptable. Christians are under an obligation to obey God, rather than human beings – and that obedience may involve deposing or killing rulers. Zwingli was careful to lay down the conditions under which a ruler may be deposed. Murder, war, and uprising were declared to be unacceptable; peaceable means must be employed wherever possible. Since Zwingli favored an aristocratic (or, at worst, an oligarchic) form of government, he was able to point to a number of peaceful means by which such rulers might be deposed – for example, by the election of a replacement. Luther's situation was somewhat different: one disadvantage of a monarchical system of government is that the prince rules for life, making regicide one of the few options available for his removal. Zwingli, however, was able to advocate less drastic electoral means of deposing unsatisfactory rulers, thus protecting more tender consciences.

Bucer on Magistrate and Ministry

The consolidation of the magisterial Reformation owed much to the close integration of the roles of preacher and magistrate in the imperial city of Strasbourg under Martin Bucer. Having been expelled from Geneva in 1538, it was to Bucer's Strasbourg that Calvin turned to receive both political refuge and ecclesiastical experience. While Bucer's relationship with the city council of Strasbourg was occasionally stormy, he nevertheless regarded that council as entrusted with a God-given task to reform the church. In view of the importance of Bucer's views, we may consider them before passing on to consider those of Calvin himself.

Bucer points out that in the New Testament period, the temporal authorities were non-Christian. God was therefore obliged to use other means – such as the agency of the Holy Spirit – to preserve and develop his church. But, Bucer argues, such has been the impact of the Christian faith since those early days that temporal authorities are now themselves Christian: God therefore uses such authorities in the sixteenth century, even if he used different ones in the first.

Whereas it is the task of the minister to preach the Word of God, it is that of the magistrate to govern according to it. This might seem to suggest that preachers have authority over magistrates: however, in that the magistrates were responsible for the appointment of preachers, the possibility of tension was lessened. For Bucer, it was axiomatic that the magistracy was godly and open to the promptings of the Holy Spirit. In common with most urban Reformed theologians, Bucer regarded "city" and "church" as so closely linked that this natural instinct for civic self-preservation directly advanced the cause of the Reformation.

Calvin on Magistrate and Ministry

Bucer's ideas were developed by John Calvin on his return from Strasbourg to Geneva in September 1541. The rulers of Geneva, having broken free from external rule in 1536, found themselves without any coherent system of church order. All the ecclesiastical changes of the 1530s had been destructive, eventually leading to something approaching chaos. A comprehensive set of ecclesiastical ordinances was required, and Calvin was recalled to Geneva to help with this task. The magistrates were prepared to let Calvin have his way (within reason) in organizing the Genevan church, provided that their civil authority was not affected (a principle which they eventually regarded as compromised by Calvin's views on the role of the Consistory: see pp. 155–7).

Calvin's original idea was that ecclesiastical discipline should rest with the Consistory, made up of pastors and 12 magistrates of their choice. This Consistory would have the right, for example, to excommunicate anyone whose moral conduct or religious beliefs were unacceptable. The magistrates, scenting a challenge to their authority, vigorously affirmed their right over all temporal matters. A compromise was reached, which Calvin interpreted as a recognition of the right of the Consistory to recommend excommunication, and which the magistrates interpreted as a recognition of their authority to excommunicate. The history of Geneva over the next 15 years indicates how unsatisfactory this compromise turned out to be.

For all the compromises made in light of the political realities of Geneva, the fundamental basis of Calvin's understanding of the relation of church and state is clear. While the political authority must not be allowed to abolish the spiritual, the Anabaptist view that the spiritual authority abrogates the political was unequivocally rejected. When the present order passes away at the Day of Judgment, there will be no need for a political authority – but while human beings remain tied to this earth, the political authority is essential in order "to foster and maintain the external worship of God, to defend sound doctrine and the condition of the church, to adapt our conduct to human society, to form our manners to civil justice, to reconcile us to one another, to cherish peace and common tranquility."

Calvin thus assigned to the magistrates two roles: the maintenance of political and ecclesiastical order and the provision of the teaching of right doctrine. Both the political and spiritual authorities were to use the distinctive resources committed to them by God for the disciplining of the same body of people:

For the church has not the right of the sword to punish or restrain, has no power to coerce, no prison nor other punishments which the magistrate is wont to inflict. Then the object in view is not to punish the sinner against his will, but to obtain a profession of penitence by voluntary chastisement. The two things, then, are widely different, because neither does the church assume anything to herself which is proper to the magistrate, nor is the magistrate competent to do what is done by the church. (*Institutes*, IV.xi.3)

The political authority was to use its right to coercion (generally through the threat of exile or execution; Geneva did not have a long-term prison) and the spiritual authority its teaching ministry for the promotion of virtue. Calvin also stated that the ministry had the right to explain to the magistracy what the Word of God required in a given situation, suggesting that the ministry was the legislative and the magistracy the executive arm of the Genevan theocracy. However, the magistracy appears to have felt able to resist the ministry sufficiently frequently to weaken the latter's role in the government of the city.

For Calvin, both magistrates and ministers were committed to the same task, the difference between them lying in the tools they had available and their respective spheres of authority. Their responsibilities were complementary rather than competitive. Both magistrates and ministers were agents and servants of the same God, committed to the same cause, differing only in their spheres and means of action. Where the Anabaptists regarded church discipline as a matter for the church itself, Calvin regarded it as a matter of public concern, within the legitimate authority of the magistracy. Although Calvin's Geneva was troubled more than once through tensions between the two authorities, spiritual and temporal, the strong sense of social organization which became an essential part of "Calvinism" may be traced back to the political theorizing of Calvin's Geneva. When the Puritans set foot in the New World, they brought with them not merely a religion, but a social vision, whose roots lay in a small town in modern-day Switzerland.

One further aspect of Calvin's political thought is of interest. Like Zwingli, Calvin had a profound mistrust of monarchy. Monarchs are prone to become tyrants; they are motivated by their personal concerns, rather than the well-being of their people. Even the Old Testament kings were prone to this tendency; and their sixteenth-century equivalents are worse. Although Calvin tends to condemn monarchs rather than monarchy, his misgivings concerning the very idea of absolute rule by one individual are unmistakable. The subsequent threat posed by "Calvinism" to monarchies throughout Europe, evident in the challenge to and subsequent execution of Charles I of England (1649), testifies to the subsequent importance of Genevan political theology. The relative merits of Lutheranism and "Calvinism" were often assessed on the basis of their political views, the former being regarded as monarchical, the latter as republican. The political circumstances of the founders of these religious systems seem to have become elevated into fundamental beliefs of those systems.

On the basis of the above analysis, it will be obvious that the phrase "Calvin's Geneva" is misleading. Calvin was no Genevan dictator, ruling the population with a rod of iron. He was not even a citizen of Geneva throughout his time there, and was thus denied access to political authority. His status was simply that of a pastor who was in no position to dictate to the magisterial authorities who administered the city. Indeed, those authorities retained to the end the right to dismiss Calvin, even if they chose not to exercise that right. As a member of the Consistory, he was certainly able to make representations to the magistracy on behalf of the ministers – representations which were frequently ignored, however. In any case, Calvin had no legal right to act independently of the ministry, whose collegiality he is known to have valued and respected. Calvin's influence over Geneva rested ultimately not in his formal legal standing (which was insignificant) but in his considerable personal authority as a preacher and pastor.

In this chapter, we have focused on Continental Europe. But what of other situations? What about England, where supreme secular authority was vested in the person of the king? In the following chapter, we shall consider the ideas associated with the English Reformation, and how these relate to their Continental counterparts.

Notes

1   *The Schleitheim Confession of Faith* (1527), Articles 6, 7.
2   *The Schleitheim Confession of Faith* (1527), Article 2.
3   WA 6.406–7.
4   WA 6.407–8.
5   WA 6.407–8.
6   David C. Steinmetz, "Luther and the Two Kingdoms," in *Luther in Context* (Bloomington, IN, 1986), pp. 112–25.

Further Reading

Cargill Thompson, W. D. J., "The "Two Kingdoms" and the "Two Regiments": Some Problems of Luther's *Zwei-Reiche-Lehre*," in *Studies in the Reformation: Luther to Hooker*, ed. W. D. J. Cargill Thompson (London, 1980), pp. 42–59.

Cargill Thompson, W. D. J., *The Political Thought of Martin Luther* (Brighton, 1984).

Cranz, F. E., *An Essay on the Development of Luther's Thought on Justice, Law and Society* (Cambridge, MA, 1959).

Green, R. W., ed., *Protestantism and Capitalism: The Weber Thesis and Its Critics* (Boston, MA, 1959).

Green, R. W., ed., *Protestantism, Capitalism and Social Science: The Weber Thesis Controversy* (Boston, MA, 1973).

Höpfl, H., *The Christian Polity of John Calvin* (Cambridge, 1985).

Höpfl, H., ed., *Luther and Calvin on Secular Authority* (Cambridge, 1991).

Hunt, R. N. C., "Zwingli's Theory of Church and State," *Church Quarterly Review* 112 (1931), 20–36.

Marshall, G., *Presbyteries and Profits: Calvinism and the Development of Capitalism in Scotland, 1560–1707* (Oxford, 1980).

O'Donovan, J. L., *Theology of Law and Authority in the English Reformation* (Atlanta, GA, 1991).

Skinner, Q., *The Foundations of Modern Political Thought*, 2 vols (Cambridge, 1978).

Skinner, Q., "The Origins of the Calvinist Theory of Revolution," in *After the Reformation*, ed.

B. C. Malament (Philadelphia, 1980), pp. 309–30.

Steinmetz, D. C., "Luther and the Two Kingdoms," in D. C. Steinmetz, *Luther in Context* (Bloomington, IN, 1986), pp. 112–25.

Tonkin, J., *The Church and Secular Order in Reformation Thought* (New York and London, 1971).

Torrance, T. F., *Kingdom and Church: A Study in the Theology of the Reformation* (Edinburgh, 1956).

Zaret, D., *The Heavenly Contract: Ideology and Organization in Pre-Revolutionary Puritanism* (Chicago, IL, 1985).

12

The Religious Ideas of the English Reformation

Much of the discussion in this volume has concentrated on the Reformation in Continental Europe. However, the Reformation also had an impact in England, in which it took a distinctive course. In view of the considerable interest and importance of the Reformation in England, the present chapter will consider its leading themes.

It is important to appreciate that not every part of Europe was equally influenced by the new religious ideas emerging from the crucible of the Continental Reformation. Germany was deeply affected, in a direct manner, by religious ideas; England was significantly less affected, with a more political style of Reformation developing. In view of the importance of this point, we shall consider the social role of religious ideas in a little more detail before proceeding further.

The Social Role of Religious Ideas: Germany and England

The sixteenth-century English Reformation under Henry VIII bore little relation to its German equivalent. The influential English historian F. M. Powicke (1879–1963) once remarked that "the one thing that can be said about the Reformation in England is that it was an act of State." For Powicke, "the Reformation in England was a parliamentary transaction."[1] There is enough truth in Powicke's generalization to suggest that there is a key difference between the German and English Reformations.

Reformation Thought: An Introduction, Fourth Edition. Alister E. McGrath.
© 2012 John Wiley & Sons, Ltd. Published 2012 by John Wiley & Sons, Ltd.

In Germany, there was a protracted struggle between evangelical and Catholic writers and ecclesiastics during the 1530s, as each attempted to gain influence in a disputed region and define its distinct identity. The situation in Germany became even more complicated during the 1560s and 1570s, as Calvinism began to make major inroads into previously Lutheran territory. Three major Christian denominations were now firmly established in the same area: Lutheranism, the Reformed churches, and Catholicism. All three were under major pressure to identify themselves. Lutherans were obliged to explain how they differed from Calvinists on the one hand and Catholics on the other. Thus doctrine proved the most reliable way of identifying and explaining these differences: "we believe this, but they believe that."

The period 1559–1622, characterized by a new emphasis on the need for purity of doctrine, is generally referred to as the "period of orthodoxy." Lutheran, Reformed, and Catholic churches found it necessary to define and defend themselves, a process which inevitably led to the construction of theological foundations for that definition and defense. Religious ideas were integral to church identity in Germany at that time.

The situation in England from 1530 onward was totally different. Henry VIII – and his Tudor successors – simply declared that there would be only one national church within his realm. By royal command, there would be a single Christian body in England, with the monarch as its head or "supreme governor." The reformed English church was thus under no pressure to define itself in relation to any other Christian body in the region, in that no rival ecclesial bodies were permitted. The Act of Uniformity ensured that there was only one national church.

The manner in which the English Reformation initially proceeded thus demanded no doctrinal self-definition, in that the church in England was defined socially in precisely the same way before the Reformation as after, whatever political alterations may have been introduced. This is not to say that no theological debates took place in England at the time of the Reformation; it is simply to note that they were not regarded as identity giving.

Niklas Luhmann, perhaps the most significant recent sociological writer to study the question of the social function of Christian doctrine, stresses that doctrine arises partly in response to perceived threats to the distinctive religious identity of a group, which may come about through encounters or conflict with other religious systems. Doctrine is, according to Luhmann, the self-reflection of a religious community, by which it maintains its identity and regulates its relations with other such communities. The case of Lutheranism maintaining its distinctive identity within the German territories in the face of Reformed and Catholic opposition illustrates this principle well. It will also be clear why there was no need for the emerging Reformed church in England to maintain its identity against any such internal opposition; there was none, on account of the Act of Uniformity.

The Henrician church in England thus regarded itself as sufficiently well defined as a social unit to require no further definition at the doctrinal level. The situation remained much the same under Elizabeth I. The "Elizabethan Settlement" (1559) laid down that there would be only one Christian church in England, the Church of England, which retained the religious monopoly of the pre-Reformation church, while recognizing royal, rather than papal, authority. The phrase "Church of England," as defined legally in Halsbury's *Laws of England*, makes no reference to its doctrine: the "Church of England" is regarded as continuous with the church established in England during the period 597–686. Catholicism, Lutheranism, and Calvinism – the three Christian churches fighting it out for dominance of the continent of Europe – would not be tolerated in England.

The social pressures which made religious ideas so important in the German context never really developed during the period of the English Reformation. There was thus no particular reason for the Church of England to pay much attention to doctrinal questions. Elizabeth ensured that it had no rivals in England. One of the purposes of doctrine is to divide – and there was nothing for the Church of England to divide itself from. England was insulated from the factors which made doctrine so significant a matter on the mainland of Europe in the Reformation and immediate post-Reformation periods.

Indeed, the need to ensure that all English Christians (whether inclined toward some form of Protestantism or toward Catholicism) felt reasonably at home in the Church of England led to the necessity of doctrine being played down: an emphasis on doctrine might lead to divisions within the new church and hence internal weakness. As Elizabeth tried to ensure England's safety in the dangerous world of the late sixteenth century, the last thing she wanted was an England torn apart by doctrinal differences. A divided English church would mean a divided England; and a divided England would be a weak and vulnerable England.

The social context of the Reformation thus has a significant influence on the extent to which religious ideas affected events. In Germany, such ideas proved to be enormously important; in England, considerably less so. It is only with the rise of Puritanism as a significant religious and political force in England toward the end of the sixteenth century that religious ideas began to become significant in the English situation.

Yet Germany perhaps provides a more reliable paradigm than England for understanding the enormous impact that religious ideas had within France, the Lowlands, northern Italy, or Switzerland. Cut off from mainland Europe by the North Sea and the English Channel, England enjoyed an untypical isolation from the power of the religious ideas that were sweeping through Europe and occasionally evoking wars of religion in their wake. The student of the English Reformation may perhaps be excused for gaining the impression that religious ideas played a secondary role at the time; elsewhere, the story was very different. England cannot be allowed to be the controlling paradigm for an understanding of the role and influence of religious ideas at the time.

English Humanism

Three major religious and intellectual elements may be argued to lie behind the English Reformation at the time of Henry VIII: Lollardy (see pp. 32–4), **Lutheranism**, and humanism. Each of these was involved, at least to some extent, in the generation of pressure for religious and theological change in England in the 1520s and 1530s. Our concern here is with the form of humanism that proved to be so influential in this debate.

> **Lutheranism** Religious ideas associated with Martin Luther, particularly as expressed in the *Lesser Catechism*.

Perhaps the most important center of humanism in early sixteenth-century England was the University of Cambridge, although the importance of Oxford and London must not be underestimated. Cambridge was the home of the early English Reformation, which centered on the "White Horse" circle (named after a now demolished tavern close to Queen's College), a group of individuals such as Robert Barnes who met to devour and discuss the latest writings of Martin Luther during the early 1520s. It was only to be expected that the tavern would soon be nicknamed "little Germany," just as the King Street area – once home of Cambridge's Communist Party – came to be known as "little Moscow" during the 1930s.

Since the publication of Frederick Seebohm's *Oxford Reformers* (1867), it has become part of the received tradition of English intellectual history to refer to the flowering of humanism at Cambridge and elsewhere as "the new learning." However, contemporary sources suggest that this phrase was used in the 1530s to refer to the ideas of early Protestantism. Thus Hugh Latimer's letter to William Huberdin (1531) refers to the "new learning" made available to the English church through the activities of the Protestant reformers.

English humanism, far from being an indigenous movement, was, to all intents and purposes, a foreign import. Roberto Weiss, a noted scholar of the Renaissance, has demonstrated beyond reasonable doubt that the origins of English humanism may be traced to fifteenth-century Italy. Poggio Bracciolini visited England in the 1430s, and was followed by a succession of Italian Renaissance thinkers. The University of Cambridge was prone to employ Italians – amongst whose numbers we may note Gaio Auberino, Stefano Surigone, and Lorenzo Traversagni – in the late fifteenth and early sixteenth centuries, not on account of any shortage of native English teachers, but on account of the acknowledged excellence of their Italian counterparts. Traversagni, a Franciscan friar from Savarona, delivered what appear to have been very well received lectures on rhetoric at Cambridge, which (by popular demand, we are told) soon appeared in print.

But the traffic of personnel was not unidirectional. Noted English scholars traveled to Italy to absorb the spirit of the Renaissance at first hand. John Gunthorpe and William Selling are early examples of this trend; their Italian peregrinations, dating from the first half of the fifteenth century, set the pattern for those of countless others over the next century. William Grocyn (1446–1519),

Thomas Linacre, (c.1460–1524), and John Colet (1466–1519) were all important and influential scholars of the early sixteenth century who had studied in Italy, and then advocated its teaching methods on their return to England. Having imbibed the spirit of Italian humanism, it was inevitable that they should propagate its ideals on their return to England.

Perhaps one appointment in Renaissance Cambridge stands out above all others as a witness to the receptivity of England to Renaissance ideas. In 1511, a noted humanist writer from the Lowlands was appointed to a university lectureship in divinity, which had recently been established by Lady Margaret Beaufort (the center of a circle of reformist devotion in the early sixteenth century). His name was Erasmus.

The Origins of the English Reformation: Henry VIII

Recent studies of English church life on the eve of the Reformation have pointed to its vitality and diversity. There is no doubt that there was some degree of internal dissatisfaction with the state of the English church in the late Middle Ages. Visitation records show a degree of concern being felt at episcopal level over the low quality of the clergy, and misgivings being expressed over various aspects of church life. There were also clear signs of external dissatisfaction. Hostility toward the clergy in many places, most notably in London, was the cause of much concern. Nevertheless, animosity toward the clergy was by no means universal. In parts of England – such as Lancashire and Yorkshire – the clergy were, on the whole, well liked, and there was no great enthusiasm for any radical change.

Luther's ideas began to be discussed in England in the early 1520s. Perhaps the greatest interest in his writings at this stage was among academics, particularly at Cambridge University. The "White Horse" group included some of the future leaders of the Reformation in England. Luther's doctrine of justification by faith, along with his criticisms of certain aspects of late medieval Catholicism, found considerable support in Cambridge. It is entirely possible that the extent of that appeal may have been enhanced through the influence of Lollardy, a pre-reformational movement, indigenous to England, which was severely critical of many aspects of church life (see pp. 32–4).

Nevertheless, the evidence suggests that the origins of the Reformation cannot be convincingly attributed to criticism of the late medieval church, or to Lutheran influence. These factors may well have served as catalysts to that Reformation, once it had begun. The evidence strongly points to the personal influence of Henry VIII (Figure 12.1) having been of fundamental importance to the origins and subsequent direction of the English Reformation.

The background lies in Henry's concern to ensure a smooth transition of power after his death through producing a son as heir to the English throne. His marriage to Catherine of Aragon had produced a daughter, the future queen,

Figure 12.1 Henry VIII, King of England (1509–47), portrait, 1536, by Hans Holbein the Younger (1497–1543). Resin tempera on wood, 26 × 19 cm. Lugano, Thyssen-Bornemisza Collection. Photo: akg-images/André Held

Mary Tudor. The marriage had not only failed to produce the requisite son and heir; it also reflected the political realities of an earlier generation, which saw an alliance between England and Spain as essential to a sound foreign policy. The weakness of this assumption had become clear by 1525, when Charles V declined to marry Henry's daughter by Catherine. Henry therefore began the process by which he could divorce Catherine.

Under normal circumstances, this procedure might not have encountered any formidable obstacles. An appeal to the pope to annul the marriage could have been expected to have secured the desired outcome. However, the situation was not normal. Rome was under virtual siege by the army of Charles V, and the pope (Clement VII) was feeling somewhat insecure. Catherine of Aragon was the aunt of Charles V, and it was inevitable that the pope would wish to avoid offending the emperor at such a sensitive moment. The request for a divorce failed. As if to add insult to injury, Clement VII informed Henry that he would be excommunicated if he married again.

Henry's response was to begin a program of persuasion, designed to assert both the independence of England as a separate province of the church, and the autonomy of the English king. On November 3, 1529, Henry convened a parliament which attempted to reduce the power of both church and clergy. The English clergy initially refused to concede these points, prompting Henry to undertake more severe measures in order to persuade them. The most important of these took place over the period 1530–1, during which Henry argued that the English clergy, by virtue of their support for Rome, were guilty of *praemunire* (a technical offense which can be thought of as a form of treason, in that it involves allegiance to a foreign power – namely, the papacy). With this threat hanging over them, the clergy reluctantly agreed to at least some of Henry's demands for recognition of his ecclesiastical authority.

Henry was presented with an opportunity for advancement of his aims when the Archbishop of Canterbury, William Warham, died in August 1532. Henry replaced Warham with Thomas Cranmer, who had earlier indicated his strong support for Henry's divorce proceedings. Cranmer was finally consecrated as archbishop (possibly against his will) on March 30, 1533. Meanwhile, Henry had begun an affair with Anne Boleyn. Anne became pregnant in December 1532. The pregnancy raised all kinds of legal niceties. Henry's marriage to Catherine of Aragon was annulled by an English court in May 1533, allowing Anne to be crowned queen on June 1. Her daughter, Elizabeth Tudor, was born on September 7.

Henry's divorce of Catherine immediately led to the threat of papal excommunication. Henry now determined to follow through the course of action on which he had embarked, by which his supreme political and religious authority within England would be recognized. A series of Acts were imposed in 1534. The *Succession Act* declared that the crown would pass to Henry's children. The *Supremacy Act* declared that Henry was to be recognized as the "supreme head" of the English church. The *Treasons Act* made denial of Henry's supremacy an act of treason, punishable by death. This final act led to the execution of two prominent Catholic churchmen, Thomas More and John Fisher, both of whom refused to recognize Henry as supreme head of the English church – a title which they believed belonged only to the pope.

Henry now found himself under threat of invasion from neighboring Catholic states. The mandate of restoring papal authority would have been a more than adequate pretext for either France or Spain to launch a crusade against England. Henry was thus obliged to undertake a series of defensive measures to ensure the nation's safety. These measures reached their climax in 1536. The dissolution of the monasteries provided Henry with funds for his military preparations. Negotiations with German Lutherans were begun with the object of entering into military alliances.

At this point, Lutheran ideas began to be adopted in some official formularies of faith, such as the Ten Articles. Nevertheless, this theological enthusiasm for Lutheranism appears to have been little more than a temporary political maneuver. When it became clear that there was serious opposition within England to his reforming measures, Henry backtracked. The 1543 *King's Book* shows every evidence of Henry's desire to avoid giving offense to Catholics. By the time of Henry's death in January 1547, the religious situation in England was somewhat ambivalent. Although Henry had made some concessions to Lutheranism, his own preference appears to have remained for at least some traditional Catholic beliefs and practices. For example, his will made provision for prayers to be said for his soul – despite the fact that Henry had, less than two years earlier, tried to close down the chantries, which existed for precisely this purpose!

From this brief account of the origins of the English Reformation under Henry VIII, it will be clear that there are reasons for supposing that Henry's aims were of critical importance for the genesis of that Reformation. Henry's agenda was political, and was dominated by the desire to safeguard the succession. Through a series of developments, this required a schism with Rome, and an increasingly tolerant attitude toward Lutheranism, both in Germany and in England. Yet Henry's tolerance for Lutheranism, which peaked around 1536, does not seem to have been grounded primarily on religious considerations.

This does not mean that Lutheran ideas were without influence in England. As we shall see, many significant English churchmen were sympathetic to the new ideas, and made it a matter of principle to secure a favorable hearing for them in both church and society at large. In fact, there are reasons for arguing that at least some degree of popular support for Lutheran ideas led Henry to pursue his policies in certain manners, rather than others. Indeed, at points Henry deliberately allied himself with Lutherans, in order to secure support for his programs in certain quarters. Yet Henry's religious and political maneuvering to consolidate the changes he introduced must not be allowed to obscure the fact that the *origins* of Henry's reforming policies are not themselves religious in nature.

In the end, the English Reformation has to be recognized as an act of state. The comparison with the situation in Germany is highly instructive. Luther's Reformation was conducted on the basis of a theological foundation and platform. The fundamental impetus was religious (in that it addressed the life of the church directly) and theological (in that the proposals for reform rested on a set of theological presuppositions). In England, the Reformation was primarily political and pragmatic. The reformation of the church was, in effect, the price paid by Henry (rather against his instincts) in order to secure and safeguard his personal authority within England.

The Consolidation of the English Reformation: Edward VI to Elizabeth I

With the death of Henry VIII, an important era in the English Reformation came to an end. In many ways, the first phase of the English Reformation was both driven and directed by the personal agenda of Henry, and the various compromises in which this involved him. At the time of his death in January 1547, Henry had failed to make the fundamental changes which would institutionalize his reforms. The diocesan and parish structures of England had been left virtually as they were, particularly in relation to their forms of worship. Thomas Cranmer might well have had ambitious ideas for the reform of the **liturgy** and theology of the English church; Henry VIII gave him no opportunity to pursue them.

> **liturgy** The written text of public services, especially of the Eucharist.

During the final years of Henry's reign, a subtle power struggle had developed within the court, with a clique based on Edward Seymour gradually gaining the ascendancy. The Seymour family had strongly Protestant inclinations. As Edward VI was still a child, his authority was delegated to the Privy Council, which was initially dominated by Seymour (who had by then become Duke of Somerset, and Lord Protector). The Church of England began to move in a distinctively Protestant direction. Cranmer, now able to flex his theological muscles in a manner which had been impossible under Henry VIII, began to introduce a series of reforms.

Of these, the most important is thought to be the revision of the Prayer Books in 1549 and again in 1552. The revisions proved to be of considerable importance, particularly in relation to Eucharistic theology. Yet Cranmer was also responsible for a series of further developments, designed to consolidate Protestantism. Recognizing the theological weakness of the reforms introduced to date, Cranmer invited leading Protestant theologians from Continental Europe to settle in England and give a new theological direction and foundation to the English Reformation. Peter Martyr was appointed as Regius Professor of Divinity at Oxford University, and Martin Bucer as Regius Professor of Divinity at Cambridge University. Their arrival pointed to a new determination to align the English Reformation with its European counterpart, particularly its Reformed constituency. The Forty-Two Articles (1553) drawn up by Cranmer were strongly Protestant in orientation, as was the Book of Homilies (a set of approved sermons for delivery in parish churches).

The text of the Forty-Two Articles is strongly Protestant, and resonates with the leading themes of the mainstream Reformation in Continental Europe. For example, consider Article 5, which affirms the central place of the Bible in Christian life and thought:

> Holy Scripture containeth all things necessary to salvation: so that whatsoever is neither read therein, nor may be proved thereby, although it be sometime received of the faithful as godly and profitable for an order and comeliness: yet no man ought to be constrained to believe it as an article of the Faith or repute it requisite to the necessity of salvation.[2]

John Colet had earlier declared that "in the choice and well-stored table of Holy Scripture, all things are contained that belong to the truth." This article develops this point, setting out the basic theme of the sufficiency of Scripture, a hallmark of the writings of Luther, Zwingli, and Calvin. Note how the article explicitly endorses the magisterial Reformation's interpretation of the *sola scriptura* principle: nobody is required to believe anything unless it can either be shown to be explicitly stated in the Bible or can be "proved" on the basis of what is explicitly stated.

Similarly, Article 20 sets out the two fundamental characteristics of the church indicated by Luther, and later given a more rigorous foundation by Calvin – the preaching of the gospel, and the right administration of the sacraments:

> The visible Church of Christ is a congregation of faithful men, in which the pure Word of God is preached, and the Sacraments be duly ministered according to Christ's ordinance, in all those things that of necessity are requisite to the same.[3]

Edward's early death (1553) put an end to this state-sponsored Protestantization of the English national church. Mary Tudor, who succeeded to the throne, put in place a series of measures designed to bring about a restoration of Catholicism within England. She appointed Reginald Pole – a loyal Catholic bishop deposed under Henry VIII – as Archbishop of Canterbury. The reversionary measures became particularly unpopular when Cranmer was executed by being publicly burned at Oxford.

By then, most Protestants with the ability and means to do so had fled England for refuges in Europe. Some 800 are known to have accepted exile in this way, waiting their chance to return to England and begin the Reformation all over again. Their exile in cities such as Geneva and Zurich brought them directly into contact with the leading representatives of Continental Protestantism, and in effect created a theologically literate and highly motivated fifth column that was merely awaiting an opportunity to put their ideas into practice. The famous Geneva Bible (1560) is an excellent example of the theological works that emerged from within these Protestant émigré communities.

Perhaps to their surprise, that opportunity came sooner rather than later. Mary Tudor and Reginald Pole both died on November 17, 1558. Both monarch and primate had been removed from the scene, which was now set for a radical change in direction. Elizabeth I (Figure 12.2), initially cautious in revealing her religious inclinations, soon put in place measures to establish a "Settlement of Religion," which would eventually lead to the creation of a more explicitly Protestant state church. Of particular importance was the formulation of the Thirty-Nine Articles (1563) – based largely on the earlier Forty-Two Articles – which gave a distinctive theological identity to the Church of England.

It will be clear from this analysis that theology did not play the major role in shaping the English Reformation that can be observed in, for example, the Lutheran Reformation. Yet the relative lack of influence of theology over developments cannot be taken to mean that there were no theological factors involved in the English Reformation, nor that there was an absence of theological debates at the time.

Figure 12.2 Portrait of Queen Elizabeth I, the Drewe Portrait, late 1580s, oil on panel, by George Gower (1540–96, attr. to). Private collection. Photo © Philip Mould Ltd, London/ The Bridgeman Art Library

In the following sections we shall explore two themes of the thought of the Continental Reformation which were appropriated by English theologians: the doctrine of justification by faith and the "supper strife" (the debate over the nature of the real presence in the Lord's Supper). The manner in which each debate was conducted offers important insights into the distinctive nature of the English Reformation, not least in indicating its largely derivative character. The English reformers might have added their own harmonies, but the tunes were written in Germany and Switzerland.

Justification by Faith in the English Reformation

As noted in Chapter 7, the doctrine of justification by faith was of fundamental importance to the first phase of the Reformation. The doctrine can be seen as central to Luther's own theological agenda, and unquestionably shaped the development of the Lutheran reforming movement throughout the 1520s and 1530s. So what of its development and appropriation within England?

In our discussion of the development of the doctrine of justification in the Continental Reformation, we noted the emergence of the concept of *forensic justification* (see pp. 125–7). This idea, although arguably implicit in the writings of Luther during the 1520s, was explicitly stated in the Augsburg Confession (1530). In view of the importance of this point to the appropriation of the doctrine in English Reforming circles, we may offer a summary of the distinction between Augustine's views on justification and those associated with Philipp Melanchthon. The most significant elements of these understandings have been emphasized, in order to help compare them:

> Augustine: Justification is an *internal process of making righteous*, in which the righteousness of Christ is *imparted* to us.

> Melanchthon: Justification is an *external event of being declared righteous*, in which the righteousness of Christ is *imputed* to us.

Melanchthon drew a distinction between "justification" and "regeneration" along the following lines. *Justification* is an external event in which God declares us to be righteous; *regeneration* is an internal process by which God makes us righteous.

The thinkers of the early English Reformation tended to understand justification as "being made righteous," showing a clear preference for the Augustinian rather than the Melanchthonian approach to justification. It is not clear whether this reflects a deliberate decision to reject Melanchthon's views, or an implicit assumption that, since the Reformation represented a return to Augustine, it was therefore entirely in order to define justification in Augustinian terms. Although the Lutheran position on justification was set out correctly and fully in the writings of Robert Barnes (c.1495–1540), who is known to have attended the University of Wittenberg and who was an enthusiastic advocate of Luther's views from the early 1520s onward, this proves to be the exception rather than the rule.

To illustrate this point, we may consider the Ten Articles of July 1536. These articles date from a period in which Henry VIII was actively pursuing closer relationships with German Lutherans for political reasons. It is widely accepted that the political links that were developed around this time were directly reflected in the official theological statements put out on behalf of the English church. Yet Article 5 still defines justification in essentially Augustinian terms as the forgiveness and the renewal of the individual believer, with no mention being made of the distinctive Protestant notion of the imputation of the righteousness of Christ:

> As touching the order and cause of our justification, we will that all bishops and preachers shall instruct and teach our people committed by us to their spiritual charge, that this word Justification signifieth remission of our sins, and our acceptation or reconciliation into the grace and favour of God, that is to say, our perfect renovation in Christ.[4]

The *King's Book* (1543) is widely regarded as representing a retreat from Reformation views, in the light of growing unrest within England. Henry's desire to reassure Catholics within England is clearly reflected in its view of justification, which is defined as "the making of us righteous afore God, where before we were unrighteous." This is an explicitly Augustinian definition, suggesting that there was no great official enthusiasm for the Continental Reformation views on the nature of justification toward the end of Henry's reign.

With the death of Henry and accession of Edward VI (1547), the scene was set for the development of more explicitly Protestant theological views within the Church of England. The most important document to deal with justification dating from this period is the homily entitled "A Sermon of the Salvation of Mankind," generally thought to have been composed by Cranmer. The homily sets out a theology of justification which makes virtually no reference to the concept of "imputed righteousness" so typical of Lutheranism during the 1540s:

> Because all men be sinners and offenders against God, and breakers of his law and commandments, therefore can no man by his own acts, works and deeds, seem they never so good, be justified and made righteous before God: but every man of necessity is constrained to seek for another righteousness or justification, to be received at God's own hands, that is to say, the remission, pardon and forgiveness of his sins and trespasses in such things as he has offended. And this justification or righteousness, which we receive by God's mercy and Christ's merits, embraced by faith, is taken, accepted and allowed of God for our perfect and full justification [5]

Note how justification is defined in terms of forgiveness and receiving righteousness. What is of particular interest is that there are clear indications that Cranmer – assuming that he is the author of this piece – has incorporated material directly from Melanchthon's writings at several points, yet appears to have deliberately omitted his statements on the imputation of righteousness.

The significance of this observation is difficult to assess. Virtually every aspect of the Lutheran doctrine of justification by faith alone is incorporated into this homily; the one exception is an explicit statement of the notion of imputed righteousness. Was this simply a misunderstanding? Or were there some deeper issues involved? For example, was there an anxiety that the notion of "imputed righteousness" might lead to moral laxity – a fear which is known to have been expressed in Swiss Reforming circles in the 1520s?

From the above discussion, it will be clear that Cranmer had a high regard for Luther's doctrine of justification by faith, particularly as he found it in the writings of Melanchthon. The fact that Cranmer married a German Lutheran woman can either be seen as a reflection or as a cause of this positive evaluation! Yet this did not mean that Cranmer held an equally high regard for every aspect of Luther's thought. As we shall see, Cranmer rejected Luther's views on the real presence in favor of the more radical views of Zwingli and Oecolampadius. In the following section, we shall explore this matter in a little more detail.

The Real Presence in the English Reformation

The most significant statements of the English Reformation concerning the real presence are found in the writings of Thomas Cranmer (1489–1556). Born in Nottinghamshire in 1489, Thomas Cranmer went up to Jesus College, Cambridge, in 1503. He first came to Henry VIII's attention in 1529, when he became involved in the attempt to gain international recognition for Henry's proposed divorce from Catherine of Aragon. Henry VIII invited Cranmer to succeed William Warham as Archbishop of Canterbury on the latter's death in 1532. Cranmer eventually accepted, apparently with some reluctance. Although his opportunities to influence the course and shape of the English Reformation under Henry VIII were somewhat limited, a new situation developed under Edward VI. Cranmer's influence was at its height during Edward's reign, as noted above (pp. 231–2).

One of Cranmer's most significant achievements was the revision of the Prayer Book. Recognizing that one of the most effective ways of changing what people think is to change the way they worship, Cranmer saw the revision of the Prayer Book as a vitally important means of consolidating the principles of the Reformation, and bringing them into direct contact with the parish clergy and the laity. The revisions which Cranmer introduced are of considerable intrinsic interest; our attention here will focus on his views on the real presence, which can be inferred clearly from the Prayer Books of 1549 and 1552.

The 1549 Prayer Book adopted a fairly traditional view of the real presence, showing strong resonance with the position of Luther. This was to be expected. Cranmer had already shown himself to be a strong opponent of the kind of "memorialist" views which were associated with Zwingli. He presided over the public execution of John Frith in 1533, in response to the latter's denial of the real presence in the Eucharist. He was also severely critical of the memorialist views of the Swiss reformer Joachim von Watt (Vadian). The generally Lutheran understanding of the real presence in the 1549 Prayer Book is evident in the following words, directed to be spoken to those about to receive the Communion: "The Body [Blood] of our Lord Jesus Christ, which was given for thee, preserve the body and soul unto everlasting life." These words, however, would be dropped in the 1552 Prayer Book, which sets out Cranmer's mature position on the matter – a position which does not include any notion of a physical "real presence."

Cranmer's mature Eucharistic views are set out with particular clarity in his *Defence of the True and Catholic Doctrine of the Sacrament*, first published in 1550. Cranmer's mature view is remarkably close to that developed by Zwingli and Oecolampadius. Cranmer rejects what he terms the "papistical doctrine of transubstantiation" as "directly contrary to God's word." Although Cranmer's early views can be argued to be something similar to transubstantiation (perhaps reflecting a familiarity with Luther's views), it is clear that his later position is significantly different. For the later Cranmer, the Lord's Supper serves three central functions:

1 It is a memorial of Christ's sacrifice.
2 It represents a "sacrifice of praise" for that sacrifice.
3 It stresses the importance of "spiritually feeding upon Christ."

Cranmer is aware that one of the issues under debate is the nature of the language used by the New Testament. As we noted earlier (pp. 168–81), the precise interpretation of the phrase "this is my body" was intensely debated in the 1520s, with Luther arguing for a literal interpretation of the phrase, and Zwingli for a metaphorical or symbolic reading of the text. Cranmer makes it clear that he prefers Zwingli's approach:

> And marvel not, good reader, that Christ at that time spoke in figures, when he did institute that sacrament, seeing that it is in the nature of all sacraments to be figures. And although the Scripture can be full of schemes, tropes and figures, yet specially it uses them when it speaks of sacraments.[6]

Having established that the New Testament uses "tropes" and other non-literal modes of expression, particularly in relation to the sacraments, it is only a small step for Cranmer to argue that the Eucharist represents a memorial of Christ's saving death:

> Christ calls the bread his body (as the old authors report) because it represents his body, and signifies to them which eat that bread according to Christ's ordinance, that they do spiritually eat his body, and be spiritually fed and nourished by him. And yet the bread remains still there, as a sacrament to signify the same.[7]

In other words, the bread does not change; it remains as it was. Note how Cranmer speaks of "the old authors" – meaning the patristic writers, who had been cited by Oecolampadius in support of his memorialist view of the Eucharist.

Among the arguments which Cranmer marshals in support of his memorialist view of the Eucharist, we may note one in particular. Cranmer argues – following Zwingli, and particularly Zwingli's English disciple John Frith (1503–33) – that Christ is now sitting at God's right hand. If he is indeed at God's right hand, he cannot be anywhere else. Therefore, Christ cannot be present in the Eucharist: "[The Lord] now sits at the right hand of his Father, and there shall remain until the last day, when he shall come to judge the quick and the dead."[8]

Cranmer also insists that the Lord's Supper offers no benefits to those who do not have faith. All people, whether they have faith or not, may physically consume the sacramental elements. Yet the benefits which they represent or signify are only applied to those who believe:

It is evident and manifest that all men, good and evil, may with their mouths visibly and sensibly eat the sacrament of Christ's body and blood; but the very body and blood themselves be not eaten but spiritually, and that of the spiritual members of Christ, which dwell in Christ, and have Christ dwelling in them, by whom they be refreshed, and have everlasting life.[9]

Cranmer's essentially Zwinglian views on the real presence would not have been welcomed by either Lutherans or Catholics. Under Edward VI, this was not an especially important issue. However, a very different situation developed under Elizabeth I. Faced with a complex political agenda at home and abroad on her accession, Elizabeth judged that a "Settlement of Religion" was a matter of priority. Alterations were introduced to the 1552 Prayer Book to make it more acceptable across a broad spectrum of theological positions. For example, consider the words spoken to those about to receive communion:

1549: "The Body [Blood] of our Lord Jesus Christ, which was given for thee, preserve thy body and soul unto everlasting life."

1552: "Take and eat [drink] this in remembrance that Christ died for thee, and feed on him in thy heart with thanksgiving."

1559: "The Body [Blood] of our Lord Jesus Christ, which was given for thee, preserve thy body and soul unto everlasting life. Take and eat [drink] this in remembrance that Christ died for thee, and feed on him in thy heart with thanksgiving."

The 1549 words reflect an essentially Lutheran position, the 1552 words a more Zwinglian stance. The 1559 statement sets both positions alongside one another, without attempting any form of theological resolution. Both Lutheran and Zwinglian found something which they could approve, and there, it seems, it was hoped the matter would rest. The Elizabethan "Settlement of Religion" was essentially pragmatic rather than theological. Perhaps this could be seen as the most distinctive characteristic of the English Reformation under Elizabeth: a desire to reconcile all parties within the theologically and socially fragmented nation, and recover a sense of national unity.

Notes

1 F. M. Powicke, *The Reformation in England* (London, 1941), pp. 1, 34.

2 The Forty-Two Articles (1553), Article 5.

3 The Forty-Two Articles (1553), Article 20.

4 The Ten Articles (1536), Article 5.

5 "A Sermon of the Salvation of Mankind," in *The Two Books of Homilies* (Oxford, 1859), p. 24.

6 *Archbishop Cranmer on the True and Catholic Doctrine and Use of the Sacrament of the Lord's Supper*, ed. C. H. H. Wright (London, 1907),

p. 156. Note that the spelling has been modernized to facilitate understanding of the meaning of this text.

7   *True and Catholic Doctrine*, p. 36.
8   *True and Catholic Doctrine*, p. 97.
9   *True and Catholic Doctrine*, p. 213.

Further Reading

Bernard, G. W., *The King's Reformation: Henry VIII and the Remaking of the English Church* (New Haven, CT, 2005).

Clebsch, W. A., *England's Earliest Protestants 1520–1535* (New Haven, CT, 1964).

Collinson, P., *The Birthpangs of Protestant England: Religious and Cultural Change in the Sixteenth and Seventeenth Centuries* (London, 1988).

Cross, C., "No Continuing City: Exiles in the English Reformation, 1520–1570," *History Review* 32 (1998), 17–22.

Dickens, A. G., *The English Reformation*, rev. edn (London, 1989).

Duffy, E., *Marking the Hours: English People and Their Prayers, 1240–1570* (New Haven, CT, 2007).

Haigh, C., ed., *The English Reformation Revised* (Cambridge, 1987).

Haugaard, W. P., *Elizabeth and the English Reformation: The Struggle for a Stable Settlement of Religion* (Cambridge, 1970).

Houston, J., "Transubstantiation and the Sign: Cranmer's Drama of the Last Supper," *Journal of Medieval and Renaissance Studies* 24 (1994), 115–30.

Luhmann, N., *Religious Dogmatics and the Evolution of Societies* (New York, 1984).

MacCulloch, D., *Thomas Cranmer* (New Haven, CT, 1996).

Nischan, B., *Lutherans and Calvinists in the Age of Confessionalism* (Aldershot, 1999).

O'Day, R., *The Debate on the English Reformation* (London, 1986).

Ryrie, A., "Divine Kingship and Royal Theology in Henry VIII's Reformation," *Reformation* 7 (2002), 49–77.

Ryrie, A., "The Strange Death of Lutheran England," *Journal of Ecclesiastical History* 53 (2002), 64–92.

13

The Diffusion of the Thought of the Reformation

In previous chapters we explored some of the major themes of the emerging theology of the Reformation, including some of the debates within the movement that would contribute to its diversification and polarization. Yet this has largely ignored a major question: how were the ideas and practices of the Reformation diffused throughout Europe? The present chapter examines some of the means by which the beliefs and practices of the Reformation were disseminated beyond their original contexts.

The Physical Agencies of Diffusion

In an earlier chapter, we noted the means by which the ideas of the Italian Renaissance were diffused to northern Europe. The three main agencies of transmission were identified as people, books, and correspondence (see pp. 42–3). Those factors continue to be of importance in relation to the spread of the Reformation. In what follows, we shall look at some general issues concerning the transmission of the ideas of the Reformation, before looking at some more specific items in subsequent sections.

The Vernacular

One of the most distinctive emphases of the Reformation was the use of the vernacular. Luther published his major reforming treatises of 1520 in German,

Reformation Thought: An Introduction, Fourth Edition. Alister E. McGrath.
© 2012 John Wiley & Sons, Ltd. Published 2012 by John Wiley & Sons, Ltd.

to ensure a wide readership for his ideas. Similarly, Zwingli ensured that his ideas were published in his native Swiss-German, and Calvin in his native French. The result was not merely an enhanced accessibility of the ideas and practices of the Reformation; the shapes of most modern western European languages were decisively shaped by the writings of the Reformers, particularly through the publication of the Bible in the vernacular. The Reformers were also aware of the importance of preaching in the vernacular, and of ensuring that the liturgy was also understood by all those taking part in worship.

Sociologically, this all fits in well with the general thesis of the "democratization" of faith, so characteristic of the early Reformation. The gospel must be made accessible to all people, not just academics and clerics who were able to read Latin. The removal of linguistic barriers to the ideas of the gospel gave the Reformation a sociological breadth which had no real parallel within Catholicism for some decades.

One of the most significant moments in the history of the Reformation is Martin Luther's decision in 1520 to switch from being an academic reformer (arguing in Latin to an academic public) to a popular reformer (arguing in German to a broader public). The Reformation witnessed a major challenge being laid down to existing understandings of the way that the Bible could and should be read, structures of the church, and Christian doctrine. Time and time again, the Reformers appealed over the heads of the clergy and theologians to the people. The people, they insisted, must decide. The practice of the Swiss Reformation, in which a public disputation between evangelicals and Catholics in the vernacular was followed by a plenary vote by the assembly body of citizens on whether to accept the Reformation, reflects this basic principle.

Books

The invention and widespread adoption of printing revolutionized the transmission of ideas. The diffusion of the ideas of both the Renaissance and Reformation was closely linked with printing. There is no doubt that the relative ease with which books and religious pamphlets could be transported across national boundaries contributed significantly to the spread of the Reformation. Luther never visited England; his ideas, however, were surprisingly widely discussed and assessed there, simply because the flow of his books into the country proved virtually impossible to staunch.

A similar situation can be discerned in France. Calvin never returned to France after 1536. (Although Calvin spent 1538–41 in Strasbourg, this imperial city was not, as it is today, part of France.) Yet Calvin's works, and especially those published in the French language, found a substantial readership in Paris. As we noted earlier (p. 15), a crucial turning point is marked by the publication of the French-language edition of the *Institutes of the Christian Religion* in 1541. Calvin's *Institutes* were seen as the spearhead of a Genevan assault upon the French church, mediated through the printed word. Yet, despite the efforts of the authorities to suppress it, the flood of Genevan literature into Paris continued. The attempt to regulate the public sale of books to exclude those originating from Geneva merely forced the trade to go underground. Until the wars of religion finally put a brake on the expansion of the Genevan publishing industry's sector of the French religious market in the years 1565–80, it was not difficult to obtain such works in Paris.

The Interchange of People

In an earlier chapter (pp. 42–3), we noted how one of the major means by which the leading themes of the Italian Renaissance were transmitted to northern Europe was through individual scholars visiting Italy and taking the ideas of the Renaissance home with them. It should not be any cause for surprise that a similarly important role was played by such individuals in relation to the Reformation. Luther's ideas were taken to England by both William Tyndale and Robert Barnes, the former of whom is believed and the latter known to have studied under Luther at Wittenberg.

The repressive religious policies introduced during the reign of Mary Tudor led many English Protestants to seek refuge in European Protestant cities (such as Frankfurt, Geneva, and Zurich). On their return to England, these individuals brought the experience of Reformed church life back to their homeland, accelerating the pace of Protestant reform under Elizabeth I. Twelve of the 18 bishops appointed by Elizabeth I in the aftermath of the mass episcopal resignations of 1559 had sought refuge in Europe during Mary's reign.

As noted above, severe limits were placed upon the movements of leading Reformers. Luther, for example, found that the ban placed upon him in the 1520s prevented him from traveling outside his native Saxony. His younger Wittenberg colleague Philipp Melanchthon thus had to travel on his behalf, promoting the Lutheran Reformation elsewhere in Germany. Similarly, Calvin's movements were restricted. While at the peak of his influence, he was virtually confined to his adopted city of Geneva. Yet Calvin was still able to exercise influence by proxy. This influence was perhaps at its greatest in his native France, the target of a major campaign of infiltration organized from Geneva from 1555 onward.

In response to requests from French-speaking Reformed congregations, particularly in the southeast of the country, Calvin arranged for reformed pastors to be smuggled into the region. Secrecy was essential to the entire operation, at both the Genevan and French ends of the operation. Safe houses, complete with hiding places, were established a day's journey apart. An underground network, similar to that employed by the French Resistance during World War II, allowed the men from Geneva to slip across the ill-defined frontier into France. The Company of Pastors made every effort to maintain total secrecy, even to the point of concealing its operations from the theoretically all-knowing city council.

By 1557, however, the Company of Pastors realized it could not hope to keep its activities abroad clandestine indefinitely; late that year Calvin appeared before the city council to explain the situation and request permission to send further agents. The city council was evidently aware of the serious danger posed to the city by these activities: if it were thought that the Genevan government itself was organizing the infiltration of religious activists, it could be held guilty of seditious action against its larger neighbor, with unpredictable (but probably unpleasant) consequences. The council, however, agreed to the secret continuation of the policy, providing that they could not be held to be associated with it. This successful policy was unquestionably one of the factors contributing to the rapid growth of Calvinism in France, which eventually led to the outbreak of the wars of religion in the region.

Other Calvinist-minded intellectuals traveled abroad to propagate his ideas, perhaps most successfully in England. Under the reign of Edward VI, leading divines, either Calvinist or sympathetic to Calvinism, were encouraged to settle in England and give a sense of theological direction to the nascent Reformed church. Individuals such as Martin Bucer, Pietro Martire Vermigli (perhaps better known as Peter Martyr), and John à Lasco gave the Church of England a new impetus that moved it away from its earlier flirtations with Lutheranism and toward at least some of the ideas associated with Calvin's Geneva. In May 1559, John Knox returned to his native Scotland after a period of exile in Geneva; within days of his arrival, riots broke out at Perth, precipitating the Reformation crisis.

The Diffusion of Ideas: The Key Texts

Having considered some general factors involved in the diffusion of the thought of the Reformation, we now turn to deal with some more specific works which are known to have been instrumental in the dissemination of the new theology of this period. We begin by considering the "catechism," by which the ideas of the Reformation could be taught to a new generation.

The Catechisms

Although what would now be agreed to be "catechisms" can be found in the medieval church, it is generally agreed that the extensive use of **catechisms** is especially associated with the Reformation. A visitation of Lutheran churches in Saxony over the period 1528–9 showed that most pastors and just about every layperson were ignorant of basic Christian teachings. Luther was shocked by his findings, and decided to put in place measures to increase public knowledge of basic Christian teachings.

catechism Popular manual of Christian doctrine intended for religious instruction.

The first result of Luther's new concern in this area made its appearance in April 1529. Although Luther himself termed it a "German Catechism," it is now more generally known as the *Greater Catechism*. The work provides a detailed analysis of the Ten Commandments, the Apostles' Creed, and the Lord's Prayer. These sections were followed by discussions of the two sacraments of the church – baptism and the "sacrament of the altar" (or Communion service). The work does not show Luther at his best. It draws upon earlier sermonical material, and was not written specifically for the purpose of catechizing. As a result, it failed to meet its goals.

This was followed in May 1529 by what is now known as the *Lesser Catechism*. This work was written specifically for this purpose, and shows a lightness of touch, an ease of communication, and a general simplicity of expression which ensured that it was widely used and appreciated. The work was a remarkable success and was widely adopted within Lutheran institutions. Its question-and-answer format was ideally suited to learning by rote, and the work was widely adopted within the schools of the region. It is important to note that both Luther's 1529 catechisms were written in German, the language of the people. Luther avoided the use of Latin for this purpose, recognizing the severe limitations which the use of this scholarly language would have on the appeal and readership of the works.

To illustrate the approach Luther adopted, we may consider the following passage from the *Lesser Catechism*. Note particularly the question-and-answer format, designed to facilitate both teaching and learning.

Q.   What is baptism?
A.   Baptism is not just water on its own, but it is water used according to God's command and linked with God's Word.
Q.   What is this Word of God?
A.   Our Lord Christ, as recorded in Matthew 28:19, said, "Go therefore and make disciples of all nations, baptizing them in the name of the Father and of the Son and of the Holy Spirit."
Q.   What gifts or benefits does Baptism bring?
A.   It brings about the forgiveness of sins, saves us from death and the devil, and grants eternal blessedness to all who believe, as the Word and promise of God declare.
Q.   What is this Word and promise of God?
A.   Our Lord Christ, as recorded in Mark 16:16, said, "Anyone who believes and is baptized will be saved; but those who do not believe will be condemned."
Q.   How can water bring about such a great thing?
A.   Water does not; but it is the Word of God with and through the water, and our faith which trusts in the Word of God in the water. For without the Word of God, that water is nothing but water, and there is no Baptism. But when it is linked with the Word of God, it is a Baptism, that is, a gracious water of life and a bath of new birth in the Holy Spirit.[1]

The Reformed churches were not slow to appreciate the importance of this literary genre and the educational advantages which it so clearly offered. After some experimentation, Calvin finally produced a "Geneva Catechism" in French (1542) and Latin (1545). This catechism was widely used within the Reformed constituency until 1563. It was at this point that the "Heidelberg Catechism" made its appearance.

The origins of this major work lie in the growth of the Reformed church within Germany. Aware of the need to ensure a well-educated Reformed laity, able to defend their ideas against Lutheran and Catholic critics, Elector Frederick III commissioned two Reformed theologians (Kaspar Olevianus and Zacharias Ursinus) to produce a catechism suitable for use in his churches. The result was a German-language catechism of 129 questions, which could be arranged in 52 blocks of material to permit regular teaching on each Sunday throughout the 52 weeks of the year. The leading themes of the Reformed faith are set out in the by now obligatory question-and-answer format.

The extensive Protestant use of catechisms, and the significant results that they achieved, led their Catholic opponents to develop the format. Earlier Catholic catechisms tended to avoid the question-and-answer format, and offered extensive discussions of points of theological importance. An excellent example of this may be found in Johann Dietenberger's 1537 catechism, which takes the form of a discussion of the Apostles' Creed, the Lord's Prayer, the Ten Commandments, the "Hail Mary," and the seven sacraments. However, the superiority of the question-and-answer approach became obvious, and was incorporated into Peter Canisius's three catechisms, published over the period 1554–8. This work was published in Latin, as was the more substantial Tridentine Catechism of 1566. While its cumbersome format ensured that it was hardly ever used, the work's appearance in the aftermath of the Council of Trent may be regarded as an important recognition of the significance of the genre.

Confessions of Faith

We have already noted how the Reformation placed considerable emphasis upon the authority of Scripture. Yet the Bible needed to be interpreted. As the controversy between the magisterial and radical Reformers made clear, there were issues of interpretation which were both divisive and elusive. There was clearly a need for some form of "official" means of setting out the ideas of the Reformation, to avoid confusion. This role was played by the "Confessions of Faith." In view of the importance of these documents, we may consider their place within the thought of the Reformation.

The magisterial Reformation, while placing considerable emphasis upon the authority of Scripture, also recognized a role for the Christian consensus of the past – an idea which we discussed earlier in relation to tradition (see pp. 100–2). In general terms, Protestant theologians can be thought of as recognizing three levels or strata of authority:

1   *Scripture.* This was regarded by the magisterial Reformers as possessing supreme authority in matters of Christian belief and conduct.
2   *The Creeds of Christendom.* These documents, such as the Apostles' Creed and the Nicene Creed, were regarded by the magisterial Reformers as

representing the consensus of the early church, and as being accurate and authoritative interpretations of Scripture. Although they were to be regarded a *derivative* or *secondary* in terms of their authority, they were seen as an important check against the individualism of the radical Reformation (which generally declined to regard these creeds as having any authority). The authority of the creeds was recognized by both Protestants and Catholics, as well as by the various constituent elements within the mainline Reformation.

3 *Confessions of Faith.* These documents were regarded as authoritative by specific groupings within the Reformation. Thus the Augsburg Confession (1530) was recognized by early Lutheran churches as possessing authority. Other groups within the Reformation did not, however, regard it in this way. Specific confessions of faith were, for example, drawn up by other groups within the Reformation. Some were linked with the Reformation in specific cities – for example, the First Confession of Basle (1534) and the Geneva Confession (1536).

The basic pattern within the Reformation was thus to acknowledge Scripture as possessing primary and universal authority; the Creeds as secondary and universal authority; and the Confessions as tertiary and local authority (in that such confessions were only regarded as binding by a denomination or church in a specific region). The development of the Reformed wing of the Reformation was complex, with the result that a number of Confessions – each linked with a specific region – came to be influential. The following are of particular importance:

Date	Title	Geographical region
1559	Gallic Confession	France
1560	Scottish Confession	Scotland
1561	Belgic Confession	The Lowlands
1563	Thirty-Nine Articles	England
1566	Second Helvetic Confession	Western Switzerland

We now turn to consider one of the most influential means of transmission of the ideas of the Reformation, in their Reformed embodiment – Calvin's *Institutes of the Christian Religion*.

Calvin's *Institutes of the Christian Religion*

The first edition of the *Institutes of the Christian Religion* was published by the Basle printers Thomas Platter and Balthasar Lasius in March 1536 (Figure 13.1). The translation of the Latin title – *Institutio Christianae Religionis* – poses some problems. The Latin word *Institutio* suggests a parallel with the Institutes of Justinian, a foundational Roman legal code of the classical period, familiar to Calvin from his Orléans period. In terms of its structure or content, however, Calvin's work bears little resemblance to a legal code.

·VI· Januarij   1538

CHRISTIA

NAE RELIGIONIS INSTI-
tutio, totam ferè pietatis summã, & quic
quid est in doctrina salutis cognitu ne=
cessarium, complectens: omnibus pie=
tatis studiosis lectu dignissi=
mum opus, ac re
cens edi=
tum.

PRAEFATIO AD CHRI
stianißimum REGEM FRANCIAE, qua
hic ei liber pro confeßione fidei
offertur.

IOANNE CALVINO
Noniodunensi autore.

Ex Biblioth: Julient. S.t B.n. pavilien.s.

BASILEAE,
M. D. XXXVI.

Figure 13.1   Title page of the first edition of John Calvin's *Institutes of the Christian Religion*, published at Basle in 1536. The Granger Collection/TopFoto, TopFoto.co.uk

Erasmus used the same Latin word *Institutio* in a rather different sense, meaning "instruction," or perhaps even "primer" (for example, his *Institutio principis Christiani* of 1516, which may have served as an inspiration for Calvin's title). The English word "Institution" perhaps conveys another of Calvin's concerns – to return to a more authentic form of Christianity than that encountered in the late medieval period. It is Christianity as originally instituted which concerns Calvin, not as it was developed (or deformed, in Calvin's view) in the Middle Ages. In practice, most English translations choose to render the Latin title as *Institutes of the Christian Religion*, despite the alternatives suggested by the Latin original, and we shall follow this practice.

The first edition of the *Institutes* was modeled on Luther's *Lesser Catechism* (see pp. 108, 245) of 1529. Both its structure and substance indicate the extent to which Calvin has drawn upon this major educational work of the early German Reformation. Its 516 small-format pages comprise six chapters, the first four of which are modeled on Luther's catechism. Calvin, however, is able to engage in more detailed discussion of questions than Luther, for the simple reason that his work is not a question-and-answer catechism which had to be learned by rote. The first chapter is essentially an exposition of the Ten Commandments (or Decalogue); the second is an exposition of the Apostles' Creed. Where Luther's discussion of the creed has three sections (the Father, the Son, and the Holy Spirit), Calvin adds a substantial fourth section on the church, recognizing both the theoretical and practical importance of this question. After expositions of "The Law," "Faith," "Prayer," and "The Sacraments," Calvin includes two chapters of a more polemical nature on "false sacraments" and "the liberty of a Christian."

The second edition of the *Institutes* dates from Calvin's Strasbourg period, and was published in Latin in 1539. The most obvious and important difference between the volumes is that of size: the new work is about three times as long as the first edition of 1536, with 17 chapters instead of six. Two opening chapters now deal with the knowledge of God and the knowledge of human nature. Additional material was added on the doctrine of the Trinity, the relation of the Old and New Testaments, penitence, justification by faith, the nature and relation of providence and predestination, and the nature of the Christian life. Although the work retained much material drawn from the earlier edition, it is evident that its character and status have changed. It is no longer a catechism; it is well on the way to being a definitive statement of the nature of the Christian faith, inviting comparison with the *Summa Theologiae* of Thomas Aquinas.

"My object in this work," wrote Calvin, "is to so prepare and train students of sacred theology for the study of the word of God that they might have an easy access into it, and be able to proceed in it without hindrance." In other words, the book is intended to be a guide to Scripture, functioning as a *vade mecum* and commentary to its often intricate and complex depths of meaning.

This is an important point, as Calvin himself later stressed, in that it establishes Calvin's *Institutes* as the primary resource for his religious thought. His other writings – such as biblical commentaries and sermons – are of secondary importance in this respect, whatever their merits might otherwise be. In writing his *Institutes*, Calvin intended to provide what is essentially a doctrinal commentary on Scripture, allowing the reader of Scripture direct access to its authentic meaning.

A French edition of the *Institutes* was published in 1541. Curiously, the work is not a direct translation of the 1539 edition; there are several points at which the French translation includes material drawn from the 1536 edition, even though this had been altered in 1539. This has led to speculation that Calvin may originally have intended to produce a French translation of the 1536 edition, and, abandoning this project, included material already translated into the 1541 edition without the modifications introduced in 1539. The work shows numerous minor alterations, all of which may be explained with reference to the intended popular readership. Scholarly points likely to cause difficulty are omitted (for example, all Greek words and references to Aristotle are omitted), and additional material likely to be familiar to the intended readership (for example, French proverbs and idioms) are added.

A further Latin edition appeared in 1543, with a French translation in 1545. Now expanded to 21 chapters, it included as its most significant addition a major section on the doctrine of the church. Minor alterations include the addition of two chapters on vows and human traditions, and the creation of a separate chapter for the material relating to angels. The impact of experience upon Calvin's religious reflections is evident in this edition, particularly in the discussion of the importance of ecclesiastical organization.

Despite the obvious merits of this edition, an inherent defect, already noticeable in 1539, now becomes transparently obvious. The work is poorly organized. New chapters are added without thought being given to the overall impact such addition has upon the structure and organization of the work. Many chapters are impossibly long, without any attempt to subdivide them into sections. The Latin edition of 1550, and the subsequent French translation of 1551, attempted to remedy this deficiency by subdividing their 21 chapters into paragraphs. A few additions may be noted, such as new sections dealing with biblical authority and human conscience. The fundamental flaw remains, however: the edition of 1550, like that of 1543, must be regarded as a remarkably poorly organized work.

Recognizing both the need for total revision and the limited time available in which to achieve this (illness was a recurring feature of Calvin's final years), the reformer decided to recast the entire work. Surprisingly few additions are made; those that were made are generally unattractive, reflecting Calvin's growing irritability and tendency to abuse and vilify his opponents. The most obvious and positive change is the total reordering of the material, which virtually restores unity to what had almost degenerated into a series of unrelated fragments. The material is now distributed among four "books," arranged as follows:

1   The knowledge of God the creator;
2   the knowledge of God the redeemer;
3   the manner of participation in the grace of Jesus Christ; and
4   the external means or aids which God uses to bring us to Jesus Christ.

The 21 chapters of 1551 are now expanded to 80 chapters, each carefully subdivided for ease of reading, distributed over these four books. It is possible that Calvin adapted the fourfold structure of the edition of 1543 to create the new division of material. An alternative explanation, however, is that he noticed and adopted the fourfold division of material in the *Four Books of the Sentences* of Peter Lombard, a seminal medieval theologian to whom Calvin often refers. Was Calvin setting himself up as the Protestant successor to Peter Lombard, and his *Institutes* as the successor to his great theological textbook? We shall never know.

What we do know is that the *Institutes* were now firmly established as the most influential theological work of the Protestant Reformation, eclipsing in importance the rival works of Luther, Melanchthon, and Zwingli.

The success of the 1559 *Institutes* reflects its superb organization. As noted earlier, Philipp Melanchthon established the definitive pattern for Lutheran works of systematic theology in 1521, through the publication of his "Commonplaces" (*Loci Communes*). In its first edition, this work simply treated a number of subjects of obvious relevance to the Lutheran Reformation. Gradually, however, polemical and pedagogical considerations obliged Melanchthon to expand the work considerably. Melanchthon met this challenge in a surprisingly inadequate manner; he merely added additional material, regardless of the impression of a lack of unified structure this created. It soon became evident that this way of handling material was clumsy and disorganized, incapable of achieving the systematic analysis needed for the theological debates of the late sixteenth and seventeenth centuries.

Calvin, however, bequeathed to his heirs an intensely systematic and organized structure, which proved ideally suited not merely to the needs of his own generation, but also for those of at least a century to come. Lutheranism never really recovered from the false start given to it by Melanchthon; the intellectual domination of Protestantism by theologians of the Reformed tradition is due to both the substance and structure of Calvin's final edition of the *Institutes*.

Calvin's *Institutes* were widely read and appreciated in western Europe, often to the point of being cited extensively in other works. The anonymous Italian treatise *The Benefits of Christ* (1541) – which rapidly attained the status of a religious bestseller before being suppressed by the Inquisition – draws heavily upon the 1539 edition of the *Institutes*. Calvin's work was evidently familiar to front-rank Protestant theologians in the Netherlands by the later 1550s. The work rapidly established itself as a neat and elegant one-stop and free-standing introduction to the ideas of the second wave of the Reformation. Where Calvinism took root at the institutional level, it had often been preceded at the intellectual level by the *Institutes*.

The success of Calvin's 1559 *Institutes* gave rise to a publishing spin-off – the "summary" or "compendium." Even in the sixteenth century, numerous abridgments of this work were in circulation, apparently enjoying considerable commercial success. In 1562, Augustin Marlorat published a set of indexes to the work, facilitating the location of subjects and biblical passages within the work. In 1576, Nicolas Colladon, one of Calvin's early biographers, produced an edition which included brief marginal summaries of the contents of significant passages. Thomas Vautrollier, the Huguenot refugee who became one of London's more important religious publishers, printed two study guides to the *Institutes*. Edmund Bunny's *Compendium* (1576) attempted to deal with Calvin's difficult style and subtleties of argumentation for the benefit of perplexed students; Guillaume Delaune (a Huguenot refugee who Anglicized his name as William Lawne) produced a summary of the *Institutes* in a mere 370 pages seven years later. In addition to summarizing Calvin, the work provided flow charts or diagrams to allow the puzzled reader to follow the intricate structure of the work. Through their medium, the ideas of Calvin became increasingly accessible and comprehensible to an ever-widening circle of readers.

Notes

1   Martin Luther, *The Lesser Catechism* (1529); in *D. Martin Luthers Werke: Kritische Gesamtausgabe*, vol. 30, part 1 (Weimar, 1910), 225.20–257.24.

Further Reading

Armstrong, B., "The Nature and Structure of Calvin's Thought According to the *Institutes: Another Look,*" in *John Calvin's Magnum Opus* (Potchefstroom, South Africa, 1986), pp. 55–82.

Cochrane, A., ed., *Reformed Confessions of the Sixteenth Century* (Philadelphia, 1966).

Eisenstein, E. L., *The Printing Press as an Agent of Change*, 2 vols (Cambridge, 1979).

Farge, J. K., "Early Censorship of Printed Books in Paris: New Insights and Perspectives," in *Le contrôle des idées à la Renaissance*, ed. J. M. de Bujanda (Geneva, 1996), pp. 75–91.

Forell, W., and J. McCue, eds, *Confessing One Faith: A Joint Commentary on the Augsburg Confession by Lutheran and Catholic Theologians* (Minneapolis, 1982).

Haugaard, W. P., *Elizabeth and the English Reformation* (Cambridge, 1968), pp. 233–90.

Kolb, R. "The Ordering of the *Loci Communes Theologici*: The Structuring of the Melanchthonian Dogmatic Tradition," *Concordia Journal* 23 (1997), 317–37.

Kingdon, R. M., ed., *The Formula of Concord: Quadricentennial Essays* (Kirksville, MO, 1977).

Robinson-Hammerstein, H., ed., *The Transmission of Ideas in the Lutheran Reformation* (Blackrock, Republic of Ireland, 1989).

Torrance, T. F., *The School of Faith: The Catechisms of the Reformed Church* (London, 1959).

Vajta, V., ed., *Confessio Augustana: Commemoration and Self-Examination* (Stuttgart, 1980).

14

The Impact of Reformation Thought upon History

Everyone studying a subject likes to be reassured of its wider relevance. This concluding chapter explores some of the ways in which the religious ideas of the Reformation may be argued to have had a significant impact on history, whether by laying the foundations for new attitudes and outlooks or by clearing away intellectual obstacles to these developments. It will trace the trajectory of some of the ideas and values developed during the period, and consider their longer-term impact upon Western culture. As we shall see, there is an excellent case for suggesting that the Reformation injected a distinctive creative impulse into history, with major results for the shaping of our own world.

A failure to realize the extent to which values, attitudes, and actions rest upon *intellectual* foundations has undoubtedly contributed much to the shallowness of some historical writing in recent years. Of course, there is more to history than an understanding of ideas. Ideas are affected by history; yet history is also affected by ideas. It is the complexity of this mutual interplay of ideas and history which is so irritating to those who, for one reason or another, want to ignore either religious ideas on the one hand or the historical context of those ideas on the other. In the remainder of this chapter, we shall explore some of the cultural consequences of the religious ideas developed at the time of the Reformation.

An Affirmative Attitude Toward the World

Recent studies have noted how most of the intellectual and spiritual leaders of medieval Christianity were monastic, isolated from many of the harsher realities of everyday life by the walls of their monasteries and convents. Protestantism chose to inhabit the more dangerous world of the city and marketplace, exposing its thinkers to pressures and problems that their Catholic forebears had not been required to consider. It is of the utmost importance to appreciate that the intellectual lights of the first phase of Protestantism – Martin Luther, Huldrych Zwingli, Martin Bucer, Heinrich Bullinger, and John Calvin – lived, thought, and wrote in an urban context.

Yet the transition from the monastery to marketplace was dangerous. Protestantism was exposed to precisely the dangers, threats, and problems that had led to the emergence of the monastic movement in the first place. How could Christianity maintain its integrity when it was now immersed in, and confronted with, the challenges of the world? As Roland Bainton, one of the most distinguished analysts of the early sixteenth century, remarked: when Christianity takes itself seriously, it must either renounce or master the world.[1] If the former attitude was characteristic of much medieval Christianity, the latter dominated the thought of the reformers.

The Reformation witnessed a remarkable turnabout in attitudes toward the secular order. Monastic Christianity, which had been the source of virtually all the best Christian theology and spiritual writings during the Middle Ages, treated the world and those who lived and worked in it with a certain degree of disdain. *Real* Christians would withdraw from the world, and enter the spiritual security of a monastery. Yet, for the reformers, the real vocation of a Christian lay in serving God in the world. Monasteries were something of an irrelevance to this task. The real business of Christian living was in the cities, marketplaces, and council chambers of the secular world, not in the splendid isolation of the monastic cell.

The importance of this shift in outlook cannot be overstated. It might be thought that monastic Christianity was only one component – and perhaps not even the most significant component – of medieval Christianity. Yet much of what is referred to in the literature as "medieval Christianity" is actually *monastic Christianity*; all too often, the everyday life and ideas of Christians in the wider world are overlooked or discounted. Many of the attitudes within monastic Christianity at this time were critical of Christians who opted to stay in the world, and declined to enter the religious life in its various forms. To live in the everyday world was seen as being a second-rate option. Furthermore, living in the everyday world was seen as a spiritual absurdity, which could lead to all kinds of spiritual degeneration.

An illustration will make this point clearer. The most famous writing of the movement generally known as the *Devotio Moderna* is Thomas à Kempis's *De imitatione Christi*, written around 1425. The full title of this work, in English, is *On the Imitation of Christ and Contempt for the World*. A positive response to Jesus Christ is seen as entailing a negative response to the world. For à Kempis, cultivating a detached or negative attitude toward the world is a mark of spiritual maturity.

During the Middle Ages, the monasteries became increasingly isolated from ordinary people. Increasingly firmly wedded to the fading medieval world, the monasteries seemed unable to relate to the new interest in religion among the laity and the technological advance of printing. Monastic approaches to the Christian life came to have a diminishing impact outside the monasteries, even upon the clergy. The everyday life of the laity was often virtually untouched by what went on behind monastic walls. Monastic attitudes to Christian living envisaged a lifestyle and outlook quite alien to laypersons.

With the Reformation, the formative centers of Christian thought and life gradually shifted from the monasteries to the marketplaces, as the great cities of Europe became the cradle and crucible of new modes of Christian thinking and acting. Mirrored in this shift are the political, social, economic, and ecclesiastical changes which lie at the heart of the formation of modern Western culture. The mainstream Reformation rejected the monastic impulse to withdraw from the world – but primarily on the basis of *theological*, not *social*, considerations.

Two of these theological considerations may be noted briefly:

1   *A new emphasis on the doctrines of creation and redemption.* Calvin's impressively world-affirming theology may be said to rest upon asserting the utter ontological distinction between God and the world, while denying the possibility of separating the two. The theme *distinctio sed non separatio*, which underlies so many aspects of Calvin's theology, reappears in his understanding of the Christian's relationship to society. A knowledge of God the Creator cannot be isolated from knowledge of his creation; Christians are expected to show respect, concern, and commitment to the world on account of a loyalty, obedience, and love for God its creator. The world does not have a direct claim to a Christian's loyalty; it is an indirect claim, resting on a recognition of the unique relation of origin which exists between God and his creation. In revering nature as God's creation, one is worshipping God, not worshipping nature.

To be a Christian thus does not – indeed, *cannot* – mean renouncing the world; for to renounce the world is to renounce the God who so wondrously created it. The world, though fallen, is not evil. The Christian is called to work in the world, in order to redeem the world. Commitment to the world is a vital aspect of the working out of the Christian doctrine of redemption. A failure to commit oneself to and work in the world is tantamount to declaring that it cannot, and should not, be redeemed.

2   *A recovery of the idea of the calling of a Christian.* The monastic idea of calling entailed leaving the world behind. Believers are "called out" of the world. The

reformers vigorously repudiated this idea. A person is called, in the first place, to be a Christian, and, in the second, to live out his or her faith in a quite definite sphere of activity in the world. The impact of Reformation thought in this respect may be judged from the fact that the Latin term *vocatio*, "calling," has now come to mean "a worldly activity or career." Behind this modern habit lies an idea which achieved wide acceptance in the sixteenth-century Reformation – that the Christian is called to serve God in the world.

This idea, linked with the central doctrine of the priesthood of all believers (pp. 210–12), gave a vital new motivation for committed faithful action within the everyday world. As we have seen, the reformers rejected the vital medieval distinction between the "sacred" and the "secular." There was no genuine difference of status between the "spiritual" and the "temporal" order (see p. 107). All Christians are called to be priests, and that calling extends to the everyday world. They are called to purify and sanctify its everyday life from within. Luther stated this point succinctly: "What seem to be secular works are actually the praise of God and represent an obedience which is well pleasing to him."

This point needs to be developed further, since it is a vital aspect of the Protestant work ethic – unquestionably one of the most significant contributions of the Reformation to the shaping of Western culture.

The Protestant Work Ethic

To appreciate the significance of the emergence of the Protestant work ethic, we need to understand the intense distaste with which the early Christian tradition, illustrated by the monastic writers, regarded work. For Eusebius of Caesarea, the perfect Christian life was one devoted to serving God, untainted by physical labor. Those who chose to work for a living were second-rate Christians. To live and work in the world was to forfeit a first-rate Christian calling, with all that this implied.

The early monastic tradition appears to have inherited this attitude, with the result that work often came to be seen as a debasing, demeaning activity, best left to one's social – and spiritual – inferiors. If the social patricians of ancient Rome regarded work as below their status, it has to be said that a spiritual aristocracy appears to have developed within early Christianity, with equally negative and dismissive attitudes toward manual labor. Such attitudes probably reached their height of influence during the Middle Ages.

The monastic spirituality of the medieval period generally regarded work as degrading. This widespread stigma against manual labor was pervasive, but not universal. Benedictine spirituality, for instance, created a genuine spiritual place for work within the monastic life. Yet the more widespread medieval attitude was that found in Geoffrey Chaucer's Pardoner in the *Canterbury Tales*, who boasted he would not stoop so low as to weave baskets with his own hands. As the Italian historian of culture Adriano Tilgher concluded in his definitive study of work in the Western world, *Homo Faber: Work through the Ages*, monastic spirituality never regarded everyday work in the world as anything of value. Those who chose to live and work in the world were merely at best "regarded with indulgent charity." Those who committed themselves – either by choice or through lack of serious alternatives – to living and working in the everyday world were regarded as inferior, devoid of any "calling." The Latin term *vocation* was understood to mean a call to the monastic life, which involved leaving the world behind.

From the outset, Protestantism rejected the critical medieval distinction between the "sacred" and "secular" orders. While this can easily be interpreted as the desacralization of the sacred, it can equally well be understood as the sacralization of the secular. As early as 1520, Luther had laid the fundamental conceptual foundations for created sacred space within the secular. His doctrine of the "priesthood of all believers" (p. 211) asserted that there was no genuine difference of status between the "spiritual" and the "temporal" or "secular" order. All Christians were called to be priests – and could exercise that calling within the everyday world. The idea of "calling" was thus fundamentally rede-fined: no longer was it about being called to serve God by leaving the world; it was now about serving God within the everyday world.

God calls his people, not just to faith, but to express that faith in quite definite areas of life. This idea of a "double calling" expressed the view that one is called, in the first place, to be a Christian, and in the second, to live out that faith in a quite definite sphere of activity within the world. Luther stated this point suc-cinctly, when commenting on Genesis 13:13: "what seem to be secular works are actually the praise of God and represent an obedience which is well pleasing to him." There were no limits to this notion of calling. Luther even extolled the religious value of housework, declaring that although "it had no obvious appear-ance of holiness, yet these very household chores are more to be valued than all the works of monks and nuns." Luther's English follower William Tyndale com-mented that while the "washing of dishes and preaching the word of God" clearly represented different human activities, "as touching to please God," there was no essential difference between them.

The historical transformation of the status of work through this ethic is quite remarkable. In his magisterial study of the status of work from Aristotle to Calvin, Vittorio Tranquilli showed how Calvin's theology led directly from a view of work as a socially demeaning, if pragmatically necessary, activity, best left to one's social inferiors, to a dignified and glorious means of praising and affirming God in and through his creation, while adding further to its well-being. It is no acci-dent that those regions of Europe which adopted Protestantism soon found themselves prospering economically – a spin-off, rather than an intended and premeditated consequence, of the new religious importance attached to work (Figure 14.1).

Figure 14.1   Detail of fruit and grain merchants, from *De Sphaera*, c.1470, vellum, by Cristoforo De Predis (c.1440/45–86) (attr. to). MS Lat 209 fol.6v Jupiter. Biblioteca Estense, Modena, Italy/Giraudon/The Bridgeman Art Library

This brings us to consider the economic impact of Reformation thought, including its attitude to work. One theme of especial importance in this connection is the celebrated "Weber thesis" concerning the relation of Protestantism to capitalism.

Reformation Thought and the Origins of Capitalism

Max Weber (1864–1920) (Figure 14.2) set out to identify the characteristics of "modern capitalism" by comparing it with what he termed the "adventurer capitalism" of the medieval period. This earlier form of capitalism, he argued, was opportunistic and unscrupulous; it tended to consume its capital gains in flamboyant and decadent lifestyles. The forms of capitalism to emerge in the early modern period, however, possessed a strong ethical basis, which was often linked to personal asceticism in respect to material goods.

Under Catholicism, the accumulation of capital was seen as intrinsically sinful; under Calvinism, it was seen as praiseworthy. Weber found this fundamental change in attitude particularly well illustrated by a number of seventeenth-century Calvinist writers such as Benjamin Franklin, whose writings combined commendation of the accumulation of capital through engagement with the world, while

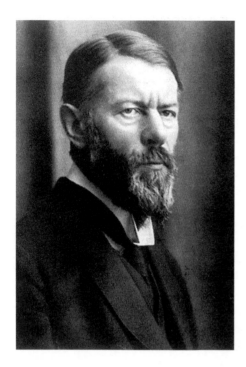

Figure 14.2   Max Weber (1864–1920), sociologist, sociopolitical advocate. Germany, c.1917. Photo akg-images/Ullstein Bild

at the same time criticizing its consumption. Capital was to be seen as something that was to be increased, not something that was to be consumed. Calvinism, according to Weber, thus generated the psychological preconditions essential to the development of modern capitalism.

Weber's argument linking the rise of the "spirit of capitalism" with Calvinism is linked with its concept of predestination. Weber argued that Calvin's predestinarianism created religious anxiety on the part of those wondering whether they were truly elect. In attempting to overcome this anxiety, Weber argued, Calvinist writers such as William Perkins (1558–1602) developed a heightened sense of moral obligation to work, the conviction that a person's election by God was authenticated by his or her activism, and a pervasive ethos of living thriftily off the proceeds from such work, with the remainder being saved, invested, or simply given away.

The "spirit of capitalism" thus arose from the quest for the assurance of salvation – which Calvin's theological system accentuated, but did not itself resolve. Whether Weber is right about this or not, the emergence of modern Western capitalism does seem to have a connection with Calvinism, although it is open to question whether this is as cause or effect. Whereas Karl Marx had argued that the emergence of modern capitalism brought Protestantism into being, Weber argued precisely the reverse. Calvinism made commercial success respectable by declaring that the virtues that lay behind it – such as thrift, austerity, and discipline – were themselves acceptable in God's sight.

Yet clear links exist between Calvin and the rise of modern capitalism in other respects. The most important of these lies in Calvin's attitudes to usury – lending money at interest, with a view to making a profit on the loan. Throughout the patristic era and the Middle Ages, the entire consensus of the church was that usury was a mortal sin. The Old Testament explicitly prohibited this practice. Throughout the patristic and medieval periods, this prohibition was both reinforced and clarified. Three medieval councils – the Second and Third Lateran Councils (1139 and 1179), and the Council of Vienna (1314) – reinforced the Old Testament ban, even stipulating that usurers were to be denied a Christian burial.

These views were not challenged during the first phase of the Reformation. Martin Luther regarded the biblical prohibition of usury as permanently binding. In his 1524 sermon on trade and usury, Luther lashed out at any attempt to charge interest. In his view, Christians "should willingly and gladly lend money without any charge."

Yet the lending of money at interest was essential to the emergence of modern capitalism. A steadily increasing hunger for capital led many in both church and state to turn a blind eye to moneylending, and to reconsider the entire theological basis of the prohibition of usury. Calvin could not be unaware of these problems. The survival of the city of Geneva depended on being able to sustain and develop its urban economy, and remain independent of potentially dangerous neighbors.

In 1545, Calvin wrote to his friend Claude de Sachin, setting out his views on usury. In one respect, Calvin reaffirms the general Protestant idea that not all the rules set out for Jews in the Old Testament were binding upon Christians; in these instances, the Old Testament offered moral guidance only, not positive prescriptions for conduct. Yet this way of interpreting the Old Testament had been applied to cultic issues – such as the Old Testament's demand for animal sacrifices. Calvin's extension of the principle to usury broke new ground.

A fundamental theme that recurs throughout the letter is that things have moved on. The situation in sixteenth-century Europe is not the same as that in ancient Israel. The new realities of financial life in the early modern period made the uncritical application of such Old Testament texts highly problematic. The new economic realities of the sixteenth century meant that interest is simply to be seen as rent paid on capital. Calvin therefore argues for the need to probe deeper, and ascertain the general principles which seem to underlie the Old Testament ban on usury in its original context. It is the *purpose* of the prohibition, not the prohibition itself, which must govern Protestant thinking on this matter. "We ought not to judge usury according to a few passages of Scripture, but in accordance with the principle of equity." For Calvin, the real concern is the exploitation of the poor through high interest rates. This, he argues, can be dealt with in other ways – such as the fixing of interest rates at communally acceptable and morally defensible levels.

Calvin's views took some time to become accepted, being seen by many as running counter to the clear meaning of the Bible. By the middle of the seventeenth century – more than 100 years after Calvin's groundbreaking analysis – usury finally came to be regarded as acceptable. It remains an integral aspect of modern Western culture, and Calvin's role in bringing about such a change of opinion – whether this is seen as progressive or regressive – needs to be recognized.

Reformation Thought and Political Change

It may be argued that the Reformation changed the political face of Europe, partly through the political and social changes it brought about and partly on account of some dangerous new ideas which it unleashed on an unsuspecting Europe. A number of beliefs which had hitherto contributed to the political and social stability of western Europe were called into question. One such belief relates to the "givenness" of existing social structures. It has been argued by political theorists such as Quentin Skinner, in *The Foundations of Modern Political Thought*, that the Reformation, and more specifically the development of Calvinism, was instrumental in effecting the transition from a medieval notion of worldly order, founded upon "an order imagined to be natural and eternal," to a modern order "founded upon change." In other words, the medieval worldview was static: one was allocated a position within society on the basis of birth and tradition, and it was not possible to alter this situation. Calvinism, however, offered an "ideology of transition," in that the individual's position within the world was declared to rest, at least in part, upon his or her efforts.

It is not difficult to see how such a suggestion would be attractive to French peasants – or, indeed, to the bourgeoisie throughout Europe. To a social class frustrated by its inability to make significant headway in a society dominated by tradition and familial ties, the doctrine of the fundamental *changeability* of existing social orders had considerable attraction. The use made of this principle by the English Calvinists John Ponet and Christopher Goodman, who developed theories of justifiable regicide on its basis, demonstrates a fundamental break with the medieval notion that existing power structures are somehow ordained by God, and are thus inviolable and unalterable.

Similar ideas developed in France in the aftermath of the St Bartholomew's Day massacre of 1572, when a significant number of French Protestants were murdered during orchestrated public demonstrations of anti-Protestant feeling. Initially, French Calvinism had limited its political reflections to the general area of liberty of conscience. Throughout the 1550s, as Calvinist influence in France grew steadily more significant, French Calvinist political agitation increasingly focused on religious toleration. There was, it was suggested, no fundamental contradiction between being a Calvinist and being French; to be a Frenchman and a Calvinist (or a Huguenot, for the terms are more or less interchangeable) implied no disloyalty to the French crown. The logic and persuasiveness of this position, which commended it to Calvin among others, were shattered in May 1560 through the Conspiracy of Amboise, in which an attempt was made, apparently aided and abetted by a number of Calvinist pastors (to Calvin's irritation), to kidnap Francis II. It was, however, the St Bartholomew's Day massacre (1572) that precipitated a radical shift in French Calvinist political thinking.

The emergence of monarchomachs – people who wished to place severe restrictions upon the rights of kings and to uphold the *duty* (not merely the *right*) of the people to resist tyrannical monarchs – was a direct response to the atmosphere of shock which persisted in the aftermath of the 1572 massacre. In 1559, Calvin – perhaps beginning to recognize the practical and political importance of the question – had conceded that rulers might exceed the bounds of their authority by setting themselves against God; by doing this, he suggested, they had abrogated their own power.

Calvin, in effect, lays down that any ruler who exceeds the bounds of his or her authority, ordained by God, ceases to be a ruler for that reason, and can no longer exercise the rights and privileges of that rule. Calvin thereby suggests that the magistrates (but not private individuals) may be in a position to take some (somewhat vague and unspecified) action against the ruler. Vague though such reflections were, they prompted others to develop them further – most notably, his French followers, in response to the shocking events of 1572. François Hotman produced the celebrated *Franco-Gallia*, Théodore de Bèze his *Droits des Magistrats*, Philippe Duplessis-Mornay his *Vindiciae contra tyrannos*, and other minor writers produced pamphlet after pamphlet, all making the same point: tyrants are to be resisted. The duty to obey God is to be placed above any obligation to obey a human ruler.

These radical new theories, forged within the crucible of French Calvinism, may be seen as marking an important point of transition between feudalism and modern democracy, with the notion of natural human rights being articulated and defended on theological grounds. Although most French Calvinists abandoned outright opposition to monarchy during the reign of Henry IV, particularly after the promulgation of the Edict of Nantes, important new political theories had been let loose in the French political arena. It has been argued that it was these ideas, in purely secular forms, which resurfaced in the French Enlightenment, when the notion of natural human rights, shorn of its theological trimmings, was amalgamated with the republicanism of Calvin's Geneva in Jean-Jacques Rousseau's *thèse républicaine*, which – in opposition to Voltaire's modernized *thèse royale* and Montesquieu's *thèse nobilaire* – declared that sixteenth-century Geneva was an ideal republic that could serve as a model for eighteenth-century France. Thus Calvin's Geneva became a vibrant and potent ideal, which seized the imagination of pre-revolutionary France. Perhaps the

French revolution of 1789 could be seen as the final flowering of the Genevan revolution of 1535.

But even if this *political* revolution does not owe its inspiration to Calvin, the *scientific* revolution of the late sixteenth and early seventeenth centuries rests firmly upon some of the religious ideas and methods of biblical interpretation which came into being at the time of the Reformation, as we shall see in the following section.

Reformation Thought and the Emergence of the Natural Sciences

To some, the notion of any positive link between religion and science seems highly improbable from the outset. Surely science and religion have always been locked in mortal combat? Yet the stereotype of the "warfare of science and religion" is a product of the social conditions of the late nineteenth century, and is now regarded as historically unacceptable. The interaction of science and religion is far too complex and interesting to be represented in such a simplistic, inaccurate way. The massive advances made in the history of science now allow the early relationship of science and Protestantism to be seen in a much more persuasive light.

It is often noted that the emergence of the natural sciences is specifically linked with the Christian intellectual environment of western Europe. Less obvious, however, is precisely what theoretical explanation might be offered for this, if it is to remain firmly anchored to the historical evidence. A good case can be made for arguing that the Christian doctrine of creation affirmed that the universe was regular and ordered, and that the study of nature was an indirect way of recognizing and honoring the divine wisdom, as seen in the order of things.

Yet, in recent years, a growing body of scholarly work has emerged that argues that the decisive contribution to the emergence of the natural sciences is not to be attributed to Christianity in general, but to Protestantism in particular. In what follows, we shall consider why this is believed to be so. A major factor concerns changes in the ways in which the Bible was interpreted, in which Protestantism played a strategic role. The fundamental change emerged in the first years of Protestantism, which brought about a new approach to the biblical text, and in doing so, brought about a hermeneutical revolution that led to a new approach to natural objects. This arose from the new meaning it lent to the old and religiously appealing "two books" metaphor, which portrayed God as the author of both a "book of words" (the Bible) and a "book of works" (nature).

Early Christian writers were well aware that the "book of nature" could be "read" in various ways. The great Alexandrian theologian Origen held that the visible world was invested with symbols which, if correctly interpreted, would teach the diligent observer about God. Both the Bible and nature thus possessed deeper symbolic meanings. In the Middle Ages, these "symbolic" meanings tended to be given the greater weight. Natural objects were understood in terms of how they fitted into a complex web of theological and spiritual symbolism, rather than being treated as "natural" objects in their own right. Similarly, the allegorical reading of the Bible was held to disclose deeper truths than might be possible by a "surface" or literal reading of the text.

Although Luther and other reformers were fully aware of the importance of symbolic and spiritual meanings of texts, they placed their emphasis upon a literal or historical reading. What, they asked, was the *natural* sense of a biblical passage? This habit of reading the "book of Scripture," when transferred to reading the "book of nature," led to a way of engaging with the natural order which placed an emphasis upon a direct, "natural" account of things. The new **hermeneutical** strategies promoted by the first Protestants were thus of central importance in establishing the conditions that made the emergence of modern science possible.

Such a "literalist mentality" toward the Bible was transposed into what was an insistent empiricism in the field of science. Both religious and scientific truth were held to arise from the immediate, "literal" sense of what meets the human eye. No professional intermediaries, sacred or secular, are required in either case. Science and religion alike are democratized. In his *History of the Royal Society* (1667), Thomas Sprat perceptively remarked that, just as there were two "books," so there were also two "reformations," each prizing direct engagement with God's two books without the need for scholars or priests.

This emerging tendency to see nature as "natural" is linked with the Protestant hostility toward images, which further reinforced the demise of the symbolic conceptions of the natural order. Protestant iconoclasm demonstrates a deep distrust of objects which are asserted to have significance as religious symbols. The same line of thought, which held that human artifacts cannot mediate or symbolize the divine, led to natural objects and phenomena being stripped of their symbolic associations – and hence allowed to become the object of scientific investigation.

This theme of the "desacralization" or "disenchantment" of nature has been studied in depth by scholars of the early modern period, who have noted its implications for the emergence of the natural sciences – but also for secularism and atheism. Peter Berger's analysis of the role of Protestantism in causing secularization deserves mention at this point. For Berger, Protestantism can be thought of as causing "an immense shrinkage in the scope of the sacred in reality." Protestants did not see themselves as living in a world that was "ongoingly penetrated by sacred beings and forces." Instead, they understood that world to be "polarized between a radically transcendent divinity and a radically 'fallen' humanity" that was devoid of any sacred qualities or connections.[2] Catholicism had contained secularizing forces through its deeply symbolic understanding of the natural world and humanity's place within it. Without realizing what it was doing, Protestantism, for Berger, opened the floodgates of the forces that would shape modernity, and ultimately cause Protestantism such grief in its heartlands.

Yet Protestantism created a new motivation – or perhaps, some might argue, enhanced an existing one – for the scientific study of nature. A persistent theme throughout the works of John Calvin was that the wisdom of the invisible and intangible God might be discerned and studied through his works, such as the created order. Calvin thus commended – and even ventured to express some little jealousy of – natural scientists, who were able to experience and appreciate the beauty and wisdom of God through what God had created and molded.

This fundamental motivation for the scientific study of nature has since pervaded Protestantism. It can be seen in many confessional documents of the Reformed church in western Europe. For example, the Belgic Confession affirmed that nature was set "before our eyes as a most beautiful book, in which all creatures, great and small, are like so many characters leading us to contemplate the invisible things of God." The trajectory of thought could not be clearer: reading the "book of nature" enhances our appreciation of what is known of God through the "book of Scripture."

Others have noted that the Protestant motivation for studying science was not limited to factors that emerged as significant during the sixteenth century. In 1938, the sociologist Robert Merton (1910–2003) suggested that certain types of Protestantism played a significant role in stimulating the consolidation of a scientific culture in seventeenth-century England. At the heart of the "Merton thesis" is a variant of Max Weber's famous theory concerning Protestantism and the rise of the "spirit of capitalism" (pp. 258–61). The Protestant ethos – especially that found in English Puritanism and German Pietism – stimulated scientific research by giving it a religious dimension.

These ideas were taken up with enthusiasm by the Royal Society, the most significant organization devoted to the advancement of scientific research and learning in England. Many of its early members were admirers of Calvin, familiar with his writings and their potential relevance to their fields of study. Thus Richard Bentley (1662–1742) delivered a series of lectures in 1692, based on Newton's *Principia Mathematica* (1687), in which the regularity of the universe, as established by Newton, is interpreted as evidence of design. There are unambiguous hints here of Calvin's reference to the universe as a "theatre of the glory of God," in which humans are an appreciative audience. The detailed study of the creation leads to an increased awareness of the wisdom of its creator.

Calvin's second major contribution was to eliminate a significant obstacle to the development of the natural sciences: biblical literalism. This emancipation of scientific observation and theory from crudely literalist interpretations of Scripture took place at two levels. First, he declared that Scripture is not concerned with detailing the structure of the world, but with proclaiming the gospel of Jesus Christ. Second, he insisted that not all biblical statements concerning God or the world were to be taken literally. Some were "accommodated," in that they were adapted to the abilities and capacities of their audiences.

The impact of both these ideas upon scientific theorizing, especially during the seventeenth century, was considerable. For example, the English writer Edward Wright defended Copernicus's heliocentric theory of the solar system against biblical literalists by arguing, in the first place, that Scripture was not concerned with physics, and in the second, that its manner of speaking was "accommodated to the understanding and way of speech of the common people, like nurses to little children." Both these arguments derive directly from Calvin, who, it may be argued, made a fundamental contribution to the emergence of the natural sciences at these points.

Reformation Ecclesiologies and the Modern World

Earlier, we noted how reformers such as Luther and Calvin set out a new vision of what it meant to be a "Christian church" that removed any necessity for institutional continuity with the medieval church. There are two – and only two – essential elements of a Christian church: the preaching of the word of God, and the proper administration of the sacraments. While tokens of historical continuity with the apostolic church were to be welcomed, the all-important thing was continuity with the apostolic teaching.

This opened the way for one of the most characteristic features of modern Protestantism in the United States and far beyond – the radical proliferation of "churches." Catholic critics of Protestantism often point to its innate fissiparous tendencies, which they regard as showing a lack of concern for the fundamental unity of the church. This "family characteristic" of modern Protestantism can be traced back to the ecclesiologies of both Luther and Calvin. With the benefit of hindsight, these can now be seen to have laid the conceptual foundations that encouraged entrepreneurs to set up their own congregations or even denominations, where necessary breaking away from older communities.

Although this distinctive and characteristic Reformation doctrine of the church dates from the 1520s and 1530s, its full significance only became clear in the nineteenth and twentieth centuries. This ecclesiology enabled enterprising individuals, often fired up by a vision for a specific form of ministry, to start their own congregations, or even their own denominations.

There might well be one universal church, to which all Christians belonged – but there were countless local churches, each embodying a distinctive idea of what it meant to be a Christian, often adapted to the specifics of a local cultural situation, or shaped by a controversy whose theological relevance and emotional potency dwindled with each passing year. It is not unfair to suggest that the Protestant vision of the church unleashed a Darwinian process of competition and survival, gradually eliminating maladapted churches, and ensuring that what survives is well suited to the needs and opportunities of the day.

This way of looking at things allowed modern Protestantism to deal with rapid social and cultural change, which often leads to churches being locked into the realities of a bygone age. Entrepreneurial pastors and preachers can easily recast a vision of the gospel, adapted to the new situation – in much the same way as older visions were adapted to their situations – and thus prevent Protestantism being trapped in a time warp.

Conclusion

It is impossible in the limited space available to provide a detailed analysis of the possible influence of the ideas of the Reformation upon the course of subsequent human history. But what has been said in this final chapter indicates that ideas possess the potential to change things. The Reformation, like the Russian Revolution, is a reminder that ideas are not simply the product of societies; on occasion, they bring those societies into being. The telling comparison between Lenin and Calvin, frequent in recent studies of the French reformer, points to the historical importance of people with radical ideas at certain formative points in history. This book has attempted to make some of those ideas intelligible and accessible to a wider public, so that a deeper appreciation of this fascinating period may result.

A history that neglects ideas has not told its story well, and has certainly not told it fully. The Reformation is a movement in which religious ideas played a major role. There were other factors – social, economic, political, and cultural – involved in that movement. Those other factors should and must gain a hearing. But to tell the story of the Reformation without allowing for the imaginative power of religious ideas is an absurdity. It may be difficult for some modern secular interpreters of the movement to appreciate the power of religion as a historical force. Since their world has not been directly shaped by religion, they assume that this has always been the case. But it is not so. Perhaps we have yet to learn that most difficult of all historical skills: the ability to immerse ourselves in the world of a culture that is now dead and imagine ourselves in the midst of a world in which religious ideas and attitudes mattered profoundly. This book cannot wholly achieve that aim; but it has tried to draw back the curtain a little, and allow us to understand better this fascinating and important period in the history of human thought and culture, and its impact on our history.

Notes

1   Bainton, R. H., *The Medieval Church* (Princeton, NJ, 1962), p. 42.
2   Berger, P., *The Sacred Canopy: Elements of a Sociological Theory of Religion* (Garden City, NY, 1967).

Further Reading

Biéler, A., *Calvin's Economic and Social Thought* (Geneva, 2006).

Dillenberger, J., *Protestant Thought and Natural Science* (London, 1961).

Grenholm, C.-H., *Protestant Work Ethics: A Study of Work Ethical Theories in Contemporary Protestant Theology* (Uppsala, 1993).

Harrison, P., *The Bible, Protestantism, and the Rise of Natural Science* (Cambridge, 1998).

Hooykaas, R., *Religion and the Rise of Modern Science* (Edinburgh, 1972).

Howell, K. J., *God's Two Books: Copernican Cosmology and Biblical Interpretation in Early Modern Science* (Notre Dame, IN, 2002).

Marshall, G., *Presbyteries and Profits: Calvinism and the Development of Capitalism in Scotland, 1560–1707* (Oxford, 1980).

Noonan, J. T., *The Scholastic Analysis of Usury* (Cambridge, MA, 1957).

Roth, G., and H. Lehmann, *Weber's "Protestant Ethic": Origins, Evidence, Contexts* (Cambridge, 1993).

Seel, G. E., *Regicide and Republic: England 1603–1660* (Cambridge, 2001).

Skinner, Q., *The Foundations of Modern Political Thought*, 2 vols (Cambridge, 1978).

Tilgher, A. *Homo Faber: Work through the Ages* (Chicago, 1965).

Appendix 1
A Glossary of Theological and Historical Terms

The standard theological reference work in English, to which the reader is referred for further discussion, is *The Oxford Dictionary of the Christian Church* (3rd edn, Oxford, 1997). Much useful information may be found in an older reference work: *The New Schaff–Herzog Encyclopedia of Religious Knowledge* (12 vols; Grand Rapids, MI, 1957), with especially useful information on sixteenth-century Lutheran and Reformed controversies. A specialized glossary of late medieval theological terms may be found in Heiko A. Oberman, *The Harvest of Medieval Theology: Gabriel Biel and Late Medieval Nominalism* (Cambridge, MA, 1963), pp. 459–76. Glossaries of terms relating to the doctrine of justification may be found in Alister E. McGrath, *Iustitia Dei: A History of the Christian Doctrine of Justification* (Cambridge, 2005), pp. 396–8.

adiaphora Literally, "matters of indifference." Beliefs or practices which the Reformers regarded as being tolerable, in that they were neither explicitly rejected nor stipulated by Scripture. For example, what ministers wore at church services was often regarded as a "matter of indifference." The concept is of importance in that it allowed the Reformers to adopt a pragmatic approach to many beliefs and practices, thus avoiding unnecessary confrontation.

Anabaptism Literally, "re-baptism." A term used to refer to the radical wing of the Reformation, based on thinkers such as Menno Simons or Balthasar Hubmaier. See p. 9–11.

Reformation Thought: An Introduction, Fourth Edition. Alister E. McGrath.
© 2012 John Wiley & Sons, Ltd. Published 2012 by John Wiley & Sons, Ltd.

anti-Pelagian writings   The writings of Augustine relating to the Pelagian controversy, in which he defended his views on grace and justification. See "Pelagianism."

apostolic era   For humanists and reformers alike, the definitive period of the Christian church, bounded by the resurrection of Jesus Christ (c.35) and the death of the last apostle (c.90?). The ideas and practices of this period were widely regarded as normative in humanist and reforming circles.

Augustinianism   A term used in two major senses. First, it refers to the views of Augustine of Hippo concerning the doctrine of salvation, in which the need for divine grace is stressed (see pp. 65–7). In this sense, the term is the antithesis of Pelagianism. Second, it is used to refer to the body of opinion within the Augustinian Order during the Middle Ages, irrespective of whether these views derive from Augustine or not. See further David C. Steinmetz, *Luther and Staupitz: An Essay in the Intellectual Origins of the Protestant Reformation* (Durham, NC, 1980); also pp. 265–7 above.

Calvinism   An ambiguous term, used with two quite distinct meanings. First, it refers to the religious ideas of religious bodies (such as the Reformed church) and individuals (such as Theodore Beza) who were profoundly influenced by John Calvin or by documents written by him. Second, it refers to the religious ideas of John Calvin himself. Although the first sense is by far the more common, there is a growing recognition that the term is misleading. See pp. 202–4.

catechism   A popular manual of Christian doctrine, usually in the form of question and answer, intended for religious instruction. With its considerable emphasis upon religious education, the Reformation saw the appearance of a number of major catechisms, most notably Luther's *Lesser Catechism* (1529) and the celebrated *Heidelberg Catechism* (1563) (see pp. 244–6).

Christology   The section of Christian theology dealing with the identity of Jesus Christ, particularly the question of the relation of his human and divine natures. Apart from a disagreement between Luther and Zwingli at Marburg in 1529, Christology, like the doctrine of the Trinity, was not debated extensively during the Reformation.

cinquecento   The 1500s – that is, the sixteenth century. See p. 36.

confession   Although the term refers primarily to the admission of sin, it acquired a rather different technical sense in the sixteenth century – that of a document which embodies the principles of faith of a Protestant church. Thus the Augsburg Confession (1530) embodies the ideas of early Lutheranism, and the First Helvetic Confession (1536) those of the early Reformed church. The term "Confessionalism" is often used to refer to the hardening of religious attitudes in the later sixteenth century, as the Lutheran and Reformed churches became involved in a struggle for power, especially in Germany.

Donatism   A breakaway religious movement, based in Roman North Africa during the late fourth century, which stressed the need for purity and holiness on the part of church members and leaders. Donatism insisted that the church was a community of saints, rather than, as Augustine taught, a mixed body of the righteous and evil. The Donatist controversy raised the question, which reemerged at the time of the Reformation, of how the mainstream church could be reformed without the need to form splinter groups.

ecclesiology   The section of Christian theology dealing with the theory of the church (Latin *ecclesia*, "church"). At the time of the Reformation, controversy centered upon the question of whether the Protestant churches could be regarded as continuous with mainstream Christianity – in other words, were they a reformed version of Christianity or something completely new, having little or no connection with the previous 1500 years of Christian history?

evangelical   A term used to refer to the nascent reforming movements, especially in Germany and Switzerland, in the 1510s and 1520s. The term was later replaced by "Protestant" in the aftermath of the Second Diet of Speyer.

évangeliques   A term often used to refer to the French reforming movement, especially in the 1520s and 1530s, centering upon figures such as Margaret of Navarre and Guillaume Briçonnet.

evangelism   A term often used in English-language scholarship to refer to the Italian reforming movement in the period 1511–45, centering upon figures such as Gasparo Contarini and Reginald Pole.

exegesis   The science of textual interpretation, usually referring specifically to the Bible. The term "biblical exegesis" basically means "the process of interpreting the Bible." See pp. 102–5. The specific techniques employed in the exegesis of Scripture are usually referred to as "hermeneutics."

Fathers   An alternative term for "patristic writers."

hermeneutics   The principles underlying the interpretation, or exegesis, of a text, particularly of Scripture. The first phase of the Reformation witnessed the development of a number of ways of interpreting Scripture, deriving from both humanism and scholasticism. Zwingli initially used a hermeneutical scheme deriving from Erasmian humanism, and Luther a scheme deriving from scholastic theology.

humanism   A complex movement, linked with the European Renaissance, discussed in detail in Chapter 3. At the heart of the movement lay not (as the modern sense of the word might suggest) a set of secular or secularizing ideas, but a new interest in the cultural achievements of antiquity. These were seen as a major resource for the renewal of European culture and Christianity during the period of the Renaissance. The impact of humanism upon Reformation thought is considerable, and is discussed in detail at pp. 35–58.

justification by faith, doctrine of   The section of Christian theology dealing with how the individual sinner is able to enter into fellowship with God. See pp. 115–17. Although of major importance to Martin Luther and his colleagues at Wittenberg, the doctrine was of relatively little interest to the Swiss reformers, such as Zwingli. See pp. 115–39.

liturgy   The written text of public services, especially of the Eucharist. As liturgy was predetermined by theology in the Reformation, the reform of the liturgy was regarded as being of particular importance.

Lutheranism   The religious ideas associated with Martin Luther, particularly as expressed in the *Lesser Catechism* (1529) and the Augsburg Confession (1530). A series of internal disagreements within Lutheranism after Luther's death (1546) between hardliners (the so-called "Gnesio-Lutherans" or "Flacianists") and moderates ("Philippists") led to their resolution by the *Formula of Concord* (1577), which is usually regarded as the authoritative statement of Lutheran theology.

magisterial Reformation   A term used to refer to the Lutheran and Reformed wings of the Reformation, as opposed to the radical wing (Anabaptism). See pp. 5–9.

nominalism   Strictly speaking, the theory of knowledge opposed to realism. The term is, however, still used occasionally to refer to the *via moderna*.

patristic   An adjective used to refer to the first centuries in the history of the church, following the writing of the New Testament (the "patristic period") or thinkers writing during this period (the "patristic writers"). For the Reformers, the period thus designated seems to be c.100–451 (in other words, the period between the closing of the New Testament and the Council of Chalcedon). The Reformers tended to regard the New Testament and, to a lesser extent, the patristic periods as normative for Christian belief and practice.

Pelagianism   An understanding of how humans are able to merit their salvation which is diametrically opposed to that of Augustine of Hippo; it places considerable emphasis upon the role of human works and plays down the idea of divine grace. See pp. 67–9.

Protestantism   A term used in the aftermath of the Diet of Speyer (1529) to designate those who "protested" against the practices and beliefs of the Roman Catholic church. Prior to 1529, such individuals and groups had referred to themselves as "evangelicals."

quattrocento   The 1400s – that is, the fifteenth century. See p. 36.

radical Reformation   A term used with increasing frequency to refer to the Anabaptist movement – in other words, the wing of the Reformation that went beyond what Luther and Zwingli envisaged. See pp. 9–11.

sacrament   In purely historical terms, a church service or rite which was held to have been instituted by Jesus Christ himself. Although medieval theology and church practice recognized seven such sacraments, the Reformers argued that only two (baptism and Eucharist) were to be found in the New Testament itself. The theory of the sacraments proved intensely divisive, with the Reformers unable to reach agreement among themselves concerning what the sacraments actually achieved. See pp. 163–90 for further discussion.

schism   A deliberate break with the unity of the church, condemned vigorously by influential writers of the early church such as Cyprian and Augustine. The Reformers were branded as "schismatics" by their opponents. The reformers thus found themselves in the difficult situation of upholding Augustine's views on grace, but disregarding his views on schism. See pp. 143–6.

schola Augustiniana moderna   A form of late medieval scholasticism which laid emphasis upon Augustine's doctrine of grace, while adopting a nominalist position on the question of universals. See pp. 65–7.

Scotism   The scholastic philosophy associated with Duns Scotus.

Scripture principle   The theory, especially associated with Reformed theologians, that the practices and beliefs of the church should be grounded in Scripture. Nothing that could not be demonstrated to be grounded in Scripture could be regarded as binding upon the believer. The phrase *sola scriptura* ("by Scripture alone") summarizes this principle. See pp. 98–100.

Septuagint   The Greek translation of the Old Testament, dating from the third century BC.

Sermon on the Mount   The standard way of referring to Christ's moral and pastoral teaching in the specific form which it takes in chapters 5 to 7 of Matthew's gospel.

sodality   A term used generally to refer to the humanist groups associated with many northern European cities and universities in the late fifteenth and early sixteenth centuries. For example, the *sodalitas Collimitiana* at Vienna centered around Georg Collimitius, and the *sodalitas Staupitziana* at Nuremberg centered around Johannes von Staupitz.

soteriology   The section of Christian theology dealing with the doctrine of salvation (Greek *soteria*).

Thomism   The scholastic philosophy associated with Thomas Aquinas.

transubstantiation   The medieval doctrine according to which the bread and the wine are transformed into the body and blood of Christ in the Eucharist, while retaining their outward appearance. See pp. 169–70.

trecento   The 1300s – that is, the fourteenth century. See p. 36.

Turmerlebnis   A German term, literally meaning "tower experience," often used to designate Luther's moment of breakthrough. See p. 120. In a later (confused) reference, Luther mentions that his theological breakthrough took place in a tower of the Augustinian monastery at Wittenberg – hence the reference to the "tower."

via antiqua   A term used to designate forms of scholastic philosophy, such as Thomism and Scotism, which adopted a realist position on the question of universals.

via moderna   A term used broadly in two senses. First, forms of scholastic philosophy which adopted a nominalist position on the question of universals, in opposition to the realism of the *via antiqua*. See pp. 66–8. Second, and more important, the form of scholasticism (formerly known as "nominalism") based upon the writings of William of Ockham and his followers, such as Pierre d'Ailly and Gabriel Biel. See pp. 67–9.

Vulgate   The Latin translation of the Bible, mostly deriving from Jerome, upon which medieval theology was largely based. Strictly speaking, "Vulgate" designates Jerome's translation of the Old Testament (except the Psalms, which were taken from the Gallican Psalter), the Apocryphal works (except Wisdom, Ecclesiasticus, 1 and 2 Maccabees, and Baruch, which were taken from the Old

Latin Version), and all the New Testament. The recognition of its many inaccuracies was of fundamental importance to the Reformation. See pp. 94–5.

Zwinglianism   The term is used generally to refer to the thought of Huldrych Zwingli, but is also often used specifically to refer to his views on the sacraments, especially on the "real presence" (which for Zwingli was more of a "real absence"). See pp. 176–9.

Appendix 2
English Translations of Major Primary Sources

John Calvin

Calvin's most important work is the 1559 edition of the *Institutes of the Christian Religion*. This is available in a number of English translations, of which the two following are particularly recommended:

Institutes of the Christian Religion, trans. H. Beveridge (2 vols; Grand Rapids, MI, 1975).
Institutes of the Christian Religion, ed. J. T. McNeill, trans. F. L. Battles (2 vols; Library of Christian Classics 20–1: Philadelphia and London, 1975).

The 1536 edition of the *Institutes* is also available in English translation:

Institution of the Christian Religion, trans. F. L. Battles (Atlanta, 1975).

Many of Calvin's remaining works, particularly his tracts and New Testament commentaries, were translated into English by the Calvin Translation Society during the nineteenth century:

Calvin's Tracts (3 vols; Edinburgh, 1844–51).
Calvin's Commentaries (47 vols; Edinburgh, 1843–59).

Reformation Thought: An Introduction, Fourth Edition. Alister E. McGrath.
© 2012 John Wiley & Sons, Ltd. Published 2012 by John Wiley & Sons, Ltd.

A new translation of the New Testament commentaries is also available:

Calvin's Commentaries, ed. D. W. Torrance and T. F. Torrance (Edinburgh, 1959–).

The following translations should also be noted:

Calvin's Commentary on Seneca's "De Clementia", ed. F. L. Battles and A. M. Hugo (Leiden, 1969).
John Calvin and Jacopo Sadoleto: A Reformation Debate. Sadoleto's Letter to the Genevans and Calvin's Reply (New York, 1996).
Jean Calvin: Three French Treatises, ed. F. H. Higman (London, 1970).
Calvin's Theological Treatises, ed. J. K. S. Reid (Library of Christian Classics 22: Philadelphia, 1954).

Desiderius Erasmus of Rotterdam

The most comprehensive English edition of Erasmus's works is *The Collected Works of Erasmus* (81 vols; Toronto, 1969–), still in progress. This series, when complete, will be the definitive English-language edition of Erasmus. The following are of particular interest to the historian of the Reformation: The correspondence (vols 1–22), especially letters 993–1251 (vols 7–8), which deal with the period 1519–21, during which the "Lutherana tragoedia" began to dominate Erasmus's concerns; and the New Testament Scholarship (vols 41–60), which did much to lay the intellectual foundations of the Reformation. These volumes should be read in conjunction with Erika Rummel, *Erasmus' Annotations on the New Testament: From Philologist to Theologian* (Erasmus Study 8: Toronto, 1986).

Martin Luther

The most widely used English translation of Luther's works is the so-called *American Edition: Luther's Works* (55 vols; St Louis and Philadelphia, 1955–75). In addition to a companion volume, this edition includes most of Luther's exegetical works (vols 1–30), as well as tracts, sermons, and political writings (vols 31–54). The exegetical works are arranged in the order in which the scriptural books are found in the Bible, rather than in the order in which Luther wrote them.

A useful anthology is *Martin Luther: Selections from his Writings*, ed. John Dillenberger (New York, 1962). The three "Reformation treatises" of 1520 are conveniently collected together in *Three Treatises* (Philadelphia, 1973).

Huldrych Zwingli

The most complete English translations to date are the three volumes of *The Latin Works of Huldreich Zwingli*, as follows:

The Latin Works and Correspondence of Huldreich Zwingli. Vol. I: 1510–1522, ed. S. M. Jackson (New York, 1912).

The Latin Works of Huldreich Zwingli. Vol. II, ed. W. J. Hinke (Philadelphia, 1922); reprinted as *Zwingli on Providence and Other Essays* (Durham, NC., 1983).

The Latin Works of Huldreich Zwingli. Vol. III, ed. C. N. Heller (Philadelphia, 1929); reprinted as *Commentary on True and False Religion* (Durham, NC, 1981).

These have been supplemented by:

Huldrych Zwingli Writings: The Defense of the Reformed Faith, ed. E. J. Furcha (Allison Park, PA, 1984).

Huldrych Zwingli Writings: In Search of True Religion, ed. H. Wayne Pipkin (Allison Park, PA, 1984).

Two other collections are worth noting:

The Selected Works of Huldrych Zwingli, ed. S. M. Jackson (Philadelphia, 1901; reprinted 1972).

Zwingli and Bullinger, ed. G. W. Bromiley (Library of Christian Classics 24: Philadelphia, 1953).

Appendix 3

Standard Abbreviations of Major Journals and Sources

The following abbreviations are encountered regularly in the literature dealing with the history and thought of the Reformation period. The situation is made more complicated than necessary through absence of general agreement on the standard abbreviations for certain works. Where several abbreviations are in use, the preferred abbreviation is indicated. The most helpful guide to the abbreviations used to designate the secondary literature is S. Schwertner, *Internationales Abkürzungsverzeichnis für Theologie und Grenzgebiete* (Berlin and New York, 1973) ("International Glossary of Abbreviations for Theology and Related Subjects," often abbreviated as IATG).

Primary Sources

The reader will find it helpful to read these notes in conjunction with Appendixes 2 and 4.

CR   *Corpus Reformatorum* (Berlin, Leipzig, and Zurich, 1834–). The standard edition of the works of Melanchthon (vols 1–28), Calvin (vols 29–87), and Zwingli (vols 88–). The Calvin section is sometimes (confusingly) referred to as OC. See notes on Calvin and Zwingli in Appendix 4.

CWE   *Complete Works of Erasmus* (Toronto, 1969–). This series, which is still in progress, has become the standard English translation of Erasmus's works.

Reformation Thought: An Introduction, Fourth Edition. Alister E. McGrath.
© 2012 John Wiley & Sons, Ltd. Published 2012 by John Wiley & Sons, Ltd.

EE   *Erasmi Epistolae*, ed. P. S. Allen (Oxford, 1905–58). The standard
          edition of Erasmus's correspondence.

LB   *Desiderii Erasmi Opera Omnia*, ed. J. LeClerc (Leiden, 1703–6;
          reprinted London, 1962). The Leiden (Lugduni Batavorum) edition
          of Erasmus's works.

LCC   *Library of Christian Classics* (London and Philadelphia, 1953–).
          Includes useful translations of Bucer, Zwingli, and Melanchthon, as
          well as of Calvin's 1559 *Institutes*.

LW   *Luther's Works*, ed. J. Pelikan and H. Lehmann (55 vols; St Louis
          and Philadelphia, 1955–75). The "American edition" of Luther's
          works in English translation.

OC   *Opera Calvini*. An alternative, and somewhat confusing, reference to
          the Calvin section of *Corpus Reformatorum*: see CR.

OS   *Opera Selecta Ioannis Calvini*, ed. P. Barth (5 vols; Munich, 1926–
          36). A useful critical edition of Calvin's major works, including both
          the 1536 and 1559 editions of the *Institutes*.

S   *Huldrich Zwingli's Werke*, ed. M. Schuler and J. Schulthess (8 vols;
          Zurich, 1828–42). The first edition of Zwingli's works, now being
          supplanted gradually by the *Corpus Reformatorum* edition.

SS   An alternative abbreviation for the Schuler–Shulthess edition of
          Zwingli's works: see S.

WA   *D. Martin Luthers Werke: Kritische Gesamtausgabe*, ed. J. K. F.
          Knaake, G. Kawerau, *et al.* (Weimar, 1883–). The definitive
          "Weimar edition" of Luther's works, which also includes his
          correspondence (WABr), his German Bible (WADB), and his "Table-
          Talk" (WATr).

WABr   *D. Martin Luthers Werke: Briefwechsel* (15 vols; Weimar, 1930–78).
          The correspondence section of the Weimar edition of Luther's
          works.

WADB   *D. Martin Luthers Werke: Deutsches Bibel* (Weimar, 1906–). The
          "German Bible" section of the Weimar edition of Luther's works.

WATr   *D. Martin Luthers Werke: Tischreden* (6 vols; Weimar, 1912–21).
          The "Table-Talk" section of the Weimar edition of Luther's works.

Z   *Huldreich Zwinglis sämtliche Werke*, ed. E. Egli *et al.* (*Corpus
          Reformatorum*, vols 88– : Berlin, Leipzig, and Zurich, 1905–). The
          best critical edition of Zwingli's works, still in progress, replacing the
          Schuler–Schulthess edition of the nineteenth century. Two other
          methods of referring to this edition should be noted: first, CR followed
          by a volume number of 88 or greater, which refers the reader to the
          appropriate volume in the section of the *Corpus Reformatorum* series
          devoted to Zwingli; second, CR (Zwingli), which refers the reader to
          the *Corpus Reformatorum* series, vols 88–. Thus *CR (Zwingli) 1* is a
          reference to the first volume in the Zwingli section of the *Corpus
          Reformatorum* series – i.e., vol. 88. See further in Appendix 4.

ZW   Alternative abbreviation for *Huldreich Zwinglis sämtliche Werke*:
          preferred abbreviation is Z.

Secondary Sources

ADB   *Allgemeine Deutsche Biographie* (55 vols; Leipzig, 1875–1912;
          reprinted Berlin, 1967–71).
AGBR   *Aktensammlung zur Geschichte der Basler Reformation in den Jahren
          1519 bis Anfang 1534* (3 vols; Basle, 1921–37).
AGZR   *Aktensammlung zur Geschichte der Züricher Reformation in den
          Jahren 1519–33*, ed. E. Egli (Zurich, 1879; reprinted Aalen, 1973).
ARG   *Archiv für Reformationsgeschichte*
BHR   *Bibliothèque d'humanisme et Renaissance*
CIC   *Corpus Iuris Canonici* (2 vols; Leipzig, 1879; reprinted Graz, 1959).
CICiv   *Corpus Iuris Civilis* (3 vols; Berlin, 1872–1908).
EThL   *Ephemerides Theologicae Louvaniensis*
FcS   *Franciscan Studies*
FS   *Franziskanische Studien*
HThR   *Harvard Theological Review*
JThS   *Journal of Theological Studies*
QFRG   *Quellen und Forschungen zur Reformationsgeschichte* (Gütersloh,
          1911–).
RGG   *Religion in Geschichte und Gegenwart* (6 vols; 3rd edn, Tübingen,
          1957–65).
RGST   *Reformationsgeschichtliche Studien und Texte* (Münster, 1906–).
RThAM   *Recherches de théologie ancienne et médiévale*
SJTh   *Scottish Journal of Theology*
SMRT   *Studies in Medieval and Reformation Thought*, ed. H. A. Oberman
          (Leiden, 1966–).
ZKG   *Zeitschrift für Kirchengeschichte*
ZKTh   *Zeitschrift für katholische Theologie*
ZThK   *Zeitschrift für Theologie und Kirche*
Zwa   *Zwingliana: Beiträge zur Geschichte Zwinglis, der Reformation, und
          des Protestantismus in der Schweiz*

Note that some writers prefer to abbreviate "Theology" and derived words as
"T" rather than "Th" – thus *SJTh*, *JThS*, and *HThR* are often abbreviated as *SJT*,
JTS, and *HTR*.

Appendix 4
How to Refer to Major Primary Sources

Major studies of Reformation personalities or ideas frequently assume that their readers know how to interpret references to primary source materials. Experience suggests that this is a wildly optimistic assumption. This appendix aims to enable the reader to handle the most commonly encountered methods of referring to such material for the four major figures for which this is usually necessary: Calvin, Erasmus, Luther, and Zwingli.

Abbreviations used in referring to primary sources may be found in Appendix 3. English translations of major works may be found in Appendix 2.

John Calvin

Calvin's *Institutes of the Christian Religion* is almost invariably referred to in the edition of 1559. This edition is divided into four main sections (books), each dealing with a broad general theme. Each book is then divided into chapters, each of which is further subdivided into sections. A reference to the 1559 edition of this work will therefore include *three* numbers, identifying the *book*, the *chapter*, and the *section*. The book number is usually given in capital Roman numerals, the chapter in small Roman numerals, and the section in Arabic numerals. Thus book two, chapter twelve, section one, would probably be referred to as II.xii.1, although a reference might also read II, 12, 1 or 2.12.1.

In addition, reference may be given to an edition (e.g., the *Corpus Reformatorum* or *Opera Selecta*) or an English translation. For example, the reference *Institutio*

Reformation Thought: An Introduction, Fourth Edition. Alister E. McGrath.
© 2012 John Wiley & Sons, Ltd. Published 2012 by John Wiley & Sons, Ltd.

III.xi.1; *OS* 4.193.2–5 is a reference to book three, chapter eleven, section one of the 1559 edition of the *Institutes*, specifically the section to be found on lines 2–5 of page 193 of the fourth volume of the *Opera Selecta*. Similarly a reference to *Institutes* IV.v.5; tr. Beveridge, 2.243 is to the fifth section of the fifth chapter of book four of the *Institutes*, as it is found on page 243 of volume two of the celebrated translation by Henry Beveridge (see Appendix 2).

Reference to Calvin's commentaries and sermons usually involves the *Corpus Reformatorum* edition, which is referred to simply by volume and page number. Thus CR 50.437 is a reference to page 437 of volume 50. The volume number will be in the range 1–59. Occasionally, unfortunately, confusion can result from an irritating practice fortunately generally confined to older studies of Calvin. The *Corpus Reformatorum* edition consists of the works of Melanchthon (vols 1–28), Calvin (vols 29–87), and Zwingli (vols 88–). Volume one of Calvin's works is thus volume 29 within the series – and older works sometimes refer to Calvin's works using this higher volume number. If you find reference to this edition of Calvin with a volume number in the region 60–87, you should subtract 28 to obtain the correct volume number. If you find an isolated reference to Calvin, especially in an older work, which doesn't seem to make sense, subtract 28, and try again!

Desiderius Erasmus

The two most commonly encountered editions of Erasmus's Latin works are the LeClerc edition, published at Leiden in 1703 (reprinted in 1963), and the Allen edition of the correspondence.

The LeClerc edition is almost invariably referred to in the following manner. An initial number denotes the *volume*, and a second number the *column* (each page is divided into two columns, numbered individually). This is then followed by a *letter* (A–F), which indicates the position of the section being referred to in the column. These letters are printed on the page of the LeClerc edition for ease of reference. The following references are given to illustrate this: LB V.153 F; LB X.1754 C–D; and LB II.951 A–B. The first reference is to column 153 of volume 5, the letter F indicating that the section is at the bottom of the column. The second reference is to column 1754 of volume 10, the letters C–D indicating that the section being referred to is to be found toward the middle of the column. The final reference is to column 951 of volume 2, the letters A–B indicating that the section is toward the top of the page.

The Allen edition of the correspondence is generally referred to by first identifying the *volume*, followed by the *page* and *line* numbers – thus EE 2.491.133–9 refers to lines 133–9 on page 491 of the second of the twelve volumes. Occasionally, reference is made to the *letter number* – thus EE 2, no. 541, is a reference to letter number 541 (from Erasmus to Capito, dated February 26, 1517), to be found in the second volume of the Allen edition.

Martin Luther

The only critical edition of Luther's works now generally referred to is the great "Weimar edition," begun in 1883 as part of the celebrations of the 400th anniversary of the German Reformer's birth. The edition is divided into four main sections:

1   The main body of the work, containing his major theological writings (abbreviated as WA).
2   The correspondence (abbreviated as WABr). In catalogues, this section is generally designated by the German word *Briefwechsel*.
3   The so-called Table-Talk (abbreviated as WATr). In catalogues, this section is generally designated by the German word *Tischreden*. This material was not written by Luther himself, but consists of reports of Luther's mealtime conversations with his friends. The reliability of this material has frequently been challenged.
4   The "German Bible" (abbreviated as WADB). In catalogues, this section is generally designated by the German words *Deutsches Bibel*.

The first stage in deciphering a reference to the Weimar edition is thus to determine which of the four sections of the work is being referred to. For most purposes, it is likely to be the main body of the work.

This is relatively simple to handle. Reference is invariably given by volume number, page number, and line number – in that order. There is some variation in the method of referring to the volume number, some writers using Roman, others Arabic numerals. Thus WA 4.25.12–17 and WA IV.25.12–17 are both references to lines 12–17 of page 25 of the fourth volume of the main body of the work. The only difficulty to note is that some volumes are divided into parts. Where this applies, the *part* number follows immediately after the *volume* number. Three main systems are encountered for designating the part number. The references WA 55 II.109.9, WA LV/2.109.9, and WA 55.2.109.9 all refer to line nine of page 109 of the second part of volume 55 of the Weimar edition.

The correspondence (WABr) and the German Bible (WADB) are generally referred to in much the same way. Thus WABr 1.99.8–13 is a reference to lines 8–13 of page 99 of the first volume of the correspondence. In the case of the Table-Talk (WATr), however, a slightly different means of reference is generally employed. The Table-Talk is divided into nearly 6000 sections, and the general practice is to refer to the volume number, followed by the section number. Thus WATr 2.2068 is a reference to section 2068, which may be found in the second of the six volumes of the Weimar edition of the Table-Talk. On a few rare occasions, these sections are further subdivided: the subdivisions are identified by letter – for example, *WATr 3.3390b*.

Huldrych Zwingli

Reference in all modern studies is to the excellent *Corpus Reformatorum* edition, generally designated simply as Z (for other designations, see Appendix 3). Several works not in this modern edition are to be found in the Schuler–Schulthess edition. The student must therefore be able to deal with both these editions.

The *Corpus Reformatorum* edition is referred to by volume number, page number, and line number. Volume 6 is subdivided, with the subdivisions usually being designated by lower-case Roman numbers. Thus Z III.259.32 refers to line 32 on page 259 of volume 3, and Z VI iii.182.3–5 to lines 3–5 on page 182 of the third part of volume 6 of the *Corpus Reformatorum* edition. In older works, reference is occasionally made to the Zwingli section of the *Corpus Reformatorum* edition using a volume number of 88 or greater. This is because the *Corpus Reformatorum* edition brings together the works of three Reformers (the others being Melanchthon and Calvin, who take up volumes 1–87). To convert from this older system, subtract 87 from the volume number. Thus CR 90.259.32 is equivalent to Z III.259.32.

The Schuler–Schulthess edition is referred to by volume number, page number, and line number. Volumes 2 and 6 are subdivided, with the subdivisions being designated by lower-case Roman numbers. Thus S IV.45.26–8 refers to lines 26–8 on page 45 of volume 4; S VI i.602.48 refers to line 48 on page 602 of the first part of volume 6.

Appendix 5

Referring to the Psalms in the Sixteenth Century

Several major works of the sixteenth-century Reformers take the form of commentaries on the Psalter or on individual Psalms – for example, Martin Luther's famous lectures of 1513–15, generally known as *Dictata super Psalterium*. The student is likely to be confused by a major difficulty encountered in referring to the Psalms. Most sixteenth-century writers used the Latin version of the Bible known as the Vulgate. For reasons which defy a simple explanation, the numeration of the Psalms in the Vulgate is different from that found in the Hebrew text, and hence in modern English versions following the latter's numeration. Thus when Luther refers to Psalm 70, he means *Psalm 70 according to the numbering used in the Vulgate* – which is Psalm *71* in most modern English editions. This obviously raises two difficulties. First, how can we convert from the Vulgate numbers to those found in the English Bible? And second, how can we refer to the Psalms to take account of this difference in numeration? We shall deal with these questions separately.

The Vulgate Psalm Numbers

We can tabulate the differences between the Vulgate and modern English versions of the Psalter as follows:

Reformation Thought: An Introduction, Fourth Edition. Alister E. McGrath.
© 2012 John Wiley & Sons, Ltd. Published 2012 by John Wiley & Sons, Ltd.

Vulgate	English versions
1–8	1–8
9.1–21	9
9.22–39	10
10–112	11–113
113.1–8	114
113.9–26	115
114	116.1–9
115	116.10–19
116–45	117–46
146	147.1–11
147	147.12–20
148–50	148–50

It will thus be clear that the Vulgate and English Psalm numbers are identical only in the case of 11 Psalms (1–8, 148–50).

Thus when Luther refers to Psalm 22, he actually intends what most people know as Psalm 23. Some modern English translations alter references to the Psalms to make allowance for the numeration difference – but when dealing with the original text, the student must be prepared to adjust the Psalm numbers accordingly. If you find a reference to a Psalm which doesn't make sense, try altering the numbers according to the above table.

Referring to Psalms

It is now virtually universal practice within the scholarly literature dealing with the Reformation (and especially Luther) to refer to Psalms in the following manner. If there is a difference between the Psalm numbers in the English and the Vulgate texts, *the Vulgate number is given first, followed by the English number in parentheses.* Thus a discussion of "Luther's exposition of Psalm 70 (71)" means Psalm 70 *according to the Vulgate numeration* and Psalm 71 *according to the English numeration.* Similarly, a reference to Psalm 22 (23):3 is a reference to verse 3 of Psalm 22 *following the Vulgate numeration*, and Psalm 23 *following the English numeration.* Occasionally the situation is further complicated through some Psalms having different verse numbers in the Vulgate and English versions. A reference to "Psalm 84:11 (85:10)" thus means Psalm 84, verse 11, in the Vulgate version; Psalm 85, verse 10, in the English version.

Appendix 6
Updating Reformation Bibliographies

The present book includes short bibliographies (at the end of each chapter) of important works dealing with Reformation thought. Bibliographies, however, go out of date quickly, particularly in a field such as Reformation studies, in which so much scholarly activity is taking place. The student may therefore wonder how such a bibliography may be kept up to date. It is hoped that the following suggestions will be helpful.

Web Searches

The growing importance of the Internet has radically changed scholarly habits, especially in relation to compiling bibliographies. The most useful and convenient way of identifying recent works of relevance in any field relevant to the study of Reformation thought is to use a search engine, and enter search terms – such as "Reformation theology bibliography" – which are designed to identify likely resources. This method should be supplemented by those noted below. Note that in many cases, the print resources mentioned are now available online through university libraries or by private subscription.

The *Archiv für Reformationsgeschichte* Literature Supplement

The leading journal in the field of Reformation studies is *Archiv für Reformationsgeschichte* ("Archive for Reformation History"), published annually

Reformation Thought: An Introduction, Fourth Edition. Alister E. McGrath.
© 2012 John Wiley & Sons, Ltd. Published 2012 by John Wiley & Sons, Ltd.

in October. Since 1972 this journal has included a supplementary Literature Review (*Literaturbericht*), which provides details of several thousand important books or articles published recently relating to the history or the thought of the Reformation. Some are annotated, either in English or in German. The review is divided into sections and subsections, the classification being given in German. An English version of its most important sections follows:

1	General
2	Religion and Culture
2.1	Before the Reformation
2.2	Luther
2.3	Zwingli
2.4	Calvin
2.5	Protestantism
3	Spirit and Culture
3.1	Philosophy and Political Theory
3.2	Humanism
6	The Reformation in European Countries

The student should select the section or subsections of particular interest to him, and work his way through the publications listed thereunder.

Review Articles and Published Bibliographies

A number of review articles or bibliographies are published regularly. The annual *Luther-Jahrbuch, Zwingliana,* and the November issue of *Calvin Theological Journal* include invaluable reports on recent works on Luther, Zwingli, and Calvin respectively. The journal *Ephemerides Theologicae Louvaniensis* publishes an annual bibliography of works, including many relevant to the study of the Catholic Reformation. The student is also recommended to check library catalogues under the "Bibliography" sections of noted reformers – such as Luther, Calvin, or Zwingli – where works such as the following will be found:

Bigane, J. and K. Hagen, *Annotated Bibliography of Luther Studies, 1967–1976* (St Louis, MO, 1977).
Erichson, A., *Bibliographia Calviniana*, 3rd edn (Nieuwkoop, 1965).
Niesel, W., *Calvin-Bibliographie (1901–1959)* (Munich, 1961).
Ozment, S. E., ed., *Reformation Europe: A Guide to Research* (St Louis, MO, 1982).
Pipkin, H. W., *A Zwingli Bibliography* (Pittsburg, PA, 1972).

It is also useful to look through recent numbers of leading history or theology journals – such as *Church History, Journal of Ecclesiastical History,* or *Journal of*

Theological Studies – with two objectives in mind. First, look for reviews of recent books. If a book *has* been reviewed by one of these journals, it is likely to be important. Second, look for review articles – in other words, articles that summarize recent work in a given field. Examples of such reviews are:

Atkinson, J., "Luther Studies," *Journal of Ecclesiastical History* 23 (1972), 69–77.
Green, L. C., "Luther Research in English-Speaking Countries since 1971," *Luther-Jahrbuch* 44 (1977), 105–26.
White, R., "Fifteen Years of Calvin Studies in French (1965–1980)," *Journal of Religious History* 21 (1982), 140–61.

Finally, the student is recommended to browse through the bibliography section of any recent publication dealing with the Reformation and note works of relevance which appeared recently. Writers using the Harvard (author–date) system make this a particularly easy task, in that the date of publication of the work is immediately obvious.

Journal Literature Searches

A number of major journals publish important articles in English dealing with Reformation thought. You are recommended to gain access to each number of these journals as it is published and note any studies of relevance to your particular interest. The following list of major journals is arranged in descending order of importance:

Archiv für Reformationsgeschichte
Sixteenth Century Journal
Church History
Journal of Ecclesiastical History
Harvard Theological Review
Journal of Theological Studies

Readers with a particular interest in the radical Reformation should also gain access to the *Mennonite Quarterly Review*. *Archiv für Reformationsgeschichte* publishes articles in English and German in about equal number; those published in German, however, helpfully include an abstract in English. Readers with a knowledge of German should also check the following journals:

Zeitschrift für Kirchengeschichte
Zeitschrift für Theologie und Kirche
Kerygma und Dogma

Abstracting Services

A number of organizations and journals provide abstracts of articles and/or books, arranged by subject. Two major publications are provided by the American Theological Library Association:

Religion Index One: Periodicals
Index to Book Reviews in Religion

These works are to be found in most North American university and college libraries. The following are also useful:

Guide to Social Science and Religion in Periodical Literature
Religious and Theological Abstracts
Social Sciences and Humanities Index

Cataloguing practices vary from one library to another. In the event of difficulty in locating these reference works, you should consult your librarian.

Appendix 7

Chronology of Political and Intellectual History

1348	First German university founded at Prague.
1365	University of Vienna founded.
1378–1417	The Great Schism in the western church, with anti-popes in Avignon and Rome.
1386	University of Heidelberg founded. Reform of statutes of University of Vienna, leading to dominance of the *via moderna*.
1388	University of Cologne founded.
1392	University of Erfurt founded.
1409	University of Leipzig founded.
1414–18	Council of Constance, ending the Great Schism.
1425	University of Louvain founded.
1453	The Fall of Constantinople: increased migration westward of Greek-speaking scholars and their manuscripts.
1457	University of Freiburg-im-Breisgau founded.
1460	University of Basle founded.
1472	University of Ingolstadt founded.
1474	Condemnation of the *via moderna* at Paris: migration of those sympathetic to the *via moderna* to German universities.
1477	Outbreak of war between France and the house of Hapsburg.
1481	French decree against the *via moderna* rescinded.
1483	Martin Luther born at Eisleben in the Electorate of Saxony, November 10.

Reformation Thought: An Introduction, Fourth Edition. Alister E. McGrath.
© 2012 John Wiley & Sons, Ltd. Published 2012 by John Wiley & Sons, Ltd.

1484	Huldrych Zwingli born, January 1. Gabriel Biel appointed to chair at Tübingen.
1491	Johan Froben starts printing at Basle.
1492	Christobal Colon (Columbus) discovers the Americas.
1498	Zwingli begins his studies at University of Vienna.
1501	Luther begins his studies at University of Erfurt.
1502	University of Wittenberg founded by Elector Frederick of Saxony.
1503	First edition of Erasmus's *Enchiridion*.
1505	Luther enters the Augustinian monastery at Erfurt, July 17.
1506	Publication of Amerbach edition of the works of Augustine.
1508	Reform of statutes of University of Wittenberg. Luther lectures in moral philosophy at University of Wittenberg.
1509	John Calvin born at Noyon, Picardy, July 10. Erasmus publishes *Enconium Moriae*. Henry VIII assumes English throne.
1512	Luther visits Rome, January–February; begins lecturing on the Bible at Wittenberg. Philipp Melanchthon arrives at Tübingen.
1515	Publication of the *Letters of Obscure Men*, ridiculing the Cologne Dominicans. Publication of third edition of Erasmus's *Enchiridion*. Luther begins his lectures on Romans at Wittenberg. Defeat of the Swiss Confederation at the Battle of Marignano, September: Zurich announces it will henceforth enter into no further foreign alliances.
1516	First edition of Thomas More's *Utopia* published. Publication of Erasmus's *Novum Instrumentum omne*. Luther and Karlstadt clash over the interpretation of Augustine, September 25.
1517	Karlstadt defends 151 Augustinian theses, April 26. Luther posts 95 theses on indulgences, October 31.
1518	Karlstadt reforms theological curriculum at Wittenberg, with new emphasis upon Augustine and the Bible, March. Christoph Froschauer begins printing at Zurich. Luther's Heidelberg Disputation, April. Luther appears before Cajetan at Augsburg, October–November. Zwingli called to Zurich as *Leutpriest*.
1519	Zwingli begins public preaching at the Grossmu[um]nster, Zurich. Charles V elected Holy Roman Emperor. Leipzig Disputation between Luther, Karlstadt and Eck, July. Luther condemned by the University of Cologne, August 30. Luther condemned by the University of Louvain, November 7.
1520	Luther condemned by the University of Paris, April 15. Papal bull *Exsurge Domine* threatens Luther with excommunication, June 15. Luther publishes his three reforming treatises: *Appeal to the German Nobility*, *The Babylonian Captivity of the Church*, *The Freedom of a Christian*. Zurich city council issues mandate declaring that all preaching must be based upon Scripture. Luther publicly burns the papal bull and works of canon law.

1521	Melanchthon publishes first edition of his *Loci Communes*, destined to become the standard format for Lutheran works of systematic theology. Diet of Worms; Luther placed under the ban of the Empire, May 8. Luther placed in protective custody in the Wartburg. Riots and iconoclasm at Wittenberg as Karlstadt takes charge of church affairs in Luther's absence.
1522	Unrest at Wittenberg leads to Luther's return. Breaking of the Lenten fast at Zurich. Publication of Luther's German translation of the New Testament, September.
1523	First Zurich Disputation, placing city council in charge of scriptural preaching at Zurich, January 29. Basle city council issues mandate on preaching according to Scripture, based on Zurich's 1520 mandate. Second Zurich Disputation, on the Mass and images in churches, October 26–28.
1524	Battle of Novara, April 30. Zurich city council issues decree permitting removal of images from churches, June 15. German Peasants' War breaks out.
1525	Anabaptism becomes an important movement: first baptisms at Zurich, January 21. Battle of Pavia, February 25. Zwingli's *Commentary on True and False Religion*, criticizing Erasmus, published. *The Twelve Articles of Memmingen* sets out the grievances of the German peasantry: mob violence results. Zurich abolishes the Mass, April 12. Luther writes *Against the Murderous and Thieving Hordes of Peasants*, May 4. Thomas Müntzer and 53 supporters of the Peasants' Revolt publicly executed, May 27. Luther secretly marries Katharina von Bora, a former nun, June 13; public ceremony follows, June 27. Luther's *De servo arbitrio* published, confirming a serious rift with Erasmus.
1526	Diet of Speyer, June–August.
1527	Schleitheim Confession (February). Sack of Rome by the troops of Charles V. Henry VIII seeks divorce from Catherine of Aragon.
1528	Berne accepts Zwinglian Reformation, including the abolition of the Mass, February 7. St Gall abolishes the Mass, July 17. Charles V authorizes death penalty for Anabaptists.
1529	Diet of Speyer, ending toleration of Lutheranism in Catholic districts, February 21. Protest of six princes and 14 cities against the Diet of Speyer, giving rise to the term "Protestant." Treaty of Barcelona, between Charles V and Pope Clement VII, June 29. Peace of Cambrai: Francis I of France and Charles V agree peace, August 3. Philip of Hesse convenes abortive Colloquy of Marburg, October 1–4. Charles V and Venice agree peace at Bologna, December 28; Augsburg Confession of Faith promulgated at Imperial Diet of Augsburg.

1530	Pope Clement VII crowns Charles V emperor at Bologna.
1531	Founding of the Schmalkaldic League for the defense of Protestantism, February 27. Charles V leaves Germany, creating a vacuum which encourages the spread of the Reformation. Death of Zwingli in battle at Cappel, October 11.
1532	Calvin publishes his commentary on Seneca's *De clementia*. Death of William Warham, Archbishop of Canterbury.
1533	Thomas Cranmer appointed Archbishop of Canterbury. Nicolas Cop's All Saints' Day oration at Paris, November 1. Calvin flees Paris.
1534	Affair of the Placards provokes Francis I to action against French evangelicals, October 18. Calvin settles in Basle; writes *Institutes*. First edition of Luther's German Bible (including both Old and New Testaments) published. Anabaptists take over the city of Münster, sending shock waves throughout the region. Succession Act, Supremacy Act, and Treason Act give Henry VIII power over English church.
1535	City of Geneva declares itself to be a republic.
1536	First edition of Calvin's *Institutes* published, March. Bucer and Luther reach agreement on the Eucharist, May. Calvin detained in Geneva by Farel, July. Henry VIII enters into negotiations with German Lutherans. Calvin's intervention at the Lausanne Disputation (October) leads to an enhancement of his authority within Geneva. Genevan Confession published, November.
1538	Calvin expelled from Geneva; takes refuge in Strasbourg.
1539	Second edition of Calvin's *Institutes*. First volume of Luther's complete works appears. *Six Articles* published in England.
1540	Bigamy of Philip of Hesse. Calvin marries the widow Idelette de Bure. The Society of Jesus formally established. Calvin publishes his *Reply to Sadoleto* and his *Commentary on Romans*.
1541	Colloquy of Regensburg (Ratisbon), April–May. First French edition of Calvin's *Institutes*. Calvin returns to establish his theocracy at Geneva, September.
1545	Council of Trent opens, December 13.
1546	Death of Luther, February 18. Outbreak of Schmalkaldic War. Fourth Session of Council of Trent, April 8.
1547	Henry VIII dies, succeeded by Edward VI. Sixth Session of Council of Trent, January 13; Seventh Session, March 3; defeat of Schmalkaldic League at Mühlberg, April 24. *Book of Homilies* published.
1549	First Prayer Book of Edward VI published, written by Cranmer.
1552	Second Prayer Book of Edward VI published, written by Cranmer.
1553	Servetus executed at Geneva for heresy. Edward VI dies, succeeded by Mary Tudor.

1555	Religious Peace of Augsburg recognizes existing religious territorial divisions between Lutherans and Roman Catholics in the Holy Roman Empire. Charles V abdicates.
1556	Thomas Cranmer and others executed.
1558	Charles V dies. Mary Tudor dies, succeeded by Elizabeth I.
1559	Publication of 1559 edition of Calvin's *Institutes*; establishment of Genevan Academy. Henri II of France dies, leading to domination of the French court by the anti-Protestant Guise family. Elizabethan Settlement of Religion.
1560	The Conspiracy of Amboise points to growing Calvinist influence in France, and increased tension as a result. Final French edition of Calvin's *Institutes*.
1562	French Wars of Religion break out.
1563	Publication of *Heidelberg Catechism*, demonstrating an increased Calvinist presence within German territories. Council of Trent closes. Publication of *Thirty-Nine Articles*.
1564	Death of Calvin, May 27.

Index

Reformation Thought: An Introduction, Fourth Edition. Alister E. McGrath.
© 2012 John Wiley & Sons, Ltd. Published 2012 by John Wiley & Sons, Ltd.